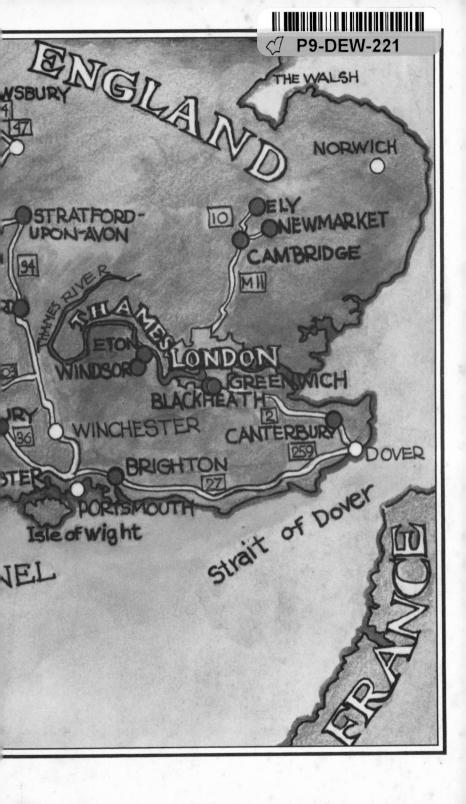

MYSTERY READER'S WALKING GUIDE:
ENGLAND

By the same authors
Mystery Reader's Walking Guide: London

MYSTERY READER'S WALKING GUIDE:
ENGLAND

ALZINA STONE DALE
BARBARA SLOAN HENDERSHOTT

INTERIOR MAPS BY ALISA MUELLER BURKEY

 **PASSPORT BOOKS**

Trade Imprint of National Textbook Company
Lincolnwood, Illinois U.S.A.

ACKNOWLEDGMENT

We are grateful to the Dorothy L. Sayers Literary Society, Rose Cottage, Malthouse Lane, Hurstpierpoint, West Sussex, England BN6 9JY for permission to quote from materials published by the Society.

Published by Passport Books, Trade Imprint of
National Textbook Company, 4255 West Touhy Avenue,
Lincolnwood, Illinois 60646-1975.
© 1988 by Alzina Stone Dale and Barbara Sloan Hendershott.
Maps by Alisa Mueller Burkey, © Alzina Stone Dale and Barbara Sloan Hendershott.
Manufactured in the United States of America.
Library of Congress Catalog Card Number: 88-60300

DEDICATION

This book is dedicated to Aidan, Dorene, and Bernadette Mackey of Bedford, England, in appreciation of their hospitality, help, and best of all, their friendship.

CONTENTS

Maps

ACKNOWLEDGMENTS

We would like to thank:

The British Tourist Authority and its personnel who were both patient and helpful, especially Wendy Young, Sandy Hunt, and Press Relations Officer Peter ffrench-Hodges.

The Dorothy L. Sayers Historical and Literary Society, Rose Cottage, Malthouse Lane, Hurstpierpoint, West Sussex, England BN6 9JY, for permission to use materials published by the Society, and especially to Ralph Clarke and Philip Scrowcroft for checking the Cambridge and Ely/Fen walks for us.

Various mystery writers for their books, letters, willingness to read and comment on walks, and for their words of encouragement. We particularly thank Catherine Aird, Marion Babson, Antonia Fraser, Paula Gosling, Harry Keating, Peter Lovesey, Susan Moody, Anne Perry, Ellis Peters, Ian Stuart, and Margaret Yorke.

Friends who assisted by walking with us or going back over territory to double-check: Susan Crowell, Ruth Howell, Bernadette and Dorene Mackey, and Carroll White.

Friends who loaned us mysteries, read our walks, or offered sound advice: Sue Chapman, Damaris Day, Lilian Gilruth, Martha Mead, Harriet Rylaarsdam, Mary McDermott Shideler.

Librarians who found books thought unfindable: Marilyn Roth; the Adult Services Staff, Elmhurst Public Library; the library staff at York Community High School.

Bookstores that lent special assistance: Mary MacLaughlin and Scotland Yard, Ltd., Winnetka, Illinois; Fifty Seventh Street Books, Chicago; and Marshall Field & Company's downtown and Oakbrook stores.

Travel Agents who got us there: Arcade Travel, Elmhurst,

Illinois; Nancy Carroll of Northshore Travel, Lake Forest, Illinois.

Technical assistance: Diana Koutny.

Our photographer, Leander Studio, Inc., Chicago, Illinois.

Our computer expert, Ronald Hendershott, who generated the special helps lists.

Our families who lived with the increasing number of mysteries piled up around us and kept the machines moving.

Mystery Writers of America, Midwest Branch, and Crime Writers Association of Great Britain for their moral support.

INTRODUCTION

England and the mystery story are firmly linked in the minds of readers everywhere. Just why Shakespeare's "demi-Paradise" has provided such an often used backdrop for murder and mayhem is open to speculation. However, ever since the unknown author of Beowulf strew the countryside with the mutilated bodies that Grendel and his malevolent mother left behind, England has provided the setting for a variety of fictional crimes. Quiet villages, the sleepy countryside, busy county towns, and teeming cities, all, it seems, are foaming cauldrons of crime.

Setting is an integral part of the English mystery. Many of the sites used are actual places with shops and churches, pubs and palaces firmly in place. Others are based on real places or are combinations of the real and the imagined. Catherine Aird, for instance, lives in the village of Sturry near Canterbury. Although she does not write about Sturry or Canterbury by name in her mysteries, she writes out of her knowledge of English villages and English town and country life.

Readers of English mystery find that the country opens up to them. They quickly become as familiar with both the fictional and the real, with St. Mary Mead, or Newmarket, Calleford or Windsor, as they do with characters in the book they are reading. They can visit the shops, attend the churches (or the races), walk the High Street or stop in a pub for a pint and some local color. As their familiarity with a locale increases, mystery fans find that their curiosity increases proportionately. Where, in Dorset, did Adam Dalgliesh go after he left the hospital in P. D. James's *The Black Tower*? Is there really an Abbey in Shrewsbury as Ellis Peters claims? Does The Dirty Duck Pub really exist in Stratford-upon-Avon, or is it a product of Martha Grimes's fertile imagination?

All of this geographical investigation is part of the "fun" of the detective story, the "normal recreation of noble minds," as Phillip Guedalla claimed. G. K. Chesterton observed that the detective story was "the earliest and only form of popular literature in which is expressed some sense of the poetry of modern life."

In *Mystery Reader's Walking Guide: London*, we brought setting and detective stories together by presenting a series of walks in selected London neighborhoods. The walks were designed to satisfy the curiosity of the mystery readers as to who did what, where. Along the way we introduced them to literary and historical sites, took them into pubs and tea shops, and filled them in with a variety of trivia about people, places, and events.

Mystery Reader's Walking Guide: England is the same sort of book. The ground rules are simple. The towns must be accessible by British Rail (each walk starts and ends at the British Railway Station). The town must have some mystery associations and it must be a place about which we were enthusiastic. As in the first book, we let our own preferences as to books and authors be our guide.

Some of the towns we chose, Oxford and Cambridge for instance, had so many associations that we had to limit what would be included. In other towns we concentrated on one or two authors' works. This was the case in Shrewsbury, Newmarket, and Canterbury. Since *Mystery Reader's Walking Guide: England* is area-oriented rather than author- or book-oriented, if you want to follow particular authors or sleuths, such as Dorothy L. Sayers or Lord Peter Wimsey, use the index to look them up and track their travels through various towns. In addition to mystery, literary, and historical details, the reader will also be given tips on where to stay, where to eat. Whenever possible we listed pubs, restaurants, and hotels involved in mysteries. In addition, we have included a list of places that we found to be of special interest in each town.

Mystery Reader's Walking Guide: England is a workable guide, one which you can carry about as you journey into the England beyond London, or that will serve you just as well if, curled up before the fire with a cup of tea or a glass of port, you choose to do your touring from your own armchair.

1

BATH

BACKGROUND

The ancient city of Bath, situated in the valley of Somerset's Avon River and on the slopes of the adjoining hills, achieved its initial fame during Roman times. Bath came back into prominence during the eighteenth century and since then has held an important place in the social history of England. Today it is noted for its classical architecture and its contribution to the cultural and intellectual life of the area.

Historically, Bath was one of the most celebrated spas in England and the only one with hot springs (nearly half a million gallons of water at forty-nine degrees Centigrade gush out of the springs each day). Modern-day Bath, one of England's most elegant cities, is still a resort center popular with both English and foreign tourists.

The story of Bath began long before either the Romans or the eighteenth-century entrepreneurs had left their mark. In the ninth century B.C., legend has it, Prince Bladud, son of the mythical King Hudibras and father of Shakespeare's King Lear, discovered the medicinal powers of the springs. Bladud, who suffered from leprosy, had been exiled from the court of his father. He became a swineherd responsible for a herd of

1

pigs. The pigs soon shared his disease. One day, as he was wandering with his herd near the River Avon, the pigs ran away to wallow in the steaming mud of a nearby swamp. To Bladud's amazement they emerged free of all signs of their disease. He immediately plunged into the mud, and at once was cured of his illness. Hudibras restored his son to favor, and Bladud eventually became king. He established his royal seat at Bath, where he built cisterns to retain the thermal waters. Under his direction the swamp became a spa.

Many years later, Charles Dickens, creator of "Inspector Bucket of the Detective," came to Bath to visit Walter Savage Landor. Dickens included a comic account of Prince Bladud in his novel, *Pickwick Papers,* which was published in 1836.

When the Romans discovered the hot springs dedicated to the Celtic god, Sul, they established their own recreational area by building a bath complex complete with a magnificent temple to the goddess Minerva, thus combining the Celtic and Roman deities. They gave the place the name of Aquae Sulis. After three and a half centuries, the Romans left Britain and, as the *Anglo-Saxon Chronicle* records, in A.D. 577 Bath, together with Gloucester and Cirencester, fell to the invading Saxon armies. The Saxons at first called the city Akemanceaster and later Hat Bathum.

In medieval times Bath was dominated by its great Benedictine monastery and the Abbey Church of St. Peter and St. Paul. The city flourished under monastic rule. The chief industry was wood, but weaving, which was introduced in the fourteenth century, made the city famous. Chaucer's "Wife of Bath," introduced in *The Canterbury Tales,* was a weaver of fine cloth.

As Bath's weaving industry declined, the city came to depend upon its attractions as a watering place and spa. The Cross Bath, Hot Bath, and King's Bath (named for Henry I) were under city control by 1554, as were the newly built Lepers' Bath and the Horse Bath. The baths became a center for the poor, and beggars filled the streets.

When influential doctors began to proclaim the curative

powers of the waters, the clientele shifted from the poor to the wealthy.

In 1576 the New Bath or Queen's Bath was opened. It was so named in 1613 after a visit by Anne of Denmark, Consort of James I. In 1692, another Anne, Princess Anne (later Queen) visited Bath. Her patronage put the royal seal on the spa as a fashionable resort. The diarist Samuel Pepys wrote in 1668 ". . . Up at four o'clock, being by appointment called up to the Cross Bath . . . methinks it cannot be clean to go so many bodies together in the same water . . ." Daniel Defoe also had a comment about Bath: "We may say it is the resort of the sound as well as the sick and a place that helps the indolent and the gay to commit that worst of murders—to kill time."

In the eighteenth century the upper classes came to Bath to take the waters and to have a good time. The coffee-houses, assembly rooms, and, of course, the Pump Room were popular gathering places for those who wished to see and be seen. During those days, Bath served England as an arbiter of taste and manners.

The mixture of classes that flocked to Bath made it a rough place until a master of ceremonies was appointed to run the spa. The position was filled in 1705 by Richard "Beau" Nash, a gambler and cardsharp, who invented the resort business. Nash inherited his honorary title when the man who held the post before him was killed in a duel. Nash remained Master of Ceremonies for the rest of his life. He came to be known as the King of Bath.

Nash brought order to the city by raising money to build better roads and streets and by building concert halls, a theater, and meeting rooms. He forbade elitist private parties and wrote and posted rules for those who attended balls and assemblies. He was also successful in forbidding dueling. He accomplished this by banning the wearing of swords in the city. The ban was generally respected, but the urge to duel persisted. In Sheridan's play, *The Rivals,* which is set in Bath, when Captain Absolute went out to duel, he had to hide his sword under his coat.

Nash was also responsible for organizing the building of an entirely new, Palladian-style city by the two John Woods, father and son. They worked under the patronage of Squire Ralph Allen, the model for Fielding's Squire Allworthy in *Tom Jones*.

Bath, like most old English towns, has a goodly supply of ghost tales. Many are associated with locations within the central areas of the city.

Bath also has numerous literary associations. Jane Austen often visited Bath and, although she disliked the city, she did use it as a partial setting for *Persuasion* and for her spoof of gothic thrillers, *Northanger Abbey*. Bath figures in the work of such other eighteenth- and nineteenth-century writers as Tobias Smollett, Charles Dickens, and Henry Fielding.

Bath is a popular city with mystery writers. Georgette Heyer used Regency Bath as a setting for her Regency mysteries as well as for her historical romances. In her *Sylvester or the Wicked Uncle,* Bath is the place to buy a frock and to visit a lending library. John Dickson Carr, in *The Problem of the Green Capsule,* had Gideon Fell in Bath for the cure. Nancy Livingston, in her *Fatality at Bath & Wells,* sent Mr. Pringle and his friend Mavis to Bath for the sights. Characters in Dick Francis's *Rat Race* go to the Bath racetrack. In *Camelot Caper,* Elizabeth Peters's dauntless sleuths found, in a black cloak dropped in the darkened ruin of Glastonbury Abbey, a letter reserving "two single rooms for Friday night" at the Regent Hotel in Bath. Anthony Price, in *Our Man in Camelot,* cites Bath as a boundary for Arthur's country as the search for the location of the Battle of Badon Hill unfolds. Mystery writer Paula Gosling, who set her short story, "Mr. Felix," in a Bath nursing home, lives in Bath. Peter Lovesey lives in the Bath area, and sets portions of *Rough Cider* in and around Bath. The West Country Branch of The Crime Writers' Association meets each month in a Bath restaurant.

Bath is an ideal center for touring the southwest. (See side trips at the end of this walk.)

How to Get There

British Rail: trains hourly from London's Paddington Station—1 hour, 10 minutes

Automobile: M4 from London to Bath exit, follow A46 south to Bath

Length of walk: 3½ miles

See also Side Trips to Chipping Sodbury and Wells.

See map on page 9 for the boundaries of this walk and page 348 for a list of detectives and stories.

Places of Interest

Abbey Churchyard, Roman Bath Museum (0225) 61111 or 6504. Britain's most complete Roman remains. (Open April–June and September–October, 9–6 daily; July–August, 9–6:30 daily; November–March, 9–5, Sunday 11–5.) Admission charge.

Pump Room, Upstairs from the Roman Baths (0225) 61111 or 6504. Place to see and be seen in the eighteenth century. Dear to the heart of Jane Austen and Georgette Heyer. You can still sample the waters, enjoy morning coffee, and listen to the string trio.

Bath Abbey. Present church was begun in 1499, but there has been a church on this site since Saxon times. Tall windows illuminate the delicate fan vaulting in this outstanding example of British Perpendicular architecture. Site of the coronation of King Edgar.

Assembly Rooms, Bennett Street (0225) 61111 or 6504. These rooms, designed by John Wood the Younger, were opened in 1771. Like the now demolished Lower Rooms, the Bennett Street Rooms were the center for fashionable gatherings when concerts, dances, and card games were the featured entertainments in these elegant surroundings. The rooms were severely damaged by bombs during World War II; the visitor today sees them in their restored splendor. (Open in summer, 9:30–6, Sunday 10–6; in winter, 10–5, Sunday 11–5.) Admission charge.

Museum of Costume, Bennett Street. Downstairs from the
Assembly Rooms. One of the largest costume collections in
the world, featuring eighteenth–century clothing. (Open daily;
see above for hours.) Admission charge.

Royal Crescent. John Wood the Younger's 1767 triumph of
residential architecture is considered the finest crescent in
Europe. It consists of thirty amber–toned Georgian stone
houses with 114 Ionic columns supporting a curving cornice
that tops the whole. Number 1 Royal Crescent has been
restored by the Bath Preservation Trust. (Open March–
October, Tuesday–Saturday, 11–5; Sunday and Bank Holiday
Mondays, 2–5.) Admission charge.

The Circus. The architectural triumph of John Wood the Elder.
Located at the end of Gay Street, the Circus consists of a ring
of identically faced stone houses surrounding a circular green
of lawn and huge plane trees.

Bath Carriage Museum, Circus Mews (0225) 25175. Over forty
antique horse–drawn carriages together with harness and livery
are featured in this unusual museum, which is housed in the
coach houses and stables that make up the Circus Mews.
During summer months, carriage rides are available around
the Circus and the Royal Crescent. (Open in summer 9:30–6,
Sunday 10–6; in winter 10–5, Sunday 11–5.) Admission
charge (rides extra).

Holburne of Menstrie Museum, Great Pulteney Street (0225)
66669. This museum, the former Sydney Hotel (built in
1796–1797), features a superb collection of silver, glass,
porcelain, bronzes, furniture, and paintings, as well as a wide
range of twentieth–century craftwork. Tea is served in the
garden during the summer months. (Open Tuesday–Saturday
11–5, Sunday 2:30–6; open Bank Holiday Mondays. Closed
December and January.)

PLACES TO STAY/EAT

Bath has many hotels and guest houses. For assistance in securing
lodgings, contact the Tourist Information Centre, 8 Abbey
Churchyard. (Telephone 60521 for accommodations; 62831
for information.)

Royal York, George Street (0225) 61541. A reasonably priced traditional hotel where such notables as Princess (later Queen) Victoria and Charles Dickens once stayed. Located just off Milsom Street.

Francis Hotel, Queen Square (0225) 2457. A moderately priced hotel in the Trusthouse Forte group. This elegant hotel occupies a group of Georgian mansions. Located with easy access to the town center.

Hole in the Wall (restaurant and hotel), 16 George Street (0225) 25242. The upper floors of this Georgian town house feature individually furnished guest bedrooms. The restaurant is one of Bath's finest, with French cuisine and an outstanding wine list. Reservations. Expensive.

The Disraeli Restaurant, the Royal York Hotel. Moderately priced traditional English food.

Popjoy's, Beau Nash's House, Sawclose (0225) 60494. High-quality English dishes at moderate prices.

Pump Room and Terrace Restaurant, the Roman Baths, Abbey Churchyard. A must. Features morning coffee, lunch, and tea. Inexpensive.

Sally Lunn House, 4 North Parade Passage (0225) 314812. Features homemade cakes in the oldest house in Bath. Open for lunch and tea. Inexpensive.

Binks, opposite the Pump Room in Abbey Churchyard (0225) 66563. Coffee shop and restaurant featuring traditional British food. Inexpensive.

Garrick's Head (pub), 8 St. John's Place, Sawclose. A town center pub near the Theatre Royale. Popular with actors, supposedly haunted. Lunchtime meals. Inexpensive.

The Saracen's Head, 42 Broad Street (0225) 26518. Oldest pub in town, serving pub food, lunchtime meals. Inexpensive.

Chipping Sodbury

Dornden Guest House, Church Lane, Old Sodbury (Chipping Sodbury) 313325. Charming former vicarage located in a quiet area. Excellent view. Bed and breakfast and half board. Inexpensive.

Wells

Red Lion Hotel, Market Place (0749) 72616. An early coaching inn adjacent to the cathedral. Features a restaurant and bar. Excellent location. Moderate.

Swan Hotel (Best Western), Sadler Street (0749) 78877. Fifteenth–century hotel with a view of the cathedral. Restaurant and bar. Moderate.

BATH WALK

Begin the walk at the Bath Spa British Rail Station, which backs up to the Avon River. In Peter Lovesey's *Rough Cider,* Theo Sinclair, who was being evacuated from London to Somerset during World War II, switched trains at Bath Spa on his way to Frome. As you leave the station, cross Dorchester Street and walk straight ahead down the left-hand side of Manvers Street past the bus station. You can take a bus from here to Lansdowne Race Course, if like Dick Francis you are horse-minded. (Dan Mallett, the expert poacher-cum-law-enforcer in Frank Parrish's *Fire in the Barley,* bought his old school friend, gamekeeper Harry Bennet, a large gin and Dubonnet at the Chestnut Horse pub in Milchester. Dan explained his largesse by claiming to have backed a winner at the Bath races.)

This is also the station for the #320 bus to Chipping Sodbury or the #173 bus to Wells, if you choose to take one of the suggested sidetrips.

Just beyond the bus station, across the street on the right-hand side, you will see the three-story, rectangular police station built of mellow-toned Bath stone. This is where Detective-Inspector Voss, CID, Bath Police, took Theo Sinclair after the death of Sally Ashenfelter in *Rough Cider*.

Jack Kemp, in Nancy Livingston's *Fatality at Bath & Wells,* was taken to the Bath police station for questioning about the murder of Christopher Gordon.

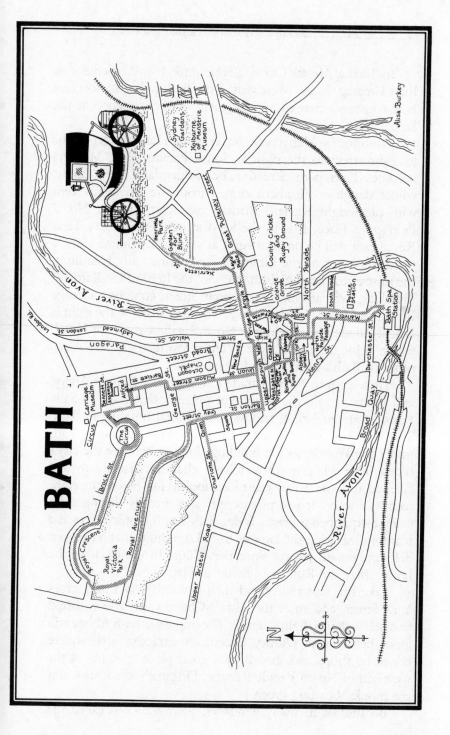

In *Theft of Magna Carta,* a Superintendent West chiller by John Creasey, Roger West visited the Bath police station first as a courtesy, then to apprise them of the presence of the Stephensens.

Continue on Manvers Street, crossing Henry Street on the left; the street to the right is South Parade. Here Manvers becomes Pierrepont Street. (The influential Linley family, whose daughter Elizabeth eloped from the Royal Crescent with playwright Richard Brinsley Sheridan, lived at No. 1 Pierrepont Place. It is to the left through the portico. Tarts Restaurant will be on your right as you turn.) Emma Hart, a maid employed by the Linleys, later became Lady Hamilton, the mistress of Lord Nelson. Nelson, the hero of the Battle of Trafalgar, lived at No. 2 Pierrepont Street; composer George Frederick Handel lived at No. 3. The next street to the right is North Parade Street, where at No. 8/9 is the Grosvenor Hotel, which belonged to the poet William Wordsworth and is another of Bath's haunted buildings.

Turn left into North Parade Passage (once Lilliput Alley), and follow it into the pedestrian precinct that leads to Sally Lunn House at No. 4, said to be the oldest building in Bath. This area was not included in the general remodeling of Bath under the Woods, so the buildings located here are the city's oldest. They will give you an idea of what the maze of crowded lanes around the Abbey must have looked like before the eighteenth century. It is a picturesque spot usually thronged by camera-equipped tourists. Today Sally Lunn House serves as a tearoom featuring the famous Sally Lunn buns that have been delighting Bath palates since the 1700s. In the cellar of the house there are Roman ruins on display.

Take the first right-hand turn beyond Sally Lunn, cross York Street, and enter the Abbey Churchyard; you will find yourself walking slightly uphill. The imposing Bath Abbey will loom before you. (Abbey Green, an attractive little square edged by shops and shaded by a great plane tree, lies at the west end of North Parade Passage. Originally the square was the monks' bowling green.)

Because of its many windows, Bath Abbey is called the

"Lantern of the West." Built in 1499 in English Gothic Perpendicular style, it includes a Norman arch that dates to 1122. Memorial tablets on the walls commemorate such past Bath greats as Beau Nash, population forecaster Thomas Robert Malthus, American Senator William Bingham, and the colonial governor of Massachusetts, Thomas Pownall, as well as Sir Isaac Pitman, the developer of shorthand. The modern window in the northeast corner celebrates the coronation of King Edgar in 973. The carved angels on the Abbey's west front represent the angels that Bishop King (1495–1503) dreamed he saw descending from heaven on a ladder.

In *Fatality at Bath & Wells,* Mr. Pringle, a quiet but highly effective private detective, and his friend, Mavis Bignall, were on holiday in Bath at the time of the murder that marked the opening of the new Bath and Wells television studio. As Mr. Pringle and Mavis searched for a tearoom after a morning of sightseeing, they paused outside the Abbey, where they noted that they could go to an Abbey concert if they stayed in Bath until Friday.

In Lovesey's *Rough Cider,* when a grown-up Theo Sinclair returned to Bath with Alice Ashenfelter in 1964, he was surprised to find himself captivated by the view of the city from the south downs. It was dusk and a shaft of sunlight "picked out the intricate levels of buildings with dazzling clarity." The streetlights make a row of light leading to the floodlighted Abbey. As a medievalist, Sinclair had always found Bath's Georgian vistas dull, but this day he was exhilarated.

Opposite the west front of the Abbey, across an open courtyard to your left are the Pump Room and the Roman Baths. In summer, the courtyard is a popular place for street musicians and sidewalk artists. The poet Shelley and his wife, Mary, stayed at No. 5, Abbey Churchyard, in the residence of William Meyler, who operated from his home one of the circulating libraries so dear to the hearts of eighteenth-century heroines. While at No. 5, Mary Godwin Shelley worked on her novel *Frankenstein.* The White Hart Inn, which was located at Westgate and Stall Streets before it was demolished in 1869, was one of the fashionable lodging places of Georgian Bath. Its proprietors were Eleezer and Moses Pickwick. Their name caught the eye and the imagination of the visiting Charles Dickens. A Barclay's Bank now occupies the site. The figure of a white hart that served as the inn sign on the old White Hart now marks a pub by that name, located at the foot of Widcombe Hill.

The Tourist Information Centre, where you can arrange lodging and get dining tips, is just across from the Pump Room in Abbey Churchyard.

You may explore these Bath landmarks now or on the return leg of this walk. Continue this part of the walk by turning right and walking along the north side of the Abbey to its east end. Here you will find the plaque marking the site of the 973 coronation of Edgar as "King of All England." He was crowned by Dunstan, the Archbishop of Canterbury, in a Saxon church that stood on this site. Continue walking around the Abbey to the spot where you entered the Churchyard. Turn left, then left again into York Street. Follow York Street to Terrace Walk.

Number 13 York Street is one of Bath's many haunted buildings. The house is built on part of the monastery that was attached to Bath Abbey. The arches in the basement were part of the site of the monastery cemetery and bones have been found beneath the flagstones there. Although several ghosts are associated with the house, the most "active" one is that of a young woman who was brutally murdered.

At the end of York Street take Terrace Walk to the left into the area known as the Orange Grove. Pre-eighteenth century, this was a squalid area called Gravel Walks. Beau Nash organized the planting of trees and set up an obelisk to commemorate a visit made by William, Prince of Orange, in 1734.

The Orange Grove by moonlight was a favored spot for clandestine duels, which, despite having been outlawed, were still a favored way of settling disagreements and affairs of honor.

Today the area is marked by the obelisk and beautiful flowers as well as a roundabout. What was a pleasant place to walk and meet friends has been turned into a hazardous traffic area. Cross the Orange Grove at the roundabout and turn left into Grand Parade. But before turning left, look beyond the river to the hillside, where you can see Sham Castle, a folly built by Ralph Allen in the eighteenth century, when England was enamored with ruins and things Gothic. At night the folly is floodlighted.

To your right along the river are Parade Gardens. A plaque marks the site of Harrison's (later Simpson's) Lower Assembly Rooms, where balls and concerts were held in the eighteenth century. The rooms, which were destroyed by fire in 1820, actually stood on Terrace Walk but the area has been altered by the building of the roundabout.

It was in these rooms that Jane Austen's intrepid heroine, Catherine Morland, was introduced to Mr. Tilney in *Northanger Abbey*. In *Bath Tangle,* despite Lady Spenborough's protests that they were in mourning, Georgette Heyer's Lady Serena, upon arriving in Bath, immediately put her own name as well as that of her stepmother down on the subscription lists for both the lower and upper Assembly Rooms.

Take Grand Parade to Bridge Street. The market will be to your left. Bath Market was founded by Royal Charter in the Middle Ages, but the present building was erected in the nineteenth century. Under its high glass dome, you will find goods ranging from second-hand paperback mysteries to buttons, from poultry and fish to sewing machines. Next to the market is the Guildhall.

Turn right and walk along the right-hand side as you cross the eighteenth-century Pulteney Bridge. It, like the Ponte Vecchio in Florence, has small shops flanking the roadway. The bridge was designed by Robert Adam in 1770. Adam was also commissioned by Sir William Pulteney to develop his Bathwick estate. After Sir William's death, the city architect, Thomas Baldwin, took over.

In *Fatality at Bath & Wells,* while Mr. Pringle was lunching in a wine bar with Mavis Bignall and her friend Mrs. Pugh, he was subjected to a discussion of the leather goods available in a shop on Pulteney Bridge. (There are a number of wine bars in Bath, several in the Abbey area—choose one and picture Mr. Pringle and Mavis passing their time there.)

Now cross the bridge and walk along the right-hand side

of Argyle Street to Laura Place. Laura Place, with its stone fountain, is the start of one of the grandest boulevards in Europe: Great Pulteney Street, a thousand feet long and a hundred feet wide. Both Laura Place and Great Pulteney were designed by Baldwin.

After a chance meeting with her long-lost love, Hector Kirkby, in Duffield's Library in Milsom Street, Lady Serena, the volatile heroine of Georgette Heyer's delightful Regency romp, *Bath Tangle,* found that they had walked all the way to Laura Place, although she did not recall crossing the bridge. Her stepmother, Lady Fanny, had signed a six-month lease on a house in Laura Place because it was described to her as "most eligible."

In *Persuasion,* Jane Austen's romantic tale of love set against the backdrop of the years following the Napoleonic Wars, a house in Laura Place was the residence for three months of Lady Dalrymple and her daughters. They were highborn relations of Sir Walter Elliot.

Moses Pickwick, the landlord of the White Hart Inn in 1835 when Charles Dickens made one of his Bath visits, lived after his retirement at No. 7 Laura Place.

Walk to the right, then left, then left again, following the diamond street pattern of Laura Place. From the fountain, look down Great Pulteney Street to the end where you will see the Holburne Museum, which was a hotel in the days of Jane Austen. The museum houses a fine collection of silver, porcelain, and paintings, including John James Masquerier's evocative portrait of Lord Nugent. Surrounding the museum are the Sydney Gardens, now a pleasant place to stroll or watch a game of bowls. During the eighteenth-century heyday, these gardens were popular pleasure gardens resembling London's famous Vauxhall Gardens.

In *Lady of Quality,* Annis Wychwood encouraged her young houseguest, Lucilla, to walk in Sydney Gardens with her friends, Corisande and Edith, and then return to their house in Laura Place, where a carriage would be sent for Lucilla.

In a letter to her sister, Cassandra, written in 1779, Jane

Austen mentions that she and her sister-in-law, Elizabeth, were hoping to attend an open-air concert and fireworks in Sydney Gardens.

The Austens lived at No. 4 Sydney Place, opposite the museum and to the left. The house, which overlooks the Sydney Gardens, is now divided into flats. A plaque records the fact that Jane Austen once lived there. At that time the four-story terraced house was lofty and elegant.

To the right of the museum, on Sydney Place, were residences of Charlotte, Queen to George III, at No. 93, and of the Duke of Clarence, later William IV, at No. 103.

The novelist Lord Bulwer Lytton lived at No. 2 Great Pulteney Street; Hannah More, writer, philanthropist, and pioneer of popular education, lived at No. 76. The elegant building-fronts on both sides of the broad street are studded with markers bearing the names of the famous people who once lived here.

One famous person who still may be around is Admiral Richard, Earl Howe, the victor in 1794 over the French in the battle off Ushant, known as the "Glorious First of June." Although Admiral Howe died in 1799, his ghost is said to haunt No. 71 Great Pulteney Street. According to Margaret Royal and Ian Girvan in their intriguing booklet, *Local Ghosts,* Mrs. Sheila Haines, who occupied a basement flat in the building, saw the ghost of the "pleasant gentleman in naval uniform" on more than one occasion.

In *Rough Cider,* Theo Sinclair and Alice Ashenfelter, after a rather frustrating search for a restaurant that was open (it was a Sunday night in 1964; restaurants were closed and hotels open to residents only), finally found a drab basement in Great Pulteney Street that was the dining room and lounge of a small hotel called the Annual Cure. They settled on an uninspired meal of plaice and French fries, skipping the "farmhouse girll" (sic). Sinclair left Alice in the dingy hotel when she accused him of murder; he angrily took the A4 out of town. Lovesey doesn't say where the hotel was in Great Pulteney Street, so pick out a likely-looking location for yourself.

Walk around Laura Place. At Henrietta Street turn right

and walk the short distance to the charming Victorian haven of Henrietta Park. Here you will find a scented garden for the blind.

Leave Henrietta Park and return to Laura Place. It is easy to picture grand ladies and dandified gentlemen walking and chatting here. Take Argyle Street and recross the bridge, following Bridge Street until it becomes Upper Borough Walls. On the way to Upper Borough Walls, you will pass Northgate Street to the right and High Street to the left. The Pelican, a comfortable although "non-fashionable" hotel according to Georgette Heyer, was located in Walcott Street, which is a continuation of Northgate Street. In *Lady of Quality,* Annis Wychwood suggested to Ninian Ellmore that he would probably find the Pelican to his liking.

Nancy Livingston's Mr. Pringle bought a copy of *The Guardian* at a newsagent's halfway down the High Street as he and Mavis made their way to Cheap Street in *Fatality at Bath & Wells*.

Follow Upper Borough Walls past Union Street on the left (it will take you back to the Abbey area) to Old Bond Street, and turn right. After you have passed New Bond Street on your right and Green Street, also on your right, Old Bond Street becomes Milsom Street. It has been Bath's number one street since before Jane Austen's time. The Octagon Chapel, the only remaining of Bath's many proprietary or subscription chapels, is on Milsom Street. Built in 1769 in the Gothic style, it today houses the *Royal Photographic Centre*. Jane Austen's letters contain numerous references to the subscription chapels.

In *Persuasion,* Jane Austen's heroine, Anne Eliot, encountered Captain Wentworth at Molland's, the pastry cook's shop at No. 2 Milsom Street. He had returned to Bath from Lyme Regis (see Dorchester/Charmouth Walk) in order to woo Anne once more.

In *Lady of Quality,* after finding a home with Annis Wychwood in Upper Camden Place, Lucilla Carleton was excited by the prospect of visiting Bath shops. She was overjoyed by the display of elegant hats and dresses that she found in Milsom Street.

Walk along the right side of Milsom Street until you reach

George Street. Cross George Street and turn right. Follow George Street to Bartlett Street and turn left. As you walk along George Street you will pass a row of houses and shops known as the Edgar Buildings. A number of noted personages lived, at one time or another, in the Edgar Buildings, among them Henry Stafford Smith, the first man to sell foreign postage stamps. He opened a shop there in No. 13. The portrait painter, William Hoare, lived at No. 6.

In *Northanger Abbey,* Isabella had lodgings with her family in the Edgar Buildings. There she was visited by her boorish brother, John. The Edgar Buildings were a perfect location for Isabella, for, with their view of fashionable Milsom Street, it was possible for her to be on the lookout for likely-appearing young men—that is, when she was not engrossed in one of the "horrid" romances she so delighted in reading. (Those "horrid" romances were Gothic thrillers, the forerunners of today's mystery stories.)

Before you turn left to walk up Bartlett Street, locate the Royal York Hotel. It is across and at the end of George Street, just before it intersects with Broad Street. Known as York House in Regency times, it was one of the favorite hostelries of the day. It served as a terminus for coaches going to and from London and other parts of the country. (Broad Street, after crossing George Street, becomes the London Road.) Charles Dickens stayed at the Royal York; so did Prime Minister Disraeli. It became the Royal York after Princess Victoria and her mother stayed there.

Ivo Barrasford, the Marquis of Totherham and Serena's nemesis in *Bath Tangle,* stayed in the York House when in Bath.

In *Lady of Quality,* Mr. Oliver Carleton, Lucilla's autocratic uncle, arranged to take his niece and Annis Wychwood to dinner at York House, where he received them in a private parlor. There they dined on green goose, pigeons, orange soufflé, Celerata cream, and a basket of pastry. Have dinner in the Disraeli Restaurant at the Royal York and imagine the scene for yourself. The menu however has changed since Oliver and Annis dined there.

If you follow George Street to the end and go to the left,

you will find the Paragon, a gently curving row of thirty-seven houses. In 1799, Jane Austen stayed here with the Leigh Perrots at No. 1. Mrs. Leigh Perrot was Jane Austen's aunt, her mother's sister. (Soon after Jane had left, Mrs. Leigh Perrot was accused of stealing lace from the haberdashers shop run by a Miss Gregory at the corner of Stall and Bath Streets. Mrs. Leigh Perrot was eventually charged with larceny and sent to jail to await trial. After a six-hour trial, it took the jury only fifteen minutes to find her "not guilty." Had she been found guilty, she would have faced a sentence of fourteen years' transportation to Australia.)

The Paragon, which stretches alongside a wide raised pavement, forms the lower end of the London Road. At the eastern end of the Paragon stands the Church of St. Swithin, Walcott Parish Church. There has been a church on this site since 1280. Jane Austen's parents were married in the old Walcott Church in 1764. The Rev. Mr. Austen is buried here in the crypt, although the grave marker is in the churchyard. Also buried in the churchyard is Madame d'Arblay, the novelist Fanny Burney, whose books Jane Austen knew and admired tremendously.

Now take Bartlett Street, which is a pedestrian walkway through the heart of Bath's antique trade, to Alfred Street and turn left. There on your right is the building that houses the Upper Assembly Rooms and the Museum of Costume. Designed by John Wood the Younger, the Rooms were the setting for balls, music, public events, and private functions.

Jane Austen danced in the great green-and-gold ballroom beneath the glitter and sparkle of the five great crystal chandeliers as musicians played from the gracefully curved balcony. Take time to explore the Assembly Rooms and the fascinating Museum of Costume on the lower level.

Now go right, past the Assembly Rooms, and walk along the side of the building until you reach Bennett Street; turn left. (A right turn on Bennett would bring you to Landsdown Road, the route followed to Camden Crescent and Landsdown Crescent.)

A right turn at Circus Place will take you to Circus Mews

and the Carriage Museum. Follow Bennett Street into the architectural circle known as the Circus. This masterpiece of John Wood the Elder is 318 feet across, and consists of three sections, each composed of eleven houses. The columns are built in Tuscan, Ionic, and Corinthian tiers. In the eighteenth century there were no trees in the center of the Circus; instead there was a well and cobblestones. William Pitt the Elder lived at No. 7, African missionary David Livingstone at No. 13, Thomas Gainsborough and William Makepeace Thackeray— at different times—at No. 17. Major John André, who was hanged in America for his negotiations with Benedict Arnold, lived at No. 22; the Arctic explorer, Admiral Sir William Parry, lived at No. 27.

Follow the curve of the Circus street to the left across Gay Street. Jane Austen lived at No. 25 with her mother and sister following her father's death. When you come to Brock Street turn left and follow Brock Street to the Royal Crescent.

You will have walked from the masterpiece of the elder John Wood to the triumph of the younger. The Royal Crescent, the most magnificent crescent in Europe, is a sweep of amber-hued stone mottled by sunlight and shadow. The Crescent is composed of thirty houses and 114 Ionic columns that unite to form a breathtakingly beautiful semi-ellipse.

In Peter Lovesey's *Rough Cider,* Theo Sinclair and Alice Ashenfelter, hot on the trail of Harry Ashenfelter, came into Bath from the south and soon were in the Circus. There they made an extra circuit before they turned into Brock Street and headed to the Royal Crescent, where Harry and his wife, Sally, lived in a house that did not live up to its Georgian potential, but instead was furnished with steel, glass, and white leather. Theo had known both Harry and Sally years before when he was a nine-year-old war evacuee.

Theo Sinclair did not particularly admire the Crescent, which he described in a depreciating tone. If time permits, visit No. 1 Crescent, a Georgian town house furnished and maintained by the Bath Preservation Trust.

Resume the walk by following the path opposite No. 1 to Royal Avenue; turn left and follow Royal Avenue to Queen

Square on the left and Charlotte Street on the right. Turn right on Charlotte Street to the Charlotte Street carpark, where Nancy Livingston located her television studio in *Fatality at Bath & Wells*. The book opens as royalty arrives to grace the first broadcast from the new facility. The studio located here becomes the focal point of the story, with much of the action taking place within the mythical building. As you look over the sea of Fords and Vauxhalls, try to imagine the modern television studio that Ms. Livingston placed here.

Walk back along Charlotte Street to Queen Square; turn right and walk to the bottom of the Square. Queen Square was the first major work in Bath of John Wood the Elder; he lived at No. 24, in a house that, according to legend, is haunted by the ghost of his mistress. Dr. William Oliver, who invented the Bath Oliver biscuit as an antidote to rich food, lived in a house on the west side of the square. It has now been replaced by the Bath Reference Library. Originally, Wood intended for all four sides of the square to be identical, but in the end he made the north side, which faces into the sun, the most magnificent. The other sides are quite simple, although some of the doorways are rather splendid.

In 1779 Jane Austen and her mother joined her brother Edward and his family in their lodgings at No. 13 Queen Square, which is on the south side of the square, on the corner at the western end. Both No. 13 Queen Square and No. 4 Sydney Place are reportedly the sites where Jane Austen wrote *Northanger Abbey*. Today the typical four-story Georgian town house is used as an office building, but it maintains much the look it had in Jane Austen's day.

The Francis Hotel, an elegant hotel that features an excellent tea, is located in Queen Square just east of No. 13. In *Rough Cider*, Theo Sinclair, taking into account Sally Ashenfelter's fondness for drink, decided to meet her for tea in the Pump Room rather than for lunch at the Francis. Walk past No. 13 and cross the square to Barton Street. Turn right on Barton Street, which becomes the Sawclose. On your right will be the Theatre Royal, which was built in 1805 and has a ghost story associated with it. It seems that the spirit of a lady dressed in gray has appeared throughout the building. She has even been seen sitting in the upper circle. One explanation of her origin is that she was an eighteenth-century lady who killed herself after her lover was killed in a duel.

Next to the theater is Popjoy's, a well-known Bath restaurant, once the home of Master of Ceremonies Beau Nash. The house is said to be haunted by the ghost of Nash's mistress, Julianna Popjoy, and the Garrick's Head public house next door to the theater, at No. 8 St. John's Place, is said to be haunted by a host of unexplained phenomena.

Continue along the Sawclose to Westgate Street and turn left. Follow Westgate Street to Stall Street, then turn right. Stall Street will lead you once again into the Abbey Churchyard, where the Roman Baths and the Pump Room are located.

Binks, the coffee shop located opposite the Roman Baths, was the destination of Mr. Pringle and his friend, Mavis, in *Fatality at Bath & Wells* by Nancy Livingston. They stood in the rain perusing a map of "Bath as it was in Jane Austen's time." Mrs. Pugh, the landlady at their B and B, had recommended Binks, and told them that it could be found "In Cheap Street, near the Roman Baths . . ." (Binks may be entered from Cheap Street or from the Abbey Churchyard.) On their way they stopped to buy a paper to see how Fleet Street was reacting to the murder at the Bath and Wells Television studio. Near the coffee shop, they met Petronella, who worked for the television studio, and they all went in for coffee and homemade cakes.

The elegant Pump Room with its Chippendale chairs was the gathering place when the *haut ton* made Bath *the* place to be. Here society gathered to gossip, flirt, play whist, and attend balls and concerts. The present Pump Room is the work of Thomas Baldwin—the same architect who designed Pulteney Street. Built in 1795, the magnificent meeting room replaced a much smaller 1709 building. Today you may stop by for morning coffee or lunch and be entertained in elegant style by the music of a string trio. A window in the Pump Room overlooks the King's Bath.

In *Northanger Abbey,* Jane Austen sent Catherine Morland to the Pump Room soon after her arrival in Bath. She was disappointed because Mr. Tilney did not appear although "Every creature in Bath, except himself, was to be seen in the room at different periods of the fashionable hours."

Lovesey's Theo Sinclair arranged to meet the alcoholic Sally Ashenfelter at the Pump Room for tea after successfully turning down her bid for a lunchtime drink at the Francis Hotel in Queen Square. Sally had laughed at the idea of cucumber sandwiches and the three-piece orchestra.

Sinclair listened to the orchestra play music from "Call Me Madam" as he looked out toward the paved area of the Abbey Churchyard. When Sally didn't show up, he left the Pump Room and headed for the Royal Crescent, where he found her house had been gutted by fire. Sally had been taken to the Royal United Hospital in Combe Park.

The Grand Pump Room Hotel occupied the building that stretches along Stall Street from Westgate and now houses a bank and a variety of shops. It is built on the site of the old White Hart Inn. This is the probable location for the fictional Beau Nash Hotel, where Inspector Eliot of Scotland Yard, despite the lateness of the hour, found Gideon Fell in John Dickson Carr's *The Problem of the Green Capsule.* Dr. Fell, dressed in a tent-sized purple-flowered flannel dressing gown, was sitting at the breakfast table drinking coffee, smoking a cigar, and reading a detective story.

This is also the probable site of the Pump Hotel, where the so-called Stephensons stayed while they waited for developments in Salisbury, in John Creasey's *Theft of Magna Carta.*

Walk through the area between the Roman Baths and the Abbey to York Street, cross York Street into the pedestrian area, go past the turning into North Parade Passage that leads to the Sally Lunn House. Continue going straight until you come to Henry Street on your left and Orchard Street on your right. Bath's first theater was opened in Orchard Street in 1750; a plaque marks its site today. It was the first theater outside London protected by a Royal Patent. In 1768 it became known as the Theatre Royal, Bath. David Garrick, for whom the haunted pub at St. John's Place in the Sawclose is named, Sarah Siddons, and the Kembles all performed here. This theater was well known to Jane Austen. In *Northanger Abbey,* as Catherine recounts her first week in Bath to Mr. Tilney, she admits to having been to a play on Tuesday. Because the Orchard Street theater was too small, a new building, designed by London architect John Dance the Younger, was erected on the Sawclose on the south side of Beaufort Square in 1804–5. The old Theatre Royale, designed by Thomas Jelly, is now the Masonic Hall.

Turn left into Henry Street. After about a block you will come to Manvers Street, where you will turn right. Take Manvers Street back to the train station and the end of the walk.

POSSIBLE SIDE TRIPS

Chipping Sodbury

An Avon town located thirteen miles northwest of Bath on the A432. Take the A46 north out of Bath for approximately ten miles; this will bring you to a junction with the A432, where you turn left (west) for three miles, or take the #320 bus from the Bath bus station on Manvers Street.

John Dickson Carr's "Sodbury Cross," where most of the action in *The Problem of the Green Capsule* took place, could very easily be based on this ancient market town. Georgian and Tudor houses line the charming main street. At one end of the main street is the Market Cross; at the other is the thirteenth-century Church of St. John the Baptist. It has a large Somerset Perpendicular tower dating from the late fifteenth century. The church, which contains an exquisitely carved, rare canopied pulpit dating from the seventeenth century, was rebuilt in the fifteenth century and restored in the nineteenth. Edward Jenner, the pioneer of the modern technique of vaccination, was apprenticed to an apothecary in Chipping Sodbury, and William Tyndale, who made the first translation of the Bible into English, lived in the Little Sodbury Manor from 1521 to 1523 while he tutored the children of Sir John Walsh.

Little streets, with names such as Hatters Lane, Horse Street, and Rouncival Street, lead off the main street and reflect the town's marketing past. The word "chipping" is the Saxon word for marketplace.

Look for a tobacco and sweet shop in the village. In John Dickson Carr's Sodbury Cross there were three, but "Mrs. Terry's was the best patronized."

Wells

England's smallest cathedral city is in Somerset, twenty-one miles southwest of Bath. Take the A39 or the A367 (Wells Road) from Bath south to Wells, or catch the #173 bus at the Bath bus station on Manvers Street.

There has been a church in Wells since the eighth century, when the West Saxon King Ina built one near the spring that gave the city its name. Archeologists have found traces of that first church east of the cloister of the present cathedral. They have also found evidence of a much earlier occupation by Neolithic man going back some five thousand years.

The Normans moved the Bishopric from Wells to Bath in 1088. It was returned to Wells in 1539 with the dissolution of Bath Abbey; however, the diocese is still known as the Diocese of Bath and Wells. The present cathedral was begun by Bishop Reginald de Bohum between 1175 and 1185. His original plan was carefully developed by later builders so that the entire resulting building achieved a harmony of design.

Visitors go to Wells to see the cathedral, and that is exactly what Jessica Tregarth and David Randall ended up doing in *The Camelot Caper*, Elizabeth Peters's fascinating chase around southern England.

They spent time pretending to be tourists, and became so enamored of the splendor of the cathedral that for a time they forgot to pretend.

It had been in the Chapter House of Salisbury Cathedral that Jess had her first encounter with Cousin John, and it was in Wells Cathedral Chapter House that Cousin John caught up with her once more. He and David grappled with each other until Cousin John fell, striking his head. Before the altercation,

Jess had been suitably moved by the splendor of the Chapter House stairway.

After the fight, Jess, David, and Bill MacAllister, the blonde giant who never left Wells, ran across the Cathedral Green and into the Market Square.

Several hours after the escapade in the Cathedral, the trio gathered for drinks at the King's Arms in the High Street. Bill had spotted Cousin John's blue convertible in the inn yard. While Jess and David sat arguing in a friendly manner, Bill noticed their quarry leaving the inn. The chase is quickly resumed, with the next destination being Glastonbury.

2

BRIGHTON

BACKGROUND

Brighton is the largest and best-known seaside resort in England. It is famous for its bracing air, seaside amusements, and places to stay, and for its glittering, stony seafront that stretches seven miles from Hove in the west to Rottingdean in the east. Originally a tiny fishing village, one of its early feudal lords was Earl Godwin, father of the ill-fated King Harold, the last of the Saxons. Harold's death in 1066 while fighting Norman William at Hastings was described by mystery writer Georgette Heyer in *The Conqueror*. The village was called "Brighthelmstone" in Domesday Book, and the center of the old village called "the Lanes" still has hilly, narrow medieval streets, which house fascinating shops and restaurants.

Brighton remained the small fishing village of Brighthelmstone for centuries, re-entering history only once, on October 14, 1651, when the fugitive Charles II, escaping to France after the Battle of Worcester, spent his last night on shore at Brighton's George Inn. He sailed next day in Nicholas Tettersell's coal boat for France and exile. After the Restoration, Tettersell used his royal reward money to buy the Old Ship Inn.

In the middle of the eighteenth century, fashionable society doctor Russell began to recommend Brighton's bracing air (ozone) and seabathing in the chilly channel waters for good health. As a result, well-known people like the great Dr. Samuel Johnson became frequent visitors. It became the ultimate in fashionable resorts—London-by-the-Sea—when the Prince Regent (later George IV) arrived in 1784. "Prinny" built himself an incredibly opulent fairy palace, known as the Royal Pavilion. The railroads changed Brighton from an aristocratic playground to a crowded resort popular with Londoners out for a day of fun in the sun.

Hove, with terraces of Regency and Victorian houses, is another seaside town with a more sedate manner, beyond Brighton to the west. In Shelley Smith's *A Grave Affair,* Cabinet Minister Edmund Burke's mistress, television personality Alys da Sylva, lived at Hove. She was murdered by Arab terrorists who wanted to ruin the peace talks Burke was coordinating as Secretary of State for Mediterranean Affairs. Her murder occurred at Horsham, halfway between London and Brighton, where Burke and da Sylva had met secretly at a pub called The Fox.

Exclusive Roedean School is at the far end of Marine Parade on the east side of Brighton. (Agatha Christie's older sister Madge went to the boarding school which became Roedean, but did not continue to Cambridge because her father had no desire to have "bluestocking" daughters.) (See Cambridge Walk.)

Susan Moody's six-foot-tall black sleuth, Penny Wanawake, also went to Roedean. Penny was the daughter of English aristocrat Lady Helena Hurley and African diplomat Dr. Benjamin Wanawake of Senangaland. In *Penny Dreadful,* Penny complained that Roedean was a cloistered, all-girl school that left her totally ignorant of "life-skills," so she had to spend nine months in Africa.

Rudyard Kipling, whose secretary was G. K. Chesterton's sister-in-law, Gertrude Blogg, lived along the chalk cliffs four miles east of Brighton at Rottingdean. Rottingdean is a quaint, artistic village with an ancient pub, the Plough Inn, on the green near Kipling's home, and the Grange, a museum with some of his books and letters.

Today Brighton is known for having the largest boat marina in Europe. It was opened by the Queen in 1979 and has berths for 2,000 yachts, protected by vast breakwaters. A World War II destroyer, the HMS *Cavalier,* is moored there. Brighton has all the typical resort and seashore fun and games, and some of the best antique shops in all England. Out of season, Brighton is also one of the most popular convention towns, much like its American counterpart, Atlantic City.

Brighton is also rich in literary and mystery associations. If the story takes place off-season, the characters usually are grim and unhappy, like Martha Grimes's Kate Sandys in *I Am the Only Running Footman.* Mysteries that take place in the fashionable season, like Peter Lovesey's *Mad Hatter's Holiday,* are less grim, but stories set in midsummer make Brighton sound alive with small-time crooks, bank clerks, and blowsy shopgirls out for a good time, like those in Graham Greene's *Brighton Rock.*

In Nicholas Blake's *Thou Shell of Death,* Oxford don Philip Starling commented that you could pick up girls like glamourous, sexy Lucilla Thrale "two a penny at Brighton any summer weekend." In *Busman's Honeymoon,* the ancient Countess of Severn and Thames, who was Lord Peter Wimsey's godmother, wrote to his mother on the occasion of Peter's engagement. Lady Severn and Thames, never mealymouthed, mentioned that her idiot great-nephew Hughie, having undertaken to provide the evidence for a divorce like a gentleman, had bungled it. Hughie had sneaked off to Brighton with a hired nobody and the judge believed neither the hotel nor the chambermaid.

Antonia Fraser used Brighton's original name, Brighthelmstone, for the name of the publisher Valentine's ancient estate and publishing house in *A Splash of Red.* G. K. Chesterton, creator of Father Brown, not only visited Brighton himself, but wrote a play about Dr. Johnson and his friend, Mrs. Thrale, who visited Brighton, and attended historic St. Nicholas Church. Chesterton began *Orthodoxy* with the story of an

Englishman who had sailed away to the South Seas, hunting new worlds to conquer, but landed instead at Brighton, armed to the teeth, to raise the Union Jack on the Royal Pavilion.

Mystery's Grand Masters like Charles Dickens, Wilkie Collins, and Sir Arthur Conan Doyle, as well as the Gothic thriller writer Harrison Ainsworth, all stayed in Brighton or used it as a setting. Agatha Christie preferred Bournemouth or her childhood home at Torquay, but she also knew Brighton. In the Miss Marple mystery, *A Pocketful of Rye,* the queen who was in the parlor eating bread and honey was Rex Fortescue's glamorous and expensive second wife. Fortescue had met Adele when she was a manicurist on the make in Brighton.

In her short story, "Evidence in Camera," Margery Allingham described a newspaper photographer who tracked down a murderer killing off middle-aged redheaded women in seaside towns. In an audiotape of her story, to give the story more verisimilitude, Allingham's imaginary place name of "Prinny's Plage" was changed to Brighton. There is also a good chance that Bognor, the seashore resort where John Creasey's Inspector West went on holiday, was really Brighton. Inspector West was soon recalled to London over the murder of a Member of Parliament in *Holiday for Inspector West.*

As World War II began, Georgette Heyer, her barrister husband, Ronald Rougier, and their small son, Richard, moved to Brighton, where they lived at No. 25 in Regency Adelaide Crescent beyond West Pier. When the war began, Georgette Heyer firewatched for the Home Front, but bombs and wartime travel troubles made the Rougiers move to London in 1942.

In *To Wake the Dead,* John Dickson Carr set one of his classic locked-room murders in a country house in Sussex called Northfield. The murder there was solved by Carr's G. K. Chesterton look-alike, Dr. Gideon Fell. In Carr's *The Problem of the Green Capsule,* Dr. Fell solved a murder near Bath which reminded him of a lady poisoner at Brighton in 1871. (See also Bath Walk.)

Brighton is also a racing town. In Dick Francis's *Break In,* the dissolute son of a press lord had his debts called in during the Hove Stakes. To pay them he gave up his shares in the family newspaper. In *Rat Race,* Francis's Matt Shore flew jockey Colin Ross from Brighton to Windsor for races only an hour and half apart. In *The Danger,* Francis's Andrew Douglas worked for Liberty Market, Ltd., a firm that specialized in working with terrorist kidnap victims and their families. Douglas got a call from his office that a little boy had been kidnapped about an hour's drive along the coast from Brighton and went to take charge of negotiations.

By all odds the most sinister Brighton thriller of them all is still Graham Greene's "entertainment," *Brighton Rock.* Its title came from the sticks of colored rock candy you buy in stalls along the Esplanade, which is as synonymous with Brighton as salt water taffy is with Atlantic City, USA.

How to Get There

British Rail: trains every half hour from London's Victoria Station—the fastest trains take about an hour

Automobile: M23, then A25; fifty-three miles from London

Length of walk: About seven miles. (The reader is warned that Brighton is all up- and downhill, so that on a map this walk looks like a four-mile hike, but our pedometer measured much more.) This mileage also does not count time spent in the Royal Pavilion, museums, or the innumerable shops. One good solution would be to take a cab from the station to the Royal Pavilion to begin the walk.

See map on page 34 for boundaries of this walk and page 350 for a list of detectives and stories covered.

Places of Interest

The Old Steine (Steen) fishing village of Brighthelmstone, now gardens with statute of George IV.

The Lanes, the honeycombed nest of ancient lanes filled with shops between the Old Steine, King's Road, West Street, and North Street.

Palace Pier, the Esplanade at Grand Junction Road and Madeira Drive. Replaced old Chain Pier. Famous Edwardian "pleasure palace" with music-hall shows and midway attractions, built in domed Pavilion style. Free.

Volk's Seafront Railway, Madeira Drive. First public electric train in England. Good way to see the Regency terraces of Madeira Drive and Marine Parade. Smart brown-and-yellow carriages with monogram VR. Open daily, summer only. Admission charge.

Brighton Marina, end of Marine Drive and Volk's Railway. Biggest boat marina in Europe. Open daily all year.

The Royal Pavilion, Castle Square. Fantastic Oriental Mogul-style palace of George IV. Inside equals the outside. (Open daily 10–6 all year except Christmas and Boxing Day.) Admission charge.

The Dome, behind Royal Pavilion on Church Street (0273) 674357. Originally the royal stables. Variety shows, concerts, exhibitions.

The Brighton Art Gallery and Museum. Special features: portraits of George IV (Prinny), Art Deco and Art Nouveau collections, exhibition on seaside resorts. (Open all year except Good Friday, Christmas, and Boxing Day; Tuesday–Saturday, 10–5:45; Sunday 2–5.) Free.

The Theatre Royal, Church Street (0273) 28488. Victorian red-plush home of musicals, thrillers, and classics. Many West End London productions. Dorothy L. Sayers's feminist comedy *Love All* did boffo business here in 1941.

Aquarium and Dolphinarium, Marine Parade next to Palace Pier. Opened in 1869 to display fish, turtles, seals, and (since 1968) dolphins in a series of underground caves. (Open all year.) Admission charge.

Brighton Race Course, off Warren Road on downs above Brighton. Races April through October. Buses from the Old Steine.

St. Nicholas Church and Churchyard, Dyke Road. Built in 1380, rebuilt in 1853. If the church is open, you can see its Norman font with memorial to the Duke of Wellington and the pew where Mrs. Thrale and her friend, Dr. Samuel Johnson (GKC's idol), worshiped in the North Aisle. In the churchyard you can find the grave of Nicholas Tettersell, who sailed Charles II to France and owned the Old Ship Hotel.

PLACES TO STAY/EAT

Brighton's famous fish and chips are best eaten out of a piece of newspaper from a seaside stall, although you might try the Palace Pier restaurant, where Graham Greene's Pinkie made his mob eat them after murdering Fred Hale.

Royal Albion Hotel, Old Steine (0273) 29202. Large yellow-and-white Regency hotel built in 1826 where Brighton promoter Dr. Russell once lived. Glassed-in veranda on the seafront. Highly fashionable 1920s scene where gay young things like Agatha Christie's Tommy and Tuppence might have stayed; likely candidate for Pavilion Plaza Hotel, where Dick Francis's jockey Alan York and his girl had tea in *Dead Cert.* Restaurant with panoramic views. Expensive.

Old Ship Hotel, King's Road (0273) 29001. Once owned by Nicholas Tettersell, who sailed Charles II to France. Cozy Georgian charm in wood-paneled parlors, low ceilings. Dickens gave readings in its Assembly Rooms; Thackeray wrote part of *Vanity Fair* here. Two restaurants serving traditional English food, parlors and bars with views of the sea. Expensive.

Hotel Metropole, King's Road (0273) 775432. Victorian favorite of Agatha Christie's Hercule Poirot. Red-and-white striped stone exterior trimmed with white iron balconies overlooking the sea. Lobby-lounge suitable for Miss Marple. Special Metropole Court with service flats. Two restaurants, the *Starlit Room* and the *Buttery.* Expensive.

Prince Regent Hotel, 29 Regency Square (0273) 29962. Small, nicely restored Georgian hotel. Inexpensive.

Wheeler's Sheridan Hotel, 64 King's Road (0273) 23221. Landmark Edwardian red brick with plush velvet, brass and crystal trimmings. Expensive.

Wheeler's Oyster Rooms and Restaurant, 17 Market Street, The Lanes. Excellent seafood. Reservations needed.

Tea Room, The Royal Pavilion, Castle Square. Small, pleasant room hung with portraits of the royal family: George III and his many children, George IV as Cupid kissing Brighton (Psyche) awake. Try the Royal Pavilion sandwich with toasted ham, cheese, pineapple, cucumber, tomato, and lettuce and a cup of soup. Inexpensive.

Skyline Restaurant, Brighton Centre (0273) 203131. Modern
    restaurant with panoramic view of the coastline. Lunch, bar,
    and evening meals before concerts at the centre. Inexpensive.

English's Oyster Bar, 30 East Street, the Lanes (0273) 27980. A
    four-hundred-year-old fisherman's cottage, housing a 150-
    year-old restaurant. Special but expensive. Reservations
    needed.

Cricketers, 15 Black Lion Street. Brighton's oldest pub, with
    stables and coachyard dating to the fifteenth century. Old
    mirrors, marble, and brass fittings in which to enjoy the
    savoury pies, jacket potatoes, daily specials, and real ale.

The Royal Pavilion Tavern, Castle Square. Central pub with oak
    paneling, old beamed ceilings. Good hot and cold bar food.

For more places to stay/eat, check at Tourist Information Centre, Marlborough House, 54 Steine Lane (0273) 23755. See
their Tourbus or Guided Walking Tours of the Lanes, June 2–
September 3, Monday–Wednesday, 10:30–7:30, or get their
leaflet "A Walk Around the Best of Brighton."

———— BRIGHTON WALK ————

Begin your walk at the Victorian Railway Station. If you don't
want to walk to the Royal Pavilion, take a taxi there, but take
care! There are doubtless many deserving taxi drivers in Brighton, but in Dick Francis's *Dead Cert,* there was a criminal gang
running a taxi business. Trying to trace them, South African
amateur jockey Alan York took a train to Brighton to keep his
expensive Lotus from being recognized. York stood outside
the railway station to observe taxi drivers, some of whom had
beaten him up for asking questions about the death of his
friend Bill Davidson. He saw four groups, one with a broad
green line, one with yellow shields, one cobalt blue, and the
fourth group, a mix.

The taxis we saw on the rack were all solid-colored cabs
with signs on top and only a few had a radio phone number.
But you should still stay away from Marconicars, the dusty
black cabs with faded yellow shields on their doors.

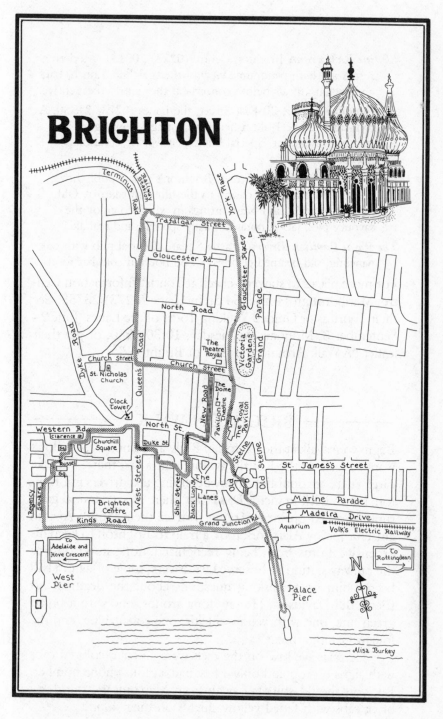

BRIGHTON

Terminus Road

Railway Station

York Place

Trafalgar Street

Gloucester Rd

Gloucester Place

North Road

Grand Parade

Dyke Road

Church Street

St. Nicholas Church

Queen's Road

The Theatre Royal

Victoria Gardens

Clock Tower

Church Street

New Road

The Dome

Pavilion Theatre

The Royal Pavilion

Old Steine

Western Rd.

Clarence Sq

North St.

Duke St.

Churchill Square

Russell Sq

West Street

Ship Street

Black Lion St.

The Lanes

Old Steine

St. James's Street

Regency Square

Brighton Centre

Kings Road

Grand Junction Rd.

Aquarium

Marine Parade

Madeira Drive

Volk's Electric Railway

To Adelaide and Hove Crescent

West Pier

Palace Pier

N

To Rottingdean

Alisa Burkey

Peter Lovesey's *Mad Hatter's Holiday* took place in 1881. Albert Moscrop, a London shopkeeper who spent each vacation at a different resort, came to Brighton, bringing along his binoculars, with which he watched the passing parade. Moscrop took care to arrive (by train) when the real season began in September, when the vulgar Londoners who liked ginger beer and Punch and Judy were gone. Now the entertainments were polo and Sarah Bernhardt at the Theatre Royal, and all the prices went up.

In David Frome's *The Black Envelope: Mr. Pinkerton Again,* Mr. Pinkerton found himself in a train compartment with a sinister couple who pretended to read the *Morning (London) Telegraph,* then accused him of being a spy. Mr. Pinkerton had come to Brighton on holiday because the late Mrs. Pinkerton regarded Brighton in general "as a sinkhole of iniquity."

Fred Hale, the newspaper reporter playing the London *Messenger's* "Kolley Kibber" for the day, dropping treasure-hunt clue cards and wearing a distinctive hat, arrived by train at high summer in Graham Greene's *Brighton Rock.*

Greene described in vivid detail the typical Bank Holiday crowd arriving from London, having stood all the way in crowded coaches. By midnight, "they would go back to the cramped streets and closed pubs of London, having with immense labor and patience extracted from their long day the small pleasures of the sun, the music, the miniature cars, the sticks of Brighton rock candy, and their paper sailors' hats." Hale himself, although frightened for his life, had to keep to a rigid schedule between Castle Square and the West Pier.

Sergeant Cribb, arriving after the discovery of a dismembered body on the beach, in Lovesey's *Mad Hatter's Holiday,* lectured Constable Thackeray, who thought it odd anyone would murder another person at the seaside. According to Cribb, it was a perfectly natural place to commit murder and he reeled off a long list of murders there, insisting that there was hardly a street in Brighton without its murderous associations. He ended his summary of crime with a Mr. Gold, done to death on the Brighton Express by a Mr. Lefroy, whose effigy was at Madame Tussaud's famous wax museum in London.

Walk out of the station. Ahead of you is Terminus Road. Cross the taxi entrance to your left and turn left again to take a sunken roadway back along the station wall. This is Trafalgar Street. Head very sharply downhill on Trafalgar Street. As is true in most English towns, the area around the railroad station is not the most scenic part of Brighton, but it has a number of comfortable-looking old pubs and secondhand-book and antique shops set in old Georgian terraces. This area is being gentrified by London commuters and students from the nearby University of Sussex; it has a seedy but trendy air about it.

You will cross nine tiny lanes before you reach York Place, which is the end of the London Road (A23). Farther down near the sea it becomes the Grand Parade. Try to imagine the heavy Brighton traffic and the summer London mobs gone. Then remember the dramatic entrance into Brighton in *Regency Buck* by Georgette Heyer's elegant Lord Worth, angrily driving his curricle and matched chestnut team with his tiger, Henry, up behind, and a furious, disheveled Judith Tavener inside.

York Place is an open roadway with the Brighton parish church, St. Peter's Church, in the center of its wide, double park. Its tall trees and colorful flower beds stretch to your right to Victoria Gardens, the Old Steine, and the sea. Although you are coming to the fashionable part of town, it seems very unlikely that this was the church where Wilkie Collins's pious Miss Clack dragged the unwilling Rachel Verinder in *The Moonstone,* declared by experts like Dorothy L. Sayers, Julian Symons, and T. S. Eliot to be one of the best detective stories ever written.

After the mysterious disappearance of the Moonstone on the night of Rachel Verinder's birthday, followed by her mother's death, poor relation Miss Clack went to Brighton to hire a house for the season for Rachel and the family of her guardian. Pious to the core, she hired only servants with sound Biblical principles, but her missionary zeal came to nothing. Upon the advice of her lawyer, Mr. Bruff, Rachel Verinder jilted her cousin, Godfrey Ablewhite, who had won her on the rebound from Franklin Blake.

Peter Lovesey's Londoner Moscrop, trying to determine which was the most fashionable church of all, asked the advice of his landlady. She said that St. Peter's, at the top of the Grand Parade, was the best known, but Moscrop decided on St. Paul's, nearer the sea on West Street, because it was closer to Montpelier Terrace where he stayed. Later promenading on Sunday, Moscrop saw the carriages sweeping down from St. Peter's into the Old Steine and concluded that matins at St. Peter's were kept short for social purposes.

Turn to your right at the stoplight and take St. George's Place to Gloucester Street. Cross Gloucester Street to Gloucester Place and take it to North Road. Cross North Road, and continue walking on what is now Marlborough Place around one side of Victoria Gardens to Church Street.

Across Victoria Gardens the roadway has become the Grand Parade. You will see terraces of bow-windowed Regency houses charmingly painted all the colors of the rainbow. This is the area of Brighton, east of the Royal Pavilion and the Old Steine, south of St. James Street and north of Marine Parade, where fashionable society stayed in Regency times. It is now occupied by people like Kate Sandys and her father in Martha Grimes's *I Am the Only Running Footman*.

Charles Dickens learned at Brighton to satirize the Regency period, which he described in his mystery, *Bleak House*. In that mystery, Turveydrop only visited Brighton at fashionable times, and the peak of his social career occurred outside the Pavilion when the Prince Regent noticed him and graciously asked, "Who the Devil is he?"

Cross Church Street and walk through the Pavilion's arched Moorish gateway. To your right is a large domed building that used to be the Royal Stables. Now called the Dome, it houses the Brighton Art Gallery and Museum with a superb collection of Art Nouveau and Art Deco, together with some Old Masters, and a collection of china, silver, furniture, and local history exhibits. There is also a concert hall where variety shows are performed. In Victorian times Lovesey's Moscrop and his Brighton acquaintances, Dr. and Mrs. Prothero, attended a regimental ball there.

Straight ahead and to your left is the Royal Pavilion, the

Oriental pleasure-palace built and rebuilt by the Prince Regent to match his increasingly ornate and florid taste. What you see is a yellow stone-and-brick structure with an amazing variety of bronze-green domes and minarets. His niece, Queen Victoria, did not approve of the Royal Pavilion's look or manners, so she sold it to the city.

George IV first came to Brighton in 1783 when he was twenty-one, the artistic, cultivated "Prince Florizel," not the stout red-faced figure of fun he would become in the pages of Georgette Heyer's *Regency Buck*. The young Prince fell in love with a Roman Catholic widow, Maria Fitzherbert, whom he secretly (and illegally) married in 1785. They lived in Brighton in two farmhouses on the Steyne (Steine), aping the simple rural life in a manner rather like the French queen Marie Antoinette at Versailles. (The results of this consciously naive behavior—for France—were illustrated by the adventures of Baroness Orczy's *The Scarlet Pimpernel*, one of the models for Dorothy L. Sayers's Lord Peter Wimsey.)

The Prince's farmhouse was the ancestor of the Royal Pavilion. In the official booklet you can see the stages it went through until it reached the Oriental splendor you tour today. It is impossible to describe adequately the unique combination of empire Regency and Chinese color and decoration; it simply has to be seen to be believed. In spite of a tendency to overdo his love of culture and luxury, George IV left England a large esthetic legacy, from a refurbished Buckingham Palace and Windsor Castle to his personal art collection, which was the foundation of the National Gallery.

In *The Black Envelope: Mr. Pinkerton Again,* Inspector Bull of Scotland Yard, called in to investigate a murder, went in the Entrance Hall of the Royal Pavilion under the large Chinese lantern suspended from a dragon's claws. He then met his friend Mr. Pinkerton, who had been present when rich old Mrs. Isom was murdered in the great Music Room with a paring knife from the kitchens.

Together with Mr. Pinkerton, Mrs. Isom's ward and her American suitor, Mrs. Isom's companion, her nurse, and her lawyer were all somewhere in the Pavilion at the time of the stabbing. Later the police reassembled all the suspects in the exotic Music Room, whose splendor Mr. Pinkerton thought stood for "all the pomp and vanity of a wicked long-dead world," to reenact the crime.

In *I Am the Only Running Footman*, Martha Grimes's Kate Sandys found the Royal Pavilion banked in scaffolding when she walked there from The Lanes through snowy slush. Later in the mystery Kate actually toured the palace. She stared at the high dome of the Music Room with its silver-winged dragon and splendid chandelier, wondering what it must have looked like when lit. She wandered, following the red velvet cords through the elaborately splendid Banqueting Room with the long table set for a princely party, into the Great Kitchen with its burnished copper canopies over the handsome wooden tables filled with gleaming pots and pans, and elaborate menus framed on the walls. Depressed, Kate could only think of the meals she fixed with carrots and cabbages, and her sister Dolly's annoyance at her plan to turn their house on Madeira Drive into a paying bed-and-breakfast place.

In Georgette Heyer's *Regency Buck,* the headstrong Miss Tavener and her young brother, Peregrine, were eager to come to Brighton, where the Prince Regent had started the season by celebrating his birthday. But after her ill-fated race, it was several tearful days before Judith pulled herself together to walk with her companion, Mrs. Scattergood, to see the Royal Pavilion. Mrs. Scattergood, who remembered the portly Prince Regent in the days of his golden youth, informed Judith that the Pavilion was begun by Henry Holland from an idea the Prince Regent got when he saw a piece of Chinese wallpaper. A wit, seeing its Taj Mahal proportions, also said it looked as if St. Paul's Cathedral in London had whelped and brought forth a litter of cupolas.

Judith Tavener and her chaperone were invited to one of the Prince Regent's parties. They entered the octagonal vestibule with its Chinese lantern, then the tent-topped entrance hall, painted to look like a clouded sky. From there they progressed into the Chinese Gallery, where the Prince Regent himself received them, creaking with corsets and bedizened with brocade. The Prince Regent affably pointed out a stained-glass portrait of Lin-Shin, god of thunder, in the ceiling.

Next they met the famous dandy, Beau Brummell, who said it was all hideously ugly. Then they went into the famous Music Room, designed by John Nash to be a blaze of red and gold, dragons, and more iron-painted bamboo. (In keeping with the sinister side of Brighton, in November 1975 a student lobbed a bomb into the Music Room and did a lot of damage, but it has been reopened.)

The chamber was overpoweringly hot, for the Prince Regent was very susceptible to drafts. Miss Tavener now met "Monk" Lewis, author of the Gothic romance *The Monk,* who also appeared in John Dickson Carr's *The Bride of Newgate.* Then the Regent asked her to slip away with him into the Yellow Drawing Room, where he had something very pretty to show her. Once there he made a portly pass at her. Judith fainted away, mainly from the heat, but Lord Worth, following them, nearly challenged his Prince to a duel.

If you are hungry, there is a pleasant, almost plain, first-floor tearoom hung with portraits of the Royal Family. One shows Farmer George III with his thirteen children; another large one is a roguish view of a naked, potbellied Regent dressed as Cupid, kissing awake a voluptuous Psyche (or Brighton). We had the Royal Pavilion Sandwich, toasted ham and cheese with pineapple, lettuce, cucumber, and tomato, a rather appropriately elaborate sandwich for tea. As you leave the Pavilion there is a gift shop where you can buy postcards and souvenirs of the Royal Pavilion and Brighton.

When you come out of the Pavilion you will be in Pavilion Park, with people sitting about in rented deck chairs or on the lawn. There are a snack stand and some bath chairs. They were the only way Mrs. Ablewhite would take exercise when she came to Brighton to chaperone Rachel Verinder in Wilkie Collins's *The Moonstone.* To your right again is the Dome, originally the Royal Stables.

Go through the southern gate, which David Frome's Inspector Bull in *The Black Envelope: Mr. Pinkerton Again* remembered was a gift from India for the hospitality given Indian soldiers in the Pavilion in World War I. You will find yourself on a street called Pavilion Buildings. Walk to the next street, called Castle Square, with a Lloyd's Bank on your right. Castle Square is an extension of North Street.

Turn left and walk along Castle Square toward the Old Steine. Across the street is a small Georgian hotel called Castle Square House with a Laura Ashley shop on the ground floor. A good pub with oaken rafters and hot and cold bar food, the Royal Pavilion Tavern, is next door. This may be the site of the Castle Inn in *Regency Buck*, where Miss Tavener's wicked uncle and cousin stayed.

As you come to the Old Steine, to your right you will see a large yellow-and-white Georgian hotel called the Royal Albion. It has a porticoed front entrance with flags flying and occupies an entire block, with a glassed-in porch that goes around the corner on the seaside.

The Royal Albion seems to be the best choice for the fictional hotel called the Pavilion Plaza Hotel. In *Dead Cert*, Dick Francis's jockey Alan York had dropped off Clifford Tudor, the suspicious horse owner who had some secret connection with the Brighton Marconicar taxis, at that hotel. York was trying to track down the criminals who had killed his friend, Major Bill Davidson, by tripping his horse with a wire, so their bet against him would be a "dead cert."

York had also fallen for Kate Ellery-Penn, whose eccentric Uncle George gave her a racehorse instead of pearls for her birthday. While sleuthing, York visited her Sussex home, then drove Kate to Brighton. They played like kids on the beach, then went to the Pavilion Plaza Hotel for tea and tried to pump the help about Tudor and the Marconicars.

The Old Steine (Regency name Steyne, or stone), where tradition says the fishermen once dried their nets, is now an open park. In *Regency Buck* Donaldson's Lending Library was here. Across the Old Steine along Grand Parade and its cross street, St. James Street, you can still see terraces of elegant Regency houses. Judith Tavener and Lord Worth had a row about his choice of a house for her to rent for the season. He wanted her to take one on Marine Parade, not the one he himself took on the Steyne. He managed it by suggesting she NOT take the one on Marine Parade. He told her the Steyne was a most eligible situation in the center of town in sight of the Pavilion, all perfectly true as you will see. No. 55 on the west side of the Steine was the home of the Regent's morganatic wife, Mrs. Fitzherbert.

Turn right to walk along the Old Steine to Steine Lane, where you will find the Brighton Information Centre at No. 54, Marlborough House. Then cross to the center of the Old Steine, where you will find the Brighton bus office. Walk toward the sea, bearing slightly to your right, and you will come to Grand Junction and Marine Parade. Straight ahead of you is the Esplanade and Brighton's famous Palace Pier. Not counting time inside the Royal Pavilion, from the palace to the pier you have walked over one mile (downhill).

To your left is the Aquarium, below Marine Parade on Madeira Drive. You will also see Volk's Electric Railway, which runs along the shoreline to Black Rock. David Frome's Mr. Pinkerton was walking there when he was pushed off a cliff by the murderer in *The Black Envelope: Mr. Pinkerton Again*. At the eastern edge of Brighton you would also come to Roedean School, a very exclusive institution where Susan Moody's black photographer, Penny Wanawake, was educated. In *Penny Dreadful,* Penny complained that Roedean was a cloistered, all-girl school that left her totally ignorant of "life-skills," so that she had to spend nine months in Africa, where she learned how to be radically chic.

If you decide to visit the Gothic grottoes of the Aquarium, remember Mr. Pinkerton followed Mrs. Isom's ward and her American admirer inside, only to be accused of being a spy in front of the octopus tank. Recall also that Peter Lovesey's Albert Moscrop followed the Prothero family inside in *Mad Hatter's Holiday.* You may prefer not to remember the experience of Sergeant Cribb and Constable Thackeray of London's Scotland Yard, who later came to the Aquarium to retrieve a human hand discovered in the Alligator and Crocodile Cavern. The monsters were drugged and Thackeray went in to retrieve the specimen, which Sergeant Cribb then carried in a brown paper bag to the police station on Grafton Street east off Marine Parade. This police station may be the one visited by Mr. Pinkerton and Inspector Bull, as well as the one where Dick Francis's Alan York went for help in *Dead Cert*. York had staked out the office of the Marconicars in a Regency building off Marine Drive, which was "lamentably vulgarized" by a flashing red neon sign. Frome's Mrs. Isom lived nearby in Sussex Square, while in Grimes's *I Am the Only Running Footman,* the Sandys family lived in a dark, high-ceilinged Victorian house on Madeira Drive, which Kate wanted to make into a paying bed-and-breakfast.

Cross to the Esplanade, which runs above the shore. This is the longest seaside walkway in Europe. It is filled with deck chairs in green-and-white stripes, arcades, food stalls and amusement park shops, punk kids, pop music, and erect old English gentlemen in tweeds taking the air. Straight ahead is the entrance to the Palace Pier, an ornate, domed Victorian structure that sticks out into the chilly sea for a quarter of a mile. Younger than its neighbor, the West Pier, which is being renovated, the Palace Pier was built to replace the 1823 Chain Pier, which Lovesey's Sergeant Cribb saw in *Mad Hatter's Holiday.*

In *Brighton Rock,* Graham Greene's cold-blooded young London punk, Pinkie, met with his gang and orchestrated the cold-blooded murder of the *Messenger's* Hale in the Palace Pier restaurant. Pinkie was eventually run down and caught by a casual, good-time Brighton type named Ida, who had spent part of the day with the terrified Hale, then ferreted out the fact that he had not deserted her, but had been murdered. Ida's strong sense of fair play meant that she then undertook and accomplished Hale's revenge.

The Palace Pier, with its palace of fun, hall of mirrors, ghost train, and all the other aspects of a Coney Island, was once a regular dock for Channel-going vessels. It is also the best place to walk out for a look at Brighton and its Downs. Chasing the murderer in Grimes's mystery, Scotland Yard's

Superintendent Jury went there with his drippy-nosed Sergeant Wiggins, who happily tried out the sideshows like "What the Butler Saw."

In *Dead Cert,* after a chase across country by a Marconicar, Dick Francis's York came back to Brighton and set up a trap for the villain. York met a friendly trainer with a horse box by the Palace Pier, and, taking his other ally, the ex-Army owner of The Lanes' pub, the Blue Duck, went to collect the race-horse, Admiral, whom York had left tied to a tree in the Sussex countryside.

It was on "Brighton Pier," presumably the Palace Pier, that British actress Jane Seymour met her first husband while filming *Oh! What a Lovely War!* Seymour has not only played the part of Lady Marguerite Blakeley in Baroness Orczy's *The Scarlet Pimpernel* and Mary Yellen in Daphne Du Maurier's *Jamaica Inn,* but she was also in the James Bond thriller *Live and Let Die.*

Once you have enjoyed all the treats and murderous associations of the Palace Pier, walk back to the entrance and turn left to take Grand Junction to King's Road, the seaside avenue of luxury hotels that stretches between Palace Pier and West Pier. In Grimes's *I Am the Only Running Footman,* the killer stalked TV personality Dolly Sands (nee Sandys) along King's Road past the arcades beneath the arches.

You should take time to climb down to walk on the rough, pebbly seashore itself. You might like to rent a green-and-white-striped deck chair like the one where Hale picked up Ida in Greene's *Brighton Rock,* or try digging up the pieces of the dismembered corpse in Lovesey's *Mad Hatter's Holiday,* or simply frolic on the shingle as Alan York and his Kate did before they went to the Pavilion Plaza Hotel in Francis's *Dead Cert.*

In Agatha Christie's short story, "The Rajah's Emerald," her clerk (with the startling name of "James Bond") had been persuaded by his girlfriend Grace to come to "Kimpton-on-Sea." James frugally stayed in an inexpensive boardinghouse, while Grace stayed at the Esplanade Hotel on the seafront, the kind of luxury hotel found all along the Brighton shore. But it was James who found an emerald in a bathing hut and through it made friends with Lord Edward Campion and the Rajah of Maraputna.

Superintendent Jury and the sneezing Sergeant Wiggins, tracking the murderer in Martha Grimes's *I Am the Only Running Footman,* found the painter Paul Swan doing a watercolor of the West Pier near the Palace Pier. Sitting on a bench by the sea, they questioned him about suspect David Marr. Wiggins managed to suggest he knew something about painting, with the result that Paul Swan shared his artistic suspicion that the poet Coleridge's poem about the stately pleasure palace of Cathay's "Kubla Khan" had been inspired by the Prince Regent's Pavilion.

Farther along the shore near the Old Penny Palace, a little museum of old slot machines, you can see the arches built under the Esplanade, with arcade shops. The Grimes killer later played hide-and-seek with Melrose Plant, the ex-aristocrat, around here. In one of the arches is a sign that reads "Annual tribute to King William called Herring Silver was 4000 herring or three day's fishing," a graphic reminder that Brighton was an ancient fishing village.

Directly across King's Road to your right as you walk west along the Esplanade there are a number of famous hotels. One is the Grand Hotel, the major Victorian hotel with a huge internal dome. It has been the meeting place of the Conservative Party for years, for Greene's Hale saw the old politicians sunning themselves in front of the Grand in *Brighton Rock.* More recently, the kind of IRA terrorists Bill Granger writes about in his November Man thrillers nearly blew up Prime Minister Thatcher and her party leaders. When we passed the Grand, it was covered, like the Royal Pavilion, with scaffolding, and there was a temporary stand in front of it selling Brighton Rock.

There used to be a Brighton institution called Mutton's, on King's Road. It was still mentioned with enthusiasm in the 1924 Baedeker's *Great Britain.* All the characters in Peter Lovesey's *Mad Hatter's Holiday* went there to dine on real turtle soup. Another institution, Brill's, which was a swimming bath for gentlemen, was nearby. Sergeant Cribb struck up an acquaintance with his suspect, Dr. Prothero, over a green-and-white towel, which ended in their lunching at Mutton's in the main dining room fulsomely decorated with mirrors, a domed skylight, and an elaborate chandelier.

The next lane running uphill to your right from King's Road is Black Lion Street, off which, to the left, runs tiny Black Lion Lane. Since there is no Black Horse Lane in the Lanes where Martha Grimes's TV weather girl Dolly Sands went to have her fortune told and was caught by the murderer, this street and its namesake lane are probably the real-life counterparts. If you are hungry or thirsty, Cricketers, the oldest pub in Brighton, is at 15 Black Lion Street and serves excellent pies and sandwiches.

Cross Black Lion Street and continue along King's Road. Just before you come to Ship Street, you see the Old Ship Hotel. It was built in three sections, and the oldest part is on the corner. Cream colored, it has Georgian bow windows, and inside, low ceilings and cozy wood-paneled lounges with elegant carpets and furniture, making it the perfect spot for tea.

The Old Ship Hotel has the most mystery associations of any hotel in Brighton. It was the inn Nicholas Tettersell bought with his reward money for helping Charles II escape to France. In *Royal Escape* Georgette Heyer unaccountably called him Stephen Tettersell. But she carefully followed history by having the King stay in Brighthelmstone at the George Inn, where the landlord recognized him but would not betray him. Early next morning Charles and his companions rode to the seashore at Shoreham just west of Hove and took ship for France in Tettersell's coal ship, *The Surprise*.

While writing *Oliver Twist*, Charles Dickens stayed at the Old Ship, and gave readings in its two-hundred-year-old Assembly Room, where Gerogette Heyer's heroine, Judith Tavener, attended balls in *Regency Buck*. Dickens's character, Mr. Dombey, also stayed in Brighton when he came to visit his son Paul in *Dombey and Son*.

In *Mad Hatter's Holiday*, Peter Lovesey's Albert Moscrop passed Black Lion Street and the Old Ship (Hotel), following

Dr. Prothero into The Lanes, where he bought a box of French chocolates. Moscrop suspected Prothero was cheating on his wife, whom Moscrop greatly admired.

Television personality Alys da Sylva in Shelley Smith's *A Grave Affair* had a second lover, Douglas Munro, an Arab sympathizer, who had expected to meet her at her apartment in Hove. The weekend she was murdered, Munro drove there, but not finding her, left a message that he would meet her at the Ship Hotel. He then buzzed down to the shore in his car and sat staring at the Promenade with the gay and grotesque people "strutting up and down against the backdrop of a sharp greeny-gray sea." Every half hour he called her Hove flat, but inevitably, Alys never arrived.

In *Brighton Rock,* Graham Greene's frantic newspaper reporter, Fred Hale, pursued by Pinkie and his gang, tried to pick up Ida when they first met in a pub near the Palace Pier. Then Hale tried to get her to stay with him by inviting her to "come and have a bite." Not really believing him, Ida called him "Sir Horace," asking sarcastically if they could go to the Old Ship.

Come out of the Old Ship Hotel and cross Ship Street to your right. In Lovesey's *Mad Hatter's Holiday* Sergeant Cribb met Moscrop to exchange information at the Seven Stars in Ship Street with a pint of East India and a large meat pie in front of him. Continue along King's Road to Middle Street, cross it, and keep going until you reach West Street.

There you will see Wheeler's Sheridan Hotel, at 64 King's Road, but its famous restaurant called Wheeler's Oyster Rooms is off to your right at 17 Market Street in The Lanes. Up West Street you can see (and hear the chimes of) St. Paul's, which Lovesey's Moscrop attended.

Across West Street you come to the Brighton Centre. It features rock and pop concerts, ice and sports shows, and on top, with a view of the sea, a restaurant called the Skyline, which is open for lunch and before many of the Centre's concerts and shows.

Beyond the Brighton Centre on King's Road you come to the Victorian, striped-brick facade of the Metropole Hotel, with its ornate white iron balconies overlooking the sea, and a terrace with café tables and chairs. You have now walked 2.2 miles from the Royal Pavilion.

This hotel seems the most appropriate one for an Agatha Christie fan, especially since in *Poirot Investigates,* Hastings dragged his friend Hercule off to Brighton for a change of air. They stayed at the Grand Metropole, where they met all the world and his wife, most of whom Poirot described as (war) profiteers. In particular they met Mrs. Opalsen, a stout lady plastered with gems, whose pearls Poirot then saved from a robbery attempt within the luxurious hotel itself.

Have tea here if you wish, or continue walking along King's Road toward the West Pier, closed for renovations. Cross Cannon Place, go past some exhibition halls, and come to the charming Georgian ambiance of Regency Square, rising uphill, with its pleasant green facing West Pier. The houses are terraced on three sides facing the sea. Many of them are small hotels or bed-and-breakfast places like the recently restored Prince Regent at No. 29. Across King's Road by the West Pier is a white candy stall called Lewington's Brighton Rock. Its sign says, "By appointment with Charles II, Royal Sweet-makers since 1672."

Turn here to walk through Regency Square unless you are feeling very energetic and want to walk another two miles west (and back) to look at Adelaide Crescent on the outskirts of Hove, where Shelley Smith's Alys da Sylva lived. Just before World War II, Georgette Heyer and her husband lived at No. 25 Adelaide Crescent with their seven-year-old son, Richard, who ran wild with the landlord's daughter until sent off to prep school in 1940.

While living there, Heyer wrote two historical novels, *The Spanish Bride* and *An Infamous Army,* about Wellington and the Battle of Waterloo, and her account of the escape of Charles II after Worcester, *Royal Escape.* Her secretary later told Heyer's biographer, Jane Aiken Hodge, that she remembered driving about Sussex to check out the inns where Charles II had hidden. (See Dorchester/Charmouth Walk and Shrewsbury Walk.) Jane Aiken Hodge's Gothic thriller, *Watch the Wall My*

Darling, took place just east of Brighton in the old walled city of Rye, as did Heyer's later Regency mystery, *The Unknown Ajax.*

In addition, Heyer wrote two modern mysteries, *No Wind of Blame* and *Penhallow,* and her Regency novel, *The Corinthian,* at Brighton. Another Regency mystery, *The Talisman Ring,* took place in Sussex, so that Sir Tristam Shield would have been obliged to ride like the wind *(ventre à terre)* from London to Brighton to appear at the deathbed of his bride.

If you do not walk farther west, you will begin to climb back up the Brighton hills through a series of charming Georgian terraces. At the back of Regency Square turn to your right and go up into Russell Square. Keep to your right to the end of Russell Square, then turn sharply left to come into Clarence Square. Keep to your right and you will come out on Western Road at Cannon Place. Turn right on Western Road. Several blocks away you will see the Victorian Clock Tower, put up to commemorate Queen Victoria's Jubilee.

At the Clock Tower, Western Road becomes North Street, one of the entrances to The Lanes. To your left is another major road called Dyke Road. It leads uphill toward St. Nicholas Church and churchyard. The grave of Nicholas Tettersell there should remind you that mystery writer Antonia Fraser also wrote a biography of "Royal Charles" (II).

In the north aisle of St. Nicholas Church there is a marker on the Thrale pew to tell you that G. K. Chesterton's hero, Dr. Samuel Johnson, worshiped there. Lilian de la Torre wrote a series of mysteries about *Dr. Sam Johnson: Detective* in which Mrs. Thrale also appeared.

In Peter Lovesey's *Mad Hatter's Holiday,* Albert Moscrop hiked up Dyke Road all the way to the Devil's Dyke on the Downs far above Brighton, where there is a great natural cleft in the chalk cliffs. There he saw Dr. Prothero meet a mysterious woman on horseback. If you want to go up Dyke Road, take Western Road to the Clock Tower, then turn left to climb uphill.

If you don't want to climb any more at the moment, walk along Western Road to the modern, open shopping center in

Churchill Square. It has all the well-known English department stores like Marks & Spencer, as well as artists doing pavement chalk drawings and mobs of tourists. Keep to your right and you will come to North Street and The Lanes. You have now walked 3.7 miles up- and downhill from the Royal Pavilion and should seriously consider some refreshment here where opportunities are all about you.

Feel free to roam along The Lanes, which are all pedestrian walkways. We cut across to Duke's Street, then into Duke's Lane. At the corner of Duke's Lane and Middle Street we found a spick-and-span old pub called The Victory, green below and yellow stucco above. It made a good stand-in for Dick Francis's Blue Duck, where the pubkeeper kept a ferocious black Alsatian dog named Prince. Alan York and his girl went there while rambling in The Lanes in *Dead Cert*.

We windowshopped, realizing why The Lanes in Brighton is a mecca for fine antiques. In Ellis Peters's *The Knocker on the Door*, Robert Macsen Martel came there to find an ancient ornament to hide a bullet hole in an abbey door. In *Malice Domestic* by Mollie Hardwick, Howell Evans, trying to avoid buying a brass bed for his antique shop, finally agreed that he could get that man in Brighton "who goes for brasses" to check it out.

David Frome's lovers in *The Black Envelope: Mr. Pinkerton Again* pottered about The Lanes, buying things for his mother, who refused to have anything that wasn't "old, cracked, chipped, or completely broken in the house." In P. D. James's *Death of an Expert Witness,* the starcrossed lovers Stella Mawson and Angela Foley bought two Victorian luster plant pots on matching pedestals in The Lanes one summer weekend.

Martha Grimes's Kate Sandys picked up a miniature porcelain box in a Lanes antique shop, then felt compelled to tell the shopkeeper she would buy it. Lovesey's Albert Moscrop spent his first Monday morning in the antique shops in East and West Streets, hoping he might find an early Venetian wooden telescope for his collection. You can find anything you are looking for, not just antiques but clothes, music boxes, luggage, china, and books, both new and second-hand.

Now locate Prince Albert's Street, and turn uphill again past the Friends Meeting House. Take the winding Meeting House Lane back to North Street, turn right and walk to New Road. Cross to New Road. On your left you will see the red-and-white marquee and white columns of the Theatre Royal, directly across from the Dome and the Royal Pavilion. In this theater at the beginning of World War II, Dorothy L. Sayers's feminist comedy, *Love All,* was put on to great applause.

Walk past the theater to Church Street, then turn left and take Church Street to Queen's Road. Both Lovesey's Moscrop and Greene's London Bank Holiday trippers went from the railway station to the seashore by way of the Queen's Road streetcars, which no longer exist. You may want to find a taxi or take a bus, for you have a long walk up Queen's Road, a busy modern thoroughfare, to the railway station where you end your walk. Measured from the Royal Pavilion, you have walked 7.5 miles in Brighton, 8.8 miles if you walked there from the station and back again.

3

CAMBRIDGE

BACKGROUND

Cambridge is the "other" university town in England. Historically, Cambridge was not only an important inland port but the best ford for the Cam River, which was navigable all the way to the North Sea. Today, as Margaret Yorke wrote in *Murder Ink*, Cambridge is "out on a limb, long ago a port, but now an end in itself."

By A.D. 43 the Romans had settled by the Cam River on Castle Hill, and later, the Anglo-Saxon kingdoms of East Anglia and Mercia met there. When he tried to conquer Fenland's Hereward the Wake, William the Conqueror built a castle at Cambridge. King John granted Cambridge's Stourbridge Fair a charter in 1211. Its international market was parodied by Bedford's John Bunyan in *Pilgrim's Progress*. Gradually, Cambridge became a thriving market town with a number of religious foundations, many of which were later absorbed into the colleges.

Depending on the source, Cambridge University began when Spanish Prince Cantaber brought students here from Athens in 4321 B.C., or when Saxon Alfred the Great, the hero of G. K. Chesterton's *Ballad of the White Horse*, began a college of priests at Ely. More likely, the university began when some students left Oxford because of town/gown riots in 1209. Oxford University is older, but St. Peter's College (or Peterhouse) was founded by 1281. Peterhouse was followed by thirty-four more colleges, the last being Robinson College in 1979.

The university began to grow about the time Cambridge lost its importance as a port to King's Lynn. Over the years there has been great deal of town/gown animosity as the colleges took over more and more land. During the Peasants' Revolt in 1381, for example, the university's royal charters were burned in the marketplace.

Cambridge University was a hotbed of the New Learning during the Renaissance (the Protestant martyrs Cranmer, Latimer, and Ridley, burned to death at Oxford by order of Mary Tudor, were students here). The town of Cambridge was Puritan during the Civil War, so the Royalist Colleges suffered considerable damage. The old town/gown disputes were finally settled by Act of Parliament in 1856, and the growth of the railroads in the nineteenth century brought industry and increased population to the town. Made a city in 1951, Cambridge is no longer merely "a town within a university."

The Cambridge colleges, however, are still the chief interest of most tourists. Like Oxford, Cambridge University is made up of a series of colleges within the university, each with a Master (sometimes called President or Provost) and Fellows (or dons) who own the College. Undergraduates live in dormitories (on "staircases") and are waited upon by "gyps" or bedmakers. They, too, when studying or seeking privacy, shut their outer doors or "sport their oaks." At night the Proctor, a university official, with two Bulldogs (or staff) patrols the town to catch drunk or disorderly students or those trying to climb back into college after the gates are shut.

At Cambridge, quadrangles are called "courts"; most colleges have a Master's Lodge and Garden, a Fellows Garden, library, chapel, and hall. It was not until the 1870s that the first women's college, Girton College, was opened; now women are accepted at most of the men's colleges. In her mystery *In the Shadow of King's*, however, American Nora Kelly took umbrage at the Cambridge Old Boys' network. She sounded very much like feminist role model Virginia Woolf in *A Room of One's Own*. (Although Woolf's father and brothers all went to Cambridge, she never went to college and was warned off the grass when she visited them.)

Oxford's crime writer, Anthony Price, sent his eccentric Intelligence Chief David Audley to Cambridge. In *Soldier No More* Price revealed that in a reversal of the Communists' recruitment of the "Cambridge Five," who spied for Russia, Audley had been secretly recruited to be a "sleeper" until British Intelligence needed him. In that same mystery, double agent Captain Roche, sent to France to "activate" Audley, found him writing best-seller historical novels. Roche remembered that "Oxford and Cambridge were notoriously addicted to whodunits and mysteries—they were even given to writing the things."

He was correct. Many mystery writers went to Cambridge. Among them were Raymond Postgate and his sister, Margaret Cole, who wrote with her Oxford husband, G. D. H. Cole. Peter Dickinson, Robert Charles, and Brian Cooper not only attended Cambridge but wrote mysteries about it.

Playwright and poet J. B. Priestley, who wrote a mystery called *Salt Is Leaving*, went to Trinity Hall, while both C. P. Snow and his wife, Pamela Hansford Johnson, also went to Cambridge. Lord Snow wrote a mystery about the Norfolk Broads called *Death Under Sail*, while his novel, *The Search*, was used as a clue in Dorothy L. Sayers's *Gaudy Night*. (See Ely, Oxford Walks.) Sayers herself had many Cambridge associations.

In addition to these mystery writers, Andrew Taylor, who wrote *Caroline Minuscule*, went to Cambridge, as did Colin Dexter, who writes about Oxford. In *The Garb of Truth*, Ian Stuart's accountant-detective, David Grierson, solved a murder based on a new will that had been drawn up by Cambridge solicitors.

Erskine Childers, who wrote the classic 1908 thriller *The Riddle of the Sands* about the possible invasion of England, went to Trinity College. Childers was later shot for treason during the Irish Troubles. C. Day Lewis, the poet laureate who wrote mysteries as Nicholas Blake, gave the Clark Lectures. The Matron of Josephine Bell's St. Edmund's Hospital in London knitted pullovers for her nephew who was "up at Cambridge."

Three generations of mystery writer Georgette Heyer's family went to Cambridge, while Margery Allingham's father, Herbert, and her husband's uncle met at Cambridge in the 1880s. Allingham was sent to Cambridge's Perse School where, according to mystery writer Jessica Mann (who went to Newnham College), she wrote long blank-verse plays for the other students to act. When she left Perse School, Allingham wrote her first book about smuggling and murder in Essex, published when she was only 17. Like Prince Charles and other members of the Royal Family, to which he supposedly belongs, Allingham's Albert Campion (aka Rudolph) was also a Cambridge man.

Agatha Christie's older sister, Madge, went to the school now called Roedean and was encouraged to apply to Girton College, but their father did not want "bluestockings" in the family so she went to a French finishing school instead. (See Brighton Walk.)

Chesterton Lane at the north end of town is a reminder that G. K. Chesterton's family may have come from here. In *Tour de Force* Christianna Brand's incredible tour guide from Gibraltar, Mr. Fernando, who was five feet four inches high and nearly as broad, tapering into infinitesimal feet, introduced himself as a "late undergrad, St. John's College."

P. D. James not only lived here and went to the Cambridge High School for Girls, but wrote about Cambridge, making Margaret Yorke suspect that Adam Dalgliesh was a Cambridge man. In *Death of an Expert Witness,* sixteen-year-old Brenda Pridmore spent her first paycheck at Cambridge's Marks & Spencer. Paul Middlemas, the Document Examiner at Hoggaths, lived on the outskirts of Cambridge and commuted to work in his Jaguar. Local Detective-Inspector Doyle lived in Scroope House, about four miles north of Cambridge, and biologist Claire Easterbrook's alibi for the murder of Lorrimer was that she and her lover had dined with the Master of his Cambridge college.

You get a bird's-eye view of Cambridge itself in a number of mysteries. In *Death of an Expert Witness,* P. D. James's Detective-Inspector, the Honorable John Massingham, saw Cambridge from the helicopter taking him and Dalgliesh from Battersea, London, to Clevisham. Above the towers and spires of Cambridge, Massingham saw the shining curve of the river and the bright avenues that lead through green lawns to miniature bridges. He watched as King's College Chapel slowly rotated beside its great square of green.

In *Rat Race,* Dick Francis's pilot Matt Shore flew the Duke of Wessex and champion jockey Colin Ross from Cambridge to a meet, then back at the end of the day. Cambridge Airport is east of town just south of the Newmarket Road. The Duke of Wessex lived near Cambridge in a stately eighteenth-century mansion open to view by the public. His mansion might well be Audley End House at Saffron Walden. (See Side Trips.) Later in *Rat Race,* Colin's sister Nancy flew her jockey brother from Cambridge to Haydock Park racecourse. A criminal had tinkered with her plane so she could not read her equipment. Matt Shore tracked her plane, then led her up the Wash, over the North Sea, and home, following the river to Cambridge.

In *No Police at the Funeral,* Margery Allingham's Campion drove his ancient Bentley to Cambridge to visit Socrates Close. The city was covered by a thick Fens mist and Campion was disappointed to find that, out of term, Cambridge was only a chill, medieval city.

HOW TO GET THERE

British Rail: trains hourly from Liverpool Station, London—63 minutes

Automobile: A10 from London; 54 miles from central London

Length of Walk: 8 miles, divided into two walks of about 4 miles each

See also Side Trips to Duxford, Saffron Walden, and Audley End House.

See map on page 59 for the boundaries of this walk and page 353 for a list of detectives and stories.

PLACES OF INTEREST

Colleges: See especially *St. John's College, St. John's Street; King's College, King's Parade; Trinity College, Trinity Street.* To view a college, ask at the Porter's Lodge or check sign in gateway.

The Backs, lawns along Cam River behind colleges.

Great St. Mary's, King's Parade. Famous view from tower.

Little St. Mary's, chapel of Peterhouse College, Trumpington Street.

Fitzwilliam Museum, Trumpington Street (6950). (Open Tuesday–Saturday 2–5; Sunday 2:15–5.) Free. Coffee bar: Tuesday–Saturday 2–4; Sunday 2:15–4.

Heffers (main bookstores), 20 Trinity Street.

Market Square, Market Hill. Open-air stalls.

The Church of the Holy Sepulchre (the Round Church), Bridge Street.

Scudamore's Boat Yards, Cam River at Bridge Street or Mill Lane, Silver Street. Place to rent a punt.

Tourist Information Centre, Wheeler Street (0223) 358977, 353363. (Monday–Saturday all year; daily May–September.)

PLACES TO STAY/EAT

Cambridge

University Arms Hotel, Regent Street (351241). Modern and expensive.

Fitzwilliam Museum Coffee Bar, Trumpington Street. (Open Tuesday–Saturday 2–4; Sunday 2:15–4.) Inexpensive.

The Oasis, Green Street. Basement restaurant. Inexpensive.

The Eagle, Bene't Street. Coaching inn with outside gallery near Cavendish Laboratory, patronized by Cambridge scientists Watson and Crick, who discovered DNA.

Fitzbillies Cake Shop, Trumpington Street. Chain famous for
sticky Chelsea buns.

Shades, King's Parade (359506). Bar below, restaurant upstairs
with English food. Expensive.

Royal Cambridge Hotel, Trumpington Street (0223 351631).
Two Regency houses. Inexpensive.

Saffron Walden

Eight Bells, Bridge Street (0799 22790). Sixteenth-century pub.

Saffron Hotel, 10 High Street (0799 22676). Georgian pub with
some bedrooms. Inexpensive.

--------- **CAMBRIDGE WALK** ---------

Begin your Cambridge walk at the Cambridge Railway Station, a landmark building featured in the opening scene of the
movie *Chariots of Fire.* Nora Kelly's American professor Gillian
Adams, who had been a history student at Newnham College,
returned there by train. She was on sabbatical and had been
invited to give a lecture by the prestigious Cambridge Historical Society. Adams felt Cambridge ought to appear in shades
of gray—skies, stones, mist, and rain—although her memory
of it was all green and gold. She arrived early on Sunday
morning and took a cab to her college friend Bea Hamilton's
house in Newnham.

A more dramatic arrival was that of V. C. Clinton-Baddeley's inoffensive Miss Banbury, who was found dead on the
train from London in *Death's Bright Dart.* In *Funeral Sites,*
Jessica Mann's fugitive architect, Rosamund Sholto, also arrived by train from London, as did P. D. James's young sleuth,
Cordelia Gray. She came with the cool and intimidating Miss
Leaming to visit Sir Ronald Callender. The two women went
to the station carpark to meet Sir Ronald's laboratory assistant, Lunn, who drove a small black van.

Go outside the station to the roundabout. On the right is
the parking lot, usually filled with bicycles. Refusing all lifts in

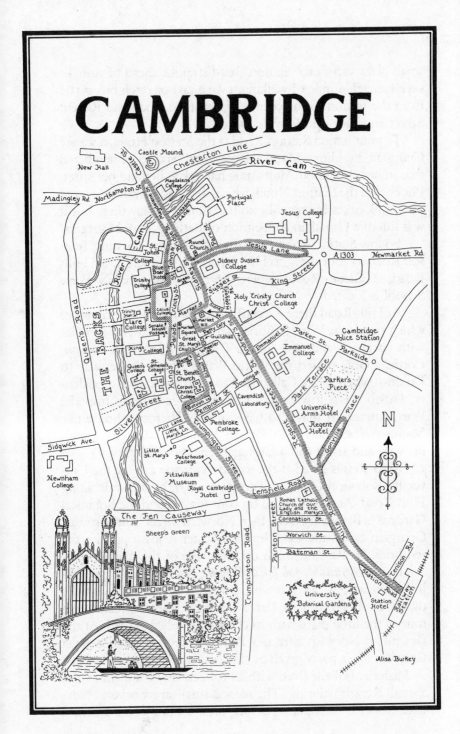

CAMBRIDGE

New Hall
Castle Mound
Chesterton Lane
River Cam
Castle St.
Madingley Rd. Northampton St.
Magdalene College
Portugal Place
Thompson's Lane
Jesus College
River Cam
St. Johns College
Park St.
Round Church
Jesus Lane
A1303 Newmarket Rd.
Blue Boar Hotel
St. Johns St.
Sidney Sussex College
King Street
Trinity College
Green St.
Sussex St.
Queen's Road
Trinity St.
Caius College
Trinity Hall
Holy Trinity Church Christ College
Clare College
Senate House Passage
Market St.
Market Hill
Petty Cury
Cambridge Police Station
Kings College
Market Square
Great St. Mary's Church
Guildhall
Emmanuel St.
Parker St.
THE BACKS
St. Mary's Church
Wheeler St.
Emmanuel College
Parkside
Queen's College
St. Catharine's College
St. Benet Church
Downing St.
Park Terrace
Parker's Piece
Silver Street
Corpus Christi College
Pembroke St.
Cavendish Laboratory
Regent Street
University Arms Hotel
St. Andrews St.
Place
Sidgwick Ave.
Mill Lane
Little St. Mary's Lane
Pembroke College
Regent Hotel
Newnham College
Little St. Mary's
Peterhouse College
Trumpington Street
Lensfield Road
Fitzwilliam Museum
Royal Cambridge Hotel
Roman Catholic Church of Our Lady and the English martyr's
Panton Street
The Fen Causeway
Coronation St.
Sheep's Green
Norwich St.
Bateman St.
Trumpington Road
Station Road
Tenison Rd.
University Botanical Gardens
Station Hotel
Railway Station
Alisa Burkey

N

59

small black vans, take Station Road straight ahead of you. To save yourself a mile of walking, take a taxi or catch bus #101 from the station to the corner of Lensfield Road and Regent Street and pick up the walk there.

To your left on Station Road is the Station Hotel, a square Georgian building. Mann's Rosamund Sholto remembered that in her childhood Aunt Anne had taken her and her sister, Phoebe, to the Station Hotel, where they had currant buns and little pink cakes for tea. Sholto had hoped to stay there but it was full of a Canadian convention of Bathing Pool Managers.

Follow Station Road away from the station, crossing Tenison Road to your right, to Hills Road. To your left down Hills Road is Glebe Road, where Margery Allingham's Perse School is located.

At Hills Road there is a traffic roundabout, in the center of which stands the War Memorial statue of a World War I soldier with backpack and rifle. In *An Unsuitable Job for a Woman*, Cordelia Gray passed the World War I soldier on her way to Duxford where Mark Callender had been working as a gardener. Duxford is a town south of Cambridge with an Imperial War Museum. It may also have an ugly Victorian house like Summertrees, where P. D. James's Major Markland lived with his wife and sister and a large garden. (See Side Trips.)

Across Hills Road at the roundabout you can see the University Botanical Gardens. Turn to your right and walk along Hills Road. Across the road on your left beyond the Botanical Gardens is Bateman Street, then Norwich Street, a little row of Georgian brick houses. (Norwich Street is just opposite the red-brick St. Paul's Church on your side of the roadway.)

In *An Unsuitable Job for a Woman*, Sophia and Hugo Tilling lived at No. 57 Norwich Street. The house is actually owned by friends of P. D. James's, and she takes her reader on a tour of the little place with its charming walled garden. At the far end of Norwich Street is Panton Street, where Cordelia Gray went to a party given by the wealthy French girl, Isabelle de Lasterie. Isabelle lived with a drunken lady companion and a small Renoir painting. The second small street beyond Norwich Street is Coronation Street, once a slum where Victoria

Mary Atkins, one of the jurors in Raymond Postgate's *Verdict of Twelve*, lived as a child.

Follow Hills Road, crossing four more streets until you reach the corner where it meets Lensfield Road/Gonville Place. The walk from the railway station to this corner is one mile. If you took a bus or taxi, get off here. At this crossroads there are signs for both Newmarket and Ely, and there are public restrooms.

On your left at the corner of Hills Road and Lensfield Road you (and Cordelia) will see the large yellow Victorian Gothic Roman Catholic Church of Our Lady and the English Martyrs. In Glyn Daniel's *The Cambridge Murders*, Inspector Wyndham of the Cambridge CID lived off Hills Road past the Roman Catholic church. Allingham's Albert Campion heard its bells when he stayed at Socrates Close in *No Police at the Funeral*.

To your right Lensfield becomes Gonville Place. Walk along it to an open area called Parker's Piece. At its far side on Parkside is the "modern and functional" concrete Cambridge police station where, in *An Unsuitable Job for a Woman*, Cordelia met the young, elegantly dressed Sergeant Maskell, who showed her the belt Mark Callender had used to hang himself. When Cordelia retured to Cambridge to trace Mark's nurse, Nanny Pilbeam, she parked her car near Parker's Piece.

In Kelly's *In the Shadow of King's*, Gillian Adams also went to the new police station with her lover, Scotland Yard detective Edward Gisborne. They were asked to make a statement after don Alastair Greenwood was shot during her Cambridge Historical Society lecture. Across Parker's Piece you can glimpse some terraced rows of houses like the one where Adams's old tutor, Basil Peters, lived. In Allingham's *No Police at the Funeral*, the American Ann Held had rooms in Cheshire Street off Parker's Piece.

Return left on Gonville Place to Lensfield Road and cross it to Regent Street. On the far right corner is a modern branch of Lloyd's Bank. It might be the branch bank that Michael Butterworth's Ernest Kitteridge "managed" for a few crazy days in *The Man in the Sopwith Camel*. Walking from his dingy

Edwardian hotel (the Station Hotel, perhaps, or the Royal Cambridge Hotel on Trumpington Street) Kitteridge saw Cambridge "as gray, gothic and unfamiliar, with a thick overcast just missing the spires and fretted battlements, swept by a Fen wind that smelled like vanilla ice cream." When a jet fighter screamed out of the murk, Kitteridge (like Snoopy in *Peanuts*, he liked to imagine he was a World War I flying ace) "took off" after it in his Sopwith Camel. Then he went in the bank to work on a scheme to defraud it of 30,000 pounds. In *Have His Carcase*, Dorothy L. Sayers's seaside masher, Henry Weldon, who was taken with Harriet Vane, kept both a bank account and a mistress in Cambridge. His mother came from St. Ives, a short distance away.

On Regent Street you will pass the Regent Hotel, an attractive Georgian building of yellow brick with white trim. Along Regent Street there are also a number of restaurants, bookstores, newsagents' shops, and grocery stores. The Featherstone family of lawyers had their offices on Regent Street in Allingham's *No Police at the Funeral*.

On your side of Regent Street, past the Post Office and a Pizza Hut, you come to the University Arms Hotel, an old establishment with a modern facade with a blue canopy and a coat of arms above the front entrance. Inside there are three bars and a spacious lobby for afternoon tea.

In *Whiphand*, Dick Francis's Sid Halley stayed there overnight, after making an appointment to see a Mr. Livingston at the Tierson Pharmaceuticals Vaccine Laboratory. In *The Cambridge Murders*, the University Arms was recommended to vague old Dr. Quibell, when he asked where young men went to party. In J. R. L. Anderson's *Death in a High Latitude*, the Home Office's Peter Blair stayed at the "University Hotel" with his wife, an Oxford don.

On Regent Street beyond the University Arms you catch another glimpse of Parker's Piece. Cross Park Terrace where Regent Street becomes Saint Andrew's Street. You pass the *Cambridge Evening News* and a Midlands Bank branch, probably the bank Sid Halley used in *Whiphand*.

Across the street is the old police station, a Victorian structure built of creamy Cotswold stone. It was here Glyn Daniel's Inspector Wyndham worked. He first met Scotland Yard's Superintendent Robertson-Macdonald, a mere Oxford graduate, when he arrived to take over in *The Cambridge Murders*. Nora Kelly's Gillian Adams also remembered that the Cambridge police station used to be in Regent Street in a sooty turn-of-the-century building when she was an undergraduate at Newnham.

Down St. Andrew's Street beyond St. Columba's Church to your left is Downing Street, site of the Cavendish Laboratory, famous for its great scientific discoveries. It was at the Cavendish that C. P. Snow's protagonist in *The Search* did research. On your side of St. Andrew's Street you are walking past the high wall of Emmanuel College.

Emmanuel College was founded in 1584 to combat popery. Many of its Puritan alumni emigrated to America. The best known was John Harvard of Stratford-upon-Avon, who, when he died in Massachusetts in 1638, left half his estate and his library to Harvard College. (See Stratford Walk.) In September 1986 Harvard University celebrated its 350th anniversary with Charles, Prince of Wales, a Cambridge graduate, speaking at the opening convocation.

Keep walking along St. Andrew's Street and cross Emmanuel Street. When you reach Christ's Lane you will see St. Andrew's Church; then walk the short distance to the gateway of Christ's College. Glyn Daniel's Detective-Superintendent Robertson-Macdonald came this way from the old police station to "Fisher College."

Christ's College has an ancient doorway that opens into a lovely round court. Inside you can see an early Tudor gateway decorated with a pair of goatlike stone beasts called "yales." These yales come from the coat of arms of Lady Margaret Beaufort who "refounded" the college in 1505. A great patron of Cambridge University, Margaret Beaufort was a descendant of John of Gaunt, and the pious mother of Henry VII. He seized the throne from Richard III, who was the subject of Josephine Tey's *The Daughter of Time*. John Milton, the Puritan poet, was also at Christ's College, after attending St. Paul's

School in London where, much later, mystery writers E. C. Bentley and G. K. Chesterton were to meet as schoolboys.

Past Christ's College on St. Andrew's Street to your right you come to Hobson's Street with another Lloyd's Bank. To your left is narrow Petty Cury, which leads to Cambridge's open-air marketplace. In Margery Allingham's *No Police at the Funeral*, the old reprobate Uncle William Faraday had been walking along Petty Cury one hot day when suddenly he found himself in front of the Roman Catholic church at Lensfield Road with a glass in his hand.

Take Petty Cury left to the Guildhall. It was in the Guildhall in *An Unsuitable Job for a Woman* that Cordelia Gray attended the inquest on the death of Sir Ronald Callender.

Walk around the market square with its open-air stalls. In *Death's Bright Dart*, Clinton-Baddeley's amateur sleuth, Dr. Davie, came here one morning when Cambridge, without students or tourists, was quiet, fresh, and beautiful, and pottered for half an hour among books and flowers. He then paid a duty call at the Missionary Exhibition being held in a small room on a side street behind the Guildhall. There was a display of artifacts from Borneo, including a blowpipe that was later stolen to use for murder.

Turn right at the end of Petty Cury and walk along Market Hill past the back of Great St. Mary's Church. Turn again to your right on Market Street and take it to Market Passage. Across the street is Holy Trinity Church. Its stone spire has been cleaned so that it stands out startlingly against the rest of the church's dirty Cotswold stone. In *The Cambridge Murders*, Detective-Superintendent Robertson-Macdonald, heading for Sidney Sussex College, passed Trinity Church, where groups of shoppers were waiting for buses back to Ely and St. Ives.

Cross Market Passage and keep going on Market Street until you reach Sidney Street. Cross Sidney Street and go left, passing tiny Sussex Street, to reach Sidney Sussex College. This was another Puritan college, and was attended by Oliver Cromwell. His skull is buried near the chapel entrance and his famous portrait, with warts and all, hangs in his college. Mystery writer Antonia Fraser has written a Cromwell biography.

Georgette Heyer's beloved father, George, also attended Sidney Sussex and wrote for *Granta*, as did her brother Frank.

Sidney Sussex College was also the alma mater of Wilfrid Scott-Giles, who was the Fitzalan Pursuivant of Arms Extraordinary and founding member of the Dorothy L. Sayers Society. With Sayers, he co-authored *The Wimsey Family*. On March 7, 1937, Muriel St. Clare Byrne, Helen Simpson, Dorothy L. Sayers, and Scott-Giles came to Sidney Sussex College to read papers on the Wimsey Family to the Confraternitas Historica. Scott-Giles talked about the medieval Wimseys, Byrne discussed the theory that the Elizabethan Duke of Denver collaborated with the Earl of Oxford to write Shakespeare's plays, and Simpson read from an eighteenth-century Household Book belonging to a Mary Wimsey, whose descendants had gone to Australia. Sayers herself read the history of Lord Mortimer Wimsey, the Hermit of the Wash, known as Old Scaley, who thought he was part of the miraculous draught of fishes caught by St. Peter. (See Ely Walk.)

Continue along Sidney Street past Sidney Sussex College to Green Street, which is on your left. In *The Cambridge Murders* Superintendent Robertson-Macdonald went from Sidney Sussex College to Green Street, where he paused to look at the cozy, curtained warmth of Miss Palliser's tea shop. Sir Richard Cherrington also took the dean's maid there to pump her.

Follow Sidney Street past Green Street, noticing that there is a red pillar-box (mailbox) in the wall of Sidney Sussex College. In *The Cambridge Murders* the "Fisher College" porters took the college mail there every evening. A letter sent by don Evan Fothergill to his fiancee, June Westmacott, was crucial to the plot. Continue walking until you reach Jesus Lane on your right.

Cross Jesus Lane and turn right to walk along it, crossing Park Street on your left. You can see the whitewashed ADC Theatre with bright red doors, where Welsh boy-soprano Aled Jones sang the role of Christopher Robin in a musical version of A. A. Milne's *Winnie the Pooh*. Milne also wrote *The Red House Mystery*.

Across Park Street on Jesus Lane you begin to follow a

high red-brick wall to Jesus College. It has a long, narrow
entrance lined by more red brick walls, which is known as the
Chimney. As we walked along its cobblestones, we met a sleek
black-and-white cat, who sat for her photograph. No one
could have been a more appropriate "mysterious" greeter,
since Dorothy L. Sayers had many associations with Jesus
College. Sayers also adored cats and housed lots of them in her
house at Witham.

At the end of the Chimney, Jesus College has a crenellated
Tudor gatehouse in an intricate red-and-white brick design
with bright shields. Through its arch you can see into a lovely
three-sided court. The college, founded by Bishop Alcock of
Ely in the fifteenth century, replaced scandal-ridden St. Radegund's nunnery, where there were only two nuns left, one not
all she should be. North of the cloisters is the nine-hundred-
year-old Hall, once the nuns' refectory, with a handsome hammerbeam roof.

In this ancient hall on a summer evening in 1946 Dorothy
L. Sayers came to talk on Dante to the Summer School for the
Society for Italian Studies. One of the graduate students, who
was also the organizing secretary, Barbara Reynolds, had read
that Sayers was doing a Dante translation for Penguin, and
decided she would be a "draw." Later, as she listened to this
impressive woman with swept-back hair, long, dangling earrings, and a shimmering silvery gown, who spoke in her deep,
resonant, faintly amused voice about "Dante the storyteller,"
Reynolds was enchanted. She and Sayers became friends, with
the result that at Sayers's death in 1957, Muriel St. Clare
Byrne and the Penguin editor, Dr. Rieu, asked Reynolds to
finish Sayers's incomplete translation of *Paradise*.

Among other Jesus graduates was Archbishop Cranmer,
chief author of the *Book of Common Prayer*, which Sayers parodied in her Initiation Rite for the Detection Club. The poet
Coleridge also went there, and wrote *liberty and equality* in
gunpowder on the college lawn, then lit a match. North of
Jesus College is the part of the Cam River where the Eights
Races are held in May Week (which takes place in June).

Looking at the map, it is obvious that Clinton-Baddeley

put his mythical "College of St. Nicholas, St. Anastasius, and the Magnificent Virgin Edwina" about where Jesus College actually is. (Added proof is that Jesus College's full name is the College of Jesus, the Blessed Virgin Mary, St. John the Evangelist, and St. Radegund.) In *Death's Bright Dart* "St. Nicholas College" stretches from St. Nicholas Lane (Jesus Lane) to the Backs of the Cam, with several handsome courts, a medieval hall, once a refectory, a library, an Abbott's Lodge, now the Master's Lodge, and a chapel. Dr. Davie's chambers looked out on the Dutch Garden and the Backs.

As you walk back out of the Chimney, to the left Jesus Lane will become the Newmarket Road (A1303). There were several pubs and roadhouses on the Newmarket Road where students and townspeople congregated in Glyn Daniel's *The Cambridge Murders* and in Michael Butterworth's zany *The Man in the Sopwith Camel.*

Turn right on Jesus Lane to return to Sidney Street and walk to the junction with St. John's Street, where Sidney Street becomes Bridge Street. You will pass the famous twelfth-century Church of the Holy Sepulchre, commonly known as the Round Church. It is built of stone like some of the colleges, although there are no quarries near Cambridge. The Round Church is a squat little building with its Norman doorway covered like a candlesnuffer by its conical roof. It is one of five surviving round churches in England, all built in the shape of the Church of the Holy Sepulchre in Jerusalem.

Keep going on Bridge Street past St. Clement's Church, which becomes a Greek Orthodox church every two weeks. St. Clement's is on tiny Portugal Place. In Daniel's *The Cambridge Murders*, Sir Richard Cherrington, trying to solve the "Fisher College" murders, went to Portugal Place to talk to Diana Gostlin, the daughter of the murdered porter. She worked at a tobacco shop there. "Fisher College" undergraduate John Parrott also met Diana Gostlin in Bridge Street at the Cam Tea Shoppe.

Cross Thompson Lane to the Cam River. At the river's edge there is a large yellow sign saying "Boats." This is one of Scudamore's Boat Yards, where you can rent a punt to row on the Backs, working your way along the river past the many college bridges. (The Backs are the college grounds that stretch to the river at the backs of the colleges on Trinity Street and King's Parade.)

If you don't want to punt now, cross the bridge to the red-brick buildings of Magdalene College on what has become Magdalene Street. It is the only ancient college on the west bank of the river. Toward the end of his life, C. S. Lewis, an admirer of G. K. Chesterton and friend of mystery writers Charles Williams and Dorothy L. Sayers, was a don here, commuting from Oxford, where he lived. Across Magdalene Street from the college is an old pub called the Pickerel where you might stop for a snack or pub lunch. There are a number of other inns along this roadway on what was one of the main routes into town.

Magdalene College was established for young monks from Crowland Abbey, where, according to Josephine Tey, wily Bishop Morton of Ely hid from Richard III. When the monasteries were dissolved, it went to Lord Audley of Audley End House, and the College Master is still appointed by the Audley heirs, not elected. (See Side Trips.) Samuel Pepys also went to Magdalene College, and left it his library, which is housed in the Pepys Building in his own book presses. Among the books is his famous cipher diary.

To the north Magdalene Street crosses Chesterton Lane, which in turn becomes Chesterton Road. These street names are a reminder that G. K. Chesterton's family came from here. Past Chesterton Lane, Magdalene Street becomes Castle Street, where the Roman and Norman forts once stood. Then Castle Street becomes Huntington Road, where you will find New Hall, the women's college founded in 1954.

In *An Unsuitable Job for a Woman*, P. D. James described New Hall as having a strangely Byzantine air, and its sunken court and its shining domes reminded Cordelia Gray of a harem. They may remind you more of an observatory. Even farther out of town is Girton College, the first women's college at Cambridge. It was founded in 1869 and located as far away from men as possible. In Nora Kelly's *In the Shadow of*

King's, Pamela Ditton, the cousin and heir of murdered historian Alastair Greenwood, had been a student there.

Across from Magdalene College is Northampton Street, which runs south into Queens' Road, the main avenue on the other side of the Backs. Northampton Road then becomes the Madingley Road, where Glyn Daniel placed St. John's Close, convenient to the new buildings across the Cam where the college had its garage. Several of his characters in *The Cambridge Murders*, among them Dean Landon and his wife, Anne, live out that way. In Allingham's *No Police at the Funeral*, Albert Campion's very proper Ignatius College friend, Marcus Featherstone, lived off Queens' Road at Number Two, Soul's Court.

This walk will continue to go past the magnificent front gates of the colleges. You can then decide whether to go in their front gates and walk through their courts to the river, or to double back on yourself at the end of this walk to see the Backs. To explore the Backs now, cross Magdalene Street and find the pathway along the Cam at the back of St. John's College.

In Daniel's *The Cambridge Murders* various characters come this way to admire the gorgeous flowers and lawns as they cross to "Fisher College's" new building. St. John's, upon which "Fisher College" was based, has a nineteenth-century building across the Backs. It is called New Court, but popularly known as the Wedding Cake. Farther down by King's College in Julian Gloag's *Sleeping Dogs Lie*, Cambridge psychiatrist Dr. Hugh Welchman liked to come to the Backs and meditate on King's Bridge.

If you follow the Cam through the Backs, you will pass by a series of lovely bridges, beginning with the Bridge of Sighs, linking the two parts of St. John's, Trinity Bridge, Garret Hostel Bridge, Clare Bridge, King's Bridge, and finally, the Mathematical, or Queen's Bridge, made without nails. At this point the River Cam is called the River Granta. You could reverse this route by crossing Queen's Bridge to Silver Street, and turning left to walk up Trumpington Street, which becomes King's Parade, Trinity Street, and finally St. John's

Street. In *An Unsuitable Job for a Woman*, P. D. James's students began their punting at the Silver Street Bridge and went north on the river toward Trinity and St. John's.

If you choose not to explore the Backs now, on foot or by punt, turn left at Magdalene College on Magdalene Street and recross the river. At Bridge Street, cross the street to walk along the high brick wall of St. John's College. As you come to the corner with the Round Church, where Bridge Street becomes Sidney Street to your left and St. John's Street to your right, stop to look across at a building with the name "Harrison & Simmons" on it. It was in a flat in that building that Dorothy L. Sayers's young friend Barbara Reynolds and her husband, Professor Lewis Thorpe, lived with their small children. Sayers stayed with them several times, cheerfully sleeping in their "spare room," which was a huge Victorian bathroom. When Adrian Thorpe was fourteen, Sayers bestowed upon him "the Collar of the Ancient Order of the Bull Dog, First Class with Studs," for having spent a holiday with his mother reading straight through Dante's *Hell*.

You have now walked four miles and may wish to stop and eat, or quit for the day and pick up the walk here another time. To return to the Cambridge Railway Station either take a taxicab, or turn right on St. John's Street to Trinity Street, then past Great St. Mary's Church and walk around it to Market Hill. Go right again to Petty Cury bus stop where you can catch a #101 bus back to the station.

Walk Part Two: 4.2 miles from St. John's College to the Railroad Station.

You can begin this walk by taking a taxi or bus (#101) from the railway station on Station Road. Get off at the Petty Cury stop, walk along Petty Cury to Market Hill, and walk around Great St. Mary's Church to the left to St. John's Street.

Go right on St. John's Street until you reach the great red-brick gatehouse of St. John's College, trimmed with blue crosses and stone. The college was built on the site of a Hospital of the Knights of St. John of Jerusalem, which, like Christ's College, was "refounded" by Lady Margaret Beaufort, mother of Henry VII. (Her deputy and great admirer was Bishop Fisher, which was no doubt why Daniel chose to name his mythical college, which lies between St. John's and Trinity, "Fisher College.")

St. John's College has the distinction of having two bridges across the Cam; one is the Cambridge Bridge of Sighs, modeled after the famous bridge in Venice. Among St. John's most illustrious graduates were Roger Ascham, tutor to Elizabeth I, Thomas Wyatt, the Elizabethan poet, and later, Wordsworth, who described his rooms above the kitchen in his poem, "The Prelude." Gigantic New Court, known as the Wedding Cake, was built across the Cam in 1831. The modern blazer seems to have originated with St. John's College, where the oarsmen wear scarlet jackets.

Architecturally, Glyn Daniel's "Fisher College" was very like St. John's. It too had two Tudor courts of brickwork and a screens, or open passageway between the hall and kitchens. Since we cannot re-create "Fisher College," walk through St. John's to see the chapel whose choir is world-famous, then walk to the Backs to see New Court.

Return to St. John's Street and turn right. At tiny All Saints Passage (across the street) St. John's Street becomes Trinity Street, a lovely old medieval way with many bookstores, small shops, and restaurants. The main Heffer's Bookstores are here. Kelly's Gillian Adams went there to find a copy of don Alastair Green's masterpiece called *Ruling Ideas: The Tranformation of European Thought in the Eighteenth Century.*

One of the old Cambridge landmarks on Trinity Street was closed to the public during 1986. It was the seventeenth-century Blue Boar Hotel, which was the favorite meeting place of many mystery characters. Your authors had arranged to meet mystery writer Anne Perry at the Blue Boar for lunch to talk about her Victorian mysteries that feature Inspector Pitt and his wife, Charlotte. We had to settle for meeting her on the steps of the ex-Blue Boar's bright blue-and-white timbered building, then going to the Oasis, a Green Street basement restaurant, to eat jacket potatoes and talk crime.

In Daniel's *The Cambridge Murders,* Scotland Yard's Robertson-Macdonald stayed at the Blue Boar. He lunched or dined there regularly with his sidekick, Inspector Fleming, whom he called "Flamingo." In *Death's Bright Dart*, Dr. Davie, coming from All Saints Passage, came out on Trinity Street near the Blue Boar, where he saw Mr. Bondini and Colonel Vorloff, both suspects in the killing of Dr. Brauer. Dorothy L. Sayers and her friend Barbara Reynolds had lunch there three days before Sayers's sudden death in December 1957.

In Margery Allingham's *No Police at the Funeral*, Campion asked if missing Uncle Andrew had just gone off to stay at the Boar. In *Caroline Minuscule*, Andrew Taylor sent his young history graduate student, William Dougal, and his girl Amanda to drink pink gins at the Blue Boar. They were hunting a hidden diamond necklace. They had wanted to stay at the Royal Cambridge Hotel on Trumpington Street, but it was full of tourists and newly minted M.A.'s. They ended by cadging a bed from an obnoxious scholar named Primrose (or Madam Pee-Pee).

Continue along the right side of Trinity Street to the gateway of the largest and most splendid of the Cambridge colleges, Trinity College. The college has a huge roster of famous men, poets, prime ministers, scientists, historians, and members of the royal family like Edward VII, George VI, and Prince Charles. Trinity College, therefore, may be Margery Allingham's "St. Ignatius College," where John Faraday had been Master in *No Police at the Funeral*. Albert Campion, Marcus Featherstone, a lawyer in Cambridge, and Giles Paget, lord of the manor of *Mystery Mile*, all went to "St. Ignatius" together. Trinity was also the college attended by Dorothy L. Sayers's surgeon, Sir Julian Freke, in *Whose Body?*

Henry VIII founded the College of the Holy and Undivided Trinity to outdo Cardinal Wolsey's Christ Church College at Oxford. Henry took over nine existing hostels, including King's Hall, founded in 1336 by Edward III, which gives Trinity a claim to be a fourteenth-century foundation.

Enter by its famous Great Gate, built to honor Edward III (the statue of Henry VIII was mounted there instead), and go into the gigantic Great Court. It was designed by Thomas

Nevile, a favorite of Elizabeth I, and Master of Trinity. The present Prince of Wales lived in Great Court when he was an undergraduate at Cambridge.

Trinity's Clock Tower, with a statue of Edward III, finished at the time of the Battle of Agincourt, strikes the hour twice. At noon the ringing lasts forty-three seconds and undergraduates test their speed by trying to circle the Great Court before it stops. Nevile's Italianate fountain in the center of Great Court was a favorite bathing spot of Lord Byron, who also kept a pet bear in Merton Corner. Queen (Bloody) Mary built Trinity Chapel.

Beyond Great Court is Nevile Court, with its hugh hall modeled after the Middle Temple in London with a portrait of Henry VIII, and the famous Wren Library with carvings by Grinling Gibbons. Despite his clubfoot, athletic Lord Byron is said to have climbed to the roof of Nevile Court and decorated its statues with graffiti.

Another popular undergraduate sport at Cambridge is getting back in college after midnight, either across the bridges in back or by roof-climbing. This popular Cambridge sport was an important clue in V. C. Clinton-Baddeley's *Death's Bright Dart*. Enterprising student Mostyn-Humphries had spent the evening of the murder on the Cam with Tilly Pool, the prettiest waitress at the Cozy Pantry, then made his way back over the spikes that separate the Close from New Court at "St. Nicholas College."

In Daniel's *The Cambridge Murders* the police and the "Fisher College" officials assume that any undergraduate would be adept at getting in over the roofs of his college after hours. Furthermore, the clocks of the Cambridge colleges all strike twelve one after another, a process that involves over fifty clocks and takes nearly five minutes, making it, as Daniel commented, conveniently difficult to make an exact computation of the time.

In Kelly's *In the Shadow of King's,* Alastair Greenwood, Cambridge Regius Professor of History, taught at Trinity. Kelly's Gillian Adams found herself thinking of Trinity's dark, forbidding gateway and the serene geometry of its vast courts as she went to meet him again. She preferred King's College as the ultimate "ikon" of Cambridge, under whose shadow she felt "it is not simple to live."

If it is open to visitors, Trinity would be a good college to walk through toward the Cam to take a look at the Backs. Cross Trinity Bridge, then walk left along the river to the Garret Hostel Bridge. Then return to Garret Hostel Lane, which leads into Trinity Lane, and follow it back to Trinity Street.

Across Trinity Street is Great St. Mary's Church. Kelly's Gillian Adams came here (in a mood reminiscent of Sayers's Harriet Vane with Lord Peter in *Gaudy Night*). She took her London lover up the tower to see the best view of Cambridge.

An impressive Perpendicular building, Great St. Mary's is the University Church. To gain their degrees, scholars used to dispute here, sitting on three-legged stools, or tripos. In Dorothy L. Sayers's *Clouds of Witness* Denis Cathcart had passed his tripos examination. If you have time and energy, go inside and climb the tower to look out over Cambridge.

Return to Trinity Street and recross it to walk along until you come to small Trinity Lane to your right. Follow this narrow alleyway as the lane turns left. There you will find the back of the College of Gonville and Caius (pronounced Keys), which Dorothy L. Sayers's Reverend Theodore Venables of Fenchurch St. Paul attended. So possibly did Sayers's artist Henry Strachen in *The Five Red Herrings* and, in keeping with the college reputation for doctors, her medical student, Leader, in *The Documents in the Case,* and prim Mr. Hankin of Pyms' Publicity in *Murder Must Advertise*. Andrew Taylor's upwardly mobile, intellectual Primrose (Madame Pee-Pee) claimed to have been in Cambridge to attend a concert at Caius on the weekend William Dougal arrived looking for the diamonds in *Caroline Minuscule*.

At the point where Trinity Lane turns to the left, ahead down Garret Hostel Lane toward the Cam River lies Trinity Hall. Kelly's Gillian Adams as an undergraduate had reclined there à la Barbara Pym on a velvet sofa while a dazzling boy removed her clothes and recited John Donne.

Caius College has three famous gates that symbolize the stages in a student's life. The first, a plain gate called Humility, once opened on Trinity Street, but now stands in the Master's Garden. Inside the college between Caius and Tree Courts is the second, the massive Gate of Virtue, and finally, the third, the tall Gate of Honour with its facing sundials, opens on Senate House Passage.

As you turn the corner of Trinity Lane left into Senate House Passage, to your right is the entrance to Clare College. Its beautiful gardens and lovely ironwork gate lead to its graceful seventeenth-century bridge. In J. R. L. Anderson's *Death in a High Latitude,* the Home Office's Peter Blair went to the Clare Gardens to ponder the case.

Clare College was founded by Lady Elizabeth de Clare, a cousin of John of Gaunt and the Countess of Pembroke, who founded Pembroke College. They were all historical personages with whom Georgette Heyer became very well acquainted doing research for *Lord John.* (See Newmarket Walk.)

At the end of Senate House Passage you come out again on Trinity Street, which now becomes King's Parade. In *Funeral Sites,* Jessica Mann's Rosamund Sholto was taken to dinner there Michaelmas Term 1956 by her future brother-in-law, Aidan Brittan. Brittan then went off to Hungary's revolt like other young "Scarlet Pimpernels," and Rosamund alone suspected he came back a Communist like the "Cambridge Five," who spied for Russia. Nora Kelly's Gillian Adams was greatly annoyed to find that Cambridge University people seemed to admire Anthony Blunt, the most recently exposed spy from this group, for his superb knowledge of art and did not regard his treachery as equally important.

Keep right on King's Parade to King's College. It was founded by saintly Henry VI as the college for students from his school at Eton, and its choristers still wear Eton collars and top hats. (See Windsor/Eton Walk.) Go inside the Victorian Gothic gateway. To your right is the most famous building in Cambridge, Kelly's "ikon," spectacular King's College Chapel.

The chapel has a breathtaking fan-vaulted roof of limestone from Yorkshire. It was painted by Turner and Canaletto, written about by Wordsworth and Betjeman, and even Puritan Milton adored King's College Chapel, and may have pled with Oliver Cromwell, the MP for Cambridge, not to let his men destroy its sixteenth-century windows. They are the biggest and most complete set of Flemish glass paintings in the world. Above the altar hangs Rubens's painting of the Adoration of the Magi. The chapel's chief claim to fame, however, is the music of its choir, which is broadcast worldwide every Christmas Eve on the BBC.

In Michael Butterworth's *The Man in the Sopwith Camel,* two fanatic bank employees marched outside the chapel with signs saying "The End's in Sight." In P. D. James's *An Unsuitable Job for a Woman,* Cordelia Gray secretly met Sir Ronald Callender's secretary, Miss Leaming, in the chapel at Evensong. Miss Leaming went through the screen into the chancel, while Cordelia sat in the nave so that they met "by chance."

As they went outside they saw a frail and elderly don limping across the grass instead of keeping to the paths. With an irony reminiscent of feminist Virginia Woolf's *A Room of One's Own,* Miss Leaming said, "He's a Fellow. The sacred turf is, therefore, uncontaminated by his feet." Other laymen, like mystery walkers, will discover that if they walk on the grass they are warned off at once.

Cordelia and Miss Leaming strolled through King's College, discussing the inquest. At King's Bridge they leaned over to look into the bright water together, and having settled how to handle their roles in Sir Ronald's death, they walked back along the elm-lined path toward the Backs, passed through King's Gate, and turned right to find their cars.

By contrast, in Kelly's *In the Shadow of Kings,* Gillian Adams came to King's College Chapel to find the cool silence that to her represented the still point of the turning world (another Kelly echo from Dorothy L. Sayers's *Gaudy Night*). Adams sat a long time, then, feeling that the sordid history of humanity had been redeemed by the rich, magniloquent beauty of the chapel, she went back to Newnham to prepare for her ordeal by scholarship.

Adams gave her lecture to the Cambridge Historical Society after tea in the Chetwynd Room at King's College. It was an unattractive room off King's Lane, with modern fluorescent lighting and an acoustical tile ceiling. At the back was an open serving hatch, through which the teacups were shoved, the clink still sounding faintly as she spoke. During the applause someone shot Regius Professor Alastair Greenwood through the opening.

Leave King's College and cross King's Parade. Turn right past St. Edward's Passage to Bene't Street. This area is the oldest part of Cambridge. Turn left on Bene't Street to St. Benet's Church with its gilded weathervane at the top of its pointed Saxon tower. The church building is connected to Corpus Christi College by a covered passage like one in "St. Nicholas College."

This tower is the oldest building in Cambridge. Francis Stedman, born in 1631, was Clerk of the parish. He is best known to Sayers fans as the "father of English change ringing," who was mentioned in pious tones by the rector of Fenchurch St. Paul in *The Nine Tailors*.

On Bene't Street you pass the entrance to the Eagle, a historic inn with an outside gallery and cobbled courtyard. Nobel Prize–winning Cambridge scientists Watson and Crick liked to drink at the Eagle while they were working on their discovery of DNA (the double helix). Farther along, St. Bene't Street becomes Wheeler Street, where the British Tourist Office is located.

Turn right off Bene't Street on Free School Lane and walk along it. On your left you pass the Cavendish Laboratory, where scientists like C. P. Snow worked. On your right you will come to Corpus Christi College. Corpus Christi was founded by two Cambridge Guilds, with the result that it is the only college to be placed in the heart of the town. Its Old Court is the best example of a medieval quadrangle still standing. The ghost of a seventeenth-century Master of the College who hanged himself just before he was supposed to deliver the University Sermon allegedly has been seen at one of the windows. Shakespeare's contemporary and fellow playwright,

Christopher Marlowe, took his degree at Corpus Christi in 1587, the same year he wrote *Tamburlaine*. Marlowe's murder was the subject of great speculation in Martha Grimes's mystery *The Dirty Duck*.

At the end of Free School Lane turn right on Botolph Lane, a very tiny alley lined with irregular medieval buildings, where you catch a glimpse of the churchyard of St. Botolph's, filled with hollyhocks among its gravestones. Then come out on King's Parade once more at the point where it becomes Trumpington Street, a wide roadway with open drains on either side. Cross Trumpington Street and turn left to walk past the main court of St. Catherine's College, where John Addenbrooke was a student. Across the street is the Cambridge University Press.

Keep going until you reach Silver Street. To your right you will see the entrance to Queens' College, founded by two queens who were deadly enemies, the Red Rose Margaret d'Anjou, queen of Henry VI, and the White Rose Elizabeth Woodville, queen of Edward IV. Queens' has an Erasmus Tower where the Renaissance scholar Erasmus, lured to Cambridge by Sir Thomas More and Bishop Fisher, lived as Lady Margaret Reader in Greek and Professor of Divinity. Erasmus complained about the damp weather and small, windy ale. Silver Street has another Scudamore Boat Yard where students can punt up the Backs. The Cam River here has its Roman name, the Granta.

Farther down Trumpington Street you come to Mill Lane. To your right is the bridge over the Granta, where the body of Hampstead model Fiona Clay was found in Kelly's *In the Shadow of King's*. Across Trumpington Street is Pembroke Street, the site of Pembroke College. Its "New Chapel" was built for the Bishop of Ely by his young nephew, Christopher Wren. After his military service Georgette Heyer's son, Richard Rougier, went there as an Exhibitioner from his public school. His mother financed his education by writing such mysteries as *Detection Unlimited*, for which her lawyer-husband, Ronald Rougier, provided her with the plot and legal background.

Continue on Trumpington Street until you come to Little St. Mary's Lane with its delightful row of tiny, whitewashed cottages with thatched roofs. Cross the lane to the oldest college of all, St. Peter's or Peterhouse. Although it was established first, most of its buildings date from the eighteenth or nineteenth century.

Beyond Peterhouse to your right down a long walkway is the Peterhouse chapel, which is also the church of St. Mary's the Less, or Little St. Mary's. It is a tiny gem of the Decorated Period. Go inside, then turn to look above the door, where you will see a plaque in memory of the Reverend Godfrey Washington of County York who was a Fellow of St. Peter's College in the early eighteenth century. It has the Washington coat of arms, a black eagle crest above three red stars and three red stripes, which is probably the source of the American flag.

Just beyond Little St. Mary's is the grandly classical portico of the Fitzwilliam Museum with its green lawns and handsome stone and ironwork fence. Just ahead to your right is the road to the Cambridge suburb of Newnham. There on Sidgwick Avenue you would find Newnham College, attended by mystery writer Jessica Mann and her sleuth, Tamara Hoyland. Newnham is also the college attended by June Westmacott, the jilted fiancée of "Fisher College" don Evan Fothergill in Daniel's *The Cambridge Murders,* and American Gillian Adams and British Beatrix Hamilton in Kelly's *In the Shadow of King's.*

You should allow enough time to stop at the Fitzwilliam Museum, but check on the times it is open. The Fitzwilliam houses one of the finest art and antiquities collections outside London. In addition it has as well superb collections of Italian, Dutch, and English paintings and prints. Its brightly painted galleries, like its elaborate entrance hall, are some of the most ornate in all Cambridge. In addition to a coffee shop, the Fitzwilliam Museum also has a gift shop.

Just a few days before her death in December 1957 at the age of 64, Dorothy L. Sayers came to Cambridge to visit Barbara Reynolds. The two of them went to the Fitzwilliam Museum to see a special William Blake exhibit. In P. D. James's *Death of an Expert Witness,* the eccentric father of Hoggath

Laboratory's director Maxim Howarth and his sister, Domenica, refused to allow his fifteen-year-old daughter to stay with him in Florence. The elder Howarth told his Cambridge University son that it would be better to get Domenica a room near him in Cambridge, where the Fitzwilliam Museum had some "quite agreeable pictures."

Those paintings include a Claude Lorrain, whose style the embezzler in Michael Butterworth's *The Man in the Sopwith Camel* imitated. In the rose gallery you will find a 1765 Stubbs painting of "Gimcrack with John Pratt Up." In Kelly's *In the Shadow of King's* the murdered Regius Professor left his Stubbs to his cousin.

Behind the Fitzwilliam Museum is the Sheep's Green (Meadows) where Uncle William and his murdered cousin, Roger Faraday, quarreled coming home from church in Margery Allingham's *No Police at the Funeral.*

Across Trumpington Street is the original Addenbrookes Hospital. Its new building is much farther out beyond the railroad station on Hills Road. In Mann's *Funeral Sites,* Thea Crawford and Rosamund Sholto had lived together in a place called the Gatehouse during their last year at Cambridge. Thea was working on a Roman dig and Rosamund was helping design a new hospital. One day Rosamund saved a small silver dish with animals and a chain from a bulldozer, and it ended up on display in the Fitzwilliam Museum.

You have now walked over three miles and may want to take a taxi back to the railroad station. If not, continue down Trumpington Street until you reach Lensfield Road. At the corner is the Royal Cambridge Hotel, where Andrew Taylor's characters wanted to stay in *Caroline Minuscule,* and where Butterworth's bank clerk may have stayed in *The Man in the Sopwith Camel.* If you were to stay on Trumpington Street until it became Trumpington Road, you would pass the majestic Victorian house called Socrates Close, where Great Aunt Caroline Faraday, the widow of the Master of Ignatius College, lived with her assorted relatives in Allingham's *No Police at the Funeral.*

Cross Lensfield Road and turn left to follow it back to the

large Roman Catholic Church of Our Lady and the English Martyrs on the corner of Hills Road. Turn right to follow Hills Road back to the World War I memorial, where you turn left to take Station Road back to the train station to end your walk.

POSSIBLE SIDE TRIPS

Duxford
Nine miles south of Cambridge on the A5056, M16. Site of an airfield and fighter station of the Royal Air Force during the Battle of Britain, now an Imperial War Museum with a gift shop and cafeteria. Admission charge.

It is a good site for the abandoned airstrip in Patricia Moyes's *Johnny Underground,* where Emmy Tibbett, wife of Scotland Yard Inspector Henry Tibbett, worked during World War II. It is also the village where Mark Callender worked as a gardener in P. D. James's *An Unsuitable Job for a Woman.*

Saffron Walden
Fifteen miles south of Cambridge, the next train stop en route to London from Cambridge. One of the best-preserved medieval towns in England, named for the Saffron Crocus, which is raised there. The home and laboratory of Sir Ronald Callender was there in James's *An Unsuitable Job for a Woman.*

Audley End House
Sixteen miles south of Cambridge, near Saffron Walden. Historic country mansion that got its name from Sir Thomas Audley, Henry VIII's Speaker of the House of Commons. When the monasteries were dissolved, Audley was given Walden Abbey, whose stones he used to build the house. It was later bought by Charles II after the Restoration because it was handy to Newmarket. In the eighteenth century Robert Adam redid the interiors and the parks were laid out by Capability Brown.

This house may be the model for the eighteenth-century mansion of the Duke of Wessex, who used its attics for his toy train setup in Dick Francis's *Whiphand*. Its name and location also make it a likely suspect for Antonia Fraser's "Saffron Ivy," the stately home of Lord St. Ives, a former Foreign Secretary. His son and heir, Lord Saffron, was the Oxford undergraduate whose lifestyle Jemima Shore was investigating in *Oxford Blood*. Its history also makes it a candidate for Montfort Abbey in Susan Kenney's *Garden of Malice*. It is now a museum with a restaurant. Admission charge.

4

CANTERBURY

BACKGROUND

Canterbury, an ancient city that has a history going back two thousand years, was one of the most venerated pilgrim shrines of the Middle Ages. Since the Reformation, it has been the see of the Primate of All England, the Archbishop of Canterbury, who heads the worldwide Anglican Communion. St. Augustine, a missionary sent from Rome by Pope Gregory, established the Roman Christian Church here in A.D. 598. He founded a Benedictine monastery that became the burial ground of the royal family on land given him by the Saxon Ethelbert, King of Kent.

In 1070 Lanfranc became the first Norman archbishop, and the oldest stones in Canterbury Cathedral come from the one he built. One hundred years later, in 1170, Archbishop Thomas à Becket was murdered in the cathedral. In 1175 William of Sens, a master-mason, was asked to design a new choir to replace the one destroyed by fire and to create a suitable tomb for the martyred archbishop. William of Sens had a crippling fall from the scaffolding, and after completing the east transepts, handed his work to another architect to finish.

Although the Normans established the modern city of Canterbury, it was the Romans who first got things going. As they moved inland from the coast of Kent, they came upon a huddle of huts at the ford of the River Stour, where there had been a settlement since the Iron Age. The Romans subdued the village, then built it up as a trade center under the name "Durovernum Cantiacorum," later the Saxon "Cantwara-byrig." They fortified the town and built a road to London. The Romans left England at the end of the fifth century, but the road between London and Canterbury continued to be heavily traveled. G. K. Chesterton's friend, Hilaire Belloc, described the importance of the Canterbury Road in the development of the church and English life in his book *The Road to Rome*.

Important as the city became, it was actually murder that put Canterbury "on the map." On December 29, 1170, four knights who were "henchmen" of King Henry II, thinking they were carrying out the King's wishes, rode to Canterbury and, entering the cathedral by the cloister, attacked and killed Archbishop Thomas à Becket. A new Triple Cross now marks the murder site, where Pope John Paul II and Archbishop Robert Runcie knelt together in prayer on May 29, 1982.

By murdering the archbishop, the four knights created a martyr, for Becket was canonized two years later. King Henry was forced by the pope to undergo a humiliating public pilgrimage of penance. The martyrdom also turned Canterbury into a very important pilgrimage center where for 350 years hordes of pilgrims journeyed to pray at St. Thomas's splendid tomb.

Geoffrey Chaucer's pilgrims in his fourteenth-century *Canterbury Tales* were on their way from London's Southwark to Canterbury. (See Thames River Trip.) In a talk she gave at the Chaucer Festival on August 7, 1985, mystery writer Catherine Aird made a strong case for Chaucer as a crime writer. She suggested that an appropriate, up-to-date title for "The Pardoner's Tale" would be "Death Steps In."

In 1538, with the dissolution of the monasteries, Henry VIII had Becket's tomb dismantled and the precious jewels and treasures went into the King's coffers. Canterbury Cathedral became the center of the Protestant Church of England, and the archbishop continued to be the Primate, or chief bishop, who crowns the English kings and queens. The archbishop also has a Tudor town house in Lambeth, London. (See Thames River Trip.)

The city of Canterbury retains many traces of the Middle Ages, such as its impressive Westgate, parts of the ancient walls, old houses, inns, and churches. But Canterbury is also a modern city featuring excellent shops, cinemas, the Marlowe Theatre, and the new (postwar) University of Kent, located beyond Westgate past Canterbury West Railway Station. Unlike that ancient and venerable institution, the University of Calleshire, where student sit-ins mixed with lost letters about Jane Austen, described by Catherine Aird in *Parting Breath*, the University of Kent is a modern foundation.

At the end of September each year the New Canterbury Festival of Arts is held in the Marlowe Theatre and other historic buildings like the Cathedral. It was here at Canterbury that Bishop George Bell of Chichester, then Dean of Canterbury, began the Canterbury Festival. Under its aegis the Friends of Canterbury during the 1930s commissioned and produced religious plays by mystery writers T. S. Eliot, Dorothy L. Sayers, and Charles Williams.

During World War II, Canterbury suffered considerable bombing damage, but the cathedral itself was not harmed. In the course of postwar reconstruction, the remains of a Roman theater, town walls, houses, and streets were uncovered. No ancient or modern dead bodies were discovered, however, as they were in Catherine Aird's *A Late Phoenix*, set, like all of her mysteries, in her mythical Calleshire which is based on Kent.

Canterbury has many literary associations. In *Written City: A Literary Guide to Canterbury,* the authors state that "outside London, Oxford, and Cambridge, there can hardly be a town in England that has attracted so many writers." To name some of the more famous, the Elizabethan playwright Christopher Marlowe was born in Canterbury in 1564. Marlowe was baptized at St. George's Church, and went to Canterbury's King's

School. Cavalier poet Richard Lovelace inherited lands in Kent and lived in Canterbury, where his great-grandfather is buried in the cathedral nave, and Daniel Defoe, who wrote *Robinson Crusoe,* preached at Canterbury in 1724.

Horace Walpole, the author of the gothic novel *The Castle of Otranto,* which was a forerunner of today's mystery story, claimed to know Canterbury by heart. He wrote that the cathedral was "the most magnificent I have seen" and he imitated some of its architectural details at Strawberry Hill, his gothic home at Twickenham. (See Thames River Trip.) His gothic novel inspired Jane Austen's spoof, *Northanger Abbey,* and many of mystery writer Georgette Heyer's Regency romances. Since Canterbury is on the direct road to Dover and France, in Heyer's *Sylvester or the Wicked Uncle,* Lady Ingham, Tom Orde, and Phoebe Marlow came that way when they fled London after the publication of Phoebe's gothic romance.

In 1869 Charles Dickens took a group of American visitors to evensong at the cathedral, then conducted them on a tour of the building. Dickens's Miss Betsy Trotwood sent David Copperfield to a school in Canterbury, for which King's School may be the model, and David's second wife, Agnes Wickfield, lived in a Canterbury house in St. Dunstan's Street just beyond Westgate on the London Road.

Dickens and his friend and fellow mystery writer Wilkie Collins often went from Canterbury to the coast at Broadstairs, and Collins "found" the title for *The Woman in White* while there. Much later John Buchan changed "Broadstairs" to "Bradgate," the place where his hero, Richard Hannay, found the *Thirty-Nine Steps* (to the sea).

Novelist Joseph Conrad, who wrote *The Secret Agent,* lived near Canterbury and is buried there. Both Hugh Walpole and Somerset Maugham attended Canterbury's King School, which Maugham satirized as "Tercanbury" in *Of Human Bondage.*

Present-day mystery writers also use Canterbury and Kent. A number of Michael Gilbert's mysteries have scenes set in Kentish towns like Sevenoaks, where the highly efficient legal secretary, Miss Cornel, lived in *Smallbone Deceased.* In Michael

Underwood's *The Uninvited Corpse,* Philip Tresant told his wife that he was going for a job in Canterbury.

Deepacres Park, the family seat of Ngaio Marsh's zany but aristocratic Lampreys, was in Kent. In *A Surfeit of Lampreys,* Chief Detective Inspector Roderick Alleyn, with his faithful Fox and his reporter friend, Nigel Bathgate, went to Canterbury by train, then took a branch line to the village to investigate the background of the family chauffeur, Giggle.

It is easy to assume that Catherine Aird is writing about Kent and Canterbury in her wise and witty chronicles of Inspector C. D. (Seedy) Sloan and Detective Constable Crosby, who deal with the criminal element in and around the County of Calleshire and the city of Calleford. Actually, however, although her countryside is Kentish and Calleford has much in common with Canterbury, including a cathedral and a university, Catherine Aird told us she is only writing about "English" countryside, "English" towns, and "English" villages because her locales are really composites. (Ellis Peters wrote us the same thing about her "Comerbourne.") (See Shrewsbury Walk.)

Catherine Aird herself lives with her mother in a charming Edwardian villa in Sturry, a village a few miles from Canterbury. Her oaken staircase has a newel post with a removable knob (see *The Religious Body*). In her garden she grows roses in an arbor she created, using the white iron pillars of an abandoned church.

HOW TO GET THERE

British Rail: trains from London's Charing Cross and Waterloo
    Stations arrive at Canterbury West Station; those from
    Victoria Station arrive at Canterbury East Station (Be sure to
    get into the right car; the Victoria train divides at Faversham)
    —about 80 minutes

Automobile: A2 and M2; 58 miles from London

Length of walk: About 2½ miles

See map on page 91 for boundaries of this walk and page 356 for a list of detectives and stories covered.

PLACES OF INTEREST

Christ Church (Canterbury Cathedral), Mother Church of Christianity. The cathedral represents five centuries of architecture. Special things to see include: Northwest Transept (site of the murder of Thomas à Becket); Bell Tower Harry; the Choir; Trinity Chapel (site of the Becket tomb and tomb of the Black Prince); crypt; Chapter House; Chapter Library; the Dark Entry; the Great Cloister.

Christchurch Gate, Mercery Lane. Main entrance to cathedral precincts. Built in memory of Arthur, Prince of Wales.

The King's School, through Green Court on cathedral grounds. Established by Henry VIII on site of seventh-century monastery. Famous for its outdoor Norman staircase.

St. Augustine's College, Lady Wootton Green. Now part of the King's School, built on the site of St. Augustine's Abbey, founded in A.D. 604. As a result of recent excavations, you can see the foundations of the old abbey and the graves of St. Augustine, Saxon King Ethelbert, his Frankish Queen Bertha, and nine of Augustine's successors as archbishop. (Open all year Monday through Saturday; Sunday P.M. only.)

Roman Pavement, Longmarket. Tessellated pavement from Roman courtyard. (Open all day in summer; winter P.M. only.)

St. Martin's Church, Longport. Oldest Christian church in continuous use in England. May be the site of earlier Romano-British church. Notice orange Roman brick in stonework.

City Walls, Pin Hill. About half of Canterbury's medieval walls, built on Roman foundations, survive and can be walked along.

St. George the Martyr Church, St. George's Street. Bombed church has only tower standing where Christopher Marlowe was baptized.

Weaver's House, River Stour. This half-timbered house, which was built in 1561 by a rich merchant, became a refuge for Huguenot weavers from France.

Westgate, St. Duncan's Street. Only remaining city gate of seven. Built by Archbishop Sudbury in 1380. (Archbishop Sudbury was dragged from the Chapel of St. John at the Tower of London and murdered by some of Wat Tyler's men during the Peasants' Revolt in 1381.) Westgate was the city jail; it now has a small museum of weapons and armor. Good view of the cathedral from the top. (Open all year. All day in summer; P.M. only in winter.) Admission charge.

PLACES TO STAY/EAT

Abbots Barton, 36 New Dover Road (0227) 460341. Large country house set in attractive grounds. Old-fashioned, comfortable atmosphere. Inexpensive.

The George and Dragon, Fordwich near Sturry on River Stour (old port of Canterbury) (0227) 710661. Sixteenth-century inn serves delicious dinners, hot and cold lunches. Inexpensive.

County Hotel, High Street (0227) 66266. First licensed in 1629, probably the best hotel in Canterbury. Furnished with antiques, big beamed lobby, private baths. *Sully's* (restaurant) a la carte. Expensive.

Alberry's Wine and Food Bar, 381 St. Margaret's Street (0227) 52378.

The House of Agnes, 71 St. Dunstan's Street (0227) 65077. Home of Charles Dickens's Agnes in *David Copperfield,* now a hotel. Restaurant serves English food. Inexpensive.

Weavers, Kings Bridge. Restaurant serves morning coffee, lunch, or French table d'hôte. Expensive.

Queen Elizabeth Restaurant, High Street (0227) 464080. In Tudor house where Elizabeth I once stayed as guest of the cathedral. Restaurant known for good lunch and tea. Inexpensive.

Olive Branch, 39 Burgate (0227) 462170. Opposite the cathedral gates. Probably the most atmospheric pub in town.

———— CANTERBURY WALK ————

Begin this walk by leaving the Canterbury East Railway Station. Take the footbridge that crosses Pin Hill and turn right on the walkway on the old City Walls. These walls, which date from the thirteenth and fourteenth centuries, were built on Roman foundations. In Elizabeth Cadell's *Remains to Be Seen,*

Philippa Lyle who had come home to England to tie up some loose ends in her life before marrying a Canadian, arrived at Canterbury (East) Station to take a bus to her hometown of Montoak, which lay twenty miles north of Canterbury.

Follow the walk on City Wall as it curves around Dane John Gardens, a pleasant eighteenth-century park that contains a mound of probable prehistoric origins. Continue until you come to the city bus station, where Philippa Lyle caught her bus. Take the ramp walkway from the walls to St. George's Street and turn left.

On the right is the tower of St. George's Church. This is all that remains of the church where Elizabethan playwright Christopher Marlowe was baptized. In Martha Grimes's *The Dirty Duck,* American tourist Harvey Schoenberg cornered ex-aristocrat Melrose Plant to regale him with an account of Schoenberg's book *Who Killed Marlowe?* Schoenberg claimed to have proved that Shakespeare murdered Marlowe. (See also Stratford Walk and Thames River Trip.)

Walk along St. George's Street, which becomes Parade Street, then High Street at Mercery Lane. Penny Wanawake, the six-foot-tall, very sexy black photographer-cum-detective in Susan Moody's *Penny Dreadful,* had gone to the library in High Street to find out more about schoolmaster Dominick Austen, whom she had caught watching her movements. Penny, who had attended the exclusive Roedean School in Brighton, now earned her living taking photographs. (See Brighton Walk.) On her way to High Street, Penny passed a bookstore with a book of her own photographs in the window and felt a thrill at seeing her work on display.

Another time Penny and American Charles Yeoman had a cold supper in a pub on High Street, and there are any number that fit the bill. Still later in the mystery when Dominick Austen came upon Penny at the Abbey, he grasped her arm and hustled her to High Street. By night without the crowds, she noticed that Canterbury took on a seedy look, with its windows filled with reject china, second-hand books, and gold rings, mixed with the jumble of ordinary chain stores like W. H. Smith, Woolworths, and Boots.

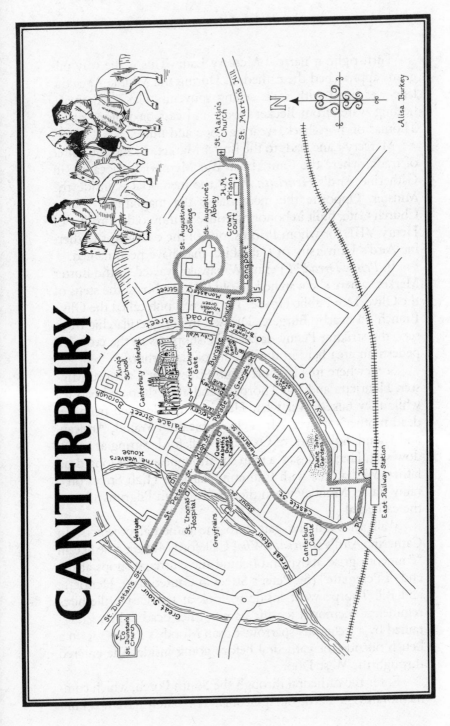

CANTERBURY

Alisa Burkey

N

St. Martin's Church
St. Martin's Hill
St. Augustine's College
St. Augustine's Abbey
H.M. Prison
Crown Court
Longport
Monastery Street
Broad Street
Lady Wootton's Green
Love Lane
Church St.
Lower Bridge St.
City Wall
Burgate
St. George's Tower
Christ Church Gate
Canterbury Cathedral
King's School
Borough
Palace Street
The Weavers House
Butchery
St. Margaret's St.
Parade
Mercery
St. George's St.
Guildhall
Bus Station
St. Peter's St.
St. Thomas's Hospital
Greyfriars
Queen Elizabeth's Guest Chamber
Stour St.
Dane John Gardens
Castle St.
City Wall
East Railway Station
Pin Hill
Canterbury Castle
Great Stour
Westgate
St. Dunstan's St.
St. Dunstan's Church

Turn right at narrow Mercery Lane. This is the way pilgrims approached the cathedral. During the Middle Ages the lane was lined with stalls selling souvenirs like cockleshells, healing water from Becket's well, and cast medallions of St. Thomas on horseback, wearing cope and mitre.

Mercery Lane leads to the Butter Market, an ancient center of trade, where the Canterbury War Memorial is located. In Catherine Aird's *Henrietta Who?* the memorial is inside the Minster. Opposite the memorial is the magnificent Christ Church Gate, built in honor of Prince Arthur, older brother of Henry VIII, for whom Princes, one of the colleges at Catherine Aird's University of Calleshire, may have been named.

In *Penny Dreadful* Penny Wanawake walked to the Butter Market, where she watched an old lady scrubbing the steps of the Olive Tree Public House. Try the real pub called the Olive Branch on nearby Burgate. Dressed in her guerilla-chic trousers, the striking Penny dazzled the shoppers in the crowded pedestrian area here in the middle of Canterbury.

Somewhere in a lane off High Street near Calleford Minster, Henrietta and Bill Thorpe found a tea shop and had tea while they talked over what Henrietta had learned from her dead mother's lawyer, Mr. Felix Arbican of Waind, Arbican, and Waind, Solicitors, of Ox Lane, Calleford. Sitting at a window seat, Henrietta saw a man she thought was her long dead father. We had tea with Catherine Aird on High Street on a rainy Easter Monday when there were Youth Pilgrims all over the cathedral.

Walk through the gate into the cathedral precincts. In Catherine Aird's *Henrietta Who?* Calleford Minster rose like an "éminence grise above and behind the clustered shops at the end of Petergate" (St. Peter's Street in Canterbury). Henrietta and Bill Thorpe went inside to look at the East Calleshires regimental memorial for the name of her dead father. Entertained by a lecherous sparrow, Susan Moody's Penny sat on a bench outside the cathedral before going inside. She entered through the West Door.

Enter the cathedral through the South Porch, which commemorates the Battle of Agincourt. The stately nave was built by Henry Yevele during the fourteenth century in Perpendicular style. At its crossing you can look up into the magnificent Bell Harry Tower, built in 1490 by John Wastell, the master mason at King's College, Cambridge. (See Cambridge Walk.) The tower, which dominates the exterior of the cathedral, is open inside to a height of one hundred fifty-three feet, with an elaborate fan-vaulted ceiling. Bell Harry has a single bell, which is rung every evening at curfew and tolled at the death of a sovereign or an archbishop.

The stairs to your right by the screen lead into the choir, which is the longest in England. It was rebuilt by the French master-mason William of Sens, who suffered a crippling fall from the scaffolding and had to give up the work before it was completed. Dorothy L. Sayers dramatized William's story in her 1937 Canterbury play called *The Zeal of Thy House.*

There are worn steps here that lead down to the crypt. This is the oldest part of the cathedral, with a low roof and heavy, rounded Norman arches. Along its south aisle there is a Huguenot chapel where services are still held in French. Thomas à Becket was first buried in the crypt, where Henry II completed his papal penance for Becket's murder. Along the aisle also is the tomb of Bishop Morton of Ely, whose treachery Josephine Tey's Inspector Alan Grant thought doomed Richard III.

Upstairs, follow the South Aisle to Trinity Chapel, which is at the end of the choir behind the high altar. On your right is St. Michael's Chapel, built by Margaret Holland for herself and two noble husbands. It contains the tomb of Archbishop Stephen Langton, who helped the barons force King John to sign Magna Carta. According to *The Wimsey Family,* an ancestor of Dorothy L. Sayers's Lord Peter Wimsey was one of the barons. John Creasey's Inspector West prevented the theft of the Sarum copy of Magna Carta in *Theft of Magna Carta.* (See Ely and Salisbury Walks.)

St. Michael's Chapel displays the Honor Roll of the Buffs, now the Royal Kent Regiment. Every day at 11 A.M., a page is turned by a soldier of the regiment, as the bell from HMS *Canterbury* is struck. This chapel therefore makes a good substitute for the War Memorial for the East Calleshires in Calleford Minster, where Henrietta and Bill Thorpe looked for the name of her dead father in Aird's *Henrietta Who?*

Continue past the choir to Trinity Chapel. Murdered Archbishop Thomas à Becket's impressive tomb was here until Henry VIII had it destroyed and the saint's bones scattered in 1538. Here are the tombs of Lancastrian Henry IV, the only king buried at Canterbury, and his uncle, Edward the Black Prince (of Wales). Edward was the oldest son of Edward III, who was the villain of Patrick Doherty's mystery *The Death of a King*.

The Black Prince died before coming to the throne. His effigy-tomb is copper-gilt, with his war panoply (replicas) hanging above. He had married his cousin Joan, the Fair Maid of Kent, and was a great patron of the cathedral. Their son was the boy King Richard II, whose misrule began the Wars of the Roses, which led to the murder of the princes in the Tower, and the Tudor monarchy. Mystery writers wrote about these historical characters in Georgette Heyer's *Lord John*, Josephine Tey's *The Daugher of Time*, and Audrey Williamson's *The Mystery of the Princes*.

At the far end of the cathedral is the Corona, the chapel where St. Thomas's skull was once preserved. Turn left and take the north aisle past the choir to the Northwest Transept, also called Martyrdom, the site of the murder of Archbishop Thomas à Becket. Catherine Aird, who was escorting us through the cathedral, especially pointed out the new Triple Cross, placed there in 1986 with a plaque that states, "In this place hallowed by the martyrdom of St. Thomas à Becket, Pope John Paul II and Robert Runcie, Archbishop of Canterbury, knelt together in prayer. May 29, 1982."

Walk through the Northwest transept into the fifteenth-century Great Cloister, once the center of the monastery. The first building opening off the cloister is the Chapter House, a high, narrow room with stone seats around the walls. It was in the Chapter House, without a real stage or any way to enter or leave except one door, that T. S. Eliot's play *Murder in the Cathedral* was performed for the Canterbury Festival in 1935. In Moody's *Penny Dreadful*, Penny Wanawake used a concert in the cathedral cloisters as an excuse not to return to her flat in Chelsea. (The third week in July a series of excellent concerts are given yearly at the King's School in the cathedral environs.) Before the concert Penny had wandered about the cathedral, admiring the stones commemorating important churchmen. Then she walked up the long nave and looked back, thinking about how Thomas à Becket's death was interpreted by T. S. Eliot.

In 1936 Charles Williams's play, *Thomas Cranmer of Canterbury*, was performed and in 1937, Dorothy L. Sayers's play about master-mason William of Sens, *The Zeal of Thy House*, was presented. Sayers took a lively interest in the production, even helping to make the archangels' tall feathered wings and raising money to send it on tour. In 1987 the Dorothy L. Sayers Historical and Literary Society sponsored a production of the play at their annual conference, which was held in Canterbury.

Between the Chapter House and the Chapter Library is a long passageway called the Dark Entry. According to legend, the ghost of a Nell Cook, who poisoned a Cathedral Canon and his mistress, walks there on Friday nights. It was one of many stories about horrible physical dismemberments or "the dark underside of morbid themes" that were described by a Canterbury-born writer, Canon Richard Harris Barham, in *The Ingoldsby Legends*. In Ngaio Marsh's *Death in a White Tie*, the painter Troy confessed to Chief Detective Inspector Roderick Alleyn that she had read *The Ingoldsby Legends* as a child and been frightened to death by them. Beyond the Dark Entry is the Chapter Library, which has a fine collection of old manuscripts.

Keep walking through the Great Cloister to Prior Selling's Gate, which leads into the Green Court, where you can see the outside Norman staircase. Beyond are the old monastery buildings that house the famous King's School, founded by Henry VIII. King's School is one of the English public schools that are really expensive and exclusive private secondary schools. Moody's Penny Wanawake was staying at the Abbots School at Canterbury, which was supposed to co-exist in Canterbury with the real King's School, but the Abbots School is obviously a fictionalized version of the real thing.

The King's School has taught many writers, among them Christopher Marlowe, Walter Pater, and Somerset Maugham. Maugham hated the school but made large donations to its Maugham Library, which has his books and papers, and his ashes are buried at the school, too. Maugham had worked for British Intelligence during World War I and based his thriller *Ashenden, or the British Agent* on his adventures.

Walk around the grounds of the King's School, then go left around the back of the cathedral to the Kent War Memorial Gardens. Pass through the gate in the far corner and cross Broad Street past Lady Wootton Green. Cross Monastery Street to reach the ruins of St. Augustine's Abbey. When Moody's Penny Wanawake was searching for schoolmaster Dominick Austen, she discovered that he had rooms in Prebend Street, just across Broad Street. Penny herself had a room near the abbey ruins. Although it is far older, the abbey is less well known than the cathedral and as Penny found her way there, she wondered if she could give the abbey the fame with her camera that Monet had given Rheims Cathedral with his paintbrush.

The abbey was founded by St. Augustine in A.D. 598 and rebuilt several times, then destroyed by Henry VIII. It is the burial place of King Ethelbert, his Frankish wife, Queen Bertha, who was a Christian, St. Augustine, and nine of his successors. Excavations have revealed the layout of the church, the monks' dormitory, kitchens, refectory (dining room), and cloisters.

Adjacent to the abbey ruins is St. Augustine's College. Walk about the college, now an annex of the King's School, then turn left into Monastery Street. Take Monastery Street left to Longport and turn left again to take Longport past the Crown Court and the Prison. In Catherine Aird's *A Dead Liberty,* the accused Lucy Durmast was not remanded to the prison in Calleford, but sent to "Her Majesty's Prison Establishment for Women and Girls at Cottingham Grange." Many scenes in that mystery took place in court, however, which may have been here.

Walk the length of Longport to reach St. Martin's Church. It is said to be the oldest church in England still in use. Built of local stone mixed with orange Roman brick, it stands where there may have been a Romano-British Church and was in use before St. Augustine arrived from Rome. As you explore the simple, dark interior, notice the Saxon baptismal font.

Leave St. Martin's Church and return to town along Longport. At Love Lane turn right, then left on Church Street. Cross Lower Bridge Street to take Burgate to Butchery Lane and turn left on Longmarket. Here, in a basement beneath a shopping center, you can see the excavated tessellated Roman pavement that was part of a Roman villa built in A.D. 100.

Follow Butchery Lane to High Street and turn right. Moody's Penny Wanawake and her mysterious American friend, Charles Yeoman, found a Chinese restaurant on High Street decorated with "big blowups of Hong Kong's waterfront all around the walls."

Continue along High Street, crossing Mercery Lane, Jewry Lane, and Palace Street to come to the River Stour. Look to your right to see the famous Weaver's House on the river's edge. Built for a rich merchant in 1561, the house was then occupied by refugee Huguenot weavers who settled in Canterbury after escaping from religious persecution in seventeenth-century France. In front of the Weaver's you can see a dunking stool that was once used to discipline nagging wives. Moody's Penny watched a party of Italians making gestures about the stool, then realized it was teatime.

High Street now becomes St. Peter's Street. Take St. Peter's Street to Westgate. The fourteenth-century gate is the only one remaining in Canterbury and is considered the finest city gate in England. It once guarded the western approach to Canterbury and its upper floor was the city prison until 1829. It is now a small museum with armor, weapons, and instruments of torture.

Beyond Westgate you will find that St. Peter's Street becomes St. Dunstan's Street, then the London Road. The Canterbury West Railway Station is a little way past the old Falstaff Inn and the House of Agnes, thought to be the home of Charles Dickens's Agnes in *David Copperfield*. Past the railway station is St. Dunstan's Church with the Roper family vault. Sir Thomas More's head was placed there by his daughter, Margaret Roper, after his execution. Like all traitors, his head had been exposed on London Bridge. (See Thames River Ride.) Josephine Tey's Inspector Alan Grant had a poor opinion of More's *Historie of Richard III*.

Turn back on St. Peter's Street and walk toward the river again. Opposite the Weavers is St. Thomas (Eastbridge) Hospital, which was built in the twelfth century as a hostel for poor pilgrims. It has a Norman undercroft and a fourteenth-century chapel inside. It is open to visitors.

Turn right at Stour Street, then turn right again into a tiny lane marked "To Greyfriars." Follow this path to picturesque Greyfriars, the first Franciscan friary in England. You can still see the small building's thirteenth-century beams and half-timber work. The seventeenth-century Cavalier poet, Richard Lovelace, who inherited lands in Kent, lived at Greyfriars for a time. During the Civil War he languished in a London prison, where he wrote his famous lines, which many a murder suspect might disagree with, "Stone Walls do not a Prison make/ Nor Iron bars a Cage."

Return to St. Peter's Street again. Walk along the right-hand side of the street; you will pass Queen Elizabeth (I)'s Guest Chamber, which is now a tearoom and restaurant. It was in this Tudor house that the Queen entertained her French suitor, the Duke of Alençon, one of the sons of Catherine de Medicis, who was accused of poisoning her husband's mistress, Diane de Poitiers. This is a pleasant place to stop and eat, although it may be very crowded.

Continue along High Street until it becomes Parade Street again. There are many shops in the side streets like those in Moody's *Penny Dreadful* where the French schoolchildren, on a day trip to England, bought "le junk anglais."

Turn right at Parade Street follow it to St. Margaret's Street and turn right. Walk along St. Margaret's Street, which becomes Castle Street. At the corner of Castle Street and Pin Hill on the right is Canterbury Castle, one of the largest and earliest Norman keeps in England. It is not, however, any longer a suitable stronghold for the current Duke of Calleshire, whose daughter had eloped with a disk jockey in Catherine Aird's *Parting Breath*. Take the City Walls walk to the left and walk back to the railway station to end this walk.

5

DORCHESTER/ CHARMOUTH

DORCHESTER BACKGROUND

Dorchester, or Casterbridge, as Thomas Hardy called it in his novel, *The Mayor of Casterbridge,* is the county town of Dorset. It is a small town with a rich past.

About one mile northwest of town is Poundbury Camp, an Iron Age earthwork where, in Aaron Elkins's *Murder in the Queen's Armes,* the fossil remains of Poundbury Man were discovered as a result of World War II bombing.

Although the site of Dorchester has been settled since prehistoric times, the Romans were the first to locate a town there, when, in A.D. 70, the people of the great entrenched camp of Maiden Castle were transferred to the site of the present town. The Romans called the new settlement Durnovaria. It was laid out in the Roman manner and surrounded by a wall. Today, the wall, except for one small section, is gone; however, in the eighteenth century the lines of the Roman wall were marked by the planting of avenues of trees which are called "the Walks." These include Bowling Alley Walk, West Walk, and Colliton Walk. Other Roman remains include an excavated Roman house in Colliton Park near the county hall.

Present-day Dorchester was rebuilt after a series of fires in the seventeenth and eighteenth centuries had destroyed most of its medieval buildings.

Between pre-Roman and modern times the history of Dorchester has been varied: in the tenth century, the Saxon King Athelstan, grandson of Alfred the Great, established a mint there; in medieval times, the forests were the hunting grounds of King John of Magna Carta fame. (The castle in which he stayed is gone; the county prison now stands on the site.)

At the beginning of the Civil War of 1642–49, John White persuaded the townspeople to support Parliament, but the Royalist forces under Prince Rupert were able to capture the town quite easily. In 1644 there was another battle, and this time it was the Parliamentary forces that captured the town.

In 1685, the Duke of Monmouth's forces attempted to seize the crown from James II, but were defeated at Sedgemoor. The Duke's followers were rounded up and tried before Judge Jeffreys in the infamous "Bloody Assize." Hundreds were transported to Barbados to live out their lives as slaves; 320 were hanged. Seventy-four of those hangings were in Dorchester. (See also Thames River Trip.)

South of Dorchester are the Maumbury Rings, the site of a Stone Age circle adapted by the Romans as an amphitheater capable of seating ten thousand people. It was used for gladiatorial combats on the scale of those in the Colosseum in Rome.

In the Middle Ages the amphitheater was used for bear-baiting, and later as a place for public executions. In 1705, ten thousand people witnessed the public hanging (or burning—sources disagree on the method of execution) of Mary Channing for the murder of her husband. As late as 1767, "hanging fairs" were held in Maumbury Rings.

Dorchester is an excellent base for exploring the West country. The wild heartland of mid-Dorset is Thomas Hardy country. In Anthony Price's *Gunner Kelly,* the West German secret agent, Benedikt Schneider, used a desire to see Hardy's country as one of his reasons for being in Dorset.

Hardy lived in the Dorchester area for his entire life and used the landscape as the memorable background for his novels. For instance, in *The Return of the Native,* there is a vivid description of "Egdon Heath" which will add pleasure to a visit to the area. Egdon Heath is the great expanse of wild moorland that stretches from Dorchester to Bournemouth. Hardy celebrated its austere dignity, not only in *The Return of the Native,* but in book after book.

Thomas Hardy was born in Upper Bockhampton, which is about three miles east of Dorchester. His house is now owned by the National Trust and can be seen by special arrangement. Although Hardy's ashes are buried in Westminster Abbey's Poets' Corner, his heart is buried in the churchyard at Stinsford, two miles east of Dorchester. (Stinsford is "Mellestock" in *Under the Greenwood Tree.)*

Scattered among the bracken and wildflowers of the vast heathland are the towns that appeared in Hardy's novels: Dorchester (Casterbridge), Weymouth (Budmouth), Bere Regis (Kingsbere), and Puddleton (Wetherbury).

The Dorset County Museum, which is located in Dorchester's West High Street, has a good collection of Roman and pre-Roman antiquities in addition to its collection of fossils and natural history. The museum also has a collection of Thomas Hardy manuscripts, including *The Mayor of Casterbridge.* Hardy's study from Max Gate, the home that he built on the Wareham Road, was transferred to the museum after his death.

William Barnes, the Dorset poet, is commemorated by a statue outside St. Peter's Church in High West Street. Barnes ran a school in Dungated Street and lived in South Street. Dorchester and Dorset are often used by mystery writers. Geoffrey Household is hither and yon in Dorchester and the countryside in *A Rough Shoot.* P. D. James used the Purbeck Hills to the south and east of Dorchester as the setting for *The Black Tower.* In *The Skull Beneath the Skin,* the fictional Courey Island with its Victorian castle lies off the Dorset coast. In *Before the Fact,* Francis Iles has Lina McLaidlaw meet her husband in a Dorsetshire village called Abbot Monckford, which may be Abbotsbury. Ngaio Marsh calls upon Dorset as a backdrop for portions of *Overture to Death* and *Hand in Glove.* Jonathan Royal, a character in her *Death and the Dancing Footman,* is from Highfold Manor in Cloudyfold, Dorset.

Anne Maybury's Gothic thriller, *The Pavilion at Monkshood,* is set in the fictional Dorset coastal village of Argent. Anthony Price sets his *Gunner Kelly* in Dorset, particularly in the village of Duntisbury Royal.

How to Get There

British Rail: Trains from London's Waterloo Station. Get off at Dorchester South Station. 2½ hours

Automobile: Take M3 west from London, then A31 just before Winchester

Length of walk: 4 miles

See also Side Trips at the end of this walk.

See page 106 for boundaries of this walk and page 359 for list of detectives, authors, and works referred to in this walk.

Places of Interest

The Dorset County Museum, West High Street. Contains good collections of fossils, natural history, Roman antiquities, a very extensive collection of Thomas Hardy materials, William Barnes relics, and the papers of Sylvia Townsend Warner. (Open weekdays 10–1, 2–8.) Admission charge.

Dorset Military Museum, The Keep, Bridport Road (0305) 64066. This museum covers three hundred years of military history. (Open Monday–Friday 2–5, Saturday 9–12; July–September 9–1, 2–5.) Admission charge.

Old Crown Court, Shire Hall, High West Street. Built in 1797, contains the Council Chamber, originally the Nisi Prius Court, and the Crown Court. The Tolpuddle Martyrs were tried here in 1834 for forming a union and were sentenced to transportation to Australia for swearing an illegal oath. (Open Monday–Friday 10–12, November–April; 10–4, May–October.)

Thomas Hardy Monument, High West Street and The Grove.

Market Day on Wednesday.

PLACES TO STAY/EAT

The Casterbridge Hotel, High East Street (0305) 6403. Affords the comfortable atmosphere of a small Georgian residence. Moderate prices.

King's Arms Hotel and Restaurant, High East Street (0305) 65353. A carefully modernized historic eighteenth-century coaching inn. Moderate.

The Horse with the Red Umbrella, 10 High West Street (0305) 6209. Specializes in homemade bread and pastries. Inexpensive.

Royal Oak, High West Street (0305) 62423. Once the terminal for horse-drawn carrier routes. A family-run pub with a restaurant for a la carte meals; pub meals served in the main bar. Inexpensive.

Judge Jeffreys's Restaurant, High West Street, opposite the Dorset County Museum (0305) 2660. The building dates to the fourteenth century. Its distinction comes from being the lodging of the disagreeable Judge Jeffreys during the Bloody Assize. The restaurant is purportedly haunted. Parts of a human skeleton were discovered in a bricked-up portion of the east wall during restoration work in 1928. The food is traditional English fare and the prices are moderate. (Open for lunch only.)

Mock Turtle, 34 High West Street (0305) 64011. Bright modern restaurant, featuring a varied menu. Open for lunch and dinner; dinner tables should be booked in advance. Moderate.

The Old Tea House, 44 High West Street (0305) 63719. Charming 1635 building. Serves morning coffee, light lunches, and afternoon tea. Snacks are served throughout the day. Inexpensive.

West Dorset Tourist Information Centre, 7 Acland Road, Dorchester (0305) 67992. The people here will assist you in finding lodging and will recommend restaurants, etc.

——— DORCHESTER WALK ———

Begin the Dorchester walk at the Dorchester South British Railway Station. Leave the station to your left, crossing Weymouth Avenue. A left turn on Weymouth Avenue would take you to the Maumbury Rings and farther along to Maiden Castle. (See Side Trips.) You should, however, cross Weymouth Avenue and enter Fairfield Road, where you will see the market to your left. This market is of fairly recent origin. It succeeds a biweekly market that was held into the mid-1800s at the "cross roads" on the High Street. Wednesday is now market day in Dorchester. Follow Fairfield Road to Maumbury Road and turn right. On the corner of Maumbury Road and Great Western Road is the Great Western Hotel in what was an old coaching inn. Turn right into the footpath at the north end of the hotel. This will take you into Bowling Alley Walk. Follow Bowling Alley Walk to West Walk and turn left and take West Walk. On your left, as you walk along, you will see a bright blue, Oriental-looking clock; it will undoubtedly remind you of the Brighton Pavilion. West Walk is a tree-shaded lane that takes you through lovely gardens on your left and past fine old houses on your right. In Thomas Hardy's *The Mayor of Casterbridge,* Susan Henchard's house was located on the right-hand side of the West Walk about midway between Bowling Alley Walk and Princess Street. At one time, the town ended at the walls that are marked by these walks; the open countryside lay beyond. The house that Susan and Elizabeth-Jane lived in soon after coming to Casterbridge is described as being near the Roman Wall with views across the fields.

Follow West Walk to where it gives into Albert Road on the left and Princess Street on the right. Here on the right at Princess Street you will find Dorchester's only remaining bit of Roman wall.

In Aaron Elkins's paleontological mystery, *Murder in the Queen's Armes,* when "bone detective" Gideon Oliver and his bride, Julie, took in the sights of Dorchester, they stopped to admire the bit of Roman wall.

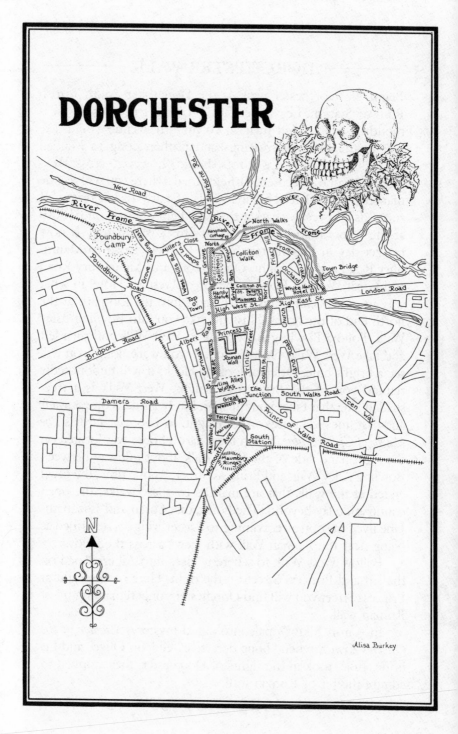

DORCHESTER

N

Alisa Burkey

Continue across Albert Street and Princess Street to High West Street (to the left it is Bridport Road). The Military Museum is in the castle-like building on Bridport Road.

You are now at the crossroads known as the "top o'town." Here was the site of the Roman West gate. Being careful of the traffic in the roundabout, cross to the north side of High West Street to the entrance to Colliton Park, where you will find the memorial to Thomas Hardy. The statue faces west, looking across the street called The Grove toward the "Top o'Town" carpark. This is very likely the carpark where Roger Taine, in Geoffrey Household's *A Rough Shoot,* left his car and collected his bicycle before his ride into the country to check the shoot.

The Hardy statue was unveiled in 1931 by Hardy's friend, Sir James Barrie. Eric Kennington designed the bronze statue, which has Hardy seated with heartland vegetation about his feet.

After you have examined the Hardy statue, as Gideon and Julie Oliver did in their tour of Hardy sights in *Murder in the Queen's Armes,* enter, also as they did, the tree-lined Colliton Walk (Chalk Walk in *The Mayor of Casterbridge*), which runs north along The Grove and through the park. This is the site of the Roman wall that encircled Durnovaria. The steep, grassy embankment makes the walker well aware of the great Roman earthwork, topped at one time by walls over eight feet thick and nineteen feet high, which surrounded Dorchester on all sides except for the northeast, which had the natural defense of the river Frome.

As you follow Colliton Walk, the area behind the flint wall to the right are parking area, County Hall, and Library. It was formerly the large park of Colliton House.

Follow Colliton Walk to North Walk, and turn right. North Walk is a raised walkway; to the left you can look down on Northernhay and the gardens of the houses beyond. Follow the North Walk through the surprisingly rural landscape to where it curves to cross Northernhay. Stone steps will take you down to the level of Northernhay, which you should cross. After crossing Northernhay, enter the right-hand lane; it curves to the left around Hangman's Cottage, an attractive thatched building surrounded by flowers, which is said to be the home of a former town executioner. It was also the home of the hangman in Hardy's "The Withered Arm"; it was here that Gertrude Lodge called on the executioner and arranged with him for her to touch the neck of the corpse after it was taken down from the gallows.

In Hardy's *The Three Strangers,* the new executioner was on his way to take residence in the cottage when he met the man he was supposed to hang, the condemned man having escaped from prison.

It was at one time the practice for each county to have its own hangman. Since it was the practice to hang a man for a crime such as sheep stealing, the hangman was kept adequately busy, or as Hardy said of the profession of hangman, it was "monopolized by a single gentleman."

Beyond the cottage, take the left fork of the lane over a branch of the river and enter the paved path to the right that follows the river. As you walk along, the river will be on your right and there will be wildflowers and alders and elderberries, as well as black-and-white cows, on your left. This was a favorite walk of both Hardy and the poet William Barnes. Just before the Friary Hill Road, which leads to the river from the south, you will see part of the old mill buildings. Here also is the site of the town's first prison. Gertrude Lodge saw the prison building for the first time from Rushy Pond on Egdon Heath and later sat beneath it in Hardy's "The Withered Arm."

Boldwood, after shooting Troy, in *Far from the Madding Crowd,* went through the "archway of heavy stonework, which was closed by an iron studded pair of doors." In the summer, the building is screened by trees so it can be seen much more clearly from the meadows. The meadows, or the moor, was where the mobs used to gather whenever there was a hanging. The hangings took place on a gallows erected on the flat roof of the archway in full view of the inmates as well as the spectators outside. When he was a teenager, Hardy was part of such a crowd and witnessed the hanging of a woman. The memory stayed with him all of his life.

Continue to follow the river walk as it curves its way back to Town Bridge. Here at the end of the walk you will find public toilets to your right. Just beyond is the White Hart Hotel. You will emerge at the east end of High East Street where you will see a sign marked "London Road." Turn right.

As Gideon and Julie Oliver wandered this way, they decided to forget the Hardy associations and enjoy the deserted path for its own sake. As they strolled along the gently flowing river with the haze-covered Durnover Moor in the distance, they speculated about the theft of the Poundbury skull from the Dorchester Museum. They were soon surprised to find themselves emerging from the shady country walk back onto the High Street at a point just a few blocks from where they'd started. Instead of walking more, the newlyweds elected to return to the hotel.

Adjacent to the point where the Olivers emerged from the river walk, there is a red postbox bearing the monogram of George V. Walk along the north side of High East Street past the White Hart Hotel. The White Hart is located next to the Riverwalk and is set back from the street. In "The Withered Arm," Gertrude Lodge stayed at the White Hart after crossing Egdon Heath. Before having her evening meal, she walked "by a path along the waterside" to the hangman's cottage.

Sergeant Troy and Pennyways met and schemed in the White Hart before Troy set out to Boldwood's farm to get his wife in *Far from the Madding Crowd.*

Beyond the White Hart is the Casterbridge Hotel, attractively housed in a comfortable Georgian building. The entire street is essentially Georgian in character, interspersed with some Victorian buildings. It was built after the disastrous fires of 1613 and 1735. There are many old shop fronts and bow windows.

On the north side of the street where you are walking, you will soon come to the friendly-looking, bow-windowed King's Arms hotel, "the chief hotel in Casterbridge." It was in this hotel in *The Mayor of Casterbridge* that Henchard faced the Commissioners and his creditors at his bankruptcy.

Across High East street from the King's Arms is the former All Saints Church, which is now part of the Dorset County Museum and houses the archeological overflow. The present building was built in 1843 on the foundation of the old church.

Continue walking along the right-hand side of High East Street, past the Victorian Town Hall with its clock tower. Turn left into South Street (called Cornhill by Hardy); North Square Street will be to your right. In the center of South Street is an obelisk that marks the location of the town pump. It is dated 1784 and replaces an old cupola. The townspeople came to the pump for water and lingered to exchange gossip. This is the area where the old biweekly market was held. On the right-hand side of South Street, just beyond the obelisk, is the Antelope Hotel. An oak-paneled room in this hotel is thought to be the trial room for Judge Jeffreys's "Bloody Assize." In Frank Branston's *Sergeant Ritchie's Conscience,* Judge Jeffreys's notorious actions prompted a disturbed CID officer, Jack Ritchie, to comment that Detective Chief Inspector Cyril Pryke's briefing was ". . . like a Judge Jeffreys's summing up."

Continue down the right-hand side of South Street until you come to No. 39, where Thomas Hardy worked as a pupil to John Hicks, architect; William Barnes lived in No. 40 from 1847 to 1862. Now cross South Street to inspect the tiny shopping center called Nappers Mite. It was built in 1616 by Sir Robert Napper as an almshouse to house ten poor men. As you walk back up South Street on the right side, you will pass No. 10, the home of Hardy's mayor of Casterbridge. It is now a bank. A plaque states: "This house is reputed to have been lived in by the Mayor of Casterbridge in the Thomas Hardy story of that name, written in 1885."

Return to the crossroads. St. Peter's Church with its great square tower is here on the corner of High West Street and North Square Street (High East Street becomes High West after South Street). There was a twelfth-century church on this site, and before that, a Roman temple. The present building is fifteenth century. It was restored in 1856–57 under the direction of John Hicks and his pupil, Thomas Hardy. The bronze statue in front of St. Peter's is of William Barnes, the Dorset poet who is known for his dialectal verse. It was in St. Peter's that a memorial service for Thomas Hardy was held at the same time that his heart was being buried in the churchyard at Stimsford.

Next to St. Peter's is the Dorset County Museum. This is the museum where Gideon Oliver stopped to pay a courtesy call and discovered that the skull on display was not that of the Poundbury Man. This is the first of several mysteries delightfully woven together by Aaron Elkins in *Murder in the Queen's Armes*.

The museum is more than worth a visit. It is everyone's idea of what a museum should be. It is friendly and small, but absolutely filled with the most fascinating collections that one would want to find. You will find yourself actually walking on a Roman mosaic tile floor. The staff is knowledgeable and willing to talk with you. The holdings are fairly eclectic, ranging from fossils to superb literary collections. The best collection of Hardy materials in the world is here, and in addition, the library is collecting the papers of novelist Sylvia Townsend Warner, who lived in Dorsetshire in Maiden Newton until her death in 1978.

Spend as much time as you dare in the museum, and when you leave cross what is now High West Street and take a look at the two very different restaurants where the honeymooning Olivers stopped to eat in *Murder in the Queen's Armes*. Directly across the street from the museum is No. 6, High West Street, the early-seventeenth-century lodgings where Judge Jeffreys stayed during the Bloody Assize of 1685, following the Battle of Sedgemoor. It is now a restaurant.

Gideon and Julie Oliver, two hours after completing the river walk, were seated in a cozy dining room "with rough-beamed ceiling and stone-mullioned, multipaned windows of wavy, leaded glass." Starting with pints of bitter, they ate their way through a meal of smoked mackerel followed by steak and kidney pie. It was at dinner that Gideon promised Julie that the rest of the trip would be "cream teas, country walks, and pub lunches, . . . and no more bones"—a promise he did not keep. Although the Olivers enjoyed dinner here, the restaurant is actually open only in the afternoon.

The other restaurant where the Olivers found memorable food is the Horse with the Red Umbrella. When you leave the Judge Jeffreys, turn left and walk up the left side of High West Street to No. 10. Soon after arriving in Dorchester, the newly-wed Olivers, with guidebook in hand, set out to see the sights the town had to offer. The aroma of fresh-baked goods com-ing from a shop caught their attention and soon they were sitting at a tiny wooden table with two big wedges of warm Dorset apple cake and a pot of tea before them. The Horse with the Red Umbrella, which stands at 10 High West Street, is probably the restaurant Elkins had in mind when he sent the Olivers in to dine. Following suit is an opportunity too good to miss.

There are several excellent guides available to the many Hardy sites in and around town. If you are interested in more material, secure one of the guides from the Tourist Informa-tion Centre at 7 Acland Road. If, on the other hand, you are ready to push on with the Olivers to the second part of this walk, which will take you to Charmouth, follow West High Street on the left-hand side back to the Top o'Town. On the north side of the street at Grey School Passage is the Shire building, which was built in 1797. It contains the Council Chamber, originally the Nisi Prius Court, and the Crown Court, where the Tolpuddle Martyrs were tried in 1834 and sentenced to be transported to Australia. At Albert Road turn left into West Walk. Follow West Walk to Bowling Alley Walk, then turn right and walk along Bowling Alley Walk to Maum-bury Road. Follow Maumbury Road to Fairfield and turn left and walk along Fairfield Road across Weymouth Avenue to the South Station. End this walk there.

CHARMOUTH BACKGROUND

The history of the delightful West Dorset village of Charmouth goes back to 500 B.C., when Iron Age man lived in the area. The local Celtic tribe was the Durotriges, who built the impressive hillfort at Maiden Castle. The Saxons, led by King Egbert in 833, and in 840 by King Ethelwulf, tried to ward off Danish attacks. Concy's Castle, which survives as an earthwork, is believed to have been the Saxon encampment. An early chronicle records that "A.D. 833, King Egbert fought against the men of the thirty-five ships at Charmouth, and there was great slaughter made, and the Danish men maintained possession of the field."

Soon after the Norman Conquest, the Manor of Charmouth passed into the hands of a Norman family, the Beauchamps. They gave it to the Abbot of Forde Abbey sometime before the end of the eleventh century. Monks would ride from Forde Abbey to Charmouth to collect the rents and taxes due. It is believed that they would stay in an abbot's house in the building that is now the Queen's Armes Hotel. The building, which has since been adapted for various uses, is one of the oldest in Charmouth. In 1501, Catherine of Aragon, while on her way to marry Henry VIII's brother, Arthur, stayed there. After other uses, the building is once more a hotel called the Queen's Armes after Catherine. In 1651, after the defeat of Royalist troops by Cromwell's men at the Battle of Worcester, it was necessary for the King, Charles II, to flee the country. A Charmouth sea captain, Stephen Limbry, agreed to take the unnamed gentleman across to France for sixty pounds. Limbry's wife interfered with the plan, and the King ended up finding a safe haven at the Queen's Armes.

This is the same Queen's Armes where the honeymooning "Skeleton Detective" Gideon Oliver and his wife, Julie, were staying when they became embroiled in the mysterious goings-on at Stonebarrow Fell.

Most of the town of Charmouth is arranged on either side of the steeply inclined A35 Trunk Road, called The Street within the boundaries of the village. The entire village lies within an "area of outstanding Beauty," as designated under the "National Parks and Access to the Countryside Act, 1949." The area along The Street has been designated as a Conservation Area under the West Dorset Heritage Coast.

HOW TO GET THERE

British Rail: From Salisbury to Axminster, taxi from Axminster to Charmouth. (Check with your Charmouth hotel; someone will meet the train.)

Automobile: Take the A35 south and west from Salisbury.

Length of Walk: varies

PLACES OF INTEREST

The Queen's Armes Hotel, The Street. Ancient inn associated with Catherine of Aragon and Charles II.

The Coastal Walks

PLACES TO STAY/EAT

The Queen's Armes, The Street (0297) 60339. An ancient inn with comfortable rooms and a homey, warm atmosphere. Serves pub lunches and dinners to nonresidents. This charming inn is the star of Aaron Elkins's *Murder in the Queen's Armes.*

The George, The Street (0297) 60280. A fourteenth-century traveler's rest and a seventeenth-century coaching inn. In *Murder in the Queen's Armes,* Julie and Gideon had dinner here.

Stow House, The Street (0297) 60603. Eighteenth-century tearoom and guest house. Once a rest for the monks of Abbotsbury. Excellent spot for tea, either in the charming tearoom or in the picturesque walled gardens.

CHARMOUTH WALK

Begin your walk at the Queen's Armes Hotel, where you should take time to examine the hotel itself. If you are not staying there, plan to take lunch or dinner in the pleasant dining room. Be sure to ask host Peter Miles to show you the Tudor room, the comfortable lounge where Gideon and Julie spent romantic hours before the fire, and where, as the novel nears its resolution, a body is found sprawled on the stone floor of the hearth. Leave the hotel and head to your left up The Street past the small shops to Lower Sea Lane, where you should turn left. Follow Lower Sea Lane past Wesley Close to the left and past the Charmouth School. Continue past Meadow Way on the left, and past a carpark with public toilets across the street on the right. After walking about half a mile you will come to the area of the beach. Turn left into the lane just before the carpark on the left and follow it as it crosses the bridge over the tiny River Char. Head up the path over the slope of the "wide grassy cliff that sweeps up to Stonebarrow Hill." In Elkins's book, the dig where the various nefarious doings took place was located on top of Stonebarrow Hill. A few miles beyond Stonebarrow, the squarish Golden Cap (from the summit of which you can see Dartmoor) looms over the Dorset coast. You can continue your coastal walk along the rugged terrain, or, after resting, return to the beach the way you came.

The walk that Gideon and Julie took in *Murder in the Queen's Armes* that almost led to their deaths was the one to the tiny village of Wooton Fitzpaine. We took the walk ourselves one sunny July afternoon, and found, instead of a man-eating dog, a delightful view of the countryside and two churches and a manor house well worth the viewing.

Once again, turn left as you leave the Queen's Armes and walk up the hill to the traffic light. Turn right to cross The Street, and then turn left. Turn right into Barr's Lane and walk along its paved surface to the playing fields. This is where Gideon and Julie encountered Colonel Conley's ill-tempered half-mastiff, Bowser. As we walked along here, the most fearsome animal we met was a playful Collie who was determined that we play ball. Go straight ahead from Barr's Lane past the playing fields, following the unpaved footpath. The footpath is quite well worn and will lead you along the stream to the wooden kissing bridge. Julie and Gideon did not complete their walk across the fields but we did, using as our guide John Hobson's excellent *Country Walks,* which is sold locally. Continue on the footpath over a second bridge and on across the fields as it leads you into the village of Wooton Fitzpaine about a mile and a half from Charmouth. Return the same way or continue to Catherston manor and church.

POSSIBLE SIDE TRIPS

Poundbury Camp

Iron Age earthwork situated about one mile northwest of Dorchester.

Getting There: By car or on foot, take the Poundbury Road that runs between the Top o'Town carpark and the Military Museum. A half mile out of town, a metal gate on the right will give you access to what Hardy described in *The Mayor of Casterbridge* as an "elevated green spot." It was here that Henchard, the Mayor of Casterbridge, plotted his ill-fated activities.

Poundbury covers about twenty acres, surrounded by an embankment. The steep slope on the north side drops to the River Frome. Here was "Pummery" weir, where the old man on his way to the workhouse attempted to drown himself after a well-intentioned act of mercy, in Hardy's poem, "The Curate's Kindness."

Poundbury was refortified prior to the Roman invasion in the first century A.D. Between A.D. 300 and 400, a vast graveyard occupied the area between the East Wall and Dorchester. In *Murder in the Queen's Armes* by Aaron Elkins, the Poundbury skull fragment that so mysteriously disappeared from the Greater Dorchester Museum of History and Archaeology was first discovered here. Hardy called Poundbury by its original name, Pummery. It is mentioned in several of his poems, including "The Dance at the Phoenix," "The Fight on Durnover Moor," and "My Cecily."

Maumbury Rings

Neolithic in origin, the ring is located at the juncture of Weymouth Avenue with Maumbury Road, just past South Station. *Getting There:* By auto or by foot: From the "Junction" follow the Weymouth Road (A354) south past South Station. A short distance beyond on the left-hand (east) side is the earthwork.

In early times, "The Ring" stood alone in the fields with views across to Maiden Castle, Poundbury, and the Dorset hills. Hardy gives a very full account of "The Ring" in chapter 2 of *The Mayor of Casterbridge:* "It was to Casterbridge what the ruined Coliseum is to modern Rome, and was nearly of the same magnitude."

In 1908, after excavations had been carried out at "The Ring," Hardy was asked to write an article for *The Times,* which appeared on October 9. By that time it had been established that the earthwork was from the New Stone Age.

Maumbury Rings was constructed as an earthwork about two thousand years ago. It was a sacred circle; excavations have determined its use in fertility rites. The Romans raised the banks of the oval-shaped arena to form an amphitheater. The spectators sat on the sloping banks while gladiators battled one another and wild beasts.

After the Romans, the amphitheater was abandoned until 1642 when Parliamentary troops used it as a fortification guarding the road to Weymouth. In the eighteenth century it was used as a place of execution.

Maiden Castle

Located about two miles southwest of the center of Dorchester.

Getting There: By bus, car, or on foot: Follow the Weymouth road south out of Dorchester for about two miles, then turn right at the Maiden Castle Road. Or, for the most scenic approach to Maiden Castle, take Weymouth Road to the Winterbourne Monkton Lane. Turn west (right) and at the village school turn right again. Follow the country road to a footpath gate on the right. From there climb straight up to Maiden Castle. You will walk a little over two miles.

Maiden Castle, which stands alone on a chalk hill, is a huge earthwork and one of the finest of its kind in Europe. Originally it was a Late Stone Age village. It was enlarged and the first rampart built during the Iron Age. In about 100 B.C., the castle was transformed into a massive complex covering forty-seven acres. It reached its prime during this time, with over five thousand people living in crowded huts.

When Dorchester was established around 44 B.C., Maiden Castle was abandoned. It lay dormant until A.D. 400, when a Romano-British temple was built on the site.

In the fifth century A.D., Maiden Castle was completely abandoned and has remained so. If you walk alone there on one of England's cold and misty days, you will find it awesome. It is what Thomas Hardy called a "stupendous ruin."

In 1934 a dig at Maiden Castle resulted in many of the finds that you can see at the Greater Dorchester Museum. Today, what is left for the explorer is an area half a mile long enclosed by steep earth walls that run from sixty to ninety feet high. The hill is encircled by three or four lines of these walls. The outer defenses are nearly two miles around and a very complicated earthwork guards the entrance.

There are references to Maiden Castle in Hardy's works, particularly in *The Mayor of Casterbridge*. It is mentioned in at least two of his poems, "The Alarm" and "My Cecily."

In the film version of *Far from the Madding Crowd*, Troy's demonstration to Bathsheba of the sword drill was shot between the ramparts of Maiden Castle.

Bridport

Located about six miles east of Charmouth on the A35, which forms East and West Street, the top of the T-shaped town layout. East Street is famous for many interesting inns. The Greyhound there dates back to 1300. One old inn has undergone a number of name changes. The "King of Russia" changed to the "King of the Belgians" in World War I, then became the "Lord Nelson" during World War II.

If you follow East Road to Lee Lane, you will find the stone commemorating the flight from town of the disguised Charles II in 1651.

The most interesting and the oldest street in town is South Street, which runs south toward the sea from the Town Hall junction. The Town Hall site was an open market prior to 1261.

The museum, which is located on South Street in an elegant building with a sixteenth-century facade, houses exhibits of flora, fauna, and fossils with emphasis on those found between Bridport and Lyme Regis. There are also some Roman artifacts, as well as an outstanding collection of dolls that dates from the end of the nineteenth century.

The mystery connection to Bridport takes you back to the A35. Gideon Oliver, accompanied by the Bridport coroner, Dr. Merrill, came into the pretty little town to see what he could deduce about a body that had been found in the sea. They drove from West Street to East Street and turned left on Barrack Street and drove "to the very edge of town, where a large hospital and a small police station shared a block of grassy land."

Lyme Regis

Located on Lyme Bay near the Devonshire border about one mile west of Charmouth.

Getting There: By foot, Lyme Regis can be reached by walking west along the beach at low tide for about a mile. It can also be reached by auto by taking the A35 northwest out of Charmouth and turning right at the junction with the A3052, which will take you directly into Lyme. Lyme, as listed in the Domesday Book, had four farms and twenty fishermen. It became Lyme Regis in 1284 when its first charter was issued by Edward I. The eight-hundred-foot-long stone pier known as the Cobb, for which Lyme Regis is famous, dates from Edward's time, although later monarchs also contributed to its improvement and upkeep. The Cobb was very important to the development of the town's harbor, since it protected both the town and the incoming ships from the southwesterly gales.

Lyme Regis's darkest time was in 1348 when the Black Death struck, reducing both the population and trade, for which it had become a center.

Lyme has played its part in strengthening the royal navy. It sent four ships to the siege of Calais in 1347, and in 1588 provided five to fight against the Spanish Armada.

Although the surrounding area was Royalist territory, Lyme was a Parliamentarian enclave during the Civil War. It was attacked by Prince Maurice and four thousand of his Cavaliers in 1644, but after a period of two months' fierce fighting, the Royalists withdrew. In 1685, the Duke of Monmouth, Charles II's illegitimate son, challenged the throne of his uncle, James II. Monmouth landed on the beach west of the Cobb and rallied Dorset men to his cause. They were soundly defeated at the battle of Sedgemore. Later, when the Duke was on the run after his defeat, he disguised himself as a peasant and fell asleep under a hedge near Cranborne Chase. His disguise was seen through, however, when the Star of the Order of the Garter, which he so proudly wore, was found in his pocket.

In the eighteenth century, Lyme Regis developed as a seaside resort. Bathing machines were introduced in 1760 and the resort became fashionable. The thatched cottages where wealthy Victorians spent their holidays can still be seen along the seafront. Princess (later Queen) Victoria visited Lyme Regis and sailed from the arm of the Cobb which now bears her name.

Jane Austen knew Lyme Regis well. It was from the Cobb that Louisa Musgrove, in *Persuasion,* had her famous fall. Visitors who admire Austen's works always begin their tour of Lyme at the Cobb. (Even Tennyson came to Lyme Regis to see the spot where the fictitious Louisa fell.)

Like Charmouth, Lyme Regis is an area of exceptional geological interest. Casts of plants and animals dating back millions of years have been found here. The Philpot museum, with its fine displays of local fauna and fossils, has as its prize exhibit the fossilized fish-lizard called an ichthyosaurus, which is estimated to have lived over 140 million years ago.

The museum's honorary curator is John Fowles, one of England's leading authors. In 1980, Lyme was transformed into a Victorian town for the filming of his *The French Lieutenant's Woman*.

Gideon and Julie Oliver, the reluctant detectives in Aaron Elkins's *Murder in the Queen's Armes,* did not go to Lyme for any of the usual reasons. They went instead to find the editor of the West Dorset *Times* and to try to get behind the coverage of the dig at Stonebarrow Fell.

After a less-than-satisfying discussion with the editor, Ralph Chanty, Gideon met Julie and they decided to be tourists and explore the hilly seaside town.

They had a hearty Dorset cream tea in the Goose House, a tiny white cottage near the foot of the crooked, climbing main street. As they ate their way through Dorset dumplings filled with a rum-and-apple mixture, a pile of buttered scones, jam, and tea, and of course a bowl heaped with clotted cream, they looked out at the quiet beach and watched the fossil hunters picking their way along. If you visit Lyme in July you will have cause to wonder at the peaceful beach the Olivers saw; but remember, they were there in November.

Later, when they were standing at the end of the Cobb facing east, they could see across the smooth expanse of water to the green coast of Dorset and the rounded dome of Stonebarrow Fell.

Start your walk in Lyme Regis at the Cobb and walk eastward along the traffic-free marine drive. This is a place to wander, which we will leave you to do, as Gideon and Julie did.

6

ELY

BACKGROUND

Ely's history goes back to the time when the town was really an island in the marshy Fens. There were quantities of eels in the marsh, and according to the Venerable Bede, its name came from Elig, or eel island. Legend later had it that when St. Dunstan came to Ely and found to his displeasure that the monks were married, he turned them into eels.

The written history of Ely began about A.D. 700 with the establishment of an abbey for both men and women by St. Etheldreda. She was a daughter of Anna, the Wuffinga king of East Anglia, whose family came from Exning. (See Newmarket Walk.) Etheldreda was married several times for reasons of state, but she was finally allowed to enter a cloister. She then founded the abbey at Ely, which had been part of her dowry. Later, she was made a saint, and her grave at Ely became the site of pilgrimages.

One hundred years later, after the Danes had sacked Ely in 870, King Edgar refounded the abbey and started the King's School, which is the oldest public school in England. The saintly King Edward the Confessor, who left the throne of England to his cousin William the Conqueror in his will, was educated there. William had invaded England to claim his inheritance, and under the outlaw Hereward the Wake, Ely was the last stronghold to hold out against him. Either by trick or treachery, a path for the Normans across the Fens was made with bundles of faggots, so that Ely fell.

In 1081 the Norman Simeon became abbot and began building the present-day cathedral. It is known as "The Monarch of the Fens" and dedicated to the Holy and Undivided Trinity. The cathedral was completed just before the Black Death struck in 1349. Its crowning glory, the Octagon, was built in 1322 to replace a central tower that had collapsed.

Ely's marshy isolation continued to protect the abbey even when Henry VIII dissolved the monasteries, giving the spiritual lord of Ely temporal powers like those of the warrior bishops of Durham in the north of England. Ely did not become easily accessible until dikes, roads, and bridges began to be built in the seventeenth century.

Mystery fans come to Ely to see the Fens themselves, with their characteristic high skies, windmills, drainage ditches, and flat farmlands, so beautifully described in all kinds of weather by Dorothy L. Sayers in *The Nine Tailors*. This is the Sayers heartland. She was raised northwest of Ely at Bluntisham and later lived at Christchurch. (See Side Trips.)

Ely also appeared in Margery Allingham's *No Police at the Funeral* when Albert Campion found himself sitting opposite a large steel engraving of Ely Cathedral in Great-aunt Caroline Faraday's dining room at Socrates Close. (See Cambridge Walk.) In Robert Player's *Oh, Where Are Bloody Mary's Earrings?* the Prince of Wales (later Edward VII) and his entourage sped north past the Isle of Ely on the Flying Scotsman to a rendezvous with the Duke of Argyll at Balmoral.

Ely is also P. D. James territory. Hoggath's Forensic Scientific Laboratory was in a Palladian mansion with a Wren chapel in the small village of Clevisham, ten miles from Ely. Inspector Blakelock, who ran the lab's front desk, drove from Ely every day to work, and, until she went to live with writer Stella Mawson, Angela Foley had lived in rooms in Ely and commuted to work. An Ely firm even did the lab's heavy cleaning.

In Glyn Daniel's *The Cambridge Murders,* Oliver Hartley, an ex-undergraduate from Fisher College and brother-in-law of Dean Landon, had driven the dean over to visit Canon Henry Boyce Cooper-Leigh of Ely Cathedral. The canon turned out to be the uncle of Scotland Yard's Detective-Superintendent Robertson-Macdonald. (See Cambridge Walk.)

Other mystery writers use fictitious places in "East Anglia," the name used to mean either Norfolk or Suffolk, where the Wuffinga, or East English, settled. In Josephine Bell's *Fall over Cliff,* her detective, Dr. David Wintringham, visited Oreborough near the sea in "East Anglia" to investigate a suspicious drowning. Jonathan Gash's Lovejoy, the shady antique dealer-detective in *The Tartan Sell,* came from a market town in East Anglia.

In E. X. Giroux's *Death for a Darling,* Robert Forsythe's secretary, Abigail Saunderson, lured him into joining her on an annual visit to an old friend in Norfolk. The Georgian mansion was in "Bury-Sutton" on the River Carey. A film company was there, remaking Emily Bronte's *Wuthering Heights,* casting the owner's niece, Erika Von Farr, as Cathy.

HOW TO GET THERE

British Rail: Major rail junction. Trains every two hours from London's Liverpool Station or every hour by changing at Cambridge. About 1½ hours
Trains also to Norwich, Ipswich, and King's Lynn.

Automobile: M11 from London to Cambridge, then the A10. A142 from Newmarket. 71 miles from London; 16 miles from Cambridge; 55 miles from Norwich; 13 miles from Newmarket.

Length of walk: 4.5 miles

See also Side Trips by car to Sandringham, Norfolk Broads, Norwich, and the Fens (courtesy the Dorothy L. Sayers Society © 1987).

See map on page 127 for boundaries of this walk, and page 360 for a list of detectives and stories.

PLACES OF INTEREST

Ely Cathedral, Cathedral Close (67735/6). See especially the Octagon, the Lady Chapel, Shrine of St. Etheldreda, angel roof in transepts, and stained glass exhibition. (Open 7:30–7 in summer; 7:30–6 Sundays and winter weekdays.) Ely Festival late May–early June.

Bishop's Palace, Palace Green. Begun by Bishop Alcock, founder of Jesus College, Cambridge. A Sue Ryder Home (hospice).

King's School, Firmary Lane.

The Ely Porta, the Gallery.

Steeple Gate, High Street. Tudor entrance to Cathedral Close.

Ely Museum, Sacrist's Gate, High Street. (Open Saturday–Sunday P.M.: Thursday in summer.)

The Market Place, Fore Hill and Market Street. Open-air market Thursday. Annual Etheldreda Fair since the twelfth century.

The Church of St. Mary the Virgin, Church Lane.

Cromwell's House, St. Mary's Street. Now St. Mary's vicarage, closed to the public.

Lamb Hotel, 2 Lynn Road. Originally the Sign of the Lamb of God, or Holy Lamb Inn, circa 1416.

Tourist Authority, Minster Place between High Street and Cathedral Close.

PLACES TO STAY/EAT

Lamb Hotel, 2 Lynn Road (Ely 3574). Georgian hotel with a cathedral view. Bar and restaurant. English food. Inexpensive.

The Cutter Inn, Riverside Walk. Waterside pub. Also Queen's Mote House Hotel chain.

Old Fire Engine House, St. Mary's Street (Ely 2582). Old fire engine still in yard. Lunch, tea, or dinner. English food. Teas inexpensive, other expensive.

Ely Cathedral, The Refectory, to left of West Door. Open for morning coffee, lunch, and tea.

ELY WALK

Begin your walk in this ancient cathedral town at the Ely Railroad Station with its welcome sign in five languages. Walk out of the station yard and turn left on Station Road. Continue walking until you reach a crossroads. On your left is Gas Lane, where you will see the pink Angel Inn and on your right a sign saying "River" and a lane called Annesdale. Take Annesdale to the right. It runs directly into the Riverside Walk along the Great Ouse.

The Riverside Walk, filled in summer with boats and people, goes between Annesdale and Waterside Quays. Now a holiday resort area, it has been a harbor since the fifteenth century, when it was called the "Broad Hithe." Part is now called the Quai d'Orsay in recognition of the "twinning" of East Cambridgeshire and Orsay in France.

Walking along Annesdale you pass Victoria Street, then reach Cutter Lane. Sitting beside the wide River Ouse is the Cutter Inn, a large, three-story red-tiled and whitewashed pub. You might like to sit at the benches and tables outside to enjoy the river view, and sample Greene King ale, which is the family business of mystery writer Graham Greene. Across the river is the shipyard of Messrs. Appleyard, Lincoln, and Company, where you can hire cabin cruisers (or have one built) for taking to the water in the Fen country.

In Ngaio Marsh's *Clutch of Constables* Troy took ship on the *Zodiak* at "Norminster," which might have been King's Lynn, for a five-day canal-boat excursion along a river, through locks, past weirs, seeing spires, fens, trees, even a Saxon Wapentake, or council circle. Troy had been north opening a new one-man show by herself because Superintendent Alleyn was lecturing on crime in America. Her trip as described was half fact, half fancy, but Troy might have sailed past Ely (Longminster) with her crew of art thieves, led by an international criminal known as the Jampot.

On the other hand, since the Fens do not have locks, and since real "Constable Country" is in Suffolk, south and east of Bury St. Edmunds along the Stour River, the mystery may

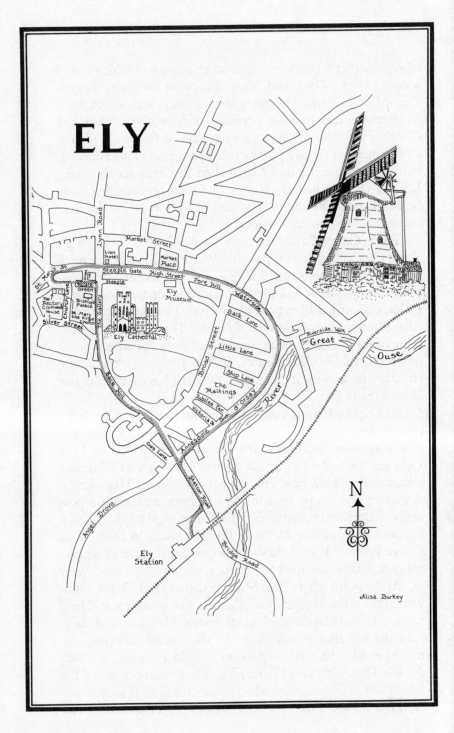

ELY

Lynn Road

Market Street

Lion Hotel

Steeple Gate

Market Place

St Maria St

High Street

Steeple

Green

The Gallery

Fore Hill

Waterside

The Rectory Cromwell House

Church Lane

Bishop's Palace

Ely Museum

Silver Street

St. Mary the Virgin Church

Back Lane

Riverside Walk

Ely Cathedral

Broad Street

Little Lane

Great

Ship Lane

Ouse

Back Hill

The Maltings

River

Jubilee Ter.

Victoria St

Quai d'Orsay

Gas Lane

Kingsdale

Angel Drove

Station Road

Ely Station

Bridge Road

N

Alisa Burkey

take place there. (It also may be an imaginary combination of several places.) On board, Troy, gazing at the shoreline, exclaimed "Oh, look! The place is swarming with Constables. Everywhere you look—a perfect clutch of them." Since *A Clutch of Constables* is about an art scam to fake and sell false Constables, her remark put the other passengers into a nervous twit. To confuse her trail Marsh then had Troy see the Long Minster (Ely Cathedral—King's Lynn has no cathedral, only St. Margaret's Church, built as part of a priory) from the river and get off to consult the local police.

From Cutter Lane you cross Jubilee Terrace. As you go along Quai d'Orsay, you pass the Victorian Maltings, a brick brewery with a high tower at one end that recently was converted into a public hall used for concerts, drama, and dance. Its location makes Ely a possible site for "Thwaite Maltings" in Alan Hunter's *Gently Between the Tides*. That town, where the body of murdered Hannah Stoven had drifted, had an annual music festival like Aldeburgh's, held in a huge brick-and-slate structure famous for its acoustics. Ely itself has a festival in late May or early June.

At Ship Lane your walk begins to curve left away from the river to take you uphill. Cross Little Lane and Back Lane and take Waterside. Still going toward your left, you cross Lisle Lane on the right and Broad Street on the left as Waterside becomes Fore Hill. Fore Hill in turn will become High Street. You have now come to a major shopping area, with a post office, stores, and restaurants. Unfortunately, the Peking Duck Chinese restaurant at 26 Fore Hill has closed. In *Death of an Expert Witness,* P. D. James's Inspector Doyle offered to take his dissatisfied wife to the Chinese restaurant on Fore Street.

At the point where Fore Street becomes High Street, off to your right is the Market Place. An open-air market is still held there on Thursday, as well as an annual May Fair and Saint Etheldreda's Fair in October. In the twelfth century, the monks at Ely obtained permission to hold a fair on St. Etheldreda's Day, October 17, making it a contemporary of the Abbey fair at Shrewsbury, which is described by Ellis Peters in *St. Peter's Fair*. Like St. Peter's Fair, St. Etheldreda's Fair lasted for several days and drew merchants from all parts of the country. It was famous for selling bright silk necklaces called Etheldreda's Chains, or "Audreys," a corruption of Etheldreda, which gave us the word *tawdry* for cheap or gaudy goods.

On your left as Fore Street becomes High Street is the medieval Sacrist's Gate, with buildings that held his offices and stores; part is now the Ely Museum. It is open Saturday and Sunday afternoons, and Thursday afternoons in summer. At the far end of High Street where it meets Minster Place, Steeple Gate is on your left. It is a plaster-and-timber building with Ely's coat of arms carved on its beams. This gate lets people into the Cathedral Close through the churchyard of St. Cross. High Street itself was once called Steeple Row.

Walk along High Street to Lynn Road. On your right at the corner is the Lamb Hotel. An attractive cream-and-brown Georgian building on the site of a much older inn, its rooms have views of Ely Cathedral, just a block away. The hotel restaurant looks out on High Street, and toward the rear on Lynn Road there is a small wood-paneled lounge with a skylight where you can stop for tea or a drink.

In the twelfth century the Lamb had its own cockpit for cockfighting, a rough sport that was popular with young Martin Frant in Georgette Heyer's Regency mystery *The Quiet Gentleman*. William Cobbett, an outspoken Tory radical whose biography was written by his great admirer G. K. Chesterton, stayed at the Lamb in Ely and "preached" in the Market Place.

Cross Lynn Road where the High Street widens to become St. Mary's Street. There are a number of old two- and three-story Georgian houses along St. Mary's Street that are being restored by the Ely Preservation Trust. Several have brass plates for offices. In *The Death of an Expert Witness,* a new will for P. D. James's forensic scientist Lorrimer had been drawn up by a firm of Ely solicitors—Messrs. Pargeter, Coleby, and Hunt. When Lorrimer was murdered, Scotland Yard's Dalgliesh was called by Major Hunt, so Dalgliesh and his assistant, Massingham, went to Ely to see him. Messrs. Pargeter, Coleby, and Hunt were in a "well-preserved" Regency house with a view of the cathedral green. The firm also had a thin, elderly Dickensian clerk and a waiting room like a men's club "in its comfort and controlled disorder." Dalgliesh found out that Lorrimer had cut his cousin Angela Foley out of his will and left a thousand pounds to sixteen-year-old Brenda Pridmore.

Cross Green Street, which leads into the Cathedral Close, and continue following St. Mary's Street. It bends to your left until you come to the triangular village green with a rose garden in its center, where Oliver Cromwell drilled his Puritan troops. Cromwell also drove the clergy out of the cathedral, but did not allow it to be destroyed.

Cromwell was related to the first Dean of Ely. For eleven years before the Civil War Cromwell had been the farmer of the cathedral tithes and lived across the green in the large white timbered house with four chimneys that is now the vicarage of St. Mary's Church. Two of his children were baptized next door in St. Mary the Virgin Church, a tall early-Gothic building with a gate into the churchyard and a steeple. Built in the fourteenth century, Cromwell's former house has stone walls two feet thick and a gigantic chimney serving both the parlor and the kitchen. At one time it was used as an inn, but it is now closed to the public. For more details about Cromwell's life, see Antonia Fraser's biography.

To your left beside the green is the Old Fire Engine House, now an attractive restaurant which you enter through the kitchen. It may be the pub off the cathedral green in *Garden of Malice,* where Susan Kenney's visiting American scholar, Roz Howard, and artist Alan Stewart ate thick cheese slabs with country bread and tomatoes and drank pints of bitters. But there are others nearby to choose from.

Cross the green and turn to your left past St. Mary's Church, then cross Church Lane. Beyond the Old Fire Engine House you will see a row of yellow brick buildings that house the canons and other cathedral personnel who live in the close.

It was within the cathedral close, or precincts, that

Hereward the Wake made his last stand against William the Conqueror. In *The Wimsey Family,* we learned that the Sieur de Guimsey had sent his sons off with the Norman to conquer England. His eldest son, Roger, served in the expedition against Ely in 1071 and as a reward received a manor in Norfolk near the River Wissey, which Wilfred Scott-Giles suggested led to the name change from "Guimsey" to "Wimsey"—as in Dorothy L. Sayers's Lord Peter Wimsey.

In Glyn Daniel's *The Cambridge Murders,* Canon Henry Boyce Cooper-Leigh, the tall, white-haired, scholarly uncle of Detective-Superintendent Robertson-Macdonald lived in the Cathedral Close, minded by his housekeeper, Miss Skilbeck. Even she could not make the canon remember that Dean Landon of Fisher College had been murdered. When his nephew came to see him, the canon did remember, however, that he had once lost the cathedral keys and without telling anyone had managed to get a new set made by Thoday in Littleport Road. (Notice the Fenland last name, which was also used by Sayers in *The Nine Tailors.* It is the name on some gravestones in Bluntisham churchyard where her father was rector.)

You are now at the Palace Green. Stop and admire the grace of one of the loveliest cathedrals in the world. In P. D. James's *Death of an Expert Witness,* Dalgliesh flew from London in a helicopter like some "deus ex machina." (See Thames River Trip.) When his assistant, the Honorable John Massingham, noticed the soaring west towers and pinnacles of Ely Cathedral, he knew that they were nearly at Hoggath's Laboratory.

Later, Dalgliesh drove to the very modern house rented by the laboratory's new director, Maxim Howarth. It was built of concrete and wood and glass and stood in splendid isolation, with no other building in sight, but hanging over the eastern skyline was the marvelous single tower and octagon of Ely Cathedral. Dalgliesh had a strange interview with Domenica Howith in her studio there.

In *Garden of Malice,* Susan Kenney's Roz Howard saw Ely Cathedral rise up before them as she and Stewart drove to Ely from Newmarket. Its shape "shimmered in the haze, a faded outline of blue with towers as faint and elusive as a ship far at sea with a single central tower impossibly massive." Then as Roz Howard walked across the close toward the Cathedral Church of the Holy and Undivided Trinity, she felt she had never seen anything like Ely's soaring ramparts, or its octagon and columns of honey-colored stone that dwarfed the row of little houses in the close. The huge cathedral stood alone, dominating the sky.

Ely Cathedral's collection of medieval buildings is the largest still in use in Europe. The castellated west tower is 217 feet high with a spectacular view out over the Fens to Cambridge and the Wash. (This tower, which you may climb, has a view like the one described by Dorothy L. Sayers in *The Nine Tailors*, when Hilary Thorpe goes up in Fenchurch St. Paul's to see the Fen Country.)

Enter the cathedral's West Door by the thirteenth-century Galilee Porch and go under the great West Tower with its bell. Kenney's Roz Howard heard it tolling like a huge round stone dropped into the Fen silence. To your left is the cathedral shop and the Refectory, where you can get morning coffee, lunch, or tea.

Look down the narrow Norman nave, which Stewart told Roz Howard was the second longest still standing in England, then walk to the center to see the spectacular central octagon, designed by Alan of Walsingham to replace the central Norman tower that collapsed in 1322. Both it and the lovely Lady Chapel were built in the Decorated style, and completed just before the Black Death struck England in 1349.

On either side of you below the Octagon are the transepts, which are the oldest parts of the cathedral. They were built soon after Hereward the Wake was defeated and the Normans took charge of Ely. The transepts have gorgeous, colorful roofs decorated with angel hammer-beams—carved in the fifteenth century, their widespread wings are tipped with gold. If you cannot see one of the Fen churches that Dorothy L. Sayers knew, with their angel roofs, at Ely you can appreciate Lord Peter's awe that cold New Year's Eve in *The Nine Tailors* as he gazed up at the massed ranks of seraphim and cherubim at Fenchurch St. Paul's.

Farther east before the High Altar is the site of the medieval shrine of St. Etheldreda. To your left is the Lady Chapel, which was being built when the central Norman tower collapsed in 1322. In James's *Death of an Expert Witness,* Superintendent Dalgliesh told Massingham that the clunch (limestone) pit where the first body was found had produced the soft chalk used for local buildings like the Lady Chapel at Ely. There is no real stone to be found in the Fens.

Back outside the cathedral's West Door, cross the palace green to your left to the Gallery, which is a walled cobblestone walk. Across it stands the Tudor red-brick Bishop's Palace, which is now a Sue Ryder Home, a hospice for the terminally ill.

Turn left to follow the medieval Gallery past the King's School, which is housed in the remaining buildings of the old monastic foundation. They include the Prior's House, the Queen's Hall, the ruins of the Infirmary, the tiny Prior Crauden's chapel, and the Ely Porta, or main gateway to the Benedictine Priory at the end of the Gallery.

The buildings within the Porta area are known as the College. King's College is one of the oldest public (private) schools in England. It was probably founded by St. Etheldreda, then refounded in 970. In 1010, young Prince Edward, son and heir of King Ethelred the Unready, came here to be educated. He was later known as Edward the Confessor.

In Susan Kenney's *Garden of Malice,* Alan Stewart and Roz Howard left the cathedral to peer companionably at the dining hall, the ruins of the Infirmary, the Prior's House, and the Chapel, imagining the people who had lived there. As they retraced their steps up the rutted roadway past the ruined cloister, Roz Howard suddenly understood the mystery of Montfort Abbey's murders. But Stewart persuaded her to spend the night at Ely with him in a pub called the Sheep and Goats near the Cathedral Close, so she did not act on her suspicions that night.

At the end of the Gallery, cross Silver Street. Then turn left along Silver Street, which becomes Back Hill and will lead you to Station Road again, where you turn left to reach the railway station and the end of the walk.

POSSIBLE SIDE TRIPS

Sandringham

Northeast near King's Lynn. Royal residence built by Edward VII. (See Newmarket Walk.) George V was not only born there, but he also died there in 1936. His body was brought to London by train. In Dorothy L. Sayers's unfinished mystery called *Thrones, Dominations,* Lord and Lady Peter Wimsey watched his cortege march up Whitehall to Westminster Abbey. (Open to view.)

Norwich

Medieval port city with magnificent cathedral, over thirty parish churches, and the medieval Elm Street. The museum is in the twelfth-century Norman castle. British Rail from Liverpool Station takes about 2½ hours; driving it is 115 miles from London on M11, then on A11.

In Agatha Christie's Miss Marple story, *A Pocketful of Rye,* the fleeing Lance and his wife headed for Norwich to take a plane to the Continent. In C. P. Snow's first mystery, *Death Under Sail,* in which he paid tribute to Dorothy L. Sayers, the police came from Norwich to the part of the Norfolk Broads where the six suspects were cruising.

Norfolk Broads

This area near Norwich has a network of water roads where thousands of people take a river holiday. G. K. Chesterton took his bride, Frances, there on their honeymoon and set his Father Brown story, "The Sins of Prince Sarradine" there, too. In "The Blue Cross," Father Brown was described as "the essence of those Eastern flats: he had a face as round and dull as a Norfolk dumpling; he had eyes as empty as the North Sea; he had several brown-paper parcels which he was quite incapable of collecting." Near the Wash, which opens into the North

Sea, Erskine Childers tried to prepare England for the danger of German invasion in World War I in *The Riddle of the Sands*. G. K. Chesterton also wrote an "invasion" novel called *The Flying Inn*. Dorothy Cannell's *Thin Woman* was an interior decorator. Her best client, Lady Violet Witherspoon, found relief from her midlife crisis by redecorating her cottage on the Norfolk Broads every six months.

Blickling Hall
Henry VIII's Queen Anne Boleyn grew up near Norwich, where her grandfather, Sir William Boleyn, was buried in the cathedral. Her great-grandfather, Sir Geoffrey Boleyn, who had gone to London to make his fortune, became Lord Mayor and bought Blickling from Sir John Fastolf. (See Shrewsbury Walk.) Anne and her brother George, who were later accused of incest, grew up at an older mansion on the site of Blickling Hall. The present Jacobean mansion and gardens closely resemble "Bullen Hall," home of Anne Boleyn in S. T. Haymon's *Stately Homicide*. (Blickling Hall is operated by the National Trust and is open to view.)

Downfield Mill, Soham.
A working windmill with sweeps (sails). To reach Soham, take the A142 from Newmarket to Ely and you will drive past it on your left about half way. The windmill is open Sunday 11–5, Bank Holiday Mondays except Christmas and New Years.

A Sayers Trip in the Fen Country
(This tour, created by Ralph Clarke, is published here courtesy of the Dorothy L. Sayers Literary and Historical Society, Rose Cottage, Malthouse Lane, Hurstperpoint, Sussex, Eng. BN6 9JY.)

Bluntisham and Christchurch: Childhood Homes of Dorothy L. Sayers.
Take the A10 southwest out of Ely and the A1123 to Earith, one of the so-called ports or bridges to the Isle of Ely with the remains of a Roman camp, which Dorothy L. Sayers com-

mented upon in "The Teaching of Latin." You are driving slightly north of the Great Ouse River (known here as Old West River), which flows past Ely and Littleport, and crosses the Wissey River to Denver. A sluice was built near Denver to prevent floodingback; and a straight twenty-mile bypass called the Bedford River was cut from Earith toward the sea. As you enter Earith you cross the New Bedford River, or Hundred Foot Drain, and the upper sluice of the old Bedford River, designed by Sir Cornelius Vermuyden, for the Earl of Bedford.

Continue on the A1123 through Earith to Bluntisham Church, which is two miles on your left. The Reverend Henry Sayers, Dorothy L. Sayers's father, was the rector here until 1917 when he transferred to Christchurch. If the church is locked, the key is hanging inside the outer door. In the south aisle of the church is a sign that says,

"December 1897 Institution of Henry Sayers MA. Patron: Christ Church Oxford. This board was erected in 1929 . . . by many who wished to put on record the loving care for the fabric of the church exercised by the Rev. Henry Sayers in whose time the foundations were indeed rendered more secure. He died at Upwell/Christchurch in 1928." Be sure to relock the church and note the Thoday graves in the churchyard, which are the names of several characters in *The Nine Tailors*. Dorothy L. Sayers used to play the violin in the little hall southwest of the church.

Continue half a mile to the former rectory where the Sayers family lived. It is a big yellow Georgian house in a wood on your right. There is a plaque by the front door, put there by the members of the Dorothy L. Sayers Historical and Literary Society in 1981 which reads, "Bluntisham House, the childhood home of Dorothy L. Sayers 1893–1957 Writer and Scholar." The plaque is one of three placed by the Sayers society; the other two are at her Newland Street house in Witham, Essex, and at St. Anne's, Soho, London, where her ashes were buried. Sayers's night nursery was in the north wing.

Drive through the village of Bluntisham, then return to Earith. Cross the Bedfords and go left on B13811 along the

New Bedford River. Turn left at Sutton, turn left again on A142 for Mepal. Go two miles along Ireton's Way, turn right at Horseway at the turn marked "Alternative Route to March," and after another two miles you cross the Forty Foot (Van Vermuyden's) Drain. Your road goes left, then right, along the Sixteen Foot Drain. (Sayers called it the Thirty Foot Drain in *The Nine Tailors*.)

Continue up the B1098 to Christchurch, turning right one mile beyond Bedlam Bridge, where Sayers used to sit and smoke cigars. It appears to be the humped-back bridge that Lord Peter Wimsey overshot in the snow storm that opened *The Nine Tailors*.

At Christchurch take the first turn to the left to the church and rectory, a red-brick Victorian house which is now a boys' home. The Victorian church was built to a design of famous architect Gilbert Scott. If the church is locked, the key hangs inside the porch. There is a photograph of the Reverend Henry Sayers in the vestry and at the west end of the nave is a tablet that says "In grateful memory of the service of Henry Sayers, Priest, from 1917 to 1928 Rector of this Parish, and of Helen Mary, his wife, this tablet is placed by the parishioners." The Sayerses' unmarked grave lies to the northeast of the church, reminding mystery fans of young Hilary Thorpe in *The Nine Tailors*, who looked down on the graves of her parents into which a strange body had been dumped. Drive on past a right-hand lane to the Dun Cow (called the Red Cow in *The Nine Tailors*). Sayers used to go there with an umbrella, a macintosh, sandwiches, and a notebook, amazing the villagers with her odd costumes.

Rejoin the Sixteen Foot Drain at Iron Bridge, turn right on B1098, cross the Drain, and Popham's Eau (Potters Lode in *The Nine Tailors*). Turn left at the T junction to take B1412 to Upwell Church. Mrs. Venables told Lord Peter Wimsey that Fenchurch St. Paul's once had had a gallery like Upwell Church, as well as its angel roof, which you may go see. Then go on to Outwell, turn right at the church and right again on the A1122 toward Downham Market.

Sayers's fictional town of Walbech is something like both

Wisbech and King's Lynn, two ancient port cities on the Wash. Wisbech is to your left and King's Lynn ahead to your right. Sayers's mythical Fenchurch St. Paul and the larger villages of Fenchurch St. Peter and Fenchurch St. Stephen are matched in real life by Walpole St. Andrew, Walpole St. Peter, and Terrington St. John, all located between Wisbech and King's Lynn. You may now explore those towns or take the A10 to your right to return to Ely, passing the village of Denver as you go.

Sayers admitted that she "borrowed" the name of Denver for the title of her noble family of Wimseys. According to *The Wimsey Family,* an early Peter de Guimsey (Wimsey) helped lead Magna Carta's King John across the Wash, where the King unfortunately lost all his baggage. In the eighteenth century an eccentric hermit, Lord Mortimer Wimsey (known as Old Scaley), lived by the Wash. One day, thinking he saw Christ walking on the waters of the North Sea, he swam out to meet Him and drowned.

7

GREENWICH/ BLACKHEATH

BACKGROUND

There has been a royal palace at Greenwich since the days of "Good Duke" Humphrey of Gloucester in 1428. He was the brother of Henry V and John, Duke of Bedford, whom Georgette Heyer wrote about in *Lord John*. Duke Humphrey began the Bodleian library at Oxford, where Dorothy L. Sayers's Harriet Vane fell asleep day after day in *Gaudy Night*.

After the Wars of the Roses, Royal Greenwich was closely associated with the Tudors and Stuarts. Henry VIII was born here, lived here with his first wife, Catherine of Aragon, took up with Anne Boleyn, married her, then sent her from Greenwich to the Tower of London to be beheaded for treason. Henry's daughters, Mary I and Elizabeth I, were born at Greenwich and his son, Edward VI, died there. It was at Greenwich that a young courtier named Walter Raleigh spread his cloak over a dirty roadway for "Good Queen Bess."

The Stuart kings, James I, Charles I, and later, Charles II, who was welcomed back from exile at Greenwich at the Restoration, built a series of splendid Italianate palaces. Today the Royal Naval College and the Maritime Museum occupy the royal buildings. Both honor Britain's Rule of the Waves. Parts of the palaces open to the public are the famous Queen's House, the huge Painted Hall, and the classical chapel.

Greenwich also has mystery associations. Josephine Bell, who died in 1987, was at Godolphin School with Dorothy L. Sayers. (See Salisbury Walk.) Bell became a doctor and married a doctor and they practiced together like Doctors Dick and Rachel Williams in *Death on the Borough Council*. Together with John Creasey (aka J. J. Marric), Bell founded the British Crime Writers Association.

To the south is Greenwich Park. It was laid out by the French architect Lenôtre for Charles II. Its open space dates from Duke Humphrey, so it is the oldest of London's royal parks. From its heights Roman soldiers on Watling Street could see London. Now the Old Royal Observatory shares the hillside with a statue of General Wolfe, who died defeating French General Montcalm at Quebec in Canada. Still a favorite public haunt, Greenwich Park used to have a fair that was described by one of mystery's Grand Masters, Charles Dickens, who also liked to come to Greenwich to eat whitebait on the riverside.

Beyond (and above) Greenwich Park lies Blackheath, as high above the Thames to the south as Hampstead Heath is to the north. Blackheath is an open, grassy area with a panoramic view north to London. Traditionally it has not only been the place where forces gathered to attack London, but also the haunt of highwaymen.

HOW TO GET THERE

British Rail: Trains to Greenwich from Charing Cross Station (about 15 minutes). Return trip from Blackheath Station to Charing Cross (about 20 minutes). Three trains an hour. Also trains from Cannon Street Station every hour.

Automobile: Leave London on A200, the Dover road (Great Dover Street); 5½ miles downstream (east) from central London

River: Daily from April to October.
    Downstream, to Greenwich:

From Westminster Pier (01-930-4087) two trips an hour beginning 10:30 A.M.

From Charing Cross Pier (01-930-0971) two trips an hour beginning 10 A.M., also evening cruise

From Tower Pier (01-488-0344) two trips an hour beginning 11 A.M.

Travel time about 45 minutes. Stops made at Festival Pier (south side) and Tower of London (north side). ½ hour to Greenwich.

Always check time of last boat back.

Length of Walk: About 2 miles from Greenwich to Blackheath, and 2 miles back. Much of the walk is up- or downhill.

See map on page 145 for boundaries of this walk, and page 362 for list of detectives and stories referred to.

PLACES OF INTEREST

Greenwich

The Royal Naval College. Built to be the Royal Hospital for Seamen by Sir Christopher Wren on site of Greenwich Palace. Painted Hall and Chapel open to the public. (Open Friday–Wednesday, 2:30–5; closed Thursday.) Free.

The National Maritime Museum, Greenwich Park (01-358-4422). Exhibits of British Naval History. (Open Monday–Saturday 10–6; Sunday 2–6 April–October. Closes at 5 P.M. in winter.) Admission charge.

The Queen's House, built for James I's wife in 1616 by Inigo Jones. First classical building in England. Great Hall a perfect cube, Tulip Staircase first cantilevered spiral staircase. (Open Monday–Saturday 10–6; Sunday 2–6 April–October. Closes at 5 P.M. in winter.) Admission charge.

Cutty Sark, Greenwich Pier. Last Clipper Ship of China Trade. Named for witch in Robert Burns's poem "Tam O'Shanter." (Open Monday–Saturday 11–6, Sunday 12–6 April–September. Closes 5 P.M. in winter.) Admission charge.

Gipsy Moth IV, Greenwich Pier. The ketch Sir Francis Chichester sailed single-handed round the world in 1967, landing at

Greenwich, where he was knighted by Elizabeth II with the same sword Elizabeth I used to knight Sir Francis Drake. (Open Monday–Saturday 10–6, Sunday 2–6 April–September. Closes 5 P.M. in winter.) Admission charge.

St. Alfege, Church Street. Built by Wren's pupil, Nicholas Hawksmoor. Older church on site where Henry VIII was baptized and composer Thomas Tallis was buried. Queen Anne demanded a royal pew when the church was rebuilt. Wolfe, victor at Quebec, is buried in the crypt. Present church heavily bombed in World War II. (Not always open. Check at Tourist Information Centre, Greenwich Church Street.)

Crooms Hill. One of the oldest roads in London. The name comes from Saxon word meaning "valley." Most fashionable street in Greenwich. Many seventeenth- and eighteenth-century houses, including Macartney House, where parents of General Wolfe lived. At top of Greenwich Park, Crooms Hill becomes Chesterfield Walk, overlooking Blackheath.

Ranger's House, Chesterfield Walk. Late seventeenth-century mansion once occupied by the fourth Lord Chesterfield, who probably wrote his letters to his son here. Became residence of the Ranger of Greenwich Park in 1815. Art and musical instrument collections. (Open daily February–October 10–5; November–January 10–4.) Free.

Greenwich Park. Oldest of London's Royal Parks; enclosed by Duke Humphrey of Gloucester in 1433, then became grounds for Tudors' Greenwich Palace. (Open daily dawn to dusk.)

The Old Royal Observatory, Greenwich Park. Founded by Charles II in 1675 to aid marine navigation. It is at zero longitude (or the Prime Meridian). Open Monday–Saturday 10–6, Sunday 2–6 April–October. Closes at 5 P.M. in winter.)

The Trafalgar Tavern, Park Row. Famous Dickensian riverside pub.

Greenwich Theatre, Crooms Hill (01-858-7755). Built on site of Victorian music hall. International reputation for drama from classics to modern opening nights.

For more information, contact: Tourist Information Centre, Greenwich Church Street (01-858-6376) or Tourist Information Centre, Victoria Station, London. Greenwich and Blackheath Trail Leaflet available there.

Blackheath

Blackheath, a grassy, treeless plateau overlooking London from the south. Natural point of assembly outside London. Used by Wat Tyler's Peasant Revolt in 1381; Jack Cade's Rebellion in 1450; Henry VIII's welcome for fourth wife, Anne of Cleves.

Blackheath Village, Tranquil Vale. Victorian town established by the coming of the railroad. Now a fashionable residential area like Hampstead.

Paragon House, Pond Road. Doorway brought from eighteenth-century Adam building at the Adelphi, London. (See *Mystery Reader's Walking Guide: London.)*

The Paragon, Georgian crescent off South Road. One of the best in London area. Laid out in late 1780s: seven four-story houses linked by a colonnade. Badly bombed, then restored after World War II.

Morden College, off Morden Road. Built by Wren (?) 1695. Almshouse for failed merchants. (Open by appointment only.)

Church of All Saints, Blackheath. Nineteenth-century Gothic.

Pagoda House, Pagoda Gardens. One of London's most curious residences. Built c. 1760 as garden house. Oriental features added later for the Duke of Buccleugh.

Isle of Dogs, Port of London, across the Thames River, just east of Limehouse. Once called Stepney Marsh. Its name probably came from the pack of hunting dogs Henry VIII kept there, or ducks. A quarter of a mile walk through tunnel to see the "Queen's view," the "Venetian" panorama of Greenwich palaces. Site of Limehouse, Millwall, and West India Docks.

PLACES TO STAY/EAT

London is near enough to stay there. For hotel recommendations in Greater London, see the British Tourist Authority Office, 12 Lower Regent Street or the London Tourist Board office at Victoria Station.

Greenwich is famous for its many good pubs and restaurants clustered around the market area near Church Street or on the riverside.

The Trafalgar Tavern, Park Row, Greenwich (01-858-2437).
Favorite haunt of Charles Dickens and members of Parliament.
Rooms are named for Lord Nelson's admirals; bar built like
eighteenth-century man o'war. Marvelous views of Greenwich
Reach. Famous whitebait dinners; inexpensive snack bars,
expensive restaurant open for lunch and dinner. Real ale.
(Open for lunch daily, closed for dinner Sunday and Monday.)
Reservations needed.

Cutty Sark, Ballast Quay, Greenwich (01-858-3146). Georgian
riverside pub with a nautical air, beyond Power Station and
Trinity Hospital. Bar and restaurant featuring whitebait
dinners, English food. (Open for lunch Monday–Friday;
dinner Thursday–Saturday.)

Maritime Museum, Romney Road (01-858-4422). Museum
restaurant in West Wing. Lunch or tea. Inexpensive.

— GREENWICH/BLACKHEATH WALK —

Begin your Greenwich/Blackheath Walk at the Greenwich
Railway Station. If you arrive by boat, get off at Greenwich
Pier and walk away from the river past the two ships, the *Gipsy
Moth* and the *Cutty Sark,* to Thames Street. Cross Thames
Street and go left to Greenwich Church Street. Take Green-
wich Church Street to St. Alfege's Church.

If you came by train it took about 15 minutes from Charing Cross with four stops. Come out of the station and walk to
Greenwich High Road, turn to your left, and follow it to
Greenwich Church Street to reach St. Alfege's Church. You
will pass a number of seedy shops and pubs.

St. Alfege was a Saxon archbishop of Canterbury kidnapped from his cathedral by the Danes. Imprisoned at Greenwich, he refused to be ransomed, so the Vikings murdered him
at sea. There has been a church here since the twelfth century.
Henry VIII and Elizabeth I were baptized in the old church,
and the famous sixteenth-century organist, Thomas Tallis,
whose epitaph by his pupil Purcell was quoted by Ellis Peters
in her modern mystery *The House of Green Turf,* was buried

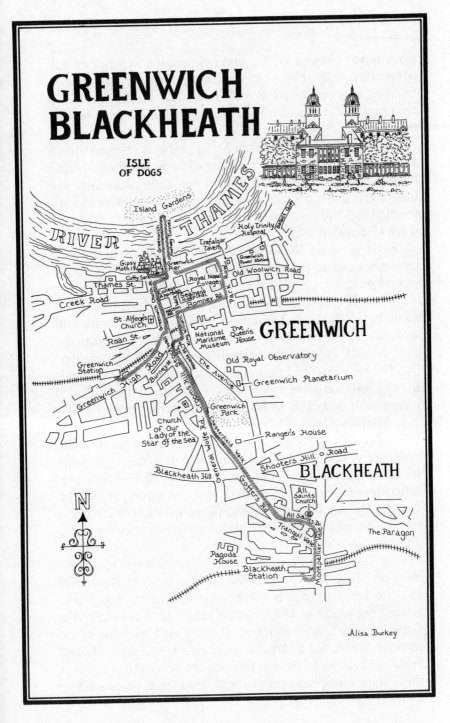

GREENWICH
BLACKHEATH

ISLE
OF DOGS

Island Gardens

RIVER THAMES

Holy Trinity
Hospital

Ballast Quay

Greenwich Foot Tunnel

Trafalgar
Tavern

Gipsy
Moth IV

Greenwich
Pier

Greenwich
Power Station

Cutty Sark

Old Woolwich Road

Thames St.

College Approach

Royal Naval
College

Creek Road

Seamen's
Hospital

Romney Rd.

St. Alfege's
Church

Park Row

National
Maritime
Museum

The
Queen's
House

GREENWICH

Roan St.

Nelson Road

Greenwich High Road

Old Royal Observatory

Greenwich
Station

Greenwich Planetarium

King William Walk

Burney St.

The Avenue

Greenwich
Park

Church
of Our
Lady of the
Star of the Sea

Chesterfield Walk

Ranger's House

General Wolfe Road

Shooters Hill o Road

BLACKHEATH

Blackheath Hill

Gaffer's Rd.

All Saints
Church

All Saints Dr.

N

Tranquil Vale

Montpelier Vale

The Paragon

Pagoda
House

Blackheath
Station

Alisa Burkey

145

here, as was General Wolfe, who defeated the French General Montcalm on the Plains of Abraham in Canada. The present building was rebuilt by Wren's pupil Hawksmoor in 1774, then much of it was restored again after World War II bombing.

Across Greenwich Church Street, between Nelson Road and College Approach, you see the old covered marketplace, where there are many charming shops and restaurants. An indoor arts and crafts market is held here every weekend. Cross Creek Road and continue down Greenwich Church Street to reach Greenwich Pier.

Mystery writer Nicholas Blake (aka C. Day Lewis, the poet laureate) came to live in Greenwich after his marriage to his second wife, actress Jill Balcon. Blake put his love of Greenwich into his mystery *The Worm of Death*, which took place there. In real life Blake himself used to hike down Crooms Hill to watch "all the river life . . . overlooked by the palace and the park, [which] enlivens their elegance with a workaday reality."

The busy Port of London that Blake described so lovingly in the 1960s has gone, so you won't see much of the bustle and commotion described in his and other, earlier mysteries like J. J. Marric's (John Creasey's) *Gideon's River* or Josephine Bell's *The Port of London Murders*. On the other hand, pollution control not only has made the Thames so clean that salmon are appearing again, but the dangerous, dirty yellow pea-soup fogs of Sherlock Holmes's day are also a thing of the past. But the Thames River Patrol still fishes up dead bodies, either murder or suicide, and the river is not yet free of either smuggling or cargo theft.

On Greenwich Pier you will see the anchored museums, the *Cutty Sark*, last of the China clippers, and the *Gipsy Moth IV*, the ketch in which Sir Francis Chichester sailed solo around the world in 1967. On his return he was knighted at Greenwich by Queen Elizabeth II, who used the same sword used by Elizabeth I to knight Sir Francis Drake on his *Golden Hind* at Greenwich. Now is the time for you to stop and visit these ships unless you plan to walk back from Blackheath to take water back to London. (If you came by train, you might take the river back.)

On the pier you will also notice a large domed building with a red-brick bottom. This is the Greenwich entrance to the foot tunnel across the Thames to the Isle of Dogs. It is a cold, damp quarter-of-a-mile walk each way, but this may be your only chance to see the "Queen's View" if the tide was wrong on your river trip or if you came by train. The Isle of Dogs will also give you a look at some remaining London docks.

In his mystery *The Worm of Death*, Blake's Nigel Strangeways and his mistress, the sculptor Clare Massinger, moved to Greenwich and, like his creator, Strangeways daily took a walk from their Queen Anne house on Crooms Hill to the pier. He saw the great brown-black hull of the *Cutty Sark* with the towering tracery of its three masts, then walked to the railed space. He saw the early workers pouring into the domed building that housed the lift that would take them to the tunnel beneath the Thames with its quarter mile of white tiled walls, while tugs, coasters, and cargo liners thrashed overhead.

You will only see the workers, not the tugs and cargo liners. Later in the mystery Strangeways took the tunnel to the Isle of Dogs to interview an old tart called Nellie, who had known the mother of Loudron's adopted son, Graham, during World War II. Strangeways walked through the white-tiled echoing tube, lighted by a long succession of electric globes in its roof. The elevator took him and the housewives going shopping up to the surface to the Island Gardens at the tip of the Isle of Dogs. Strangeways looked back at the Queen's View, painted by Canaletto, seeing the two wings of the Palace and beyond them, the Queen's House, in its plain, incomparable elegance. On the hill above the palace was the statue of General Wolfe, with Wren's observatory beside it. Strangeways remembered that in the palace over there the body of Admiral Nelson had rested on its journey between Trafalgar and its tomb in St. Paul's Cathedral, while his rough seamen swilled grog and damned their eyes and wept like babies.

If neither the Isle of Dogs nor the ships appeal to you, turn right on Greenwich Pier and go past the landing stage to take the public footpath called Riverside Walk. It runs just above the mudflats at low tide all the way to Ballast Quay and the Greenwich Power Station. Walking along it you have a tremendous view of the river to your left and, like Nigel Strangeways in Blake's *The Worm of Death*, you can observe the debris floating in the Thames and the screaming seagulls. Strangeways saw a police launch pull murder victim Dr. Piers Loudron from the river; his corpse was minus its legs, which had been chewed off by a ship's screw.

Straight uphill to your right are the magnificent buildings of the Royal Naval College, once the Royal Hospital for Seamen, built on the site of Greenwich Palace. The hospital, built by Mary II, was meant to be the Navy's equivalent of the army's Royal Hospital at Chelsea. (See Thames River Trip.) Only the green and gilded classical chapel with its huge altar painting of the shipwreck of St. Paul by the American Benjamin West, and the even more spectacular Painted Hall, are open to the public.

The Painted Hall, built under William III, Anne, and George I, has portraits of all three monarchs on its walls and ceiling. The huge ceiling portrait of William and Mary is considered the greatest example of British Baroque painting. The vast chamber's tall fluted columns flanking its high windows make this a magnificent setting for historic occasions.

In 1805 Admiral Lord Nelson lay here in state before he was buried in St. Paul's Cathedral across the Thames. The televised life of Prince Philip's uncle, Lord Mountbatten, Admiral of the Fleet and last Viceroy of India, showed him here at a great naval dinner. Mountbatten's terrorist murder by the IRA was eerily similar to the one described by Bill Granger in his thriller, *The November Man*. Mystery fans should remember, too, that Lord Mountbatten always claimed that it was he who gave Agatha Christie the plot for her mystery *The Murder of Roger Ackroyd*.

Keep walking beside the river until you reach Park Row. Across Park Row is the Trafalgar Tavern, painted a deep cream with white trim. It has wrought iron balconies off the first-floor windows overlooking the river. It was here that mystery's Grand Master Charles Dickens liked to eat whitebait dinners, which he described in his Thames River novel, *Our Mutual Friend*.

Blake's Nigel Strangeways, trying to discover a likely building where a body could have been dumped in the river at high tide, noted that the high-water mark on the Trafalgar Tavern was just below the balcony over the ground floor windows. He then went behind the tavern along Crane Street, past Holy Trinity Hospital on Ballast Quay. Holy Trinity Hospital is a seventeenth-century almshouse towered over by the Greenwich Power Station, near the Cutty Sark Inn. Strangeways was hunting for the modern riverside house of Dr. Loudron's son Harold, who worked in the City. In his note to the reader, Nicholas Blake admitted that he made this house up while he gave his own Georgian house on Crooms Hill to the murdered Dr. Loudron.

Josephine Bell set her mystery, *Death on the Borough Council*, in "Stepping," which was probably near Greenwich. She described the borough as built on the marsh and mist-laden mud flats of the Thames below London, where the river stretched in a broad shining ribbon toward the sea. This borough, once market gardens, was now rows of little brick houses with bow windows, hideous pillared porches, and iron gates and railings. It had its own railway station and a public library in what had been a private mansion. A philandering member of the Borough Council was murdered in the library while Dr. David Wintringham and his pregnant wife Jill were in "Stepping." They were minding the practice of their doctor-friends, Dick and Rachel Williams.

Unless you want to stop here for refreshments at the Cutty Sark or the Trafalgar Tavern, take a look at them and at Trinity Hospital, then turn right to walk up Park Row. Cross Old Woolwich Road and turn right again on the next unmarked road, which is Romney Road. Romney Road takes you between the Royal Naval College to your right and the Queen's House and the National Maritime Museum to your left.

Greenwich is a very steep riverside town, rising straight up to Blackheath, so each of these rows of buildings is on higher ground. Behind the National Maritime Museum you can see Greenwich Park, laid out for Charles II by Lenôtre on the site of the old Royal Park of Lancastrian Duke Humphrey, with the red-brick Old Royal Observatory and Planetarium and the statue of General Wolfe at the summit. The statue was given by the Canadian government in 1930, around the time when John Buchan of *The Thirty-Nine Steps* was Canadian Governor General.

Now is your chance to go in the Royal Naval College, the Queen's House, and the National Maritime Museum. The Queen's House is an architectural gem, well worth a good look, while the Maritime Museum could easily take your entire day.

As you observe all its mementos of the rise of British sea power, note that the American Revolutionary War and the War of 1812 are passed over very quickly. There is no mention made at all of that American pirate John Paul (Jones), who ravished the Western coast of Scotland and did time in the Kirkcudbright Tolbooth. (Dorothy L. Sayers and her artist husband, Mac Flemming, spent summers in Kirkcudbright, where she set *The Five Red Herrings*.) There is an excellent gift shop and cafeteria in the National Maritime Museum.

Past the National Maritime Museum on the corner of Romney Road at King William Walk, you come to the Dreadnought Seamen's Hospital. In Blake's *The Worm of Death* Graham Loudron, the illegitimate son of Dr. Loudron, was once a cook there.

In Julian Symons's *Three Pipe Problem* Val Haynes ran an antique shop off Romney Road near the market where she sold Victorian bric-a-brac. She was the disaffected wife of actor Sheridan Haynes, who played Sherlock Holmes in a television series and fancied himself an amateur sleuth. It was also off Romney Road in a little side street that a chemist called Morley sold poisons to the Mortimer family in Julian Symons's *The Blackheath Poisonings*.

At the end of Romney Road take King William Walk to your left. You are near the entrance to Greenwich Park, where

King William Walk becomes The Avenue and goes straight uphill to the Old Royal Observatory and Greenwich planetarium. This quaint red-brick structure was built by Charles II to improve navigation. You can still straddle the brass strip that represents the Prime Meridian, and stand with one foot in the Western Hemisphere and one in the Eastern, at the old source of Greenwich Mean Time. (It is now measured from the Royal Observatory in Sussex.) This observatory is also associated with astronomer Halley of Halley's Comet. In Symons's *The Blackheath Poisonings* Charlotte Mortimer stole out of her family house in Blackheath to walk to Greenwich Park to meet her lover, of whom her strong-minded mother disapproved.

Cross King William Walk to your right at the corner where you see a large pub called the Gloucester. Take narrow little Nevada Street past the Greenwich Theatre to the crossroads of Stockwell Street, Burney Street, and Crooms Hill, where you will see St. Alfege's Church again.

Here at the beginning of Crooms Hill was No. 6, where Nicholas Blake and his second wife lived. In *The Worm of Death* Blake installed Dr. Piers Loudron, his daughter, Rebecca, and two of his sons in this house (which was his own). He then described it as an early-Georgian house, one of two pairs, which was almost a perfect cube. In 1961 when he wrote his mystery, No. 6 was painted white and had a portico. Its drawing room had a yellow fitted carpet, glowing little landscapes set within the white wall panels, richly patterned curtains, and button-backed chairs. Doctor Loudron had exquisite taste, for his dining room was equally elegant with a rosewood table set with Georgian silverware. At the Loudrons' February dinner party Strangeways's mistress, Clare Massinger, explained to the Loudrons that she felt that marriage was for the procreation of children and the raising of families. Since her energies went into children of stone and wood, she refused to be married.

After locating the Blake/Strangeways house go left to climb up Crooms Hill. So far you have only walked about a half mile but it is another half mile straight up to Blackheath, so take a deep breath. (The view of London and the heath is

worth it.) Crooms Hill is one of London's oldest roads, leading down from Blackheath to the river. Its name comes from
the Celtic word for "crooked"—an appropriate choice, since it
winds up the western side of Greenwich Park. It is (and always
has been) the most fashionable street in Greenwich. During
the days of the Tudors and Stuarts, families with famous
names like Dudley, Cecil, and Howard lived here. When the
monarchy moved elsewhere, it became a neighborhood of
prosperous Georgian and Victorian middle-class families, with
its attractive seventeenth- and eighteenth-century houses.

Blake had Strangeways and Massinger live about halfway
up Crooms Hill on the first two floors of a Queen Anne house
that overlooked the park. They turned the ground floor double
drawing room into a studio because the floor was strong
enough to hold Clare's stone carvings.

You pass by the nineteenth-century seamen's Church of
Our Lady of the Star of the Sea on your right and the iron
railings of Greenwich Park on your left. Through the gate you
can sight the Old Royal Observatory. Near the top of Crooms
Hill you pass Macartney House, where the parents of General
Wolfe lived. Finally, you come to a pathway to your left called
Chesterfield Walk. (To your right Crooms Hill becomes Gen-
eral Wolfe Road.)

Chesterfield Walk is lined with young lime trees planted in
honor of Queen Elizabeth II's Silver Jubilee. It leads to the
Ranger's House at the top of the hill. This elegant mansion
was once the home of the fourth Earl of Chesterfield, whose
letters on manners to his illegitimate son, Philip, became the
model for eighteenth-century etiquette. In 1815 it became the
home of the Ranger of Greenwich Park. Now it is a museum
with a collection of English paintings and portraits and musical instruments. The view of London and the heath from the
earl's three bow windows is unsurpassed.

Behind the Ranger's House you can take Great Cross Avenue and then Blackheath Avenue to the Royal Observatory,
then go back down to Greenwich, or you can continue on to
Blackheath. You have now walked one mile, most of it uphill.

To see Blackheath, go to your right to General Wolfe

Road, carefully crossing Blackheath Hill (a major truck route) to your left. Then find the Avenue, which cuts across the heath past All Saints Church, Montpellier Row, and takes you into Tranquil Vale, which is Blackheath Village's high street.

You are now standing in the open grassy plain called Blackheath. Its name may come from the black gorse that once covered it or from the victims of the Black Death who were buried here or from the highwaymen who regularly plied their trade here until the nineteenth century. The Romans camped here, and so did Wat Tyler's peasant army in 1381 before they marched on London. There they raided the Tower of London, pulling the old Archbishop of Canterbury out of his chapel to murder him. Their revolt was finally stopped by the courage of young King Richard II, who rode out alone to parley with them at Smithfield.

To your left as you cross the heath is Shooters Hill. In Blake's *The Worm of Death* Strangeways was told by the local police that they were having trouble with a group of "teddy boys" who terrorized the respectable residents of Shooters Hill. Farther still to your left as you cross the heath you can also see the shining curve of the Paragon, considered the best Georgian crescent in London. Part of its colonnaded facade came from an earlier Palladian villa on this site. When we had lunch in Cambridge with Anne Perry, she told us that the Paragon was the real-life setting for her mystery *Paragon Walk*. Perry told us she had gone to nursery school in Blackheath and remembered the crescent.

In her mystery, a society cult based on sex and magic was going on under the prim Victorian surface of Paragon Walk. Charlotte Pitt's sister Emily, Lady Ashworth, lived there, together with a mixed bag of neighbors who included tall, gaunt Miss Laetitia Hornbury and her small, plump sister, Miss Lucinda. As Perry described it, Paragon Walk was a Regency road of great elegance, facing an open park with flower beds and ornamental trees. It "curved gently for about a thousand yards, white and silent in the sunlight."

In the first murder a "nice" girl was attacked and then knifed. She came in dying through the French doors at the back of her family's drawing room, which led into a small, walled garden. All the gardens of Paragon Row connected at the back.

A mile away Perry put a church with a churchyard. Charlotte Pitt's husband, CID Inspector Pitt, stood in the churchyard, trying to decide which of the gentry had been murdering his neighbors. Later Charlotte went to place flowers on one of their graves and was attacked by the murderer. As you cross the heath you will pass by the nineteenth-century Gothic All Saints Church, but it has no lynch gate or cemetery, only a modern parking lot.

All around the heath, there are elegant and eccentric villas like the ones built by Julian Symons's toy-manufacturing Mortimers. One Mortimer mansion was "Albert House," built in the style of a Gothic castle; the other, "Victorian Villa," on Belmont Hill, was in the Palladian style. There is a real Oriental mansion called Pagoda House below Shooters Hill off Pond Road, which you could detour to see.

Symons's Mortimer family often went into Blackheath Village. Young Paul Mortimer attended the Blackheath Proprietory School, but his father, Roger Mortimer, refused to pay for him to go to Oxford. Paul Mortimer also escorted his cousin, Isabel Mortimer, to the Rink Hall, where poetry recitals were held. What Paul did not know at that time was that Cousin Isabel was his father's mistress or that she would be tried for Roger's murder.

As you come into All Saints Drive, go left to the junction with Montpellier Row, which runs into Montpellier Vale, which turns into Tranquil Vale. You can see that Blackheath Village, like Hampstead Heath, has become a very fashionable, if a bit arty, London neighborhood. There are many shops and restaurants, bookstores, and a great deal of traffic.

It was in Peaceful Alley just off Peaceful Vale in Blackheath that Julian Symons's bookseller, Jonathan Jacobs, had his shop in *Bland Beginning*. In this mystery about first editions, Jacobs was described as being as broad as he was tall, running an unimpressive, dark little shop filled with cats, one for every month of the year. Jacobs fed tea to his cats as well as to his visitors, Basingstoke and Vicky Rawlings. She was the grand-daughter of the Victorian poet, Martin Rawlings, whose first editions were unaccountably disappearing. Later Jacobs was found hanged in his shop by Basingstoke and his friend, Bland.

Take Tranquil Vale straight to the Blackheath Railway Station, a typically Victorian yellow-brick building. Just before you reach it, you pass the Railway Hotel with the Railway Tavern, where you can get good, substantial pub food like a Ploughman's Lunch or macaroni. In Symons's *The Blackheath Poisonings* the Metropolitan Police admitted that the Railway Hotel and a pub called the Three Tuns in Blackheath Village caused most of the crime handled by their R Division, which covered Greenwich, Woolwich, Lewisham, and Blackheath. They were not used to handling family poisonings. It would also have been the R Division that handled the berserk police officer Micklewright who attacked his unfaithful wife at their home in Greenwich. Micklewright was disarmed by Commander Gideon himself in *Gideon's River* by J. J. Marric (aka John Creasey).

Just west of Blackheath, off the Lewisham Road, is St. John's Hospital. Since she and her doctor-husband practiced in this area, it was probably the model for Josephine Bell's St. Edmund's Hospital. In *The Trouble in Hunter Ward*, Bell said St. Edmund's had been built in the first years of the century in the green fields outside southeast London. It had been one of Edward VII's charitable outbursts made to mark the new reign, in thanks for the monarch's recovery from acute appendicitis.

The action in *The Trouble in Hunter Ward*, however, took place many years later under the postwar Labor Party. The story of the murder of mean old ex-Sister Hallet when she returned for an operation suggests that she was partly a victim of Bell's own strong dislike of nationalized medicine and the strikes it produced, as much as malice aforethought.

Look around Blackheath Village, then take the train back to London. You have walked two miles uphill and downhill from Greenwich Pier (or Greenwich Central Railway Station). If you came by train to Greenwich and want to return to

London by boat, you will have to walk two miles back or take a cab. There is no underground here, and trains do not go from Blackheath to Greenwich. You could, however, take a bus along the south bank back to the underground or the railway station at London Bridge.

8

NEWMARKET

BACKGROUND

Newmarket is THE flat-racing capital of Great Britain. It lies in a hollow of the chalk downs on the border of Suffolk east of Cambridge on the way to Bury St. Edmund's and Ipswich. Surrounded by great heaths where horses are exercised and trained, Newmarket is perfect horse country, and both the National Stud and thirty to forty private racing stables are located here. More than a thousand horses are trained every day on Newmarket Heath. Racing begins in April and continues, on and off, for eight weeks, to the end of October. Newmarket's big spring races are the Two Thousand Guineas and the One Thousand Guineas, familiarly called "the Guineas" in Dick Francis's *Bonecrack*. The Cesarewitch and the Cambridgeshire are the highlights of the fall season. In Peter Lovesey's *Bertie and the Tinman,* the 1886 Cambridgeshire race was the starting point for murder.

Newmarket was "new" in 1227 when the "old" market at Exning, a Saxon town to the north, was closed down by plague. Later the Stuart kings made Newmarket the home of the Sport of Kings. James I built the King's House, and between races, amused himself by creating nearly a hundred knights. Charles II liked to race himself and built a palace in High Street, part of which forms a section of the Rutland Arms Hotel. A fire at Newmarket in 1683 made the Royal Party leave the town, upsetting the Rye House Plot to over-throw Charles II.

The Prince Regent (George IV) raced his horses at New-market until the stewards held an enquiry into a race won by his colt, Escape. Insulted, he left, never to return. In Edwardi-an times, sportsman Edward VII was a frequent visitor, both as Prince of Wales and later as king, and a large number of pseudo-Tudor villas were built here by racing enthusiasts and members of the Jockey Club.

Newmarket today still stands for horse racing and that background is reflected in the detective stories placed near this attractive little English town. Peter Lovesey's *Bertie and the Tinman* was based on the suspicious death of famous real-life jockey Fred Archer in 1886. Archer was known for his love of money, or "tin."

In Dick Francis's *Bonecrack* Old Robinson told young Neil Griffon many horse-racing legends about Newmarket's royal past. *Bonecrack's* plot is built around horse racing, which is the chief business of Newmarket. According to mystery writer Catherine Aird, Josephine Tey's sister thinks it quite possible that Lachetts, the yeoman home (and horse stud) of the Ashby family in Josephine Tey's *Brat Farrar,* was near Newmarket, too. In the Ashby night nursery there was wallpaper featuring the Fens Saxon hero, Hereward the Wake, while Alec Loding or Ledingham, who dreamed up the impersonation of Patrick Ashby, was not only the local vicar's brother-in-law but a son of the Lord of the Manor from the village of Clare.

There is a village of Clare on the River Stour, about ten miles from Newmarket. Clare Castle was an important military fort that controlled the Icknield Way (the high land route between the Essex swamps to the south and the Fens to the north). The Clare family was royally connected. Elizabeth de Clare founded Clare College at Cambridge and entertained her royal cousin, John of Gaunt, whose grandson was the hero of Georgette Heyer's *Lord John.* (See Cambridge Walk.)

Modern-day mystery characters who like to race invariably turn up at Newmarket. Georgette Heyer's "amiable snake," Randall Mathews, used his presence at Newmarket for an alibi when his uncle was murdered in *Behold, Here's Poison*.

During the racing season, little planes fly in and out all day, taking top jockeys and trainers and owners back and forth across the country to different meets. In *Rat Race* Dick Francis's hero, Matt Shore, was flying a champion jockey to Newmarket when he felt something wrong with his plane and landed, only to have it burst into a ball of flame.

While most of his books mention Newmarket, two of Dick Francis's mysteries are set here. *Bonecrack* is about the training stable called Rowley Lodge. In it Neil Griffon tried to run his father's stables and deal with would-be jockey Alessandro Rivera, son of an international gangster, who wanted to ride the Derby favorite, Archangel.

Another Newmarket mystery is *Break In*, which has a sequel called *Bolt*. Both star a pair of rival families, the Fieldings and the Allardecks, who own training stables in Newmarket. They have been mortal enemies since the time of King Charles II. In the present generation there is a grandfather Fielding who still runs a training stable and an Allardeck who disowned his son Bobby when he married Holly Fielding, twin sister of Christmas (Kit) Fielding. A champion jockey, Kit rides for the Princess Casilia, who owns a string of horses, just as champion jockey Dick Francis once rode for the Queen Mother. Lovesey's real-life jockey, Fred Archer, had also worn the colors of the Prince of Wales.

Agatha Christie's Prudence (Tuppence) Cawley, who was seeking work in *The Secret Adversary*, was born in Suffolk, where her father was a Church of England clergyman. In Margery Allingham's *No Police at the Funeral*, the brother of the Master of Ignatius College lived in Newmarket. But he was shipped to the Colonies because he married a woman with a "touch of the tarbrush" (i.e., Black). The Master's nephew was the blackmailer, George Faraday.

Finally, between writing mysteries about TV investigator Jemima Shore, Antonia Fraser has written full-scale biographies of two kings associated with Newmarket, James I and Charles II. She also wrote about their arch-nemesis, Oliver Cromwell, who was closely associated with Ely. (See Ely Walk.)

HOW TO GET THERE

British Rail: trains from Liverpool Station, London—one hour, 34 minutes (For some, change at Cambridge. Newmarket Station is an unstaffed halt without a station, where you wait on the platform and pay on the train.)

Automobile: Take A11 from London, or A1303/1304 from Cambridge. This road is known in Cambridge as the Newmarket Road, and as the Cambridge Road in Newmarket. Newmarket is 63 miles from London, and about 13 miles from Cambridge.

Length of Walk: 2 miles. Optional walks: 4 miles to and from High Street to the National Stud, Devil's Ditch, and Newmarket Racecourse; 3 miles past some training stables to the Limekiln Training Ground.

See also Side Trips to Exning, Bury St. Edmund's, and Ipswich.

See map on page 163 for the boundaries of this walk and page 364 for a list of detectives and stories.

PLACES OF INTEREST

Newmarket

National Horseracing Museum, High Street. (Open Monday–Saturday 10–5, Sunday 2–5.) Admission charge.

The Jockey Club, High Street. (Members and guests only.)

The Rutland Arms Hotel, High Street.

Tattersall International Sale Paddock, the Avenue.

Queen Victoria Jubilee Clock Tower, High Street.

Nell Gwynne's House, Palace Street.

All Saints' Church, Sun Lane.

St. Mary's Church, St. Mary's Square.

Newmarket Cemetery, Cambridge Road. Peter Lovesey visited the grave of jockey Fred Archer, who was buried here.

To see inside training stables, racecourse, etc., contact *Newmarket Thoroughbred Tours,* Anna Ludlow, 2 The Orchard, Ashly, North Newmarket (0638 730605) or ask at the Rutland Arms.

Optional Walks
The Devil's Ditch, Cambridge Road. An ancient earthwork fortification.

The National Stud, Cambridge Road. (Closed to the public.)

The Rowley Mile Stands, Newmarket Heath. (Open on racing days.)

The Limekilns

Icknield Way

PLACES TO STAY/EAT

Newmarket
The Rutland Arms, High Street (3175). Historic coaching inn built on site of older Ram Inn. Later palace of Charles II. Very popular with trainers and top (senior) jockeys in real life and in Dick Francis's stories. Good English food and lodgings.

Bedford Lodge Hotel, Bury Road (0638) 663175. Originally Bedford Lodge, leased in 1886 to Abington Baird, "the Squire," who was the best gentleman jockey of the time. Peter Lovesey stayed there while researching *Bertie and the Tinman.* Comfortable small hotel with good meals, near stud farms and training stables, where visits may be arranged. Inexpensive.

Bury St. Edmunds
The Angel Hotel, Angel Lane (3926). Georgian building on old inn site across from the Abbey Grounds, where Dickens's Mr. Pickwick and Sam Weller stayed.

Ipswich
The Great White Horse, Oak Lane (56558). Patronized by Charles Dickens's Mr. Pickwick.

——————— NEWMARKET WALK ———————

Begin your walk at the Newmarket Railway Station whose red-brick building is now used by a company called J. Brooke Fairbairn. Facing away from the railroad building toward the town, there is a large parking lot with a row of delivery trucks waiting for copies of *The Sporting Life*. In Lovesey's mystery called *Bertie and the Tinman*, the Prince of Wales found *The Sporting Life* a very "congenial organ." Walk across the parking lot to Green Road. Across the street is the brick Coronation Hotel. Cross Green Road and pass the hotel on your right to reach Station Approach. Turn right and follow Station Approach until it runs into the Avenue. Then turn left to go up The Avenue to Newmarket's High Street.

On The Avenue as you reach Queensberry Road you pass Tattersall's International Sale Paddocks. This is the Newmarket headquarters of the famous horse market in London, a popular haunt of Georgette Heyer's heroes like Peregrine Tavener and his guardian, Lord Worth, in the mystery *Regency Buck*. Cross Queensberry Road and keep walking until you reach High Street.

High Street is really an extension of the Cambridge Road. Newmarket Race Course is about a mile away to your left on Newmarket Heath, which is also the Jockey Club Training Ground. The racecourse's Rowley Mile Stands are named for Charles II (aka Old Rowley). In Lovesey's mystery the Prince of Wales told his readers that the Cambridgeshire race was run uphill from the Rowley Mile Stands. Another mile or so west are the old Saxon earthworks called the Devil's Ditch. Traditionally anyone can have a free grandstand view of the races from there.

Across the road from the racecourse is Newmarket Cemetery, where jockey Fred Archer, the "Tinman," was buried. According to Lovesey, Archer's funeral cortege began at his home, Falmouth House on the Ely Road. It wound past the heath with a continuous line of stable lads at attention along the route, then down High Street, where all the stores were shuttered and the townspeople stood three and four deep in

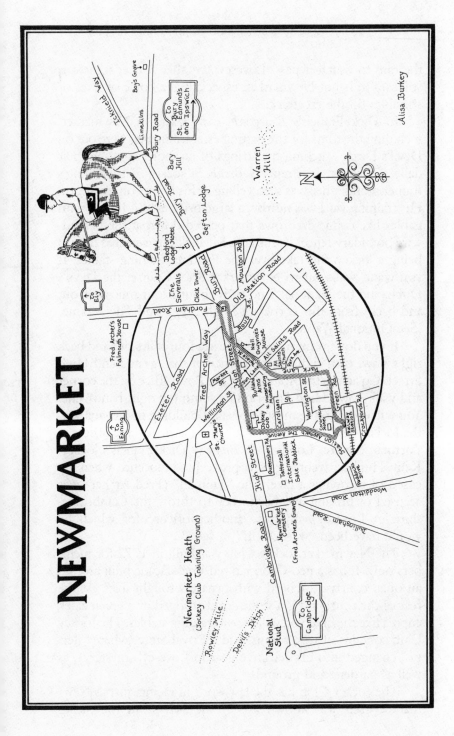

NEWMARKET

Alisa Burkey

the rain to watch it pass. Lovesey says that Archer's ghost is still said to haunt Newmarket, especially if a horse swerves or stumbles on the racetrack.

In Dick Francis's *Bonecrack,* early risers in Newmarket, including the touts for the betting establishments, were out on Devil's Ditch watching the strings of racehorses getting their daily workouts. In Francis's *Break In* jockey Kit Fielding's trainer grandfather was seen yelling at his horses on the heath. His training yard was nearby, a large brick establishment with gables like comic eyebrows that peered down at the barbed-wire boundary fence. Eventually Kit Fielding expected to quit being a jockey and take over the Fielding training stables. If you want, walk out to Newmarket Race Course, the Devil's Ditch, and the National Stud (it is about a four-mile walk out and back) from this corner of High Street and The Avenue. (See Optional Walks.)

If you don't want to walk the extra four miles out and back right now, turn right at the corner of the Avenue and High Street. Go across the Avenue past the Post Office on the corner and walk down High Street on its south (or right-hand) side. You will come to the most important building in Newmarket, the Jockey Club. The Jockey Club also has handsome offices in Portman Square, London. In *Enquiry* Dick Francis's jockey, Kelly Hughes, went there to prove his innocence when accused of throwing a race. The "Tinman" (Fred Archer) was accused of bribing another jockey to throw the Cambridgeshire in Lovesey's mystery, another offense for which he would have been "warned off."

The Newmarket Jockey Club was built in 1772 for members only. It has a neo-Georgian red-brick facade built around an open courtyard fenced with ornate wrought iron. At the rear of the courtyard is a stone arcade topped by a green clock cupola like the ones you will see on training stables. The Jockey Club contains offices, rooms, and a Royal Suite (where "Bertie" changed into his detective gear in Lovesey's mystery), as well as gardens and grounds.

The Jockey Club has the last word in racing, just as Newmarket itself was known as "Headquarters" in the racing world. In Francis's *Rat Race,* pilot Matt Shore uncovered a fraud in racecourse insurance being worked out of the Jockey Club itself. In *Bonecrack,* Neil Griffon talked to its stewards to persuade them not to "warn off" (take away his racing license) Alessandro Rivera. Griffon had found out that the elder Rivera was suffering from the same aftereffects of syphilis as Henry VIII. Both Henry VIII and Ensio Rivera were subject to towering rages that led to a lot of heads being chopped off.

Francis's *Enquiry* opened with steeplechase jockey Kelly Hughes being warned off Newmarket Heath for throwing a race. In *Break In,* jockey Kit Fielding warned his brother-in-law's father, Maynard Allardeck, that if he told the Jockey Club that a Fielding was responsible for gossip-column items about Bobby Allardeck, he would sue him for slander. Next to the Jockey Club is the brick National Racing Museum. It stands on the site of the old Subscription Rooms, where "Bertie" used to place his bets in Lovesey's *Bertie and the Tinman.* Now it has a Fred Archer exhibit that includes Archer's nightshirt and cuff links and boots, as well as the gun with which he shot himself. Across High Street from the Jockey Club is a bookstore that very properly features mysteries by Dick Francis, Dorothy L. Sayers, and Jeffery Archer in the window.

As you walk along the High Street you will see almost as many dogs as people. Newmarket's attractive brick-and-flint buildings are low, many only a story and a half high. On High Street there are a number of Dickensian-looking coaching inns with wide gates for horse carriages, where you might stop to eat. The street is lined with specialty shops and antique stores, some of which are not open on Sundays. The whole town with its narrow, crooked lanes, and sixteenth- and seventeenth-century buildings feels like a charming country cousin of the area of London around St. James's Palace.

Continue walking along High Street to Sun Lane on your right. It is one of many enchanting lanes with old houses and interesting shops. To your left across High Street is Wellington Street, which runs north into St. Mary's Square where St. Mary's Church, as old as Newmarket itself, has a church register that dates from the time of Charles I. Beyond Wellington

Street is Market Street, where the original "new" market was held.

On the south side of High Street after you cross Sun Lane, you reach the Rutland Arms Hotel. This hotel, made of dark brick with whitewashed wood trim, is world-famous, and parts of it date back to the time of Charles II. It is built on the site of an even older Ram Inn, an important coaching stop on the route from Norwich to London. Across the street is the wide white Waggon & Horses Inn and Market House. In *Bertie and the Tinman,* as the Prince of Wales sneaked past the Rutland Arms at night to do some detecting at Falmouth House, dressed in a Norfolk jacket and deerslayer hat, he saw a group of waits (carolers), who were singing the "First Noel."

Go in the front doorway beside the wide carriage arch that leads to the coachyard. The Rutland Arms is a very comfortable, friendly hotel. To your left as you come in the High Street door are a series of cozy small parlors and a double bar, with fireplaces, stuffed armchairs, and low tables, all looking out on the High Street. Although the building is much older, the decor is Edwardian. There are many horse pictures and a large map in the hall showing all the training stables in Newmarket, as well as a portrait of good sport Edward VII in a jaunty fedora.

The windows of the main dining room also open on High Street. Its walls are painted a light purple and there are a deep red carpet and white pillars, hung with gold-framed paintings. On one brick wall is a sign stating that this was part of the palace of Charles II. The dining room serves a delicious Sunday luncheon of roast Scotch sirloin of beef and all the proper English fixings. Most Francis characters either ate or stayed at the Rutland Arms and we recommend you do, too.

Once you have enjoyed luncheon, tea, or dinner, go out the back door into the courtyard of the Rutland Arms to Palace Street, which runs behind the hotel. Turn left to keep going on High Street and cross Rous Street. Soon you will reach Old Station Road and the Clock Tower, which is a late-Victorian Gothic structure of red brick with stone trim, built in honor of the 1887 Jubilee of Queen Victoria.

You are now in the center of six roads: High Street, Old Station Road, Moulton Road, Bury Road, which becomes the ancient Icknield Way, Fordham Road, and Exeter Road. To the north of High Street, Exeter Road is crossed by Fred Archer Way.

In Lovesey's *Bertie and the Tinman,* jockey Fred Archer's mansion, Falmouth House, was on Fordham Road. The Prince of Wales went there to listen in on the inquest into Archer's suicide. He felt that the multigabled red-brick structure was very impressive for a jockey and so was the cellar full of good champagne.

After trying later in the mystery to "lay Fred Archer's ghost," the Prince of Wales cut across the open area between Fordham and Bury Roads called the Severals to reach Sefton Lodge, the home of the Dowager Duchess of Montrose. She had wanted the jockey to be her third husband. The Dowager lived across Bury Road from the "Squire's" Bedford Lodge (now the Bedford Lodge Hotel, where Peter Lovesey stayed while researching the book). Her second husband was buried next door in St. Agnes Church (her middle name was Agnes), which is still there.

In Dick Francis's *Bonecrack,* the Rowley Lodge training stables, with its eighty-five thoroughbreds worth six million pounds, was also on the south side of Bury Road. The yard was built in 1870 of red brick with green trim, with its blocks of boxes put together in bays that faced each other. To reach Newmarket Heath, ordinarily the Griffon string of horses came from Rowley Training Stables on the Bury Road to the Clock Tower, then took Exeter Road to reach the system of roads north of High Street known as the Newmarket Horse Walk. According to Dick Francis, Newmarket's traffic has to wait for the horses, because the traffic patterns are for horses, not cars.

One morning in *Bonecrack,* however, the head lad, Etty Craig, took the string out on Warren Hill (between Old Station Road and Moulton Road) to exercise. A horse called Lucky Lindsay unseated his stable lad and took off down Moulton Road, knocked over a man on a bicycle, scared a woman with a baby buggy, and ended up by the Clock Tower, causing a traffic jam. Someone finally caught him at Woolworth's on High Street.

At this point you could continue along Bury Road another two miles to see the Limekilns and the Boy's Grave, or take an excursion by car to Bury St. Edmunds and Ipswich. (See Side Trips.) Otherwise, turn left to walk back on High Street to the Rutland Arms at the corner of High Street and Palace Lane.

Go down Palace Lane past the back doorway of the hotel. Walk past a series of small flint buildings, painted white with dark shutters and "eyebrow" trim over their ground-floor windows. The first house, now an art studio, is supposed to have been the house of Nell Gwynne, one of Charles II's favorite mistresses, who followed the Court here. You also pass by the high walls and gates of several horse yards.

At the corner of Palace Lane and Sun Lane, which runs back to the High Street, you will find All Saints Church. Built in 1876 on the site of the church Charles II used to attend, it is a squat flint church with a conical roof. Short Sun Lane has several specialty shops.

Continue past All Saints Church to Park Lane, then turn left on Park Lane and follow it back to Green Road. Turn right along Green Road to the Coronation Hotel and cross Green Road to the Newmarket Railway Station to end your walk. To catch the train you must walk behind the station along a red-brick wall to a red phone box, then go up an iron stairway to the platform where the trains stop to take on or discharge passengers from London or Ipswich. You pay your fare on the train.

Optional Newmarket Walks
1. *Devil's Dike, Newmarket Race Course,* and the *National Stud:* (four miles round trip)
Turn left on High Street at the Avenue and go past the fountain at Falmouth Avenue, built in 1910 in memory of Sir Daniel Cooper. Keep walking uphill about a mile past the entrance to the racecourse until you reach the Devil's Ditch.

Just beyond the Devil's Ditch on the Cambridge Road,

you come to the handsome brick-and-stucco buildings of the National Stud, painted cream, with red-tiled and thatched roofs. All along the beech-lined roadway you see the kind of brown split-rail horse fences that would be white in Lexington, Kentucky.

Nearer to Cambridge on this road there were several places mentioned in detective stories. One was a pub called the Mitre in Michael Butterworth's *The Man in the Sopwith Camel;* another was a roadhouse called the Yellow Barn in Glyn Daniel's *The Cambridge Murders,* where both dons and undergraduates went to enjoy wine, women, and song.

Somewhere along here in *Bonecrack,* Alessandro Rivera's gangster father rented a house in which his toughs beat up Neil Griffon. Just west of the National Stud there is an old inn called the White Swan that might be the Forbury Inn, where Alessandro Rivera stayed while he learned to be a jockey. The White Swan is a Greene King brewery, which is the beer manufactured by the family of thriller writer Graham Greene.

After looking at the National Stud's buildings, turn back on the Cambridge Road toward Newmarket. Walk to the Devil's Ditch, which will be on the left side of the road as you face toward town. In Susan Kenney's *Garden of Malice,* the young American professor, Roz Howard, was taken to see the Devil's Ditch by artist Alan Stewart. Howard was in England to edit the letters of Lady Viola Montfort-Snow, a famous Suffolk poet and gardener.

The Devil's Ditch, or Dyke, is an earthen rampart about twenty feet high that runs above a ditch and small gullies filled with ancient briars and brambles. The narrow ridge, which Roz and Alan climbed up to walk along, stretches seven miles from Newmarket Heath almost to the "Isle" of Ely. Stewart told Roz Howard that the Ditch was a botanist's heaven because so many kinds of plants that grow there are seen nowhere else in Britain. Later, as Roz was wildly driving from Cambridge with the murderer, she wrecked the car at the Devil's Ditch and escaped him by running along its top. Beyond the Devil's Ditch on your left along Cambridge Road is the entrance to Rowley's Stands and Newmarket Race Course.

Across from the racecourse you will find the cemetery where Fred Archer was buried.

2. *Training Stables,* the *Limekilns,* and the *Boy's Grave:*
If you want to catch a glimpse of some training stables, walk past the Clock Tower up Bury Road. You will recognize them by their typical high brick walls and clock cupolas. You cannot go inside a training stable without an invitation. (For guided tours, see Newmarket Thoroughbred Tours.) You can plan on stopping to look at St. Agnes Church and the Bedford Lodge Hotel as well. The walk from the Clock Tower to the Limekiln Training Ground is about two miles up and two miles back.

To your right as you walk along Bury Road is Warren Hill, with its famous view of Newmarket and its heaths, then Long Hill, and behind it to the south, Bury Hill, where Bury Road divides into two roads about two miles from the Clock Tower. Its left fork is the ancient high Icknield Way, which is also the modern A1304. To the right is the A45 to Bury St. Edmunds. Between the forks is the open Limekiln Training Ground, once the site of a pottery.

In *Whiphand,* Dick Francis's private investigator, Sid Halley, came to Newmarket to investigate some horse doping. Halley talked to Ken Armadale at the Equine Research Establishment Unit, then tape-recorded an account of how the trick was done. One-handed Halley had been a jockey in Newmarket, but took a stable favorite out on the Limekilns Training Ground for its morning exercise. In Lovesey's mystery, the appalling rich rascal known as "the Squire" nearly bought the Limekilns, putting the Jockey Club into an uproar.

In *Bonecrack,* Neil Griffon ran a trial race with his horses at the Limekilns just as the Champion Hurdle started at Cheltenham, hoping to keep the touts away. Nearby is the railway line where Alessandro's father's hit men brought Griffon to beat him up. Uphill from you is the Waterhall, where Rivera had his men lurking in the bushes near the (Gipsy) Boy's Grave. Neil Griffon had told Alessandro Rivera it is supposed to be some stable lad's grave, where the flowers bloom each year with the colors of the Derby winner.

POSSIBLE SIDE TRIPS

Exning

A small modern suburb a few miles north of Newmarket Race Course, Exning was the home of the Wuffinga dynasty, whose famous burial place was Sutton Hoo. St. Etheldreda, daughter of King Anna, who founded the abbey at Ely, was born there and baptized in a spring called St. Wendred's Well, to which people made pilgrimage until the shrine at Walsingham became more important.

Bury St. Edmunds

Eleventh-century Town Centre. Guided Tours Tuesday, mid-June–September; daily July and August.

Abbey Gardens and ruins, Angel Hill.

Tourist Information Centre, Angel Hill (0284) 64667 (summer); 63233 (winter). Open Monday–Saturday, May, June, and September, Daily July and August.

In P. D. James's *An Unsuitable Job for a Woman,* several characters made the hour's drive from Cambridge through Newmarket to Bury St. Edmund's. First Mark Callender and Isabelle de Lasterie went that way to visit his mother's doctor, then spent the day at the sea. Next, Cordelia Gray drove through the "gentle, unemphatic" countryside. Outside of Newmarket she noticed that Lunn's black van was following her but she threw him off at the second set of lights on the High Street. Half an hour later she, too, reached Bury St. Edmunds to interview senile old Dr. Gladwin.

Bury St. Edmunds is a small medieval town that began, like Ely, as a monastery founded around 700 by the Wuffinga dynasty. Danish King Canute established a Benedictine monastery here in 1020 in memory of the martyred Saxon king St. Edmund, who was captured by the Danes, tortured, and put to death. As a result, Bury St. Edmund's became a great shrine with a famous Abbey Church something like Ely Cathedral. (See Ely Walk.)

The Abbey was located off Angel Hill in the center of town but it was dissolved (and the stones looted) in the sixteenth century. Now there are only picturesque ruins open to the public with its Botanical Gardens at the site. You can see parts of the church and the Abbot's Palace, the Norman Gate, and the Abbey Bridge over the Lark River. There is also a Rose Garden, which was paid for with the royalties from a book written by an American serviceman.

In the Abbey gardens there is a plaque at the site of the High Altar that commemorates the moment here in 1214 when the barons swore to make King John ratify Magna Carta with its clause about "Habeas Corpus," or "Have His Carcase" (title of a Dorothy L. Sayers mystery with characters who came from nearby St. Ives). According to Wilfred Scott-Giles in *The Wimsey Family,* Peter de Guimsey (Wimsey) attended this baronial assembly. In John Creasey's *Theft of Magna Carta* Inspector West prevented the theft of the Sarum copy of Magna Carta.

Bury St. Edmunds's center is laid out in a medieval grid. It has two beautiful Gothic churches of St. Mary and St. James. In the latter is the tomb of Henry VIII's sister Mary, the young widow of Louis XII of France, who ran off and married Charles Brandon, Duke of Suffolk. Brandon was son of Henry VII's standard bearer at Bosworth Field. Richard III, whose crimes Josephine Tey investigated in *The Daughter of Time,* died there defending his crown. This Mary Tudor was also the grandmother of judicially murdered Queen Lady Jane Grey, whom Sayers's college friend and co-author Muriel Byrne felt was a "true Tudor woman."

The Abbey ruins and the Botanical Gardens, famous even in East Anglia, where the soil is the most fertile in all England, make it possible this is the "original" for Susan Kenney's *Garden of Malice.* In her mystery, there were a series of spectacular gardens, including one with poisonous plants, created by Lady Viola Montfort-Snow in the grounds and ruins of Montfort Abbey. Under Henry VIII Montfort Abbey had been taken over by Gilbert Fotheringhay who built himself a handsome Tudor mansion there. The mansion itself was later destroyed, but parts of the Abbey still stood and housed Lady Viola's son, Giles Montfort-Snow, and a group of odd family retainers.

In *An Unsuitable Job for a Woman,* after her depressing visit to the Callenders' old doctor, P. D. James's Cordelia Gray parked her car on Angel Hill and paused to refresh herself in the Bury Abbey gardens. She walked through the Abbey grounds to the riverbank, then, sitting quietly in the sun, she looked again at Mark's mother's *Book of Common Prayer,* which Nanny Pilbeam had brought Mark on his twenty-first birthday. It suddenly struck Cordelia that she should look at the page for his birthday, which was St. Mark's Day, April 25. There she found the vital clue to the mystery.

Ipswich

It seems possible that Mark Callender and Isabelle de Lasterie drove from Bury St. Edmunds to Ipswich to the sea. From Newmarket to Ipswich is only forty miles and once there, you are almost at the North Sea. Ipswich was once an old inland port on the River Orwell above Harwich on the River Stour, on the direct railway line from Bury St. Edmunds. Henry VIII's powerful Cardinal Wolsey, who arranged his divorce to marry Anne Boleyn, was born here, the son of a butcher. Much later, Charles Dickens's Mr. Pickwick had his adventure with the lady in yellow curlpapers at the Great White Horse Hotel there. Mr. Pickwick was G. K. Chesterton's favorite Dickens character. Recently, in a travel article about Suffolk painters Constable and Gainsborough, Ruth Rendell (aka Barbara Vine, who won an Edgar in 1986 for *A Dark-Adapted Eye)* talked about "her" East Anglia with its distinctive speech and customs.

It may have very few old buildings left standing, but Ipswich is the nerve center for murder investigations along the North Sea. Patricia Moyes's Scotland Yard detective, Henry Tibbett, contacted its police when murder was done among the London weekend sailors in *Down Among the Dead Men.* In the same mystery, local lord of the manor in Berrybridge, Sir Simon Trigg-Willoughby, owner of stately manor Berry Hall, claimed to have been in Ipswich the day of the murder, visiting his solicitor. In Alan Hunter's *Gently Between the Tides,* the body of murdered Czech violinist Hannah Stoven was sent there for an autopsy from the tiny village of Shinglebourne.

Beyond Ipswich on the Suffolk coast there are mysterious Suffolk fishing villages (real and imaginary) like Moyes's Berrybridge or Hunter's Shinglebourne with its Martello Tower, where the murdered Hannah lived. The next river north on the coast after the Orwell is the Deben, where the Tibbetts' hosts, Rosemary and Alastair Bensen, took them sailing in Patricia Moyes's *Down Among the Dead Men.*

In Andrew Taylor's *Caroline Minuscule,* grad student William Dougal and his girl friend, Amanda, who were treasure-hunting in Cambridge, drove to Ipswich, where they madly bought supplies (like a sharp knife). William Dougal's Cambridge friend, Malcolm, kept his boat, the Sally-Anne, moored somewhere south of the Deben and north of the Alben estuary, where they planned to lure their enemy to the boat and kill him.

Still farther up the Suffolk coast is Aldeburgh, where a yearly musical festival in mid-June was begun by composer Benjamin Britten (born nearby in Loftestowe) and singer Peter Pears. The real Aldeburgh Festival is similar to the one held at Thwaite Maltings, four miles from Shinglebourne, in Alan Hunter's *Gently Between the Tides.*

It is also mentioned as one of the big festivals by Dr. Davie in V. C. Clinton-Baddeley's *Only a Matter of Time.* In this mystery, Dr. Davie had come to the King's Lacy Festival, where he became involved in murder. The King's Lacy Festival could easily have taken place at Aldeburgh because Dr. Davie was a classics don at St. Nicholas College, Cambridge. (See Cambridge Walk.)

In P. D. James's *Unnatural Causes,* Detective Adam Dalgliesh's Aunt Jane lived on the Suffolk coast at Monksmere. To visit her, Dalgliesh took the direct route from London that went through Ipswich. Mystery writer Anne Perry lives nearby in a tiny Suffolk village called Saxmundham. Her Charlotte Pitt stories take place in Victorian London. She has also written a radio play about witchcraft in the time of Oliver Cromwell.

In *The Elberg Collection,* Anthony Oliver's arthritic ex-CID man, John Webber, retired to garden in a Suffolk village called Flaxfield. He met his energetic Welsh friend Lizzie, who helped him investigate a huge pottery scam. Sheila Bradley set *The Chief Inspector's Daughter,* her story about Jasmine Woods, who published two romantic novels a year and collected both jade and netsuke, in "unspoiled North Suffolk" near the sleepy little village of Breckham Market. Unfortunately for her, Alison Quantrill, the Chief Inspector's daughter, had come home from London and got a job as Jasmine's secretary.

Finally, although Margery Allingham's roots were in Essex, she set *Sweet Danger,* in which Campion first met Amanda Fitton, at Pontisbright. Pontisbright was the ancestral home of the young earl and his missing treasure. Her *Mystery Mile* also took place at Mystery Mile, the hereditary fiefdom of Giles Paget and his sister Biddy. Both feudal villages were near Ipswich because Albert Campion went there to get the train to London.

9

OXFORD

BACKGROUND

These walks take place in the lovely city of Oxford, the oldest and most celebrated of England's university towns. Close by is the ancient royal domain of Woodstock and the Duke of Marlborough's great palace of Blenheim, where Winston Churchill was born.

Oxford was first mentioned as Oxnaford in the *Anglo-Saxon Chronicle* of 911. The name, Oxford, comes either from the literal—a ford for oxen—or from "Osca's ford." The town, which is fifty-six miles from London, is situated at the junction of the Thames (which in Oxford, for poetic reasons, is called the Isis) and the Cherwell rivers, the site of the Saxon priory of St. Frideswide. This point marks the very middle of Middle England. It is as far from the sea as it is possible to be in England.

A river city, Oxford was part market and part fortress. For several centuries, it functioned almost as a second capital of England. A center of the Cotswold wool industry, it was a medieval borough with trade guilds and royal charters. According to tradition, the university was formed about 1167 by students who had returned to England as a result of an edict issued by Henry II when, angered that France had given refuge to the fleeing Archbishop Thomas à Becket, he ordered that all English students must return from the continent. Many of them are said to have settled at Oxford, where they tried to re-create the university atmosphere they had known abroad.

In 1209, the university closed because of strife between townspeople and students. In 1214 it started up again, prob-ably because tradesmen and merchants missed the revenue that students had brought in. A chancellor was appointed at this time and given disciplinary power. The university was once again under way. At first students simply arrived in Oxford and took lessons from various Masters of Arts. Then in 1249 Uni-versity College was founded. By the end of the thirteenth century it had been followed by Balliol, Merton, and St. Ed-mund Hall. In the next century came Exeter, Oriel, Queen's, and New College. In the fifteenth century, Lincoln, All Souls, and Magdalen (pronounced "maudlen") were founded. The sixteenth century brought Brasenose, Corpus Christi, Christ Church, St. John's, Trinity, and Jesus, and in the seventeenth, Wadham and Pembroke were added. Nineteenth-century col-leges are Worcester and Keble. Also, dating from the end of the nineteenth century are five women's colleges—Lady Margaret Hall, Somerville, St. Anne's, St. Hugh's, and St. Hilda's. St. Catherine's and Wolfson, both established since World War II, are among the latest additions.

Oxford is an industrial as well as a university city. It has a population that exceeds 120,000, only 1200 of whom are students. Its factories produce automobiles, agricultural imple-ments, printed goods, and marmalade. What has been de-scribed as "the city of dreaming spires" is now a city surround-ed by factories, housing estates, and motorways.

It is not really possible to locate The University. Like Cam-bridge, Oxford is modeled on the medieval form. There is no campus. The university is really administrative. It coordinates such things as entrance qualifications, the organization and maintenance of academic standards, and the granting of de-grees.

The academic year at Oxford consists of three terms. Each

lasts for eight weeks. The weeks are numbered one through eight. The year begins in the autumn with the Michaelmas term. The second term is the Hilary term; it begins with the New Year. The third term, Trinity, starts in the late spring, right after Easter.

Many literary greats have studied in or written about the colleges of Oxford. It is thought that Geoffrey of Monmouth, the first to present King Arthur as a romantic hero, studied at Oxford around 1100. In his "Miller's Tale" Chaucer called Oxford "Oxenford." When Alexander Pope passed through town, he drank at the Cross Inn. Oxford was mentioned in the novels of Jane Austen; she and her sister attended school there for a time. Much of Thomas Hardy's *Jude the Obscure* is set in "Christminster," which was Hardy's name for Oxford. (See Dorchester Walk.)

Percy Bysshe Shelley studied at University college until he was expelled for publishing a pamphlet on "The Necessity of Atheism." Today a fine marble sculpture of him with the muse of poetry mourning beneath sits in a domed chamber built by the college after his death. In Amanda Cross's *No Word from Winifred*, Winifred discusses in her journal the impression the sculpture made on her as a child.

Charles Lutwidge Dodgson, better known as Lewis Carroll, was a mathematics don at Christ Church when he devised the tale of *Alice's Adventures Underground*. Carroll is said to have once smiled at the infant Dorothy L. Sayers in her baby carriage.

Opposite Christ Church is Pembroke College, where Samuel Johnson spent the year 1718 living in great poverty in a room above the gatehouse. Henry James, author of the classic thriller *The Turn of the Screw*, wrote of Oxford in *Portraits of Places* (1883).

The poet William Butler Yeats, along with his wife and child, lived on the corner of Broad Street opposite Balliol, and the poet John Masefield lived at Boar's Hill in the 1920s in what is now called Masefield House. Kenneth Grahame is buried in St. Cross churchyard, as is Charles Williams, friend of C. S. Lewis and the author of such brooding metaphysical thrillers as *The Place of the Lion*. St. Cross Church is mentioned in Dorothy L. Sayers's *Busman's Honeymoon*.

Dorothy L. Sayers and P. D. James were both born in Oxford, and many other mystery writers are associated with the town either because they attended school there, as did Edmund Crispin and E. C. Bentley, and C. Day Lewis (aka Nicholas Blake), or because they live in Oxford or its environs as do Margaret Yorke, Colin Dexter, Anne Morice, Anthony Price, and James McClure.

Oxford long has been a favorite site for the plyers of the mystery trade. The list of detective stories set there is almost endless. Many came from the ordered minds of men and women who taught in the colleges, as was the case with G. K. Chesterton's friend, Ronald Knox, and J. I. M. Stewart (aka Michael Innes). Not that these academics are obsessed with crime, for as Innes notes in *Seven Suspects*, "the senior members of Oxford and Cambridge colleges are undoubtedly among the most moral and level-headed of men."

In *Gaudy Night*, Dorothy L. Sayers called Oxford "an innocent and well-ordered community."

In many ways, Oxford is England in miniature. Keats thought that it was the finest city in the world.

HOW TO GET THERE

British Rail: trains hourly from London's Paddington Station
    (Service is reduced on Sunday.)—One hour

Automobile: A40 and M40 from London; 57 miles

Length of Walk: Walk 1, The Colleges, 5 miles; Walk 2, Jericho, 4.6
    miles

See pages 182 and 199 for maps of boundaries of this walk, and page 366 for a list of detectives and stories referred to.

PLACES OF INTEREST

The individual colleges

The Carfax Tower, intersection of Queen Street, Cornmarket, the High, and St. Aldate's. Fourteenth century. The hub of the town.

Tom Tower, St. Aldate's. Crowns the entrance to Christ Church. The tower, which is dedicated to St. Thomas of Canterbury (see Canterbury Walk), was begun shortly after Cardinal Wolsey founded the college in 1525. The upper part, which was completed in 1682 by Christopher Wren, is in the Gothic style, which differs considerably from the Tudor base, which dates from Wolsey's time.

The Church of Christ, within the building of the Christ Church. Since the time of Henry VIII, it has been Oxford's Anglican cathedral. Parts of the building date back to the twelfth century, when the Priory of St. Fredeswide stood on this site.

"Bridge of Sighs," New College Lane. A modern copy of the one in Venice; this one links two parts of Hertford College.

Sheldonian Theatre, Broad Street. The first building designed by the young professor Christopher Wren. The building is guarded by a phalanx of Roman emperors. What you see are modern copies of the nineteenth-century originals. The theater is used for academic ceremonies and concerts. Visitors may have a splendid view of Oxford from the theater's cupola.

Martyrs' Memorial, Magdalen Street. Memorial to the three Protestant bishops—Cranmer, Latimer, and Ridley—who were burned at the stake by Mary Tudor.

Ashmolean Museum, Beaumont Street (0865) 57522. Collection of paintings, sculpture, and artifacts of the Stone and Bronze Ages. Other holdings include drawings by Michelangelo and Raphael as well as the Pomfret and Arundel Marbles. (The museum is closed on Monday.)

The Covered Market, Market Street. A charming street market, built in the nineteenth century.

PLACES TO STAY/EAT

The Old Parsonage Hotel, 3 Banbury Road (0865) 5483. Near St. Giles Church, a thirteenth-century building that houses a comfortable, moderately priced hotel with a carpark, but within walking distance of town center.

The Randolph Hotel, Beaumont Street (0865) 48707. A Trusthouse Forte Hotel. An Oxford institution on Beaumont Street at Magdalen, across from the Martyrs' Memorial. It has a carpark and is within walking distance of town center. Restaurant and coffee shop. Moderate.

The Eagle and the Child, St. Giles Street. Called "The Bird and the Baby" by the Inklings—Charles Williams, C. S. Lewis, J. R. R. Tolkien, etc.—who used to gather there. Also mentioned by Edmund Crispin and Jeffrey Archer. Features traditional pub fare.

The Lamb and the Flag, St. Giles Street (0865) 42883. Mentioned in *Gaudy Night* by Dorothy L. Sayers. Wide selection of pub food.

The Turf Tavern, 10 St. Helen's Passage, Bath Place (off Holywell Street). A thirteenth-century tavern, it was used by Thomas Hardy as the setting for part of *Jude the Obscure*. Features traditional English food.

The Tourist Information Centre, St. Aldate's Chambers, St. Aldate's (0865) 48707, will assist you with room and restaurant suggestions.

OXFORD I WALK

Begin your exploration of Oxford by taking a train from London's Paddington Station as David Kesler did in Jeffrey Archer's *Not a Penny More, Not a Penny Less* when he wanted to see his Harvard friend and classmate, Stephen Bradley, now a visiting Fellow of Magdalen College. Almost fifty years before David Kesler came to Oxford by train, Edmund Crispin's Richard Cadogan attempted to do the same thing, but was foiled by canceled trains at Didcot. He then hitchhiked the rest of the way and discovered a moving toy shop in the process.

The railway station is a center of activity in real-life Oxford as well as in the Oxford of literature and mystery. In mystery stories characters come and go from the Oxford station with

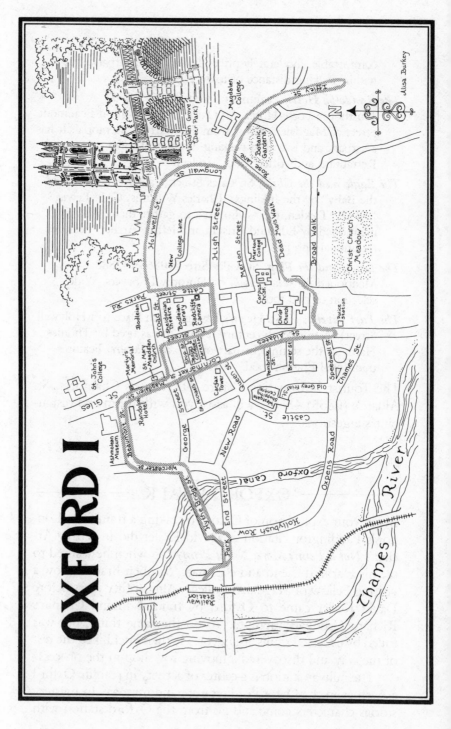

regularity. Michael Innes begins his *Hare Sitting Up* with Headmaster Juniper on a train from Oxford shamelessly listening in on the conversation of some new B.A.s who were going to London.

The Oxford station is an especially busy place at the beginning of term. In John Penn's *Mortal Term,* the summer term at Coriston College began on a gray, wet day. Trains filled with chattering girls and boys all laden with bags, and books, and various items of sports equipment disgorged their contents at Oxford station.

At the station, David Kesler hailed a taxi for the short ride down New College Lane to Magdalen College. Taxis are plentiful, and you may do the same. You may wish to be driven to the town center, where you may join the walk at any point indicated on the map. As in most English towns, the least attractive area of Oxford is around the train station. You may wish to save your energy for walking in more picturesque places. If you have come to Oxford by car, as James Brigsley did when he traveled down from London on the M40 for the team dinner at Magdalen College in *Not a Penny More, Not a Penny Less,* use the carpark near the station and join the walk at this point. (If this park is full, there are other carparks at Thames Street and Norfolk Street.)

In *Gaudy Night* by Dorothy L. Sayers, Harriet Vane, returning to Oxford for the Gaudy celebration at Shrewsbury (actually Somerville) College, rejoiced that, since she could now afford her own little car, this "entry into Oxford would bear no resemblances to those earlier arrivals by train." Despite Harriet's elation, Oxford is an extremely difficult place in which to drive. The best thing you can do with a car in Oxford is park it.

Leave the station and turn right; this will take you to Park End Street. Turn left into Park End and follow it to the junction that curves around the Royal Oxford Hotel. The air will be heavy with the smell of malt, indicating a nearby brewery. Rewley Road will be to the left and Hollybush Row to the right. Follow the curve into Hythe Bridge Street on the right fork, and walk past the modern building housing Blackwell's offices, which Kate Fanzler in Amanda Cross's *The Question of Max* contrasted with the ancient bookstore in the Broad across from the Sheldonian Theatre where Dorothy L. Sayers once worked.

Walk along Hythe Bridge Street, crossing Upper Fisher Row, to Worcester Street. Turn left at Worcester Street and follow the barbed-wire-topped college wall to the point where Beaumont Street dead-ends into Worcester College. Turn left in through the college gates and take a moment to consider this college, which was founded in 1714. Note the tile-roofed Gloucester Row of original fifteenth-century monastic buildings that form the south range of the quadrangle and contrast with the eighteenth-century buildings in the north range.

Cross the quadrangle to the gate to catch a glimpse of the lake beyond. Worcester is the only college that can boast its own lake. It was the college of the Cavalier poet Richard Lovelace, who wrote of iron bars not making a prison. It was also the college of Thomas de Quincey, author of "Confessions of an Opium Eater." In 1803, de Quincey decided to study at Oxford after wandering about the countryside and almost starving in London. He also wrote a brilliant essay "On Murder Considered as One of the Fine Arts," which was quoted by P. D. James in *The Maul and the Pear Tree,* her look at the same Radcliffe Highway murders.

Return to the main gate and cross Worcester Street into Beaumont Street, then walk east along the curving row of pleasant Regency houses. In 1894, Henry James, author of the supernatural thriller, *The Turn of the Screw,* sketched out "The Altar of the Dead" while he was lodging at 15 Beaumont Street. As you cross Gloucester Street, you will pass in front of The Playhouse, where Patrick Grant and his guest, the Greek policeman Manolakis, watched a revival production of *The Importance of Being Earnest* before driving up to London in Margaret Yorke's *Cast for Death.* The Playhouse was the location in Edmund Crispin's *Swan Song* where a Wagnerian opera was performed. Across the street, on the right, is the Ashmolean Museum, the oldest museum in the country. Its many exhibits include an outstanding collection of archeological finds from Greece, Crete, and the Near East. There are also paintings, prints, porcelain, and scientific curiosities. Its greatest treasure is the Alfred Jewel, a brooch made for King Alfred in the ninth century, which G. K. Chesterton described in *The Ballad of the White Horse.*

As you approach Magdalen Street, you will pass, on your right, the row of buildings where Father Walter Hooper, C. S. Lewis's friend, literary executor, and posthumous editor, lived for many years.

You are now passing the Randolph Hotel, an impressive Gothic-style mid-Victorian building that stretches its length along Beaumont to Magdalen Street. We met Margaret Yorke here on a warm July day and, over a delightful lunch of poached salmon and asparagus, talked mysteries.

Many people use the Randolph as a meeting place. Stephen Bradley arrived there at 9:55 A.M. and told the bellboy that he was there to meet Mr. Metcalfe in Archer's *Not a Penny More, Not a Penny Less.*

Stephen Bradley spent so much time studying the layout of the Randolph as he worked on his plan to defeat Harvey Metcalfe that the manager became suspicious.

It was no doubt at the Randolph, described by Anne Morice as ". . . that hotel . . . as far as I know . . . the only one in Oxford," that Tessa Crichton, the actress-wife of Scotland Yard Inspector Robin Price, agreed to meet the suspicious James McGrath in *Murder Post-dated.*

In *A Deadly Sickness* by John Penn, Tony Dinsley suggested that he and Celia stop at the Randolph for dinner and a drink when repairs to his car required longer than anticipated at the garage at St. Aldate's.

At the corner of Beaumont and Magdalen Streets, turn right into Magdalen Street and walk along the right-hand side of the street. Across from the Randolph where St. Giles forks into Magdalen Street is the Martyrs' Memorial. Kate Fanzler stood here and reflected on the truth of generalities about Oxford in Amanda Cross's *The Question of Max.* She then collected her just-rented bicycle from the rack behind the Memorial. She planned to cycle around Oxford in a "properly eccentric" manner.

The Memorial commemorates the Protestant Archbishop of Canterbury, Thomas Cranmer who, together with Bishops Hugh Latimer and Nicholas Ridley, was burned in 1556 at a spot in Broad Street outside Balliol College. The Memorial, which was erected three hundred years later, is modeled after the Eleanor Crosses set up by Edward I to mark the funeral procession of his wife.

The Memorial and the Carfax Tower at the end of Cornmarket are major rendezvous spots in Oxford. Both are easily accessible as well as highly visible.

Beyond the Memorial, St. John's College extends to the north (left) along the far side of St. Giles. Edmund Crispin located St. Christopher's College just north of St. John's. In *The Moving Toyshop*, Gervase Fen was a professor of English Language and Literature at St. Christophers. Crispin himself, (aka Robert Bruce Montgomery) was educated at St. John's, where he read modern languages and served as organist and choirmaster for two years.

It was between St. John's and its neighbor, Balliol, to the south that Antonia Fraser placed her mythical Hawksmoor College (named, no doubt, for architect Nicholas Hawksmoor) in *Oxford Blood*. She incorporated into the tale many of the logistical problems, i.e., the lavatories, that her daughter encountered as one of the first women students at Wadham College off Parks Road. (Dorothy L. Sayers stayed on after term at Wadham College in 1913 and went to her first convocation.)

As you walk along the right-hand side of Magdalen Street, you will pass Debenhams department store, where Moira Gale in John Penn's *Mortal Term* shopped for a gift for her auntie and lost her purse after purchasing a scarf. The parish church of St. Mary Magdalen is on your left as you come to the juncture of Broad Street to the left and George Street to the right.

In *Not a Penny More, Not a Penny Less*, Stephen Bradley and

Harvey Metcalfe strolled along Magdalen Street on their way to the Broad to view the procession of honorands to the Sheldonian Theatre for the presentation of honorary degrees.

Magdalen Street ends at George Street and becomes Cornmarket Street. (Oxford Streets are often only one block long before the name changes.) To the left down Broad Street, embedded in the concrete of the street, is an iron cross marking the actual site of the burning of Cranmer, Ridley, and Latimer. Opposite the cross on the left is Balliol College. As Stephen Bradley, in the guise of Professor Porter of Trinity College, escorted Harvey Metcalfe back to the Randolph Hotel, he pointed out the iron cross set in the street and told him the story of Archbishop Cranmer.

If you detour to enter Balliol here, you will be in the front quadrangle. An old gate hangs on the wall in the archway that leads to the garden quadrangle to your left. The gate is said to have been blackened by the fire that burned the martyrs. Through here you will see the Hall at the far end of the quadrangle. The rooms occupied by Dorothy L. Sayers's intrepid detective, Lord Peter Wimsey, were to the far left in the new (1906) Warren Building, staircase No. XXI. In *Gaudy Night,* Lord Peter took Harriet Vane to a Bach concert at Balliol. Balliol is also the college of the 1920s detective-writer Ronald Knox.

Return to the right to cross George Street into Cornmarket Street at the intersection of Broad, Magdalen, Cornmarket, and George Streets. This is an extremeley crowded area, teeming with shoppers, tourists, and students all jostling one another about as they pursue their various activities. The area is rich in its variety of eating places. It offers a string of snack bars and pubs where thirst can be quenched and weary feet rested.

As you walk south on Cornmarket, on the left, just before Ship Street, is the Saxon tower of St. Michael's at the North Gate. Dating from c. 1000, it is Oxford's oldest building and marks the site of the North Gate, which was demolished in 1771. The tower served the Saxons as lookout post and stronghold. The rest of the church is thirteenth-century.

Continue working your way through the shoppers on

Cornmarket, crossing St. Michael's Street on the right, Ship Street on the left. Here fronting on an alley that leads off to the right is the Corn Dolly, where Colin Dexter's Inspector Morse in *The Dead of Jericho* followed Edward Murdoch in time to watch the noontime "go-go" performance by the buxom dancer, "Fabulous Fiona."

Follow Cornmarket to the Carfax, the point at which it becomes St. Aldate's. The Carfax Tower, all that remains of the Church of St. Martin, which was demolished in 1896 to ease traffic congestion, is situated at Cornmarket and High Street. The tower can be climbed to obtain an excellent view of the city.

In *A Deadly Sickness* by John Penn, Tony Dinsley, Diana Postons's lover, took his car to the garage in St. Aldate's. The cross streets here are the High Street to the left, and Queen Street to the right. Somewhere around here was located the law office of Mr. Rosseter. Rosseter came close to killing Gervase Fen and Richard Cadogan, but ended up being killed himself in Edmund Crispin's *The Moving Toyshop*.

Follow St. Aldate's along the right-hand side past Job Centre and the bus stop for Woodstock. Continue past Pembroke Street and Pembroke Square on the right, where Pembroke College is located. Originally it was Broadgates Hall, one of the medieval halls that were used to house the first Oxford students. It was established as Pembroke College in 1624 by King James I. It is named for William, third Earl of Pembroke.

The next street on the right is Brewer Street, where at No. 1, Dorothy L. Sayers was born on June 13, 1893. No. 1 Brewer Street is still the Headmaster's house; it includes No. 2 next door. At the time of Sayers's birth, her father was Headmaster of Christ Church Cathedral Choir School. The school is at No. 3.

Cross St. Aldate's at a safe point, and walk back up the east side of the street past the city police station and into Christ Church Memorial Garden on your right.

In Edmund Crispin's *The Moving Toyshop*, after regaining consciousness following the attack in the toy shop that followed his finding the body, Crispin's Richard Cadogan presented his bruised and battered self to the city police. They listened to his story, bandaged his wounds, plied him with tea, and then drove him back to the toy shop on the Iffley Road, which had become a grocery store.

A boatman walked into the Oxford police station at 8:30 with information about the "three men in a boat" in Peter Lovesey's *Swing, Swing Together*.

Before you enter the Memorial Gardens, go left up St. Aldate's to the main entrance of Christ Church and look inside. Christ Church, where Lord James Brigsley in *Not a Penny More, Not a Penny Less* was educated, is one of the largest and most famous of all Oxford colleges. It was founded in 1525 by Cardinal Wolsey. Its twelfth-century chapel, where Dorothy L. Sayers was baptized, is the smallest cathedral in England. The College's Tom Tower at the main gate was designed by Christopher Wren and is one of the most dominant features on the Oxford skyline. Each evening at five minutes past nine Great Tom, the bell in Tom Tower, is tolled 101 times in accordance with the old curfew laws—once for each member of the original foundation.

Inside Tom Tower is the Tom Quad with the fountain Mercury, where Harriet Vane and Lord St. George tossed her meringues to the carp in *Gaudy Night*.

Return along St. Aldate's and walk left to the Memorial Garden and on into Christ Church Meadow. Constable Thackeray trained his binoculars on four small squares of light, the windows of a houseboat that were just distinguishable against "the dark mass of Christ Church Meadow," in Lovesey's *Swing, Swing Together*.

Later, the handcuffed Lucifer explained to Sergeant Cribb that the "ladies" he was visiting on the houseboat, he had met that afternoon while he and his two companions were "taking a constitutional through Christ Church Meadow." He and Humberstone and Gold had accepted the invitation to the houseboat even though they had planned to spend the time touring some of the colleges.

Take Dead Man's Walk, the path that runs along the north

side of Christ Church Meadow behind Merton College. In *Swing, Swing Together,* the dead man, Bonner-Hill, was a Fellow of Merton College. The gardens beyond the walls are private and the gates open only by key. If it is summer, flowers will spill over the wall in a profusion of color and fragrance.

Tony Dinsley suggested that he take Celia Fints for a walk in Christ Church Meadow after they left his car at the garage in St. Aldate's in John Penn's *A Deadly Sickness.*

The Meadow thrusts you into the countryside in the midst of a teeming, bustling city. Students and tourists recline on the grass in conversation, or read, or sleep in the warm sunlight, lulled by the muffled music of the city.

Dead Man's Walk is so called because it is the route along which high Jewish funerals passed during the Middle Ages. The synagogue was almost on the site of Tom Tower. Another account of the name has it so called because an execution was carried out there.

Follow Dead Man's Walk until it angles to the right into Rose Lane, going past the Botanic Gardens and back into the High Street. In Sayers's *Gaudy Night,* Harriet Vane and Lord Peter walked to the Botanical Gardens after sending the dean some birthday flowers.

In Archer's *Not a Penny More, Not a Penny Less,* Stephen Bradley had his rooms in Magdalen College, where he was a visiting Fellow. He rose early the morning after his trip to London and walked in a leisurely manner across the Cloisters to a Common Room breakfast, where he enjoyed eggs, bacon, coffee, and toast. After stopping in the Bursar's office, he strolled back across Magdalen Bridge and as he walked he admired the well-maintained flower beds in the university Botanical Gardens.

Cross the High and walk along the left side to Magdalen College with its historic tower. Magdalen College, which was founded in 1458, counts among its famous students Cardinal Wolsey, Sir John Betjeman, and Oscar Wilde. C. S. Lewis was a Fellow here until he left in 1954 to become a professor at Cambridge.

The Bell Tower at Magdalen is one of Oxford's most beautiful and forms the focal point of the city's May Morning celebration. The May Morning festivities became an orgy in Antonia Fraser's *Oxford Blood*. At 6 A.M. on May 1, a choir sings a Latin hymn from the top of Magdalen Tower to the crowd gathered below. Morris dancers then lead the crowd to Radcliffe Square where the dancers perform in a display that progresses from the Square to Broad Street and then to St. Giles. The program of music and dancing usually continues all day.

In *Gaudy Night*, Harriet Vane got a coveted ticket to the tower in time to prevent an undergraduate suicide.

Behind Magdalen College is Magdalen Grove and Deer Park, as well as the path leading to Addison's Walk along the Cherwell, where the noted scholar and poet, Joseph Addison, liked to walk, as did C. S. Lewis.

In *Not a Penny More, Not a Penny Less*, Stephen Bradley and David Kesler strolled along Addison's Walk before David took his reluctant leave of Oxford.

Walk eastward along the High Street with your back to the city. Cross Magdalen Bridge, beyond which the road fans and becomes three. According to Robert Robinson in *Landscape with Dead Dons*, Cambridge scientists, bent upon relaxing after a week spent with alkali reactions, would zoom across the bridge in fast cars into Oxford. In the meadow just below Magdalen Bridge, the company to which actress Tessa Crichton belonged shot scenes for a new film in Anne Morice's *Murder Post-dated*.

In Peter Lovesey's *Swing, Swing Together*, it was not until a check was made of the skiffs tied together near Magdalen Bridge and one was found to be the Lucrecia, that a lead was uncovered to the whereabouts of the three wanted men, Humberstone, Gold, and Lucifer.

High Street beyond the bridge becomes three roads. To the left is Clements Street, in the center is Cowley Road. It was on Cowley Road in a succession of dingy rooms that John Westerby, one-time husband of Anne Scott, the victim in *The Dead of Jericho*, had lived. The road to the right of Cowley is the Iffley Road.

As he walked up the Iffley Road contemplating climbing over the wall to his old college, St. Christophers, Richard Cadogan, in Crispin's *The Moving Toyshop,* reflected that in Oxford, as in no other place, a man can do anything, no matter how eccentric, and arouse neither the interest nor the emotion of those about him. Somewhere in the clutch of small shops along the left-hand side of the Iffley Road was the blue-and-white awninged toy shop where Cadogan found a body and launched his adventure. After picking out a likely spot for the toy shop and perhaps investigating to find the alley out of which Cadogan came after he was assaulted, turn and go back across the bridge. Walk along the right-hand side of High Street past Magdalen College, until you come to Longwall Street, turn right into Longwall and follow it to Holywell Street, where you will turn left. If you continue along Longwall Street, it will become St. Cross Street, which will take you to St. Cross Church and cemetery. This "obscure little church in a side street," was the scene of the marriage ceremony between Lord Peter Wimsey and Harriet Vane. In the churchyard are the graves of Charles Williams and the creator of Toad Hall, Kenneth Grahame. Just beyond St. Cross on the left-hand side of the street are the Balliol College Sports Grounds, where Dorothy L. Sayers placed "Shrewsbury College" in *Gaudy Night*.

Holywell Street takes you along the old city wall, which is now a part of New College, where a plaque commemorating 1880s undergraduate John Galsworthy is located in the cloisters.

In the area bounded by Holywell Street on the north, Longwall on the east, High Street on the south, and Catte Street on the west are all the following colleges: Hertford College, where Evelyn Waugh, author of *Brideshead Revisited,* was an undergraduate in the 1920s; All Souls' College, where T. E. Lawrence, Lawrence of Arabia, was elected a fellow in 1919; Queen's College, which made Thomas Hardy an honorary fellow in 1922; and St. Edmund's Hall.

St. Edmund's Hall is a survivor of the medieval halls, but it was only admitted to the rights and privileges of other colleges of the university in 1957. Its quadrangle with its painted sundial is one of Oxford's quietest and most charming spots. The chapel contains some beautiful seventeenth-century stalls and oak and cedar screens.

Continue along Holywell, noting that a left turn will take you into Bath Place, where the thirteenth-century Turf Tavern is located. The Turf served Thomas Hardy as a partial setting for *Jude the Obscure*. Dorothy L. Sayers lived at No. 5 when she worked at Blackwell's.

At the junction of Holywell Street with Parks Road to the right, and Catte Street to the left, turn left into Catte, noting that just ahead is Broad Street with the New Bodleian Library on the corner of Broad Street and Parks Road. As Nicholas Flower strode along, thinking lustful thoughts about Balboa Tomlin, the sunshine turned the stone of the New Bodleian to dark yellow, making the building resemble a cardboard box, according to Robert Robinson in *Landscape with Dead Dons*.

Just beyond the New Bodleian on Broad Street is the world-famous Blackwell's Book Store. In Archer's *Not a Penny More, Not a Penny Less,* Lord James Brigsley, the handsome British aristocrat, purchased an Oxford calendar here for two pounds.

In Colin Dexter's *Last Bus to Woodstock,* Jennifer, looking cool and clean in a blouse and jeans, explained to Morse that on Wednesday she had gone to Blackwell's to spend a book token.

On the corner of Catte Street and Broad Street, facing the New Bodleian, is the Clarendon Building. Built to house Oxford University Press, which it did until 1827, the Clarendon Building was designed by Nicholas Hawksmoor, Sir Christopher Wren's greatest pupil.

In *Not a Penny More, Not a Penny Less* by Jeffrey Archer, Stephen Bradley visited the office of the Vice-Chancellor of the University in the Clarendon Building. There he spent some time asking strange questions of the V-C's personal secretary, Miss Smallwood.

On Broad Street just beyond the Clarendon Building is the Sheldonian Theatre with its row of carved heads, which are known as "the Emperors." The Sheldonian was the first building designed by the young professor of astronomy, Christopher Wren, who went on to become one of England's greatest architects. In the Sheldonian, Wren created a ceiling 21.5 m × 24.5 m without any of the load-bearing columns that would have interfered with the spectators' view of ceremonies. The Sheldonian is still used for the major ceremonies of the university. It was to the Sheldonian that Archer's Stephen Bradley went to watch a brief ceremony as a group of students took their bachelor of arts degrees.

Leave the Sheldonian by the gate leading to Catte Street. You will see ahead of you, in New College Lane, the "Bridge of Sighs," a modern copy of the one in Venice. It joins two buildings belonging to Hertford College. It was in New College Lane that Lord Peter Wimsey, for the promised last time, proposed to Harriet Vane with the very academic "Placetne, magistra?"

New College Lane leads into Queen's Lane and on into the High. This route will bring you to the colleges that were passed as you walked along the High and later Long Wall Street. Unless you very much want to explore them, avoid the turning and continue along Catte Street.

Walk along the right-hand side of Catte Street. Next to the Sheldonian is the Bodleian Library; the Divinity School here is open and contains notable volumes including illustrated manuscripts that date back to the Middle Ages. The Bodleian contains over two million volumes. It is entered through the Old School Quad. In Robinson's *Landscape with Dead Dons*, as Nicholas Flower entered the Old School Quadrangle he concluded that Balboa Tomlin was really a "stupid cow" of the type that would never get over the novelty of calling a don by his first name. When Flower entered the Bodleian, he inhaled deeply; "the smell was like a cupboard full of old boots."

Flower headed up the wooden staircase to the Duke Humphrey, the most ancient section of the library with its emblazoned ceiling. He finally settled down to read in a seat by a window overlooking Exeter Garden.

In *The Dead of Jericho*, Morse canvassed Canal Reach in the guise of one doing research for the Bodleian Archives.

In *Gaudy Night,* Harriet Vane chased the Shrewsbury ghost by night and slept in the Bodleian by day.

Next to the Bodleian is the Radcliffe Camera. Built in the mid-1700s during the heyday of Palladian design, it looks most impressive. The domed circular structure stands alone in its own patch of green grass. Today the Camera, which means "chamber," is used as a Bodleian reading room.

Nicholas Flower, in Robert Robinson's *Landscape with Dead Dons* went to the Radcliffe Camera to read *Paradise Lost,* but the only available copy had double columns and small print, so he sat and stared at it, while smelling the floor polish and the radiators.

In Dorothy L. Sayers's *Gaudy Night* Lord Peter Wimsey came to the Radcliffe Camera and found Harriet Vane working in the Camera's circular chamber with other silent readers. She followed him to the roof, where the shining city of Oxford glistened before them.

Continue to the intersection of Catte Street and High Street and turn right into High Street staying on the left side of the street. You will pass All Souls College on the way. In Anthony Price's *The Alamut Ambush,* Minister David Llewelyn's car was taken from the Radcliffe Square just next to All Souls College. (All Souls has no students, only fellows.) Llewelyn was dining at All Souls with intelligence officer Colonel Shapiro.

In *Landscape with Dead Dons,* Nicholas Flower was whistling as he turned into the High and walked briskly toward the Cornmarket, dodging shoppers on his way to the Bodleian when he realized that the course he was taking was a roundabout one.

At Catte and High Street you will come to the University Church of St. Mary the Virgin, where C. S. Lewis preached. This section of the High will walk you past Brasenose College on the right. John Buchan, author of *The Thirty-Nine Steps* and other thrillers, came to Brasenose in 1897 from Glasgow University.

Miss Catherine Edgeley from Summerton House, who played bridge with Anne Scott in Dexter's *The Dead of Jericho,* was an undergraduate at Brasenose.

When Archer's Stephen Bradley and Harvey Metcalfe walked past Brasenose, Stephen explained that the name actually meant "brass nose" and that the original brass nose was a thirteenth-century sanctuary knocker still mounted in the hall.

Stephen and Harvey then turned right toward Lincoln College, as James, who was hidden in the entrance to Jesus College, quickly advised Robin. The elaborate plan of revenge was beginning to unfold. Coming from Lincoln College, Stephen and Harvey met Robin in the guise of the Vice-Chancellor. Harvey was so impressed by Robin's flattery that he invited both Robin and Stephen to tea at the Randolph.

Continue along High Street to the next street, which is Turl, the one down which Stephen and Harvey walked. At the corner of Turl and High is the Mitre. It is no longer a hotel but a Berni Inn that serves meals as well as teas and drinks. It was at the Mitre that Peter Wimsey stayed in *Gaudy Night*.

Chief Inspector Morse in Colin Dexter's *The Dead of Jericho*, after declining the Master of Lonsdale's invitation to lunch, walked from the Mitre along the curve of the High up to the Carfax.

Continue to follow Stephen Bradley and Harvey Metcalfe by turning right into Turl Street and walking north past the back of the Covered Market on your left, across Market Street. Continue on past Jesus College on your left and Lincoln and Exeter Colleges on your right. Jesus College was the location of the garden party to celebrate "Encaenia" at the end of Trinity Term. All the notables of the university gather to enjoy champagne, strawberries and cream at Jesus College. Turn left into Broad Street and cross to the far side. Trinity College, where detective writer Ronald Knox was a Fellow in 1910, will be facing you to the right; to your left is Balliol. After you turn into the Broad you will walk toward Balliol. This will bring you again to the historic Church of St. Mary Magdalen, which is located on an island between St. Giles and Magdalen Street. There was a church on this site in Saxon times, attached to the Priory of St. Frideswide, which is now Christ Church. No trace of the ancient church remains but this is a logical location for the Church of St. Frideswide in Colin Dexter's *Service of All the Dead.*

Turn right into Magdalen Street and cross to its far (west) side. At the next corner turn left into Beaumont Street. The Randolph Hotel is on the left, the Martyrs' Memorial is behind you, and on your right is the Ashmolean Museum. Follow Beaumont Street to Worcester Street. On the right is the site of Beaumont Palace, which Henry I built and where King John was probably born, as was his romantic brother, Richard I (the Lion-Heart), who was served by Robin Hood and his men.

Cross Worcester Street and turn left. Follow Worcester Street to Hythe Bridge Street, where you will turn right. Cross Upper Fisher Row and follow Hythe Bridge Street to where it Y's into Rewly Road and Hollybush Row. Angle to your left around the Royal Oxford Hotel into Park End Street. Follow Park End to the turning on the right into the British Rail Station where, in Colin Dexter's *Last Bus to Woodstock,* the train lingered and Sue kissed David "fully and freely as he leaned from the window of an empty carriage." End the first walk here.

OXFORD II WALK

The second Oxford walk also begins at the train station, and leads from there into the area known as North Oxford.

Mrs. Walsh-Atkins, in Colin Dexter's *Service of All the Dead,* lived amid the scent of lavender and silver polish in a home for elderly gentlewomen in North Oxford. Tossa Barber, in *Mourning Raga* by Ellis Peters, had undergraduate "digs" in a "genteelly decaying corner" of North Oxford. It is where the goings-on in Barbara Pyms's delightful study of the uncertain, *Crampton Hodnet,* took place. Colin Dexter's Detective Inspector Morse lives at 45 The Flats, Banbury Road, where he usually returned rather dolefully after dealing with the darker side of man's nature. Peter Lovesey's Merton don, Bonner-Hill, and his actress-wife lived in North Oxford in *Swing, Swing Together.* A number of mystery stories have occurred in the northern part of the city, particularly in Jericho and along Woodstock and Banbury Roads. Edmund Crispin's moving toyshop turned up on Banbury Road after moving from its original location on the Iffley Road (see Oxford I Walk).

Walk down from the railway station to Park End Street, turn left and take Park End to the junction, where it curves around the Royal Oxford Hotel. Rewley Road will be to the left and Hollybush Row to the right. Follow the curve into Hythe Bridge Street on the right to Worcester Street, where you will turn left. Follow Worcester Street past the college; its renowned gardens will be on your left. Along here, Worcester Street becomes Walton Street. Soon you will realize that the university area has been left behind. The red-brick Clarendon Press Centre will be on your right. It is a former Oxford University Press Building as is the Clarendon Building on The Broad (see Oxford I Walk). It was here that Detective Chief Inspector Morse of the Thames Valley Police, who, by his own admission, was "blessed with the most brilliant brain in Oxford," was heading when he detoured into Jericho and searched out the street called Canal Reach, where Anne Scott lived.

Jericho is probably the original of Thomas Hardy's "Beersheeba," where Jude the Obscure found his lodgings. A largely residential district created for the people who worked for the Oxford University Press, it was the first industrial community in the city. It stretches along the west side of Walton Street, and is bordered on the south by Great Clarendon Street, by Juxon Street on the north, and the Oxford Canal on the west, where pleasure boats are now tied up on what, when it was completed in 1790, was intended to bring new life to the river by linking it to the industrial north. This was one of the first of the English canals, a forerunner of the Industrial Revolution. Today an occasional barge will slip along the waterway, but for the most part it is the amateur boatman who holds sway. The Isis lock, where the Canal and the Thames connect, has for many years been a favorite place for suicides. The lock has steep sides that rule out a change of mind.

The neighborhood is made up of small hotels and private residences. The buildings are of brick in a variety of colors, and the street has a cozy, Georgian feel. Just beyond the Clarendon

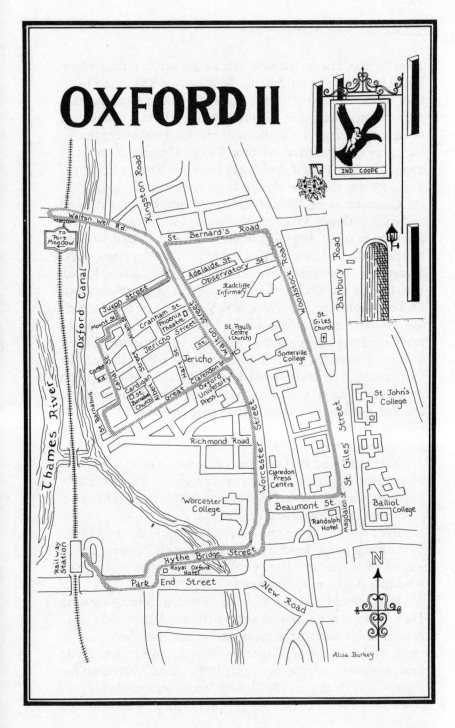

OXFORD II

IND COOPE

To Port Meadow

Walton Well Rd.

Kingston Road

Oxford Canal

Thames River

St. Bernard's Road

Adelaide St.

Observatory St.

Radcliffe Infirmary

Juxon Street

Mount St.

Cranham St.

Phoenix Theatre

St. Paul's Centre (Church)

Woodstock Road

Banbury Road

St. Giles Church

Jericho Street

Walton Street

Somerville College

Jericho

Cardigan Street

Canal St.

Combe Rd.

St. Barnabas St.

St. Barnabas Church

Albert St.

Great Clarendon St.

Hart St.

Clarendon's

Oxford University Press

St. John's College

St. Giles' Street

Magdalen St.

Richmond Road

Worcester Street

Clarendon Press Centre

Worcester College

Beaumont St.

Balliol College

Randolph Hotel

Railway Station

Hythe Bridge Street

Royal Oxford Hotel

Park End Street

New Road

N

Alisa Burkey

Press Centre, but on the west side of the street, is the turning to the left for Richmond Road. It was down Richmond Road that Morse hurried after the chairman of the Oxford Book Association mentioned to him that there was a traffic jam outside the Clarendon Institute (Press Centre), where the association had gathered to hear Dame Helen Gardner talk about *The New Oxford Book of English Verse.* The traffic tie-up, the chairman said, was due to some trouble in Jericho.

Continue along Walton Street, crossing Richmond Road and passing through the neighborhood, which now consists of a variety of small shops—antiques, books, etc.—and services, hairdressers, groceries, small restaurants. The street curves and brings you, on your left, to a mammoth pile of darkened stone that houses the Oxford University Press, a much-respected Oxford institution. The Press, which is owned by the Chancellor, Masters, and Scholars of the University, prints anything from a visiting card to an encyclopedia. It prints more Bibles, in more languages, than any other press. Together with the Cambridge Press and Her Majesty's Printers, the Press has a monopoly right to print the Authorized Version of the Bible and the Book of Common Prayer. Anyone who finds a misprint in one of its editions of the Authorized Version is entitled to a guinea reward.

Turn left just beyond the Press into Great Clarendon Street. Across Walton Street on your right St. Paul's Church, which is being converted into an arts center, stands at the top of Great Clarendon Street on the east.

Even when summer crowds swell college Oxford almost to the bursting point, Jericho goes about its daily business, which includes few tourists. The people who are about are the ones who live, work, and shop here.

Walk straight down Great Clarendon Street, crossing Hart, Albert, and Canal Streets. Between Albert and Canal, School Court leads off to the right. Beyond the school you can catch a glimpse of St. Barnabas Church. Somewhere along here, approximately twenty yards before Canal Street, on the right, Colin Dexter, in *The Dead of Jericho,* located the shop of A. Grimes, Locksmith. From outside his shop, Walters looked up Great Clarendon Street to Walton Road and the "temple-like" Church of St. Paul's at the head of the street.

At the corner of St. Barnabas Street turn right. But before you do, take the opportunity to walk into the boat yard just off St. Barnabas Street and get your first unrestricted view of the canal with its assortment of colorful houseboats. The boat yard, Black Prince Narrow Boats Limited, stretches north behind the area where Canal Reach once was. Garden walls, most of them lower than the one behind No. 9, which Morse scaled, help re-create the scene of Morse's surreptitious visit to No. 9 in *The Dead of Jericho*. There have been alterations in the area since Dexter set his mystery here. Now turn right into Cardigan Street, which runs just in front of St. Barnabas Church.

When Morse made his first, belated trip to No. 9 Canal Reach, he drove down Great Clarendon Street and turned into Canal Street. He found a parking spot "beneath the towering Italianate campanile of St. Barnabas Church" in a stretch of road bordering the canal. It was marked for restricted parking.

Follow Cardigan Street to Canal Street and turn left. Just before Victor Street there is a telephone kiosk, probably the one in which Morse noticed the odor of fish. You will cross Victor Street to your left. The parking ticket that was paid from the Lloyd's Bank account of Mr. C. Richards was for a violation at the corner of Victor and Canal, thus affording Inspector Morse with a clue in *The Dead of Jericho*.

On the left, after you cross Combe Road you will see the block of new flats that replaced Canal Reach. Walk to the end of the flats and turn left. Walk up the stairs and on to the bridge over the canal. Stop in the middle of the bridge and look back along the Canal Reach replacement flats to the old brick wall at Combe Road. This is the type of wall that figured in *The Dead of Jericho*.

Return to Canal Street and zigzag to the right into Mount Place, which becomes Mount Street. Follow Mount Street to Juxon Street. Here you will turn left and find Lucy's iron foundry, where George Jackson, who lived at No. 10 Canal Reach and kept watch on No. 9, worked for forty-two years before "becoming redundant." Now turn back right on Juxon, which you will follow back to Walton. This is a pretty residential street filled with red-brick houses.

At Walton turn left and walk up Walton Street to Walton Well Road across the two bridges to the carpark before Port Meadow.

The blackmail letter that Charles Richards received in *The Dead of Jericho* directed him to go down Walton Street and turn into Walton Well Road. He was to follow Walton Well Road over little Canal bridge, and then over the railroad bridge. When he came to the parking area off to the left, he was to turn around and face Port Meadow. The money was to be put in the fifth willow tree from the left, where he would find a big hole.

Return to Walton Well Road, retracing your steps. At Walton Street, turn right and walk on the right-hand side of the road, past the Phoenix cinema (which was playing *Sex in the Suburbs* when Morse noticed it), back to Great Clarendon Street. This gives you an opportunity to stop at one of the restaurants or pubs along the way. Just past the cinema is the Jericho Tavern with its inn sign that reads, "and the King said/ tarry at Jericho til your beards be grown."

There is a grocery at the corner of Cardigan Street and Walton Street where Jackson bought a loaf of brown bread. At Great Clarendon Street, cross Walton Street and walk back north past the locksmiths on the corner of Walton and Observatory Street. E. Smith and Co., Locksmiths Ltd. probably served as a model for A. Grimes in Great Clarendon Street.

Continue up Walton Street and cross Adelaide Street. Turn right at St. Bernard's Road and follow it to Woodstock Road. In Amanda Cross's *The Question of Max,* Kate Fanzler biked up the Woodstock Road and turned left into St. Bernard's Road, where she found Phyllis's house on the left, a third of the way down. It had the only uncut lawn. Phyllis and her husband, Hugo, were spending a year in England while he worked at All Souls College. (See Oxford I Walk.)

At Woodstock Road turn right. On the right is the Horse and Jockey Pub, where Jackson turned right on his flight home in *The Dead of Jericho*. Walk on past the telephone kiosk to

Radcliffe Infirmary on the right. (C. S. Lewis was once a patient here, as was his brother Warren.) In Edmund Crispin's *Swan Song,* the young singer named David died here after being poisoned.

On the right is Somerville College, where Margaret Thatcher was educated, and before her, Dorothy L. Sayers. Somerville served as the model for Shrewsbury College in *Gaudy Night,* although Sayers located it, rather apologetically, on Balliol's cricket ground. Kate Fanzler cycled past Somerville and was almost knocked down by a truck that lurched out of the Radcliffe Infirmary.

Go through the gate and down the long entry lane to the quad. The library and the building where Sayers stayed are on the right. Look around Somerville and admire the well-kept grounds and the mellowed stone of the attractive buildings.

Come out of Somerville and continue on Woodstock Road past St. Giles Church (which is possibly the model for the church of St. Frideswide in Colin Dexter's *Service of All the Dead*) and the War Memorial into St. Giles Street. Mrs. Walsh-Atkins hurried toward St. Giles after services at St. Frideswide.

Across from St. Giles is the Lamb and the Flag Pub. In Sayers's *Gaudy Night,* Harriet Vane walked from Somerville College one evening and found a group of undergraduates climbing the trees of St. Giles. Among them was Mr. Pomfret, who cornered her and proposed to her "in the shadow of the big horse chestnut by the Lamb and the Flag."

The Eagle and the Child Pub, known as "the bird and baby," which has associations with the Inklings, including metaphysical thriller writer Charles Williams, is on the right. Directly across the street is the Lamb and the Flag pub, where your authors and American crime writer Caroline Heilbron (aka Amanda Cross), the creator of Kate Fanzler, spent a most enjoyable evening quaffing Guinness and discussing the state of the world in general and the state of the mystery in particular.

Follow St. Giles to Beaumont Street and turn right into Beaumont. On the corner across the street is the Randolph Hotel (see Oxford I Walk), and to the right you will be walking along the Ashmolean Museum. Follow Beaumont Street to Worcester Street and go left, then turn right into Hythe Bridge Street. Follow Hythe Bridge Street to where it curves into Holly Bush. Angle to the left, around the Royal Oxford Hotel, into Park End Street. Follow Park End Street to the turning into the British Rail Station and so end your walk.

10

SALISBURY

BACKGROUND

The cathedral city of Salisbury had its beginning as an Iron Age Camp in a place called Sarum, now Old Sarum, two miles north of the present city. The old city was already in existence by the time the Romans arrived and fortified it. They called it Sorviodunum. After the Romans, it became a Saxon town called Searoburh; in the eleventh century a Norman castle and a cathedral were built there. There were frequent arguments between the cathedral clergy and the military. Physical conditions were harsh, for Sarum was dry and subject to fierce winds. In 1220 Bishop Poore decided that the cathedral and its Old Sarum site were too inconvenient. He laid the foundation for a new cathedral two miles south of Old Sarum, and built the present city of Salisbury. The new cathedral of St. Mary was built between 1220 and 1258, entirely in the Early English style; the graceful 404-foot tower was added in the next century. It is the tallest medieval spire in Europe.

Traditionally, the center of Salisbury is divided into two separate areas—the cathedral and the market place. Even today, this tradition persists and the gates to the Cathedral Close are locked each night.

The original City Charter of 1227, which was granted by Henry III, authorized Salisbury to hold a Tuesday market. This was soon increased to include Saturday as well. Salisbury continues to maintain its traditional market days. The market green is overlooked by lovely houses of medieval and Georgian architecture.

Many kings and queens have visited Salisbury. The Duke of Buckingham was executed there in 1483 for rebelling against Richard III. Salisbury was the site of some fighting during the Civil War. After the Battle of Worcester, Charles II hid nearby at Heale, while his escape was planned at the King's Arms in Salisbury. Later, he stayed in Salisbury to escape the plague in London. It was at Salisbury that James II put together an army to oppose his son-in-law, William of Orange.

Salisbury is rich in literary associations. In 1563, the year he was made Canon of Salisbury, John Foxe published his *Book of Martyrs*. Samuel Pepys, his wife, and assorted servants traveled to Salisbury from Hungerford in June 1668. They arrived after dark at the George Inn, where he "lay in a silke bed and had very good diet." The next morning, Pepys and the others found the town to be "a brave place." During visits to Salisbury from 1730 to 1734, Henry Fielding met his first wife, Charlotte Cradock. The house from which she eloped with him, a fine seventeenth-century building, is on The Friary south of Saint Ann Street. The poet Wordsworth visited Salisbury in 1793 on one of his many walking tours. Oliver Goldsmith's *Vicar of Wakefield* was first published there. Anthony Trollope's work for the post office took him to Salisbury, and in his autobiography he stated that "whilst wandering there on a mid-summer evening round the purlieus of the cathedral I conceived the story of *The Warden*." With Winchester, Salisbury forms the basis for Trollope's Barteshire novels. It is the Melchester of Thomas Hardy's Wessex novels and especially figures in *Jude the Obscure*.

Salisbury is mentioned in *Northanger Abbey* by Jane Austen. Mrs. Allen tells Mr. Tilney that Bath is a charming place and quickly adds that it has many good shops. She explains that although Salisbury also has fine shops, it is eight miles from her home and quite inconvenient to reach. On the other hand, Jessica Tregarth, the heroine of Elizabeth Peters's *The Camelot Caper,* was amazed that anyone could find something worthwhile in Salisbury's unexciting shops. She saw Salisbury as a sleepy little cathedral town.

In nearby Wilton, Wilton House, the elegant country mansion that was the home of Mary Herbert, Countess of Pembroke and sister to Sir Philip Sidney, is considered by many to be the most beautiful house of its kind in England. When Mary Herbert was in residence, it was a center for people involved in the arts. Sir Philip Sidney was a frequent visitor and did much of his writing there. (See Shrewsbury Walk.) Since then the house has been visited by many literary lights including Izaak Walton (who would walk to Salisbury twice weekly when he stayed at Wilton House), Edmund Spenser, Ben Jonson, Charles and Mary Lamb, Horace Walpole, and William Hazlitt.

Salisbury is also a recurrent location in Charles Dickens's *Martin Chuzzlewit.* Tom Pinch thought the city "a very desperate sort of place"; nevertheless, he strolled about the streets with the vague idea that "they teemed with all kinds of mystery and bedevilment." The day ended with him safely playing the organ in the cathedral.

Salisbury, especially its cathedral, is also often used by mystery authors. Michael Gilbert used it for the setting of his *Close Quarters;* like Hardy, he called it Melchester. Geoffrey Household used Salisbury Cathedral as the setting for his short story "Abner of the Porch." In Anthony Price's *Our Man in Camelot,* Major David Davies, USAF, who died under mysterious circumstances, had received a catalogue in the mail from James Barkham and Sons, New, Second-hand and Antiquarian Bookseller, Salisbury. In the same book, American secret agent Mosby Sheldon had had to sort out the various possible sites for the Battle of Badon. Salisbury made him think only of a tall spire. David Audley pointed out to him that

Winchester-Salisbury formed the north boundary of King Arthur country. Audley was convinced that British super-patriot Billy Bullitt had discovered that Major Davies had surmised that Badon Hill was in the region of Salisbury.

In Price's *Gunner Kelly,* the landlord of the Eight Bells at Duntisbury Royal claimed that he had no rooms to let, and directed West German secret agent Benedikt Schneider to Salisbury. In *Sergeant Ritchie's Conscience* by Frank Branston, Martin Tilt, the MP for the constituency of White Horse Vale, was identified as the owner of the car reported at the scene of the murder of young policeman Rodney James. A swift check revealed that the car had not long been in Tilt's hands and had not been registered in Tilt's name. Sergeants Ritchie and Gotobed were dispatched to the red-brick house that snuggled in a vale on Salisbury Plain, where the MP lived when not attending Parliament.

During the last years of his life, the prolific John Creasey lived at New Hall, Bodenham, near Salisbury. Creasey, who wrote over six hundred books, was cofounder, with Josephine Bell, of the Crime Writers Association. The Creasey Memorial Literary Museum is located in the Salisbury Library. Dorothy L. Sayers and Josephine Bell attended the Godolphin School in Salisbury before going on to university.

In William M. Green's *The Salisbury Manuscript,* a shady operator named Charles Ford had a secret rendezvous at a cottage on the Salisbury Plain near Old Sarum.

How to Get There

British Rail: from London, trains from Waterloo Station at hourly intervals; from Bath, trains from Manvers Street Station

Automobile: from London, take M3 to A30; from Bath, take A36

Length of Walk: 2½ miles

See map on page 212 for boundaries of this walk, and page 370 for a list of detectives and stories.

PLACES OF INTEREST

St. Mary's Cathedral. A magnificent example of later early English
style. The Library has one of the four existing copies of Magna
Carta, which was brought here for safekeeping around 1265.

Church of St. Thomas à Becket, St. Thomas Square. The men
working on the Cathedral and desiring a place to worship put
up a wooden chapel here in 1219. It was dedicated to St.
Thomas à Becket, the Archbishop of Canterbury who had
been murdered in his cathedral fifty years before. (See
Canterbury Walk.) The interior of St. Thomas is a fine
example of fifteenth-century splendor. The great Doom
Painting above the chancel arch is the church's world-famous
feature and is the largest existing wallpainting of the Last
Judgment. It dates from 1475 and was possibly the work of a
Flemish artist. It was whitewashed during the Reformation
and remained hidden until the nineteenth century.

Trinity Hospital, Trinity Street. Founded in 1379 by Agnes
Bottenham. Now an almshouse. The courtyard and the chapel
are open daily.

Poultry Cross, Butchers Row. The only one remaining of four
market crosses.

Hall of John Halle, New Canal. The ornate half-timbered facade
now forms the entrance to the city cinema.

Mompesson House, 53 Cathedral Close. Built in 1701, it has been
described as "the most perfect specimen of a small country
town house." Mompesson House is administered by the
National Trust. (Open May–September, Wednesday and
Saturday 2:30–6.)

Salisbury and South Wiltshire Museum, the King's House, 65
West Walk, Cathedral Close (0722) 332151. Displays include
models and relics from Stonehenge and Old Sarum, also local
history items. (Open weekdays 10–4.) Admission charge.

Old Sarum, two miles north of Salisbury. Take Castle Road.
Remains of the great earthwork and foundation of the first
cathedral.

Wilton House, on the A30 northwest of Salisbury. Buses from
outside the Cinema on New Canal Street. (Open April–

September, Tuesday–Saturday and Bank Holidays 11–6;
Sunday 2–6.) Admission charge.

Stonehenge. See Possible Side Trip at the end of this walk.

PLACES TO STAY/EAT

Red Lion Hotel, Milford Street (0722) 23334. A Best Western
Hotel. Parts of the modernized coaching inn date from 1320.
The Red Lion was the starting point for the *Salisbury Flying
Machine,* the nightly horse-drawn coach to London. The
antique-filled hotel offers warm hospitality in a traditional
English setting. Full meal service. Moderate.

Rose and Crown, Harnham Road, Harnham (0722) 27908. A
thirteenth-century building with a new wing. Hotel featured
in John Creasey's *Theft of Magna Carta.* Full meal service.
Moderate.

King's Arms Inn, St. John's Street (0722) 27629. A half-timbered
former coaching inn dating back to the building of the
Cathedral. Fireplaces in the King's Arms are made from the
same stone as the Cathedral. In *Theft of Magna Carta* by John
Creasey, Superintendent Roger West stayed here. Moderate.

Haunch of Venison Inn, Minster Street opposite the Poultry Cross
(0722) 22024. Fourteenth-century building. Moderate.

Bay Tree Restaurant, the High Street (next to W. H. Smith). The
upper stories belong to the Old George Inn, dating back to
1314. Good spot for morning coffee. Inexpensive.

The Tourist Information Centre in Fish Row (0722) 334956,
will assist you in finding lodging and will suggest places to eat.

SALISBURY WALK

Begin this walk at the Salisbury British Rail Station. Sue
Brideshead in Thomas Hardy's *Jude the Obscure* believed the
railway station had replaced the cathedral and other historic
buildings as the center of town life. When you leave the station, turn left. There will be a number of taxis waiting there

that may be hired to take you into town, or to Stonehenge, Old Sarum, or Wilton House.

The station fronts upon a wide paved area. Walk to the left along the sprawl of the station to Fisherton Street, where you will angle right. The railroad underpass will be to your left as you enter Fisherton Street. To the left under the underpass is Wilton Road and the police station where Roger West, in John Creasey's *Theft of Magna Carta,* threatened to take Sarah and Neil Stephenson for questioning after the disappearance of policewoman Linda Prell.

As you enter Fisherton Street, Dews Street will be to the right. Considerably south of here is Harnham Road (the A3094) with the Rose and Crown Hotel, which has a view across the watermeadow to the cathedral with its graceful spire. The view that Constable painted was also noted and admired by Frank Caldicott and Neil Stephenson as they plotted dark doings over dinner at the Rose and Briar (the Rose and Crown) in John Creasey's *Theft of Magna Carta.*

Cross to the right-hand side of Fisherton Street and walk past the assortment of antique shops toward High Street, where you will turn right. On the way, you will pass Griffin Court to the left, and also Malthouse Lane. The Maltings shopping precinct will also be to the left. Beyond the maltings is the main Salisbury carpark where, in Elizabeth Peters's *Camelot Caper,* David and Jess left their car on several occasions. Just before High Street you will come to the River Avon, one of four rivers that flow in or around Salisbury. As you cross the bridge, take time to notice the lovely symmetry of the houses that sweep along the river bank. At this point, Fisherton Street becomes Bridge Street. At the corner of Bridge Street and High Street, turn right. You are now in the midst of small shops, fast-food restaurants, and ancient inns.

In Elizabeth Peters's *The Camelot Caper,* Jessica Tregarth hurried along High Street on her way to Sunday service at the cathedral and the beginning of an adventure that would take her all over southern England.

Take High Street past New Canal Street on the left. Soon

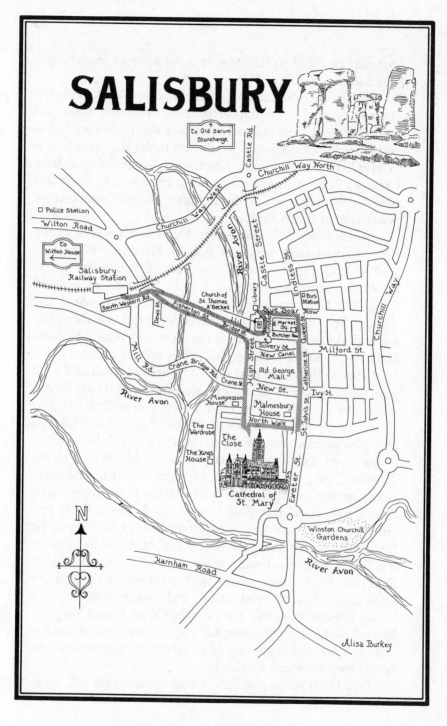

SALISBURY

To Old Sarum
Stonehenge

Castle Rd.

Churchill Way North

Police Station

Wilton Road

Churchill Way West

To
Wilton House

Salisbury
Railway Station

River Avon

Castle Street

Endless St.

Bus
Station

Library

Church of
St. Thomas
A'Becket

South Western Rd.

Fisherton St.

Dews Rd.

Bridge St.

Blue Boar Row

Market
Sq.

Butcher Row

Queen St.

Milford St.

Mill Rd.

Crane Bridge Rd.

Crane St.

High Street

Silvery St.

New Canal

Old George
Mall

St. Catherine St.

Churchill Way

River Avon

Mompesson
House

New St.

Ivy St.

St. John's St.

The
Wardrobe

Malmesbury
House

North Walk

The Kings
House

The
Close

Exeter St.

Cathedral of
St. Mary

Winston Churchill
Gardens

N

Harnham Road

River Avon

Alisa Burkey

212

you will see the heavy old timbers from the George Inn that mark the entrance to Old George Mall. Just beyond Old George Mall is the Bay Tree Restaurant, the upper story of which belonged originally to the much earlier Old George Inn, which dates back to 1314. Here diarist Samuel Pepys in 1668 "lay in a silke bed and had very good diet."

The next day he and his party did some local sightseeing and returned to the Old George. When his bill was presented, he found it so "exorbitant" that he removed his party to a cheaper inn where the beds were "good but lousy, which made us merry."

The Bay Tree Restaurant is an excellent spot for morning coffee or afternoon tea. The dining room is low-ceilinged and heavy-timbered. The assorted wooden tables and the cheerful bustle of the staff add to its charm. In Elizabeth Peters's *The Camelot Caper*, after their visit with the canon, Jessica and David had tea in a High Street tea shop, which may have been the Bay Tree.

Continue on High Street past Crane Street on the right and New Street on the left. On the corner of High Street and New Street is Mitre House, where the bishops robe for their enthronement. It is a tall, medieval building with a mitre painted on it. Bishop Poore's house stood on this site.

On the corner of High Street and Crane Street is a fourteenth-century house that is now Beach's Bookshop. Just beyond this is the Perpendicular-style gateway (North Gate) to the Cathedral Close. The gate, which once had a portcullis, protected the bishops from rebellious citizens. The gate has a royal coat of arms on the north side and a statue of Edward VII on the south.

The close at Salisbury has been called the finest in England. It is an important part of the cathedral and its life. Three sides of the close have walls made from the stones of Old Sarum. The fourth side is protected by the River Avon. The gates are closed and locked at eleven o'clock each night.

The first houses in the close were built at the same time as the cathedral; others were added as needed. The result is a rich blend of Tudor, Jacobean, and Georgian architecture. Four of the houses are open to visitors: Mompesson, the Wardrobe, the King's House, and Malmesbury.

Once inside the gate, on the left, at Nos. 39 to 34, is the College of Matrons, which was probably designed by Christopher Wren. It is a long, low, red-brick building with a cupola built in the middle over an assortment of embellishments including a crowned lion. It was intended to house clergy widows with the admonition that they live "soberly" and "respectably." The widows were forbidden to go out without an approved escort, and the gates were locked each evening at 8 P.M. If one of the widows chose to remarry, she was excluded from the college.

In *Close Quarters,* Michael Gilbert's tale of anonymous letters, broadsheets, comic flags, and murder that intruded on the quiet of a cathedral close, Mrs. Judd, the relict of old Canon Judd, who received one of the anonymous letters, was the type of woman who lived at Matron College. In Gilbert's book, the college is dispensed with and Mrs. Judd lives instead in a close cottage, to the discomfort of all.

Opposite Matron's College is The Green. On the right of The Green is Mompesson House. It was designed for Charles Mompesson, and probably was built by Wren, c. 1701. The interior features a richly carved oak staircase and excellent plaster decoration.

Like most English cathedrals, Melchester (in Gilbert's *Close Quarters)* had its own resident choir school. It was housed in two fine Queen Anne buildings located in the southwest corner of the close.

Although the houses around the close will draw your attention, the real focal point is the cathedral itself, set in its wide sweeping lawns facing the river. The best view of the cathedral is from the northeast corner of the close. Augustus Pugin, the nineteenth-century architect, was standing there when he remarked, "Well, I have travelled all over Europe in search of architecture, and I have seen nothing like this."

In *Theft of Magna Carta* when John Creasey's Superintendent Roger West came into the close he walked from the northeastern corner toward the southern porch and the western doors, admiring the carved figures of saints and patriarchs that had survived Cromwell's destruction.

The cathedral exterior, except for the upper tower and spire, is built in Early English Gothic. It is austerely beautiful, although the west front is richly ornamented with statues. The entrance will be somewhere along the west front. (The cathedral is undergoing much restoration work.) Before going inside, examine the bottom row of statues near the west door. There, holding a spireless model of the cathedral, is Bishop Poore, the illegitimate son of a bishop of Winchester, whose idea Salisbury Cathedral was.

The interior of the cathedral is considered by some critics to be rather cold-looking. Indeed, the harsh effect of the shafts of polished black marble against the gray Purbeck marble columns would be warmer with the softening effect of the old stained glass that was removed by the eighteenth-century "restorer," James Wyatt. Wyatt, who was called "the Destroyer," streamlined the interior of the cathedral by clearing it of its medieval "clutter." He removed a number of tombs, and the ones not destroyed were moved to form two long lines on either side of the nave. He included among his other "improvements" the lime-washing of ancient paintings and the sweeping away of two chantry chapels, the High Altar, and the choir screen. At the end of his destruction he received a congratulatory visit from King George III and the royal family.

In William M. Green's *The Salisbury Manuscript*, Casey Ford dreamed that her dead husband, Charles, was "as cold and smooth and unyielding as one of the polished marble effigies on the tombs in Salisbury Cathedral."

At the end of the north aisle is the still-working mechanism of the fourteenth-century clock, the oldest of its kind in England.

The Cloisters, which are approached from the southwest corner of the south transept, are thirteenth-century. The chapter house dates from the same period. It has ribbed vaulting springing from a single column in the middle, and features a fascinating series of sculptures from the Old Testament.

In Gilbert's *Close Quarters*, "Melchester Cathedral," like the other English cathedrals, is a tourist attraction, especially during the summer months. The tourists found all they could wish for at Melchester with its long, elegant nave, transepts, and choir, the beautiful Lady Chapel, the stately cloisters, and the ancient chapter house.

In *The Camelot Caper*, after a half hour spent wandering about the fascinating interior of the cathedral, where she marveled at the "stiff effigies of mailed knights," Jess was standing in the center of the chapter house when she was accosted by the men who had been shadowing her and asked to turn over her grandfather's ring. Jessica didn't understand why the men wanted her ring, but she knew that they meant business. When the bells set forth a cacophony of ringing to signal the start of the service, she slipped inside, still followed by her pursuers. At the offering she dropped the ring into the maroon velvet collection bag presented by the verger.

Creasey's Roger West found green grass and delicate arches in the Cloisters, as well as a cedar of Lebanon with its branches intertwined like the fingers of lovers with those of another tree.

Along the east walk of the Cloisters is the Cathedral Library. Among its wealth of historic treasures is one of the four existing copies of Magna Carta. In *Theft of Magna Carta*, Roger West was told about the Sarum Magna Carta by Tom Batten, Detective-Sergeant of the Wiltshire Constabulary, who had a special love for the cathedral and all its treasures. As Caldicott and Stephenson's anticipated theft of Magna Carta took shape, their major concern was just how to overcome the library security system. They solved their problem by forcing Batten to assist them in the break-in.

Returning to the walk, leave the cathedral the way you entered and turn right. Follow the walk back toward North Gate. At the first walk to the right (North Walk), turn right and follow it to St. Ann's Gate. Malmesbury House, which adjoins the gate on the left, was formerly the home of the Earl of Malmesbury. From it Lord Coventry, a supporter of King Charles II, signaled across St. John Street to other supporters in the King's Arms Inn. At the time, Charles, who was fleeing from Cromwell's forces, was hiding at Heale House near Almsbury. (See Dorchester/Charmouth Walk.)

Leave the close through St. Ann's Gate. Handel gave his first public English concert in a room above this gateway. Turn left on St. John Street, where you will see the historic King's Arms Inn. Inspector Roger West stood at the window of this small inn and looked at the cathedral spire. Its magic lured him out of the hotel and along to Queen Ann's Gate in Creasey's *Theft of Magna Carta*. Beyond the King's Arms is the imposing pillared portico of the White Hart Hotel. In *Theft of Magna Carta* the Leech Gallery exhibited a number of paintings at the Hart (White Hart) Hotel prior to the auction, which drew dealers from all over Britain. Detective-Officer Linda Prell was covering the exhibit when she was kidnapped.

Unlike most cathedral cities, Salisbury did not begin as a village because the cathedral preceded the town. Bishop Poore was able, therefore, to plan a well-organized area beside the cathedral, where people could live and work in comfort. The area consists of a rectangular grid system of five streets running parallel from north to south and six running from east to west, resulting in about twenty squares or chequers of roughly 38 × 17 yards each. This is the area you have entered.

Cross New Street to the left and Ivy Street to the right, where St. John Street becomes Catherine Street. Continue along Catherine Street to New Canal on the left and Milford Street on the right. Around the corner and on the left on New Canal Street is the Odeon Cinema. The foyer of the cinema is called the Hall of John Halle and incorporates the hall, which was built around 1470. If the cinema is open, go inside and take a look at architect Pugin's 1834 restoration. The hall is lofty, with a magnificent roof of foliated woodwork. There are three enormous mullioned windows and a chimneypiece that displays the arms and the merchant's mark of John Halle. In *The Camelot Caper* by Elizabeth Peters, David explained to Jessica that the "fifteenth-century house that is now a cinema" was on the must-see list. The historic Red Lion Inn is down Milford Street on the right-hand side of the street.

Catherine Street now becomes Queen Street. Many of Salisbury's older shops are located in this general area.

Number 8 Queen Street is one of Salisbury's fine old buildings. The early-fifteenth-century half-timbered house is now a shop specializing in pottery, china, and glass. Opposite No. 8 is the Guildhall, which was presented to the city in 1795 by Lord Rednor as a replacement for the Elizabethan Council House, which had been severely damaged by fire. The "new" building has tall pillars and enormous arched windows. It contains a number of interesting portraits by Lely, Hoppner, and Raeburn. At one time the Assizes were held here, but today the Guildhall is used for the Magistrates' Courts and for social functions.

Follow Queen Street a short distance to Fish Row on the left. Here on the corner is the Tourist Information Centre. The medieval buildings that house the shops in Fish Row put one in mind of the famous Shambles in York or the Lanes in Brighton. (See Brighton Walk.) Other street names in the area such as Butcher Row and Oatmeal Row, suggest that this was once a sort of medieval supermarket. Continue along Queen Street to the Market Place on your left. In *Theft of Magna Carta,* Roger West found, in Market Square, the shop where policewoman Linda Prell had bought the suit that she was wearing when she disappeared.

At Blue Boar Row on the north side of the Market Place, Queen Street becomes Endless Street. Just up Endless Street on the right is the bus station where Jessica Tregarth in Elizabeth Peters's *The Camelot Caper* fled from the men who terrified her in the cathedral. She caught the bus from Platform Six without the slightest idea where she was going.

Casey Ford, in William M. Green's *The Salisbury Manuscript,* stayed at the Wild Boar Inn.

Turn left into Blue Boar Row and walk to the Salisbury Library on the northwest corner of Blue Boar Row and Castle Street. As you pass Debenhams department store, notice the wall plaque. It marks the beheading for treason of the Duke of Buckingham, which took place here in 1483. He was a cousin of Richard III, whom Josephine Tey investigated in *The*

Daughter of Time. In 1556, Lord Stourton was hanged here for the murder of two men. Stourton's noose was a silken cord in concession to his noble birth. Strangely enough, Stourton's tomb is in the cathedral.

Opposite the execution site was the whipping post, pillory, and stocks. The stocks were last used in 1858. Today on the site there is a statue of a Victorian gentleman, Henry Fewcett, a Salisbury native. He is wearing a frock coat and carrying his top hat. Although blinded as a young man, he went on to become a Member of Parliament as well as Postmaster-General.

Enter the library and head up the stairs for a visit to the John Creasey Literary Museum to see the Creasey Collection of Contemporary Art, which opened in September 1980.

Creasey, who lived from 1908 until 1973, was the most prolific of all detective-story writers. He wrote over six hundred books under twenty-eight pseudonyms.

J. D. Hilesbeck and Lettie Winterbottom, trying to solve the disappearance of Stonehenge in Leela Cutter's *Who Stole Stonehenge?* found that the Institute for Innovative Celtic Studies didn't appear in the *Index of British Institutes* at the Salisbury Public Library. They had discovered that the society had a barge on the canal the night Stonehenge was stolen. After coming upon *The Journal of Innovative Celtic Studies,* Lettie and J.D. settled down in the library to read through the back issues of the journal. Visit the pleasant periodicals reading room on the first (second to U.S. readers) floor at the back.

After leaving the library, turn right and take Minster Street, which angles past St. Thomas Square, back to Bridge Street. The Church of St. Thomas à Becket is located in St. Thomas Square. The church was founded by the builders of the cathedral. In *The Camelot Caper,* David told Jess that another "must-see" was St. Thomas with its remarkable "Doom" painting. On the way you will pass the Poultry Cross on the left and the Haunch of Venison Pub on the right. The pub's history goes back to about 1320, although the present building dates from the fifteenth century. In one of the first-floor rooms is a rather grisly relic, a mummified hand holding some eighteenth-century playing cards. It was discovered during a 1905 remodeling job. The Poultry Cross at the junction of Minster and Silver Streets is the last of four market crosses. It is still in use on Market Days—Tuesdays and Saturdays.

In *Theft of Magna Carta* by John Creasey, Caldicott, one of the brains behind the planned theft, assured Inspector Roger West that on the day policewoman Linda Prell disappeared, he, Caldicott, had spent time in the cathedral, had lunch at the Haunch of Venison, and then had walked to the station. Turn right into Bridge Street, which shortly becomes Fisherton Street, and follow it to the train station, where you will end your walk. In *Theft of Magna Carta,* Frank Caldicott protestingly caught the train back to London.

POSSIBLE SIDE TRIP

Stonehenge

Located on the Salisbury Plain off the A345, ten miles north of Salisbury and thirty-five miles southeast of Bath. You may reach Stonehenge by car, or by bus or taxi from Salisbury's British Rail Station.

The origin of Stonehenge is still shrouded in mystery. One of the world's most puzzling monuments, it consists of a circular grouping of massive standing stones that were erected between the Late Neolithic and Middle Bronze ages. Speculation continues as to the purpose of the stone circle; it may have been an astronomical temple or calendar, a center for sun worship, a Druidic religious center, a palace, a trade center, or even a royal tomb, as Mary Stewart suggests in *The Crystal Cave.* Since its origin and purpose and appearance are all mysterious, and outrageous speculation is the order of the day, Stonehenge makes a perfect setting for a mystery story. For instance, did Merlin build it by magic? Edward Rutherfurd, in his epic novel *Sarum,* speculates about the origin of Stonehenge and selects the theories that suit his purpose.

In *Murder in the Queen's Armes,* Aaron Elkins's "bone-detective," Dr. Gideon Oliver, attempts to explain the dilemma behind the origin of the advanced Wessex culture that overran the earlier Beaker culture: ". . . the Beakers being the last of the Neolithic people, the ones who built Stonehenge."

In *The Camelot Caper* by Elizabeth Peters, as David and Jessica escaped from Cousin John across the countryside, "The moon threw their shadows along the grass ahead of them, strange elongated caricatures knobby with the unevenness of the ground." Soon, on the horizon they made out an irregular silhouette. At first Jessica thought it was a modern factory or a ruined castle, and it was David who realized that they had come upon Stonehenge. It was not long before they were startled by a ragged chorus of chanting men, and they met the Supreme and Exalted Eminent Archpriest of the Mystical Order of Sunworshipers, Sam Jones. After lavishly partaking of mead, a slighty intoxicated Jess and David were returned to their car by Sam and his crew.

Leela Cutter's thoroughly enjoyable, humorous tale, *Who Stole Stonehenge?,* began with mysterious goings-on and glowing lights on the Salisbury Plain. It was J. D. Hilesbeck who discovered that Stonehenge was actually gone. It took all the talent Lettie Winterbottom could muster to get to the bottom of what had actually happened.

In William M. Green's *The Salisbury Manuscript,* Charley Ford, who had a rendezvous in an old cottage on the Salisbury Plain, burned to death there under mysterious circumstances, leaving a manuscript with clues to his hidden treasure for his ex-wife Casey.

Stonehenge was also the "heathen temple" where Tess was found sleeping by the police in Thomas Hardy's *Tess of the D'Urbervilles.*

The walk around Stonehenge will put you in the mood of the place. The best time to visit is a damp, cold, mist-shrouded day when the ancient stones will best work their magic on you, and perhaps will suggest a mystery of your own.

Stonehenge is open March 15–October 15, Monday–Saturday 9:30–6:30, Sunday 2–6:30; April–September, Sunday 9:30–6:30; October 16–March 14, Monday–Saturday 9:30–4, Sunday 2–4. Closed Christmas Eve, Christmas Day, Boxing Day (December 26), New Year's Day. Admission charge.

11

SHREWSBURY

BACKGROUND

Shrewsbury, pronounced "Shrozebury" by native Salopians, is an ancient market town nearly encircled by the horseshoe curve of the River Severn. It is the county seat of Shropshire, located only twelve miles from Wales. Shrewsbury was first settled in the fifth century by people from the nearby city of Virconium after the Roman withdrawal from Britain. By the eighth century it was part of the Saxon kingdom of Mercia when the great earthwork fortification called Offa's Dyke was built to guard the Welsh border. Several historic churches like St. Chad's and St. Alkmund's were founded by the Saxons, as well as the small church of St. Peter's on the site of the future Benedictine abbey. Under the Saxon kings Shrewsbury was an important town; a royal mint was established here which existed for three hundred years.

The Norman Conquest in 1066 brought Baron Roger de Montgomery to Shrewsbury. He not only built a new castle on the site of the old Saxon fortifications, but also established the Abbey of St. Peter and St. Paul across the Severn, giving it great land and wealth. For centuries afterwards, the abbey and the town argued over markets, tolls, and fairs until the abbey was dissolved under Henry VIII in the sixteenth century. Henry I granted the town of Shrewsbury a royal charter, but under his daughter, Matilda, the castle was besieged and taken by her cousin, King Stephen. This period of Shrewsbury's history is chronicled in Ellis Peters's Brother Cadfael mysteries.

Throughout the Middle Ages, Shrewsbury's location made it an important outpost against the Welsh, with the result that it has a bloody history of sieges and battles. In 1283 Edward I used Shrewsbury as his headquarters to conquer Wales. The famous Battle of Shrewsbury between rebel Henry Percy (Hotspur) and his Welsh allies and the Lancastrian Henry IV was fought on July 21, 1403, just north of the town.

The town of Shrewsbury took the Yorkist (or White Rose) side in the Wars of the Roses. It supported first the Duke of York, then his sons, Edward IV and Richard III. Richard, Duke of York, the younger of the Princes in the Tower, was born here in 1473. But under Richard III, Thomas Mytton, the sheriff of Shropshire, had announced that Henry Tudor would enter Shrewsbury over his (dead) body. But when Henry appeared outside the gates on his way to fight Richard III for the crown at Bosworth Field, Mytton merely "lay down" on the Welsh Bridge, allowing Henry Tudor to step over him and enter Shrewsbury. By Tudor times Shrewsbury was not only an important traffic center for river trade, but also a prosperous market for wool, Welsh cloth, and weaving. Many of the town's historic "black-and-white"—or half-timbered—buildings date from this period.

Shrewsbury Grammar School, one of England's famous public schools, was founded by Tudor Edward VI in 1552. One of its famous sons was the Elizabethan poet-warrior Sir Philip Sidney. Sidney's father, Sir Henry, was President of the Court of the Marches, which ruled Wales for the king from nearby Ludlow. The four hundredth anniversary of Sir Philip's death was commemorated in 1986 by both Shrewsbury and Zutphen, the Dutch town where Sidney died in battle.

During Henry VIII's dissolution of the monasteries, the Abbey of St. Peter and St. Paul was taken over by the Crown. Later, during the seventeenth century's Civil War, its gentry were mostly Royalist. Charles I came here with his army under the command of his nephew, Prince Rupert of the Rhine, but Shrewsbury was finally captured by the Parliamentarians. The young Charles II came to Shrewsbury from Scotland, hoping to raise his standard there, but the Parliamentarian-controlled town would not surrender. As a result, after his defeat at the battle of Worcester, Charles II wandered about Shropshire in disguise until he managed to escape to Brighton and from there to exile in France. (See Brighton and Dorchester Walks.)

After the Restoration, Charles II granted the castle to the Earl of Bradford as a private residence. Shrewsbury became a social center, specializing in trades that catered to Society. By the eighteenth century, Shrewsbury's many handsome Georgian red-brick and stone houses had been built for the fashionable season.

Lord Clive of India, who added that subcontinent to the British empire, was mayor in 1762. Both Lord Hill, who served on the staff of the Duke of Wellington at Waterloo, and the young Benjamin Disraeli, the future prime minister, were MPs from Shrewsbury during the nineteenth century. The scientist Charles Darwin was born at Shrewsbury and attended Shrewsbury School at the time the writer Samuel Butler, author of *Erewhon,* was headmaster. Queen Victoria paid the school an official visit when she was thirteen.

During one of his several visits to Shrewsbury, Charles Dickens stayed at the Lion Hotel in Wyle Cop, describing its strange little rooms and ceilings he could touch with his hands, in a town that was all "downhill and slantwise" and filled with black-and-white houses. Shrewsbury's quaint, old-world look made it the perfect backdrop for the television production of Charles Dickens's *A Christmas Carol.*

Shrewsbury is best known to mystery buffs as the site of Ellis Peters's medieval and modern detective stories, written by Edith Pargeter, who lives in nearby Telford. But the Shrewsbury area was also the home of Victorian Stanley Weyman, whose historical romances were the model for those of Anthony Hope and Raphael Sabatini. Weyman wrote *Shrewsbury* about the period of the Civil War. A modern writer, Mary

Webb, who was related to Sir Walter Scott, also wrote about Shropshire.

Josephine Bell, cofounder with John Creasey of the British Crime Writers Association, grew up near Shrewsbury. Bell went to Godolphin School in Salisbury with Dorothy L. Sayers. She set *Trouble at Wrexin Farm* near the Wrexin, an ancient Shropshire hill fort, and *Murder on the Medical Board* in Shornford (Shrewsbury). Dorothy L. Sayers herself used the name of Shrewsbury for her fictional Oxford college in *Gaudy Night.*

In *Dark Side of the Street,* contemporary thriller writer Jack Higgins had Special Branch operative Chavasse follow the trail of the Baron, an international supplier of prison escapes. By using the organization's password, "Babylon," Chavasse picked up the trail of one "consignment" of escapees at the Shrewsbury home of medium Madame Rosa Hartman.

How to Get There

British Rail: Trains hourly from Euston Station, London. Trip takes nearly 3 hours. Passenger information Shrewsbury Station: (0743) 64041

Automobile: Take the M1, the M6, then A5 from London. Shrewsbury is 153 miles from London; 40 miles from Chester; 43 miles from Birmingham; 3 miles from Wroxeter (Virconium); 10 miles from Wellington (the Wrekin); 5 miles from Battlefield; 12 miles from Offa's Dyke (Welsh Border); 30 miles from Ludlow.

Length of Walk: 4.7 miles

See Side Trips to Battlefield, Wroxeter (Virconium), Ludlow, Attingham Park, the Wrekin, Ironbridge Gorge, Birmingham.

See map on page 231 for exact boundaries of this walk and page 371 for list of sleuths and stories referred to.

Places of Interest

The Castle (The Shropshire Regimental Museum), Castle Street (58516). Great Hall, West Tower, and East Tower rooms with display of Royal Charters. East Gallery display of 1403 Battle of Shrewsbury. Dungeons with display of Borough Regalia. (Open Easter–October 10–5 daily; October–Easter 10–4 Monday–Saturday.) Admission charge.

Rowley's House Museum, Barker Street (61196). Timber-framed "black-and-white" late sixteenth-century mansion. Roman material from Virconium, gallery on history of Shrewsbury. (Open all year Monday–Saturday 10–5.)

Clive House Museum, College Hill (54811). Occupied by Clive of India while Mayor of Shrewsbury. Elegant Georgian house with display of Caughley and Coalport chinaware. (Open all year Monday–Saturday 10–5.)

Shrewsbury Central Library, Castle Gates, Riggs Hall, rear of Old School (241207). Old Shrewsbury Grammar School. Library open Monday and Wednesday 9:30–6; Tuesday and Friday 9–5:30.

Old Council House Court, Castle Gates. Built about 1501. Two medieval halls at right angles to each other. Tudor prison and meeting place of Council of Welsh Marches. Occupied by Charles I and James II. Now the residence of Rt. Rev. Monsignor Grasar.

Shrewsbury Abbey (of St. Peter and St. Paul), Abbey Foregate, across from the English Bridge. Disestablished in 1540, monastery buildings largely destroyed, but a dig is going on to establish their dimensions.

Church of St. Mary's, St. Mary's Street. Original foundation by Saxon King Edgar. Rebuilt as Norman church in 1170, with one of the three tallest spires in England. Famous stained glass; Jesse Window moved there from Old St. Chad's.

Old St. Chad's, College Hill. Founded c. 780, fell down in 1788. Fifteenth-century Lady Chapel still standing. (New St. Chad's, Clairmont Hill, England's largest round church; built in 1792 to replace Old St. Chad's.)

Church of St. Alkmund, Fish Street and St. Alkmund's Square (adjoining St. Julian's, now a craft center). Founded by Ethelfleda, daughter of Alfred the Great. Medieval tower, eighteenth-century church. Original Shrewsbury marketplace.

Bear Steps, Fish Street. Restored fifteenth-century Medieval Hall and Solar joined to Link block, and three bays on west side of

St. Alkmund's Square with steps leading to Fish Street. (Open all year Monday–Saturday.)

Jones's Mansion, Church Street and Butcher Row. Early seventeenth-century half-timbered headquarters of Prince Rupert, son of Elizabeth of Bohemia and nephew of Charles I. Now part of Prince Rupert Hotel.

Ye Olde House (Rooke's House), Dogpole. Fifteenth-century timbered house where Mary Tudor supposedly stayed in 1526.

High Street (originally Gumblestal Street, also Bakers' Row). Whole group of timber-framed houses. See especially:
Owen's Mansion (1592).
Ireland's Mansion (1592).

The Square, town center since 1269 removal of market from St. Alkmund's Square. See especially:
Old Market Hall. Late Elizabethan 1596. Statue of Richard, Duke of York, father of Edward IV and Richard III, taken from the Welsh Bridge, set in north gable.
Statue of Lord Clive.

Pride Hill (originally Corvisers' or Shoemakers' Row). See especially:
High Cross and Plaques at site of execution of David III, Prince of Wales, and display of body of Harry Percy (Hotspur).

Watch Tower, Town Walls. Thirteenth-century; probably built by Henry III.

Wyle Cop (on the Wyle, or hill), probable site of original Saxon settlement. See especially:
Mytton's Mansion (Plaques 65, 66, 67, 68, 69). Timbered frame built about 1460. May be house of Sheriff Thomas Mytton, who let Henry Tudor walk over his body on Welsh Bridge in 1485.
Henry Tudor's House (Plaques 71, 72, 73). Built about 1450. Henry Tudor stayed here before Bosworth Field.
Lion Hotel. Ancient mail-coach inn. Three buildings, dating from the fifteenth to the eighteenth century. Robert Adam–style Assembly Room at rear. Bar, lounge for tea, restaurant. Expensive.

Market Days are Wednesday, Friday, and Saturday. Many historic buildings are closed on Sunday.

PLACES TO STAY/EAT

The Lion Hotel, Wyle Cop (0743) 53107. A Trusthouse Forte
Hotel. Truffles Restaurant, Tudor Bar. Expensive.

Prince Rupert's Hotel, Butcher Row and Church Street (0743)
52461. Historic fifteenth-century rooms and lounge.
Expensive. Three restaurants:
The Cavalier (inside hotel), breakfast, lunch, and dinner with
international cuisine. Expensive.
Prince Rupert Steak Bar, Fish Street. Lunch and dinner.
The Royalist, Church Street entrance. Businessmen's buffet
lunch. Inexpensive.

St. Julian's Craft Centre, Fish Lane. Once a church. Vegetarian
restaurant for coffee, lunch, tea. Open daily 10–5. Inexpensive.

Feathers Hotel, Bull Ring, Ludlow. Spectacular seventeenth-
century half-timbered inn. Lounge and bar with pub food.
Inexpensive. Restaurant with cathedral ceiling, giant menu.
Expensive. (See also the older Bull across the street.)

Midland Hotel, New Town, Birmingham. Comfortable
Birmingham "institution" in town center. Two restaurants,
four bar-lounges, suitable for coffee, tea, or drinks. Expensive.

Attingham Park, Telford Road, southwest of Shrewsbury on A5.
Georgian mansion, National Trust Museum, and festival hall.
Tearoom open 2–5. (For more information about
performances, etc., contact Tourist Information Centre,
Shrewsbury.)

For a list of other accommodations, from hotels to bed-and-
breakfasts, write or call the Tourist Information Centre and
Music Hall, The Square (236761). (Open 9:30–6:30 Easter–
October; closed Sunday October–Easter.)

———— SHREWSBURY WALK ————

Begin your walk at Shrewsbury Railway Station. You can come
out from the tracks or through the station. To your left in the
station parking lot rises up the massive red sandstone battlements of Shrewsbury Castle. This open area in front of the

station is probably the place where Brother Cadfael found the ninety-five bodies of the castle's defenders, summarily executed by order of King Stephen.

In Ellis Peters's *One Corpse Too Many,* saintly old Abbot Heribert had sent Brother Cadfael with a party of monks to give the victims Christian burial. They collected the bodies from the Foregate, brought them back into the inner ward of the castle and laid them out, whereupon Brother Cadfael discovered that one man too many had been executed. Cadfael told Sheriff Prestcote "there is . . . a leaf hidden in your forest," reminding all Chesterton fans of Father Brown's comment in "The Sign of the Broken Sword" that a wise man hides a leaf in a forest. Edgar Allan Poe used the same idea in *The Purloined Letter.*

You may want to stop now to look over the castle ramparts. Take the stone ramp to your left along the lower castle wall. It will lead you to the battlements, where you can look across the Welsh Bridge and the old suburb of Frankwell into Wales. Ellis Peters's Brother Cadfael took that route in *Dead Man's Ransom* on his way to arrange a prisoner exchange with Owain Gwynedd. Scientist Charles Darwin was born in the Mount, just beyond Frankwell.

There is a Frankwell Riverside Trail, which goes across the Severn and around the next loop of the river upstream. In Ellis Peters's *An Excellent Mystery* the wounded crusader, Godfrid Marsecot, had a small estate upriver called Salton (present-day Shelton). With his faithful Fidelis, the Lord Godfrid visited Salton the day he died, rowed there by Madog of the Dead Boat. John Benbow was born beside the river in 1653. Benbow ran away to sea, becoming a famous admiral under Charles II, as well as the namesake of a character in Robert Louis Stevenson's thriller *Treasure Island.*

As you look over the battlements, to your right beyond the station, Castle Gates becomes Castle Foregate. This was the area where armies camped on a narrow neck of land unprotected by the Severn. Henry VII, clearly the villain in Josephine Tey's *The Daughter of Time,* came this way into Shrewsbury on

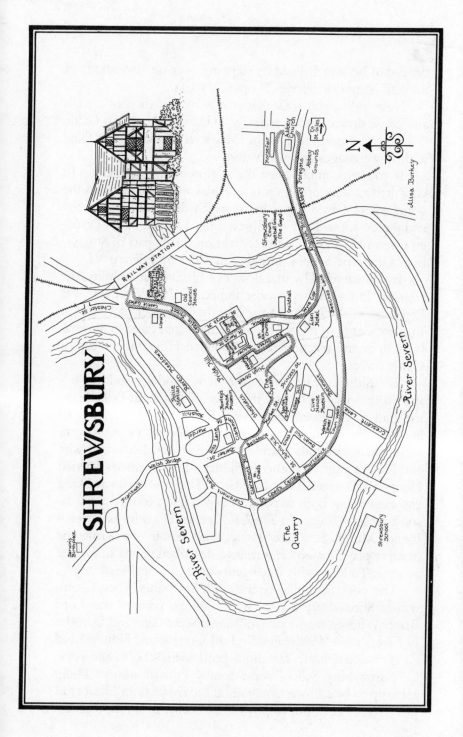

SHREWSBURY

Darwin's Birthplace

River Severn

Welsh Bridge

Frankwell

Claremont Bank

RAILWAY STATION

Chester St.

Police Station

Rowley's House Museum

Mardol

Mardol

Claremont

Barker St.

Hills Lane

Bridge St.

Claremont

Bellstone

Swan Hill

St. Chads

Good Cottage

The Quarry

River Severn

Shrewsbury School

Old Council House

Library

Castle St.

Castle Gates

St. Mary's St.

Dogpole

St. Julians

St. Mary's Church

The Square

Dogpole

Pride Hill

Shoplatch

Mardol

High St.

College Hill

Princess St.

Belmont

Wyle Cop

Guildhall

Lion Hotel

Beeches Lane

Clive House Museum

Town Wall

Murivance

Crescent Lane

River Severn

Shrewsbury Town Football Ground (The Gay)

Horsefair

Abbey Foregate

Abbey Church

Abbey Grounds

To St Giles

St. Giles

N

Alisa Burkey

231

the eve of Bosworth Field by stepping over the (live) body of the Yorkist traitor Sheriff Thomas Mytton.

Now follow the walk that winds around the castle walls and come down a steep stairway called the Dana into Castle Gates just beyond the station. (Medieval Shrewsbury is filled with tiny passages and walkways.)

If you are coming from the station, take Castle Gates to your left to walk uphill (you will pass the Dana exit) to the point where Castle Gates becomes Castle Street. Across the rising road you will see the Shrewsbury Library, built of golden Cotswold stone. The library was originally part of Shrewsbury Grammar School, founded in 1552 by Edward VI.

It was attended by that flower of Elizabethan nobility, the poet Sir Philip Sidney, whose father, Sir Henry Sidney, was President of the Court of the Marches (or ruler of Wales) at Ludlow Castle to the south. Sir Henry often came to Shrewsbury to attend meetings at the Council House at the top of Castle Street.

The Sidneys were part of the "new" Tudor nobility. Philip's mother was a Dudley, the sister of Elizabeth I's favorite, the Earl of Leicester. (Sir Walter Scott, a distant relative of another Shrewsbury writer, Mary Webb, wrote *Kenilworth* about the mysterious death of Amy Robsart, Leicester's wife and Philip's aunt.) Another of Sidney's Dudley uncles married Henry VIII's niece, Lady Jane Grey. They were crowned king and queen, but both were overthrown and executed for treason by Mary Tudor. In *The Lisle Letters,* Dorothy L. Sayers's friend, Muriel St. Clare Byrne, with whom she wrote the mystery play *Busman's Honeymoon,* described young Lady Jane as a true Tudor, highly intelligent and quite capable of ruling.

The poet Sir Fulke Greville, Philip Sidney's best friend, was at Shrewsbury School with him. So perhaps was Lord Roger Wimsey, mentioned in Wilfrid Scott-Giles and Dorothy L. Sayers's *The Wimsey Family.* Like Greville and Sidney, Lord Roger was a delicate, fastidious gentleman, scholar, and poet.

Shrewsbury School was strongly Puritan and Sir Philip grew up to be a Protestant "radical activist" whom Elizabeth I preferred to keep out of power. Ironically, Sir Philip's godfather was the Catholic Philip II of Spain. Philip II appeared in Georgette Heyer's Elizabethan romance *Beauvalet*.

Sidney died at thirty-two at Zutphen, Holland, fighting against Philip II for Protestant William of Orange. The statue in front of the library, however, is that of another Shrewsbury School Old Boy, Charles Darwin, who explored the mystery of creation itself. A statue of Sir Philip, dedicated to the memory of Shrewsbury's students who died in World War I, is in front of the new school across the Severn.

To reach the castle's main entrance, continue walking uphill past a number of shops until you come to the gateway on your left. Through the arch you can see the inner ward. When the Romans left nearby Virconium in the fifth century, first the Britons, then the Saxons, fortified the site with a watchtower and stockade.

Then in 1083 Norman Roger de Montgomery destroyed anywhere from fifty to two hundred houses to build the keep. His original moated castle was made of wood, but as Ellis Peters pointed out in our correspondence, Roger built the abbey of stone and probably followed suit with the castle. At any rate, Peters believes that by the time of her Brother Cadfael mysteries in 1140, the castle was largely built of the red sandstone you see today.

In *One Corpse Too Many*, Shrewsbury was under siege by King Stephen. Brother Cadfael, Aline Siward, her brother Giles, and Hugh Beringar of Maesbury, who later fought a duel to the death before the Royal Court, all came to Stephen's camp in the Foregate.

Later in the thirteenth century, during his Welsh wars, Edward I rebuilt the castle, which was a royalist stronghold during the Wars of the Roses, in Tudor times, and during the Civil War, until captured by Oliver Cromwell's Parliamentarians. At the restoration of Charles II, however, it became a private residence, which was modernized in 1790 by the famous engineer, Thomas Telford. When it was taken over by Shrewsbury as a museum, it was restored as much as possible to the Edwardian castle of 1300.

In Peters's *St. Peter's Fair*, after the murder of wine merchant Thomas of Bristol, his niece, Emma, came with Brother Cadfael to the chilly great hall with its smoky tapestries. She was there to bear witness to the facts about the riot on the jetty near the Gaye. She saw the provost's son, young Philip Corviser, dragged in from his cell. He looked a sorry figure, dirty, hung over, and still giddy from the blow he had taken in the riot. In *One Corpse Too Many*, the murderer was exposed by a fisherboy at a military banquet given by King Stephen in the same great hall.

In *Dead Man's Ransom* Sheriff Prestcote maintained an apartment high in the castle's corner tower, where his family stayed when in Shrewsbury. As he walked through the inner bailey with Brother Cadfael, the Welsh suspect and prisoner, Elis, saw Prestcote's blond daughter, Melicent, and fell madly in love with her.

Take time to go inside the castle as well as look over its battlements. You can see the Great Hall with its timbered roof, the octagonal Mayor's Room, the West Tower room, and the East Tower room adjoining the vestibule, with a display of the town's Royal Charters and a diagram of the 1403 Battle of Shrewsbury. In the basement of the castle you can see the dungeons and the Town Council's regalia and silver plate. Before you leave, you may want to walk around the castle's inner bailey (or courtyard) to see its northeastern Postern Gate, which dates from the fortifications added for the Civil War.

Outside the castle gate once more on Castle Gates, you will pass the Castle Gates House, a timbered black-and-white building moved here from the street called Dogpole. Keep walking on what is now called Castle Street to Council House Court. Built in Tudor times, it was used for meetings by the Council of the Marches, and perhaps as a prison. Both Charles I and his son James II used it as a residence while in Shrewsbury.

Beyond Council House to your left is an area that stretches to the Severn River. In Peters's *The Sanctuary Sparrow*, Brother Cadfael went that way to treat Dame Julian Aurifaber. The old dame lived with her son, the goldsmith Walter Aurifaber

(Latin for "gold maker"). Aurifaber had a large, prosperous town house and business (or burgage) with a rear plot that stretched to the town wall along the river. He had room enough to let the locksmith Baldwin Peche rent part for his home and business. In *The Rose Is Rent,* Judith Perle, the widow of a clothier, was kidnapped and held prisoner in a storeroom on the river near the Aurifaber house.

You next pass by the abandoned St. Nicholas Church. Beside it on your left is the narrow entrance to St. Mary's Waterlane, which will take you to The Royal Salop Hospital on the river. It may be the "Comerbourne General," where Ellis Peters's singer Maggie Tressider recovered after her car accident in *The House of Green Turf.* It might also be the hospital where Detective Chief Inspector George Felse of the Midshire CID kept a wary eye on don Stephen Paviour in *City of Gold and Shadows.* (Ellis Peters wrote us that Shrewsbury and Comerbourne can be "loosely" identified, but she was not as meticulous about details in her modern mysteries as she is being with Brother Cadfael.)

Continue walking downhill on Castle Street to St. Mary's Street across from the post office. At this corner, Castle Street becomes Pride Hill, a pedestrian walkway with a number of black-and-white timbered buildings to admire. (In medieval days Pride Hill was Corvisers', or Shoemakers' Row. In Peters's *St. Peter's Fair,* the town provost (or mayor) who asked Abbot Radulfus to share the proceeds of the abbey fair was Geoffrey Corviser, who made some of the finest shoes and riding boots in England.

At the top of Pride Hill there is a tall modern High Cross. It replaced the old High Cross, which was the town's gathering spot in *Dead Man's Ransom.* As the plaques on the Barclay's Bank at St. Mary's Street tell you, this cross is at the site where in 1283 the captured David III, the last Welsh Prince of Wales, was drawn and quartered for high treason. It is also the place where, after his death at the Battle of Shrewsbury in 1403, the body of Harry Percy (Hotspur) was displayed. Then parts of his body were sent to towns across England for display as a warning to traitors.

Ellis Peters described the battle of Shrewsbury in *The Bloody Field*. In her unfinished novel about Prince Hal's (Henry V) brother, *Lord John,* Georgette Heyer also mentioned the battle. Hal and his father, Henry IV, were on one side, opposing the Percies, the Mortimers, and the Welsh. This famous battle also forms the finale of *Henry IV, Part One* by William Shakespeare, who knew Salopians Sir Philip Sidney and Fulke Greville.

Partway down Pride Hill on the right side of the street are the thirteenth-century remains of the Royal Mint, known as Bennet's Hall. (You have walked one mile when you reach the High Cross.) Turn left and walk along St. Mary's Street. Just before you reach the medieval Church of St. Mary's, you come to St. Mary's Lane to your left. It then turns right behind the church and joins St. Mary's Water Gate, coming from Castle Street. St. Mary's Lane turns right behind the church to form the far side of St. Mary's Place.

Along St. Mary's Lane you can see some old almshouses and the Olde Yorkshire House Inn, a three-story, red-brick building, and across St. Mary's Place is the two-story Tudor Draper's Guildhall. In Peters's medieval mysteries, Sub-Sheriff Hugh Beringar and his wife, Aline, had a small house with an enclosed garden near St. Mary's Church. Their son's godfather, Brother Cadfael, played wooden soldiers there with him when he visited the family.

The Church of St. Mary's was founded around 970 by King Edgar. (Edgar was crowned king at Bath Abbey in a ceremony whose form was used for all succeeding rulers, includin Elizabeth II. See Bath Walk.) The Saxon church was demolished about 1170 and a cruciform Norman church built on its foundations. That is the church you see. It has some more recent additions, like its Perpendicular spire, one of the three tallest spires in England, and some medieval stained-glass windows, including a Jesse Window brought here from Old St. Chad's when it fell down. St. Mary's was the parish church of the family of prosperous goldsmith Walter Aurifaber, as well as Hugh and Aline Beringar, when they did not go to the abbey.

The medieval market was held in St. Mary's Place when Brother Cadfael was walking the Shrewsbury streets.

Later St. Mary's served as the Draper's Company chapel, where Shrewsbury School students like Philip Sidney went to church. In the eighteenth century a young man named Cadmon tried to slide down a rope from the spire to the river, but the rope broke and he was killed.

As you return to St. Mary's Street in front of the church, turn left to continue walking—downhill again—toward the river. On the opposite side of the street you see the corner of Church Street, which runs into Butcher Row. The Prince Rupert Hotel fronts on both Church Street and Butcher Row.

As you pass Church Street, St. Mary's Street becomes Dogpole. On your left side at No. 11 is the red-brick classical Guildhall, built about 1700. Next you come to No. 20, known as the Olde House, built in the fifteenth century, where Mary Tudor may have stayed.

Follow Dogpole as it curves into Wyle Cop, the steep road that goes down to the English Bridge across the Severn River. Wyle Cop is Anglo-Saxon for "hill top." The original settlement was probably here. This was also the route Brother Cadfael climbed when coming from the abbey into town.

Cross Wyle Cop at the junction with Dogpole. The first building to note is the Lion Hotel (Plaque 36), which is really three buildings. The golden statue of a lion stands above the main entrance. In the rear is the Assembly Room, designed in the style of Robert Adam. The Lion Hotel is a historic coaching inn, where writers Charles Dickens and Thomas De Quincey both stayed. De Quincey was the author of "Murder Considered as One of the Fine Arts," mentioned by P. D. James in *The Maul and the Pear Tree*. Opera singer Jenny Lind stayed here, as did Ellis Peters's fictional world-famous contralto, Maggie Tressider, in *The House of Green Turf*.

Maggie Tressider, who had once gone on an Austrian tour chaperoned by Detective George Felse's wife, Bunty, took a suite with a grand piano when she was discharged from the hospital following a car smash. The accident had made her remember a long-repressed fear that a young man who had loved her had committed suicide, so she hired a private detective, Francis Killian, to find out if her fear were true.

Killian, who had made the mistake of falling in love with Maggie, came to report his findings at the Lion Hotel by the "Comer" (English) Bridge. When Tressider paid him off, Killian, followed by an interested Detective George Felse, stalked out of the hotel to a church by the river to stuff her money in the alms box.

Below the Lion Hotel is a half-timbered fifteenth-century house (Plaque 35) where Henry Tudor stayed before meeting Richard III at Bosworth Field. In addition to Josephine Tey's *The Daughter of Time,* some other mysterious views on the classic mystery of the Princes in the Tower are Elizabeth Peters's entertaining book *The Murders of Richard III* and Guy Townsend's attempt to destroy Tey's case for Richard in *To Prove a Villain.* Next door (Plaque 34) is Mytton's Mansion, where the turncoat Sheriff of Shrewsbury who had sworn not to let Henry Tudor enter Shrewsbury once lived.

In Ellis Peters's *Monk's Hood* Gervase Bonel was suddenly poisoned. Brother Cadfael came up the Wyle Cop to talk to the suspected murderer, Bonel's stepson Edwin. Edwin lived there with his widowed mother, Richildis, and his brother-in-law, carpenter Martin Bellecote. (Brother Cadfael long ago had pledged his troth to Bellecote's mother-in-law, Richildis, then had run away to the Crusades.) Bellecote later reappeared as one of the delegation who came to a Chapter Meeting to ask the newly appointed Abbot Radulfus to share the abbey's fair profits with the town.

Take Wyle Cop to the English Bridge over the Severn River. Like the Thames, the Severn here is wide and swift, a truly impressive river halfway from its mouth at Bristol. Its Shrewsbury shoreline is banked with green parks on either side. This part of Shrewsbury is very modern and bustling with traffic, making it hard to imagine yourself back in the twelfth century, when it was a fortified hill town across from the wide fields and impressive buildings of a great abbey. If you would like to see more abbey ruins in situ than exist here

today, make a side trip to Buildwas Abbey, just past Virconium
on the way to Ironbridge. Its beautiful stone ruins are well
preserved and will give you a better idea of the size and layout
of a typical medieval monastery.

The first Shrewsbury bridge was here, but the present one
only dates from 1774. The one Brother Cadfael crossed had a
drawbridge at the town end. In *One Corpse Too Many,* the
drawbridge remained up when fire and smoke poured from the
besieged town. Merchant Thomas of Bristol came in his barge
with his niece, Emma, up the Severn from the port of Bristol.
Their party landed at the abbey jetty, to your left on the far
bank as you walk across the English Bridge toward the abbey.
(This is the beginning, too, of the King's Highway to London.)

In *St. Peter's Fair,* as Thomas's men were unloading his
wares, young Philip Corviser led a group of the sons of the
town's craftsmen to try to persuade the arriving merchants to
pay the town a percentage of the tolls owed the abbey. The
result was a riot.

In *One Corpse Too Many,* Brother Cadfael negotiated the
Severn in a cockleshell boat one night, closely shadowed by
Hugh Beringar. Cadfael was collecting the Empress Matilda's
treasure, hidden in the river, and helping two of her followers,
Godith Adeney and Torold Blund, to escape with the treasure
into Wales. Later in the mystery a fisherboy saw a knight toss a
dagger into the Severn here. He dived to rescue it for his own
use, helping Cadfael solve the mysterious death of one prisoner
too many. In *Monk's Hood,* Cadfael and his faithful shadow,
Brother Mark, got the river watchers to search for the small
wooden reliquary made by Edwin for his stepfather.

In *The Rose Is Rent,* Brother Cadfael found traces of the
struggle in which widow Judith Perle was kidnapped on the
abbey side of the river just before you come to the Gaye. He
also discovered the marks of a getaway boat that had been kept
nearby under the first arch of the bridge.

Once across the Severn you are in Abbey Foregate, formerly part of the lands belonging to the Benedictine Abbey of St.
Peter and St. Paul, which covered ten acres. Immediately to

your right is the Victorian Gothic United Reformed Church, which may be the one Peters's unhappy private detective Killian considered giving his fee from singer Maggie Tressider in *The House of Green Turf.*

To your left along the Severn behind a school building is the town's football field, still known as the Gay(e). In Brother Cadfael's time the abbey orchards where Rhun and Brother Fidelis picked apples in *An Excellent Mystery* were beyond the Gaye. Along Abbey Foregate itself there were market stalls and taverns on the eastern edge of the abbey property. It was in this general area in *St. Peter's Fair* that Brother Cadfael visited the temporary booths of the Horse Fair grounds. (Today the street to your left behind Abbey Foregate is called Horsefair.)

Beyond the fairgrounds, the London Highway went on past the abbey barns and stores, where Brother Cadfael hid Edwin Gurney, who was accused of poisoning his stepfather in *Monk's Hood.* Saint Giles's Church, where the abbey had a leper hospital, was near the end of Abbey Foregate on the London Road. To reach St. Giles, you would have to walk another mile to the crossroads at Hill's Column. The column was put up in honor of Lord Hill, the son of a local landowning family, who was one of the Duke of Wellington's most trusted generals at Waterloo. Mystery writer Georgette Heyer described Waterloo in *An Infamous Army.*

In *The Leper of St. Giles,* Brother Cadfael and Brother Mark stood in front of the long, low roof of the hospice, which had a wattled fence and a small church with a squat turret, to see a splendid wedding party ride by to the abbey. The middle-aged groom whipped a tall, gaunt leper out of his way, while the young bride smiled at a leper boy and threw him largesse. Later, a leper's gown that hid the face was used as a disguise for an accused murderer who hid at St. Giles. A leper's gown played a similar role in Robert Louis Stevenson's romance about the Wars of the Roses called *The Black Arrow.*

Unless you want to take the time to follow Abbey Foregate to St. Giles, follow Abbey Foregate as it curves to your left. Somewhere along the Foregate here was the house that Judith

Perle gave to the abbey for the yearly rent of a white rose from its rosebush in *The Rose Is Rent*. It was occupied when that mystery began by the bronzesmith Niall, a widower with a small daughter.

Cross the Foregate to your right to go inside the abbey's west door. The red sandstone building is now awkwardly isolated on a traffic island with major roads on either side. But at night when there is less traffic, its square west tower is lit up and it glows with a massive power appropriate to its great monastic foundation.

Built on the site of the small wooden Saxon Church of St. Peter, the abbey was one of the wealthiest religious houses in England within 150 years of its founding in 1083. It owned over seventy-one manors, twenty-four churches, and the right to the tithes of thirty-seven other parishes.

In 1137, as readers of Ellis Peters's *A Morbid Taste for Bones* know, Abbot Heribert sent Prior Robert to negotiate for the bones of the Welsh St. Winefrede, which were then (supposedly) transferred to the abbey. A great bell was later dedicated to the memory of Holy Winefrede, whose great weight and awkward position required four men to ring it.

Edward I called Parliament to meet at the abbey in 1283. This was the first Parliament in which the Commons, or representatives made up of two shire knights and two townsmen from important cities like Shrewsbury, were called to meet in council with the king and his barons. They probably met in the Chapter House or Refectory to decide the fate of the captured David, Prince of Wales. He was charged with treason and executed with great barbarity at the High Cross in Shrewsbury. In 1403 Henry IV asked the abbot to mediate between him and Henry Percy (Hotspur), but the negotiations failed, and a bloody battle in which Percy was slain was fought north of town.

Parts of the abbey church Brother Cadfael knew still remain in the present nave, where the three eastern bays are rounded Norman. They were joined in the fourteenth century to the two western bays with their pointed arches, added when the tower was built. Between the nave and the north aisle of the church is the small shrine of Saint Winefrede. Part of the stone is believed to have come from her original shrine.

In Peters's *The Pilgrim of Hate*, the lame boy Rhun touched the saint's shrine and was made whole. In *St. Peter's Fair* the body of Thomas of Bristol lay there in a coffin made by Martin Bellecote, into which his niece slipped a single rose. Later that night when Brother Cadfael found a petal from the rose on the floor of the chapel he knew that someone had broken into the coffin.

As you stand inside the church looking toward the altar, try to imagine the scene in *The Sanctuary Sparrow* when Brother Cadfael was attending Matins. The midnight service was interrupted by a hue and cry coming from the English Bridge. Then a scarecrow of a young man, reeling and panting, burst in the west door and rushed down the aisle to grab the altar cloth, followed by a quarter of the town. They were after his blood for the murder of Walter Aurifaber, the goldsmith. Abbot Radulfus stood over the wretch as he claimed sanctuary and warned the blasphemers that if they grabbed the young man they risked everlasting hell.

The abbey was dissolved in 1540 and its land sold to speculators, who used the buildings as a stone quarry. They spared only the western end of the abbey for the local parish church. (In *The Raven in the Foregate* the parish church was actually Holy Cross, familiarly known as the Foregate, where the abbot appointed a sanctimonious priest named Ailnoth.)

By the eighteenth century the abbey's owner had cleared enough monastery buildings to the south and east of the church to make the Abbey Gardens. Then in 1836, Parliament allowed Thomas Telford to run a new London Road south of the abbey, with the result that the rest of the monastery buildings were destroyed.

The cloister and other monastery buildings lay just south of the church. They included the dormitory (or dortoir), where *The Devil's Novice* had bad dreams; the Chapter House, where abbey business was conducted and Brother Cadfael lurked sleepily behind his pillar in *St. Peter's Fair*; and the refectory or dining hall, where, in *A Morbid Taste for Bones,* Brother Cadfael sat through the highly dramatic readings of his first garden helper, Brother John. The refectory pulpit is still standing in its tiny garden. Still farther south in the abbey grounds was the Abbot's House. It was occupied by Abbot Heribert, who was succeeded in *Monk's Hood* by patrician Abbot Radulfus. Both abbots routinely consulted Brother Cadfael when a murder occurred. In *Monk's Hood,* however, Prior Robert had set himself up as interim abbot in the absence of Abbot Heribert.

Next to the abbot's lodging was the Guest Hall, where the unwilling bride, Iveta, was housed before her marriage to Huon de Domville in *The Leper of St. Giles.* South of these buildings near the abbey pond and gardens was Brother Cadfael's "kingdom"—his herbarium and his workshop hut.

Today a parking lot fills most of the abbey grounds. The parking lot entrance is about where the Abbey Gatehouse used to stand. Sub-Sheriff Hugh Beringar and Brother Cadfael often sat there while conferring on a case. In *St. Peter's Fair,* just inside the gatehouse in the Great Court of the abbey, Ivo Corbriere called his servant to account for a rip in his cotte that marked him as a murderer. When the servant took Corbriere's horse to make a run for it, Corbriere ordered his archer to shoot him dead.

At the entrance to the carpark there is a sign saying that the digging is a Shrewsbury Heritage Project. The men you see working there in a trench are excavating the monastery infirmary, which was run by Brother Edmund. It was in the infirmary that the poison was stolen in *Monk's Hood* and wounded Sheriff Gilbert Prestcote was smothered in *Dead Man's Ransom.* Take a look at the dig, in which Ellis Peters herself is taking a great interest, then return to the front of the abbey. Walk back along Abbey Foregate to the English Bridge. You will pass the site of the guest house where Gervase Bonel was poisoned in *Monk's Hood* and the mill and millpond where Godith and Brother Cadfael hid Torold Blund, who had escaped from the besieged castle in *One Corpse Too Many,* pursued by King Stephen's man Hugh Beringar.

Stand by the river long enough to see for yourself that Shrewsbury is an island hill town, then recross the Severn River. At the junction of Wyle Cop and St. Julian's Friars take Beeches Lane straight ahead of you and walk along it. You will pass the Victorian Gothic Roman Catholic Cathedral of Our Lady Help of Christians and St. Peter of Alcantara, which was designed by Pugin. Beeches Lane becomes Town Walls at Belmont, a lane that runs back toward the center of town, where it becomes Milk Street.

Town Walls is actually built on top of Shrewsbury's old walls. They were not the walls the townspeople wanted the fair tolls to pay for rebuilding in Peters's *St. Peter's Fair,* but date from the time of Henry III. The sidewalks here are very narrow and the traffic is fierce. You may prefer to cross Town Walls and walk on its right-hand side where there is more room.

Just past Crescent Lane to your left and Belmont to your right, you come to a medieval (thirteenth-century) battlemented watchtower. From it you can look out toward the Welsh mountains to the west. Below you along the Severn is a huge green park called the Quarry. In Peters's *City of Gold and Shadows* Gus Hambro's car was found by a pair of lovers in a quarry, proving Charlotte Rosignol's assertion to George Felse that Hambro had not voluntarily left the Roman site of Aurae Phila. Miss Peters, however, says it is not the same quarry.

Across the river on the hill above the Quarry stands present-day Shrewsbury School, with its statue of Sir Philip Sidney. Ellis Peters says that Shrewsbury School was not the model for Dominic Felse's Comerbourne Grammar School, to which young Felse went as a day pupil. As one of the six top schools in Britain, Shrewsbury School would have been too expensive for a police detective's son, even if he later went to Oxford University.

In *Death and the Joyful Woman* schoolboy Dominic Felse became involved in a case about an ancient inn sign. In *Flight of a Witch* when young Felse was a sixth (or top) former, he had a new master called Tom Kenyon. Kenyon boarded in a neighboring village with the family of a beautiful girl who vanished from the top of the Hallowmount, a hill haunted by local legends. It had an Iron Age fort of dykes and ditches, presumably part of the eighth-century Offa's Dyke, west of Shrewsbury, which stretches from the Dee to the Wye.

In many of her modern mysteries set in Shrewsbury, like *Flight of a Witch, The Knocker on the Door,* and *City of Gold and Shadows,* Peters's characters were very aware of sharing the blood and traditions of the ancient folk who lived here before time began. Young Dominic Felse explained to Kenyon that the area's past did not scare him because he belonged to it.

Continue walking along Town Walls to Swan Hill, where Town Walls becomes Murivance. You are coming to the Georgian part of Shrewsbury, built during the city's heyday as a center for a fashionable season. You will pass a hospital on your left and then come to St. John's Hill, a reminder of the Knights of St. John of Jerusalem. It is another steep lane down to your right, which will become Shoplatch, then Pride Hill, the pedestrian walkway, in the center of town.

In Ellis Peters's *Flight of a Witch,* the new master, Tom Kenyon, was driven into town by a student's mother. She then, in Peters's words, "shot away up Castle Wylde before the light at the Cross could change." This description makes it obvious that Peters's "Comerbourne" is Shrewsbury with its High Cross at the corner of Pride Hill and Castle Street.

Cross St. John's Hill, staying on the right side of the street. Murivance now becomes St. Chad's Terrace, which leads you to the new St. Chad's Church. This Saint Chad's, a splendid example of eighteenth-century Greek revival, is England's largest round church. It seats over two thousand people and serves as Shrewsbury's civic church, where official ceremonies take place.

It was built to replace old St. Chad's on College Hill, whose tower fell with a crash on July 9, 1788, as the clock struck four. (Thomas Telford had warned that it would do so.) When you reach St. Chad's, you have walked three miles from the railway station.

Walk past St. Chad's and turn right to walk down steep

and narrow Claremont Hill where on either side there are lovely Queen Anne and Georgian houses. There are a number of bookstores on this street, too.

At the bottom of Claremont Hill you will come to a corner. Barker Street is to your left and Bellstone to your right; straight ahead across the wide intersection Claremont Hill becomes Claremont Street. Across the intersection on your right is the tall, modern Market Hall with a clock tower. In Ellis Peters's *City of Gold and Shadows,* Leslie Paviour drove Charlotte Rosignol into Comerbourne (Shrewsbury). She parked near the market (probably in the bus-station carpark to your left) and commented that this multistory monstrosity of raw concrete was brutal in a nice Tudor-cum-Georgian town. Leslie then took a large bag of pale, soft leather, filled with something heavy, out of her car. She told Charlotte that it was money belonging to Orlando (Orrie) Benyon, who worked at the dig in Uriconium. Leslie said that Orrie wanted her to keep it in her strongbox. There is a Lloyd's Bank on the corner handy for Leslie Paviour (and for you, if you have American Express traveler's checks).

To your left down Barker Street beyond the bus station, you will see Rowley's House Museum on Hill's Lane. It is really two buildings. Rowley's Mansion is a brick-and-stone building where Dr. Johnson, whom G. K. Chesterton loved to impersonate, stayed in 1774. It was then the vicarage of Old St. Chad's. Next to it is Rowley's House, an incredibly gorgeous, free-standing sixteenth-century black-and-white timbered building. It now houses the Roman artifacts from nearby Virconium (Wroxeter), especially its prize, a large silver mirror, as well as prehistoric, medieval, and natural history exhibits, and a gallery devoted to the history of Shrewsbury.

Beyond Rowley's House Museum at the end of Barker Street is Bridge Street, which leads directly to the Welsh Bridge and Frankwell. To the right of Barker Street are first Hill's Lane, then Mardol, both of which also lead to the Welsh (or Western) Bridge. In Ellis Peters's *The Rose Is Rent,* the burgage of the Vestier family, who were the most important clothiers in

Shrewsbury, was located on Maerdol (now Mardol). Brother Cadfael went there to investigate the destruction of the white rose bush and the murder of Brother Eluric. The Shrewsbury Police Station where Peters's Chief Detective Inspector George Felse worked in *The House of Green Turf* was beyond Mardol on Raven Street.

Turn to your right, taking Bellstone to Market Street, where, in *The House of Green Turf,* Ellis Peters's private detective, Francis Killian, had his austere office over a bookstore. His small brass plate said "Confidential Inquiries." Doctor Gilbert Rice came there to ask Killian to go see Maggie Tressider in hospital, although Killian thought the doctor would have much preferred to send her to a psychiatrist.

This is an area with fascinating shops of all kinds. Before you turn left into the square, walk along Market Street and look for a narrow passageway to your right called Coffee House Passage. It is one of many in Shrewsbury that date from the Middle Ages. If you detour to go right on it, you will come out on College Hill by the Clive House Museum. Lord Clive of India was not a mysterious character, but two mystery writers, E. C. Bentley and G. K. Chesterton, wrote and illustrated one of their schoolboy clerihews about him.

The Tourist Information Centre is located in the Music Hall at the Market Street end of the square. Directly in front of the Music Hall is the sixteenth-century Market Hall with the arms of Queen Elizabeth I over the entrance. They appear below the statue of Richard, Duke of York, father of Richard III, brought there from the Old Welsh Bridge. The stone market is a single-story building over open arcades.

Walk through the square toward the bronze statute of Lord Clive at the other end on High Street. Two of the most famous of Shrewsbury's many black-and-white timbered buildings are on High Street. (It was once called Gumblestal Street because it was the site of Gambol, or the ducking stool for scolds. Part was also known as Bakers' or Baxter's Row.) To your left on the square side of High Street you will see Ireland's Mansion (Plaque 16), built in Tudor times. Across

High Street is Owen's Mansion at Nos. 23, 24, and 25. Midway along High Street is another of the narrow medieval passages, Grope Lane, with some more Elizabethan buildings.

Turn right on High Street and walk to the corner of Wyle Cop and Fish Street. Cross the street, then turn left on Fish Street to walk by St. Julian's Craft Centre and St. Alkmund's Church to the Bear Steps. Across Fish Street you will see the Prince Rupert Grill, run by the Prince Rupert Hotel. You may stop and have coffee (or a vegetarian meal) at St. Julian's Craft Centre, or eat good English beef or mutton at Prince Rupert's, sitting in one of their old wooden inglenooks and looking out (really up) at the Bear Steps and St. Alkmund's and St. Julian's above you on St. Alkmund's Square.

Then take the Bear Steps up to St. Alkmund's Square, past the medieval cottages that have recently been restored. The original town market was held here. Turn right and walk over to look at St. Alkmund's Church and churchyard. The church was founded by Ethelfleda about A.D. 900. She was a daughter of Alfred the Great. He was one of G. K. Chesterton's heroes, about whom he wrote his epic poem, *The Ballad of the White Horse*. The only medieval part of the church is its tower. The rest of the church was rebuilt soon after old St. Chad's fell.

In *One Corpse Too Many*, the family of Aline Siward (who became Aline Beringar) had a family tomb in St. Alkmund's. After she had identified the body of her brother Giles at the castle, Aline took it to St. Alkmund's on a narrow litter, covered by his black cloak with the clasp of a dragon of eternity. His body was laid in the tomb of his maternal grandfather with all due ceremony.

Return to St. Alkmund's Square (then St. Alkmund's Place) along Fish Street, which now curves to become Butcher Row. On your left is a handsome fifteenth-century timber-and-brick building (Nos. 13, 14, and 15) called Abbot's House, which may have been the abbot's town house after Brother Cadfael's time.

Across Butcher Row is the main entrance of the Prince Rupert Hotel. The facade has elegant black-and-white timbering above a stucco ground floor. Inside, the low beamed ceilings and uneven floors proclaim its age. During the Civil War Charles I's nephew and general, Prince Rupert of the Rhine, had his headquarters here in what was then called Jones Mansion. (At the Prince Rupert Hotel you have walked 3.7 miles from the railway station.)

Take Butcher Row past the Prince Rupert Hotel to Pride Hill. You will go by Powney's Bookstore, where Ellis Peters's current mystery was displayed. In *One Corpse Too Many*, Edric Flesher, whose wife was the nurse of Godith Adeney, had his shop there. Both Hugh Beringar and Brother Cadfael came to visit them, seeking news about Godith, who was the daughter of one of Queen Mathilda's men. At Pride Hill turn right and walk past the High Cross to Castle Street, which becomes Castle Gates. Take Castle Gates to the railway station to end your walk. You have walked 4.7 miles in all.

POSSIBLE SIDE TRIPS

Battlefield

3 miles north of Shrewsbury on A49
Church of St. Mary Magdalene built as chantry for prayer for those killed in Battle of Shrewsbury in 1403. Scene of Edith Pargeter's (aka Ellis Peters) *The Bloody Field*, references in Georgette Heyer's *Lord John*.

Virconium (Wroxeter)

5½ miles southeast of Shrewsbury on A5 to Atcham, take B4380 (the road to Ironbridge). On Watling Street, the ancient Roman highway.
Roman capital of Britannia Secunda and fourth largest city in Britain. Founded as a fort before A.D. 70, abandoned around A.D. 400. Plateau with view of Welsh hills. Fenced open field next to a farm, not far from Severn River with one-story museum/ticket house. Extensive dig you can walk through (only part of city done as yet). You can see Roman walls and layout of Roman forum and baths. Called "Uriconium" by Ellis Peters in *City of Gold and Shadows*, where her plot centered around a Roman hoard found here. No Roman helmet found

yet, but Rowley's House Museum has a famous silver mirror with a fabulous "flower handle" and a Roman bronze eagle head.
(Open daily March 15–October 15, Monday–Saturday 9:30–6:30, Sunday 2–6:30; October 16–March 14, Monday–Saturday 9:30–4, Sunday 2–4.) Admission charge.

Attingham Park
4 miles southeast of Shrewsbury on the A5 at Atcham. Magnificent Georgian mansion in 230-acre park. Landscaped by Humphrey Repton. National Trust House.
According to Peters, its location is correct for "Follymead" in *Black Is the Colour of My True-Love's Heart,* but Attingham Park is not built in the "Gothick fantastic" style of Horace Walpole's Strawberry Hill. (See Thames River Ride.)
(Open April–September, Saturday, Sunday, Monday, Wednesday 2–5; October, Saturday and Sunday 2–5. Shop, tearoom open 2–5.) Special drama and music events. Admission charge.

Boscobel House
Halfway between Shrewsbury and Birmingham on M54 off A5. Seventeenth-century timbered home of John Giffard, where fugitive Charles II hid in an oak after Battle of Worcester in 1651. Featured in Georgette Heyer's *Royal Escape.*
(Open March 15–October 15, Monday–Saturday 9:30–6:30, Sunday 2–6:30; October 15–March 15, Monday–Saturday 9:30–4, Sunday 2–4.) Admission charge.

The Wrexin
East of Shrewsbury on A5, just south of Wellington. Site of ancient Britons' hilltop fort, rising a thousand feet above Shropshire farms. Used for warning beacon. Near Leighton Lodge, birthplace of writer Mary Webb, related on her mother's side to Sir Walter Scott, who wrote *Kenilworth* about Sir Philip Sidney's uncle, Robert Dudley. Scene of Shropshire mystery writer Josephine Bell's World War II mysteries: *Trouble at Wrexin Farm,* in which some World War II spies are routed by London evacuees; farm home of murder victim

Ursula Frinton in *Murder on the Medical Board,* which took place at the market town of Shornford (aka Shrewsbury). Possible to climb to summit from Forest Glen. This is not Ellis Peters's Hallowmount in *Flight of a Witch,* but it has remains of fortifications, etc.

Ludlow
About 25 miles south of Shrewsbury on A49.
Showpiece little market town in strong defensive position above two rivers. Its Norman keep, begun in 1086, is still standing, together with other parts of the extensive royal castle.
Prosperous as a wool trade center, Ludlow was also a Yorkist stronghold. As Prince of Wales, Edward V lived here, as did Prince Arthur, son of Henry (VII) Tudor and his wife, Catherine of Aragon. In reign of Henry VIII, Sir Philip Sidney's father, Sir Henry, lived here as President of the Court of the Marches. Later, like Shrewsbury, Ludlow became the center of a fashionable season. The grounds and ruins of the sandstone castle, with its spectacular view over Wales, include the keep, the Council Hall where Puritan poet John Milton's *Comus* was first performed, the round Norman chapel (first of five in England), and Pendover Tower, where Edward V and his brother, Richard, Duke of York, stayed before going to London, the Tower, and their mysterious deaths.

Castle open daily except Sunday, October–April. Admission charge.

At the Castle Gate go past Castle Square to Church Street. On your left off Broad Street is the Perpendicular Church of St. Lawrence, a wool church, with a spire 135 feet high. A memorial stone marking the ashes of poet A. E. Housman is on its north wall. Across Broad Street, Church becomes King Street. Continue to the Bull Ring, then turn left on Corve Street to reach the famous half-timbered Tudor Feathers Hotel. Across the street is the even older Bull Inn. Mystery writer P. D. James lived in "the very beautiful little town called Ludlow" before her family moved to Cambridge when she was eleven. Ellis Peters's *The Virgin in the Ice* took place near

Ludlow in the year 1139. The Norman keep was manned by Josce de Dinan for King Stephen, but Dinan's loyalty was in some doubt, so Hugh Beringar, deputy Sheriff of Shropshire and friend of Brother Cadfael, was keeping an eye on him. News came that a brother and sister, Ermina and Yves Hugonin, whose uncle was overseas in the Holy Land, had fled toward Ludlow with a young nun but were missing.

Just south of Ludlow lie Leominster and Hereford, also fortress Welsh border towns. In Simon Brett's *Murder in the Title,* his middle-aged actor-cum-detective, Charles Paris, played a dead body at a local rep theater in a town called Rugland Spa in Herefordshire, but people in the audience and supporters of the Regent Theatre came from Leominster and Ludlow. Between Chinese food and drinks at the pub behind the theater, Paris solved the murder of one of the cast members, just as the theater itself fell to a housing development.

Birmingham
Take A5, then A464 from Shrewsbury (or British Rail).
An ancient Midlands town that grew into the second-largest city in England during the Industrial Revolution because of its iron and coal, it has long been a city famous as a center of Nonconformists. Cardinal Newman established the Oratory of St. Philip Neri in 1847, with a private school attached, to which Hilaire Belloc, descendant of the famous Noncomformist Joseph Priestley, went before going to Oxford where he met E. C. Bentley and later, in London, G. K. Chesterton. Chesterton's hero, Dr. Samuel Johnson, worked here as a hack writer, and Chesterton's romance *The Return of Don Quixote* took place near here. Nicholas Blake's Georgia Strangeways visited the chief of the organization called the English Banner, Lord Cantalog, in Birmingham in *The Smiler with the Knife.*

Charles Dickens's Mr. Pickwick met Mr. Winkle on Easy Row near Victoria Square.

On New Street, the main shopping area just north of the New Street Railroad Station, is the old-fashioned but handsome Midland Hotel. In Josephine Tey's *The Franchise Affair,* market town solicitor Robert Blair came to the Midlands after a morning spent tracking teenager Betty Kane through Larborough (Birmingham?). Albert, the tubby little lounge waiter, did remember seeing her pick up a traveling salesman at tea. According to mystery writer Jessica Mann in *Deadlier Than the Male,* Josephine Tey had gone to the Anstey Physical Training College in Birmingham. This education later gave rise to her mystery *Miss Pym Disposes,* and it also made Tey well acquainted with the city.

In Dick Francis's *Enquiry,* warned-off jockey Hughes came to Birmingham to the office of David Oakley, about a mile from the town's center, over a bicycle shop. Oakley had framed him with a phony photograph of some money. Hughes then went to the Great Stag Hotel, where he asked its landlord, Teddy Dewar, to lunch in the bar. Hughes asked Dewar's help in tracking down who had hired David Oakley to discredit Hughes as a jockey.

12

STRATFORD-UPON-AVON

BACKGROUND

Stratford-upon-Avon is best known as the birthplace of poet and playwright William Shakespeare, who was born there on April 23, 1564. After London, Stratford is the most tourist-visited city in England. In summer its population is swelled by visitors from every corner of the world. Stratford-upon-Avon is centrally located in Warwickshire and is accessible from London, ninety-three miles away, by train, coach, and automobile.

Situated in an area of idyllic farms and scenic woodlands, Stratford lies mainly on the northwest bank of the winding river Avon. The town is dominated by the spire of the medieval Holy Trinity Church, where Shakespeare and his wife, Anne Hathaway, as well as other members of their family, are buried.

Stratford was established by King John in 1192, near the site where the Romans had a ford across the River Avon. In 1196 a market was established at Stratford and fairs were held; the town was incorporated in 1553. The layout of Stratford is basically that of a medieval grid, with three parallel streets crossed by three others at right angles.

The five buildings that are most closely associated with William Shakespeare's life are under the protection of the

Shakespeare Trust. Its purpose, as defined by Parliament, is twofold: "to preserve and maintain the Shakespearean properties as national memorials to the poet and to promote the general advancement of Shakespearean knowledge and appreciation." The properties administered by the trust are the gabled half-timbered Tudor house where Shakespeare was born; Anne Hathaway's Cottage, the early home of Shakespeare's wife (see Side Trips at the end of this walk); the site and gardens of New Place, where Shakespeare lived after his retirement and where he died; Mary Arden's House, the farm home of Shakespeare's mother (see Side Trips at the end of this walk); and Hall's Croft, the Tudor house of Shakespeare's daughter, Susanna, and her husband, Dr. John Hall. Most of the buildings associated with Shakespeare were acquired by the British government in the nineteenth century and have since been restored. Elizabethan and Jacobean stuccoed and half-timbered facades with leaded windows are to be seen throughout the town—some are genuine, some are not.

In the village of Shottery, where Anne Hathaway's Cottage is located, is a cottage that once belonged to mystery queen Agatha Christie. It was one of the many homes that she collected. The cottage, which is now privately owned, is very much like the one to which Gerald Martin took his bride in the Christie short story, "Philomel Cottage." That cottage too was near a village, just as the Christie cottage is near Shottery.

One of Stratford's greatest attractions is the Royal Shakespeare Theatre, which opened in 1932 as a replacement for an earlier theater which had been destroyed by fire. The theater now has a permanent company that has a home at the Barbican Centre in London as well as in Stratford.

Stratford's accessibility to London makes it a popular spot with characters in mystery stories. Like everyone else, they come to Stratford for the plays at the Royal Shakespeare Theatre and for the other Shakespeare associations and for a myriad of other activities.

Because so many Americans find their way to Stratford, it was appropriate that American writer Martha Grimes should select Stratford as the setting for one of her pub-based thrillers, her best-selling *The Dirty Duck*. English mystery writer Margaret Yorke, who lives near Oxford, is very familiar with Stratford. In *Cast for Death*, Tina Willoughby, the woman friend of actor Sam Irwin, was planning to move to Stratford-upon-Avon. Irwin's body had earlier been spotted floating in the Thames by Yorke's detective, the Oxford don Patrick Grant.

When Grant and the visiting Greek policeman, Manolakis, reached Stratford-upon-Avon they found the town preparing for the festival, which now is always held on the Saturday nearest Shakespeare's April 23 birthday but has been held on the birthday itself. Flagpoles flying the flags of various nations that had sent representatives were fixed in Bridge Street near the garden, and a huge marquee occupied space in the garden. Manlokis was pleased to discover that there would be some Greek people among the visitors.

Another master of the English mystery, Edmund Crispin, used Stratford and the surrounding countryside as the setting for *Love Lies Bleeding*, his tale of a lost Shakespearean manuscript.

In *Trial Run* by Dick Francis, Randall Drew, the gentleman horseman who resisted the prince's assignment to go to Moscow, spent a Saturday morning driving around his horse farm, then visited the local races at Stratford-upon-Avon in the afternoon. Charlie Salter in Eric Wright's *Death in the Old Country* was also very fond of the racetrack located south of Stratford.

Charles Dickens, a keen master of suspense and the author of two authentic tales of detection—*The Mystery of Edwin Drood* and *Bleak House*, visited the Stratford Shakespearean sites in 1838. He later donated proceeds from amateur theatricals to the curatorship of the Shakespeare birthplace. His trip to Stratford afforded him the opportunity of having Mrs. Pickwick state, in chapter 27 of the *Pickwick Papers*, "After we had seen Shakespeare's tomb and birthplace, we went back to the inn there, where we slept that night, and I recollect that all night long I dreamed of nothing but a black gentleman, at full length, in plaster-of-Paris, with a lay down collar tied with two tassels, leaning against a post and thinking: and when I woke in the morning and described him to Mr. Nickleby, he said it was Shakespeare, just as he had been when he was alive, which was very curious indeed."

Stratford makes an ideal center for touring the villages of the Cotswolds; both Warwick and Kenilworth Castles are nearby, as is Coventry Cathedral.

How to Get There

British Rail: from Paddington Station to Leamington Spa; change for Stratford-upon-Avon. Service on Sunday is limited to May through September only. Weekday schedules do not permit attendance at an evening performance at the theater and return the same evening. 2½ hours

Train/coach: "The Shakespeare Connection" leaves Euston Station each morning for Coventry; change there to a special bus. This service makes it possible, except on Sunday, to return to London after the evening performance. 2 hours

Automobile: A40 and M40 to Oxford, then the A34 to Stratford-upon-Avon. Ninety-three miles from London.

Length of walk: 4.8 miles; with Shottery Walk, 6.8 miles

See map on page 260 for exact boundaries of this walk, and page 376 for a list of detectives and books mentioned.

Places of Interest

Clopton Bridge, east end of Bridge Street. A fine example of late-medieval stone bridge. Route Shakespeare took when he left for London.

Grammar School, the upper floor of the original Guildhall, Church Street (0789) 293351. The quaint half-timbered building was built in 1417 to house the Guild of the Holy Cross. Stratford's grammar school was located here in Shakespeare's time, and it is generally believed that he was educated here. The school is now King Edward VI School; visitors are admitted to the buildings during summer vacations.

Harvard House, High Street. This half-timbered house, built in 1696, was the early home of Katherine Rogers, who married Robert Harvard. Their son, John, was the founder of Harvard University. (Open 9–1, 2–5:15.) Admission charge, except to members of Harvard University.

New Place Great Garden, Chapel Street entrance; *The Knott Garden,* entrance through Nash House. Only the foundations remain of New Place, the house where Shakespeare spent his retirement and where he died. The New Place gardens are exquisitely beautiful. The Knott Garden is a replica of an Elizabethan garden. (Open April–October, weekdays 9–6, Sunday 2–6; November–March, weekdays only 9–12:45, 2–4.) Admission charge.

Holy Trinity Church, Trinity Street. Thirteenth century. Shakespeare was baptized and is buried here.

Shakespeare's Birthplace; Shakespeare Centre, Henley Street (0789) 204016. William Shakespeare was born in the upstairs bedroom of this gabled half-timbered Tudor house on April 23, 1564. The window of the bedroom bears the scratched-in signatures of such well-known visitors as Sir Walter Scott and Alfred, Lord Tennyson. The birthplace also contains a museum of relics and a library. The garden behind the house features flowers, herbs, and other plants that Shakespeare knew. (Open daily, except Good Friday morning and Christmas.) Admission charge.

Royal Shakespeare Theatre, Waterside. Call (0789) 295623 to book seats in advance; (0789) 69191 for 24-hour information on the program and seat availability.

Gower Memorial, Bancroft Garden, near Clopton Bridge. Bronze statue of Shakespeare with Hamlet, Lady Macbeth, Falstaff, and Prince Hal at its base. Unveiled in 1888.

Stratford Motor Museum, Shakespeare Street (0789) 69413. A wonderful collection of exotic cars from the 1920s and 1930s. (Open daily except Christmas.) Admission charge.

Stratford Brass Rubbing Centre, Avonbank Gardens (0789) 297671. The center has replicas of a number of brasses and supplies of paper and wax for doing the rubbing. (Open daily except Christmas.) Admission charge.

POSSIBLE SIDE TRIPS

Shottery and Anne Hathaway's Cottage. Located one mile west of
Stratford-upon-Avon town center.

Wilmcote and Mary Arden's House.

PLACES TO STAY/EAT

The Shakespeare, Chapel Street (0789) 294771. A rambling half-
timbered Tudor hostelry located in the heart of town.
Moderate.

The Falcon, Chapel Street (0789) 205777. A big half-timbered
building in an excellent location.

Box Tree, Royal Shakespeare Theatre, Waterside (193226).
Convenient in-theater place to dine when attending a play.
Moderate.

Garrick Inn, High Street (292186). A colorful pub with
inexpensive food and snacks.

The Dirty Duck, Waterside, across from the Royal Shakespeare
Theatre. Called the Actors' pub, a fun place to play who's
who.

Tourist Information: Judith Shakespeare House, 1 High
Street (0789) 293127. Open Monday through Saturday 9–
5:30; Sunday 2–5.

——————— STRATFORD WALK ———————

Begin this walk at the Stratford British Railway Station. Upon
leaving the station, turn right on Station Road and follow it as
it runs into Alcester Road. Walk along Alcester Road, passing
assorted small shops—fish and chips, antiques—the sort of
places that seem to cluster around the station in many English
towns, easing the traveler into the whole business of tourism.
You will soon come to Arden Street to the left, and Grove
Road to the right; here Alcester becomes Greenhill Street.
Follow Greenhill Street to Rother Street and the Rother Market (the word *rother,* as used by Shakespeare, meant an ox or

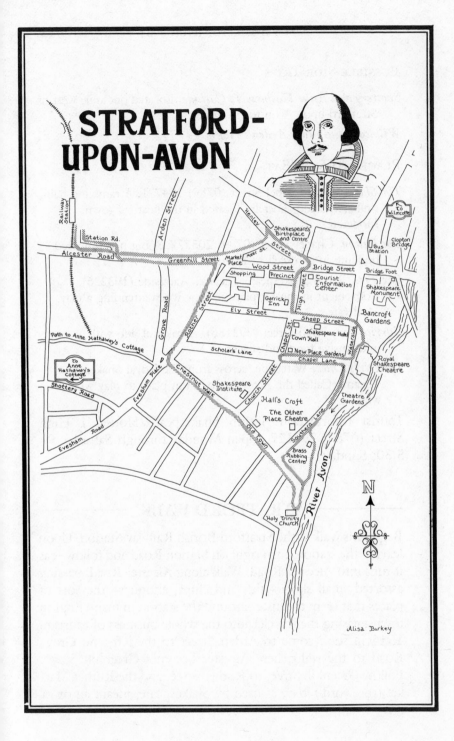

STRATFORD-UPON-AVON

Railway Station

Station Rd.

Arden Street

Henley Street

Shakespeare's Birthplace and Centre

To Wilmcote

Alcester Road

Greenhill Street

Market Place

Meer St.

Wood Street

Shopping

Precinct

Bridge Street

Bridge Foot

Bus Station

Clopton Bridge

Tourist Information Center

Shakespeare Monument

Grove Road

Rother Street

High Street

Garrick Inn

Ely Street

Sheep Street

Bancroft Gardens

Path to Anne Hathaway's Cottage

To Anne Hathaway's Cottage

Chapel St.

Shakespeare Hotel

Town Hall

New Place Gardens

Scholar's Lane

Waterside

Chapel Lane

Royal Shakespeare Theatre

Shottery Road

Chestnut Walk

Evesham Place

Shakespeare Institute

Church Street

Chapel Street

Hall's Croft

Theatre Gardens

Evesham Road

Old Town

The Other Theatre

Southern Lane

Brass Rubbing Centre

River Avon

Holy Trinity Church

N

Alisa Burkey

260

cattle). The American Fountain is located here. The fountain, given by Philadelphia journalist George W. Childs in 1887, the Jubilee Year of Queen Victoria, was unveiled by the actor, Sir Henry Irving, who drank the first cup of water.

In Eric Wright's *Death in the Old Country* visiting Canadian policeman Charlie Salter and his wife, Maud, parked their car in the Market Square in preparation for a day's exploration of Shakespeare sites, and it was to the Turf Accountant's establishment located there (whose establishment Charlie had spotted earlier) that Charlie returned to put five pounds on the nose of the horse whose name Freddy Tinsdale had given him.

Take time to admire the fountain and to look about the square at such interesting old buildings as the Old Thatch Tavern on the corner of Greenhill Street and the White Swan Hotel, which was a tavern in Shakespeare's day. Inside the White Swan there are some well-preserved wall paintings that depict scenes from the Apocryphal book of Tobias. Leave the square by going to the right on Meer Street (it is opposite Greenhill Street and leads out of the northeast corner of the square). Take Meer Street to Henley Street and Shakespeare's Birthplace, which will be across Henley and to the left. The Birthplace, which looks much as it did at the time of Shakespeare's birth, is a sixteenth-century half-timbered building built of Arden timber and Wilmcote stone; it served as both house and shop for the glover John Shakespeare.

In *The Dirty Duck* by Martha Grimes, Detective Superintendent Richard Jury and Penny Farraday went to the Birthplace to ask questions after the disappearance of Penny's brother, James Carlton Farraday. They circumvented the line of tourists at the door by showing Jury's warrant card and then showed Jimmy's picture to the guardians of the various small, cozy rooms. Finally they headed out past the garden of Shakespeare flowers and through the souvenir shop with its selection of treasures.

In *Death in the Old Country*, Charlie and Maud and their companions looked at the preserved relics displayed at the Birthplace. Charlie was not particularly enthusiastic about the Shakespeare memorabilia but the others were fascinated.

There is much to see at the Birthplace, outside as well as inside. If you plan to take advantage of this and the various other Shakespeare sites, plan additional time in your walk.

When you leave the Birthplace, turn left and walk along Henley Street to the point where it Y's into Bridge Street. Here you will find the white-faceted Barclay's Bank (formerly a Regency Market Hall) and just opposite, at the junction of Henley and Bridge Streets, the Tourist Information Centre. The Information Centre occupies Quiney's House, once the home of Shakespeare's daughter, Judith, and her husband, Thomas Quiney, a wine merchant. After stopping at the Information Centre for maps and theater schedules, as well as hotel recommendations and reservations, cross High Street and turn left. A short distance along the right-hand side of High Street is a large Tudor town house that dates from 1595 and once belonged to the mother of John Harvard, the founder of Harvard University. Harvard House, which is one of finest period houses in town, is open to the public. It was presented to Harvard University in 1909 by Edward Morris of Chicago. The restoration was accomplished through the efforts of novelist Marie Corelli, notorious Stratford gadfly. Adjoining Harvard House is the half-timbered Garrick Inn. Today, as it has been for four centuries, it is one of Stratford's most congenial pubs. The Garrick building joins up with the picturesque building on the corner of Ely Street that is called the Old Tudor House.

Cross High Street and turn left into Sheep Street at the point where the High becomes Chapel Street; Ely Street is to the right. On the southeast corner of Chapel and Sheep Streets is the impressive mid-Georgian Town Hall built by Robert Newman in 1767 of lovely Cotswold stone. The first-floor ballroom contains a number of fine paintings, including one of David Garrick as Richard III, painted by Nathaniel Dance. The bust of Shakespeare that is set high on the wall in Sheep Street was a gift to the town from David Garrick.

Follow Sheep Street, an interesting mixture of shops intermingled with a variety of restaurants, to Waterside and turn right. Cross Waterside and enter the gardens facing the Royal

Shakespeare Theatre. The Bancroft Gardens lie north of the Royal Shakespeare Theatre between Waterside Street and the river. Wander eastward here toward the river. There are two bridges that cross the Avon here—the old Tramway, now reserved for pedestrian traffic, and the Clopton, the bridge that Shakespeare crossed on his way to and from London.

In *Cast for Death,* Dr. Patrick Grant, Margaret Yorke's Oxford don-cum-sleuth, parked his car in the large parking lot beside Clopton Bridge. He crossed Bridgefoot Street and cut through the garden. There were people standing on the river bank watching the swans and others strolling in front of the theater.

Just west of the bridges is Lord Ronald Sutherland Gower's wonderfully magnificent Shakespeare Memorial. The memorial, sixty-five tons of bronze on stone plinths, was cast in Paris in 1888. Oscar Wilde was one of the speech-givers at its dedication.

The memorial shows the bard in a seated position surrounded by representatives of the types of his drama: Prince Hal with the crown represents History; Hamlet holding Yorick's skull represents philosophy; Lady Macbeth sleepwalking represents tragedy; and of course, Falstaff represents comedy. Although not a detective writer, Shakespeare was a first-class creator of suspense, mystery, and intrigue. Josephine Tey challenged the character of Richard III as depicted by Shakespeare in her *The Daughter of Time.* Elizabeth Peters picked up the same subject in *The Murders of Richard III,* as did Guy M. Townsend in *To Prove a Villain,* Jeremy Potter in *A Trail of Blood,* and Audrey Williamson in his Crime Writers' Gold Dagger Award winner, *The Mystery of the Princes.* And of course, Edmund Crispin centers his *Love Lies Bleeding* around the discovery of a lost Shakespearean manuscript.

If you look left beyond the memorial across Bridge Foot Street, you will see the incongruous bulk of the Stratford Hilton, now a Moat House International Hotel. It was the Hilton that Gwendolyn Bracegirdle in *The Dirty Duck* by Martha Grimes eschewed in favor of a lumpy-bedded B-and-B, because she wanted to stay some place "English."

It was to the Stratford Hilton that Inspector Jury in *The Dirty Duck* hurried when he was informed of trouble by Detective Sergeant Lasko. Upon their arrival in the posh modern hotel, they discovered that James Carlton Farraday had disappeared.

From the Hilton, Penny Farraday and Jury defied death and cut through traffic across Bridge Street to sit on a bench near the Shakespeare Memorial.

In *The Wimsey Family*, "A Fragmentary History compiled from correspondence with Dorothy L. Sayers," C. W. Scott-Giles explains that even Lord Peter Wimsey, through his ancestors, had a connection with the Bard. It seems that Gerald, the fourth Duke of Denver, found it politic to present Queen Elizabeth I with a manor in Warwickshire. John Shakespeare of Stratford-upon-Avon had his own claim to the property. Both John and his son, William, were so angered by the handing over of what they considered theirs to the Wimsey family, that ever after, the Shakespeares considered the Duke of Denver as their nearest and dearest enemy. When William wrote *Romeo and Juliet* he used the character of Tybalt, whom Mercutio addresses as the "Good King of Cats," to get even. When Romeo later felled Tybalt in a fight, Shakespeare had the satisfaction of knowing that every time the play was performed, his enemy would fall. It must be remembered that the domestic house cat, crouched as if to spring, occupies a dominant position on the Wimsey coat of arms.

Scott-Giles, all in good fun of course, goes on to point out that there were arguments that could be mounted both for and against the theory that the Duke of Denver, in association with the Earl of Oxford, authored some of the plays attributed to Shakespeare.

Turn your attention now to the Royal Shakespeare Festival Theatre itself. The present theater was built in 1932 after the 1879 building was destroyed by fire. The festival to honor Shakespeare dates back to 1769, the idea of the actor, David Garrick. A Shakespeare theater opened in Chapel Lane in 1827 as part of the festival, but failed to make money. The festival idea continued to grow, however, and as a result of the efforts of a local brewer, Charles Edward Flower, the 1879 building was erected. The Royal Shakespeare Company presents Shakespeare's plays continually from Easter through August. In addition, the Elizabethan-styled Swan Theatre, located at the south end of the Royal Shakespeare building, presents plays by Shakespeare's contemporaries—writers such as Christopher Marlowe, whose death was the subject of a book with which Harvey Schoenberg bored Melrose Plant in *The Dirty Duck* by Martha Grimes. The Swan was opened in 1986.

Peter Plumstead, a clerk on holiday in Edmund Crispin's *Love Lies Bleeding,* visited the Royal Shakespeare Theatre before going on to Ravenswood, where he discovered Mrs. Bly's body in a derelict Elizabethan cottage.

Yorke's Patrick Grant did not like the architectural style of the Theatre but it held good feelings for him because he had spent many happy hours there with his friends. When he arrived at the Theatre, Grant inquired for Denis Vernon at the box office.

No one there knew who he was talking about, so they sent him "round the side of the building to the office entrance." He entered the building at this point and made his way along "echoing stone corridors" past many closed doors until at last he came to a small office occupied by two girls and a young man with cropped hair. It took Grant a moment to recognize Denis because the last time he had seen him, Denis had been sporting shoulder-length locks. Denis agreed to meet Grant at a nearby pub in a half hour.

Grant was disappointed when one of the girls agreed to lead him out of the Theatre. He would very much have liked to have found his own way out and to have done some investigating on the way. The girl, Jean, explained as they walked along that "this side of the theatre had formerly been used for dressing-rooms, but now they had all been moved to the river side of the building."

Before leaving the theater environs, if you have not already done so, take time to walk around the grounds as our mystery characters did, being sure to locate the stage door on the side facing Waterside Street toward the southwest end of the building.

Denis was five minutes late arriving at the pub (The Dirty Duck). The room in which he and Grant found themselves was heavily timbered, dark, and "loaded with atmosphere, some of it genuinely old."

Martha Grimes's *The Dirty Duck* begins with theatergoers pouring out of the Festival Theatre after a performance of *As You Like It* and heading across Waterside to the Dirty Duck/ Black Swan Pub. The two-sided pub sign with its double logo leaves it up to the patron to decide which pub—since they are one and the same—that he or she is frequenting. Grimes's aristocratic amateur sleuth, Melrose Plant, after meeting the American Harvey Schoenberg in Holy Trinity Church, took time to explain to Harvey that the Black Swan is the restaurant part of the establishment. The restaurant offers moderately priced food and the pub provides excellent liquid refreshment and inexpensive pub food, but don't ask for "Old Peculiar," a brew featured in Grimes's writing, but generally available only north in Yorkshire.

It was in the Dirty Duck that Schoenberg explained to Plant that he, Schoenberg, had written a book called *Who Killed Marlowe?* In it Schoenberg advanced the theory that Shakespeare killed Marlowe. Later, over dinner in the Black Swan, Plant explained the Schoenberg theory to Inspector Jury, who was disappointed because his own plans to add Jenny Kennington to their dinner duo had fallen through.

Leave the Dirty Duck and turn left on Waterside. Walk back along Waterside to Chapel Lane and turn left. Follow Chapel Lane to New Place on your right. This is the location of the home Shakespeare built when he returned from London a successful man and it is where he died after an evening of revelry, on his fifty-seventh birthday, in 1663. The house was dismantled in 1759, and today only the foundation stones and extensive gardens remain. The gardens are open to the public and may be visited daily.

In *Death in the Old Country,* Charlie and Maud Salter, in

their ramble through Shakespeare sites, took time to admire and examine the Elizabethan Gardens at New Place.

At the corner of Church Street to the left and Chapel Street on the right, turn right if you wish to visit the New Place Museum. After visiting the museum, return to Chapel Lane, where you will turn left. Note that at the south end of Church Street, to your right is the eighteenth-century house of novelist Marie Corelli (Mary Mackay).

Return along Chapel Lane to Southern Lane and turn right to the Dirty Duck, where you can pick up Grimes's American tourist, Gwendolyn Bracegirdle. After she left the Royal Shakespeare Theatre, she crossed Waterside and walked along the right-hand side of the street past the Arden Hotel, where Jury took Plant after the first act of a "very good Hamlet" to the Dirty Duck. Once at the Dirty Duck, by all means have something to drink and enjoy the terrace out front, weather permitting. This is where Gwendolyn stood with her unidentified companion, getting "sloshed" on gin. They soon left the pub for what she hoped would be a romantic encounter. They walked west along Southern Lane until they crossed into the Avonbank Gardens and took an unlit path that curved around the Brass Rubbing Centre and led toward the church. When they had circled around the church her "friend," pleading a call of nature, conducted her to the public restrooms, where he killed her.

If you wish to follow Ms. Bracegirdle on her last journey, leave the Dirty Duck and this time turn right. Walk along Southern Lane until you come to a brick building called "The Old Ferry House." Cross the street here to enter the theater gardens where boat rentals are posted and pick up the path that leads up to and around the Brass Rubbing Centre. Follow the path through the gateway in the low, natural-wood picket fence, with the Avon to your left and the round brick building that houses the Stratford-upon-Avon Brass Rubbing Centre on your right. Here people stroll about, admiring the floral display or picnicking before a performance. The path falls off sharply to the left down to the Avon, which is extremely busy with pleasure boats of all sorts. The path now becomes quite wooded and it is easy to imagine how remote one would feel walking along here at night. Soon you will come to another opening in the picket fence; go through this into a little valley. A brick wall tops the rise at the south side of the little valley and the spire of the church rises over the wall. Now, you must scramble up the hillside, through an opening in the brick wall and into the churchyard of Holy Trinity Church. You will see the entrance to your right, but continue to the Avon end of the church and behind it, where you will find the rather dilapidated and no longer used public restrooms. It is easy to see that this would be a perfect place for a murder because it is quite remote, although the housing estate that lies just beyond another brick wall has encroached upon some of that seclusion. Return now to the entrance of the church.

Gwendolyn Bracegirdle was not the only one to walk in the gardens that surround the Theatre. In *Death in the Old Country*, after dinner in a "Frenchified" restaurant, Charlie and Maud and their friends walked down to the river, then returned to the theater for a performance of *The Taming of the Shrew*, at which time Charlie indulged himself in a light snooze.

James Brigsley, in Jeffrey Archer's *Not a Penny More, Not a Penny Less*, brought Anne Summerton down to Stratford for the weekend. They took in a performance of *Much Ado About Nothing*, and afterwards James proposed to Anne as they walked along the Avon.

In *The Dirty Duck*, when Martha Grimes's Melrose Plant walked in the gardens with his aunt, the redoubtable Lady Agatha Ardry, he briefly considered drowning as a means of escaping his unfavorite relative, then decided that she would no doubt bore him to death.

If you would rather not walk across the gardens with Gwendolyn, leave the Dirty Duck and turn right to walk along Southern Lane until you come to The Other Place Theatre on your right, where new plays are presented. Just beyond The Other Place you will come to Old Town Street. Turn left and follow Old Town as it curves to the left, then enter the avenue of lime trees (twelve left-hand trees for the twelve tribes of

Israel, eleven right-hand trees for the Apostles sans Judas) that leads to Holy Trinity Church. You are walking along a path paved with what appear to be grave markers, through the avenue of trees and across an old and interesting cemetery, into the beautiful fifteenth-century church with its fourteenth-century wall and tower. It is one of England's stateliest medieval churches. William Shakespeare is buried in the chancel together with members of his family. The parish registers, which contain entries relating to Shakespeare's christening and to his death, are located near the font. The church is open until seven each evening.

In *Death in the Old Country* by Eric Wright, Canadian policeman Charlie Salter came into the church alone. He was not prepared for the impact of the floor-slab marker placed just beyond the altar rail and bearing the inscription "Good friend, for Jesus sake forbeare/ To digg the dust encloased heare;/ Blese be ye man y spares thes stones/ And curst be he y moves my bones." Suddenly Charlie felt the reality of the man Shakespeare and wanted to return to all the Shakespeare sites he had just visited.

Melrose Plant also wanted to visit the chancel of Holy Trinity. He felt rather ghoulish as he fished out ten pence to pay for a look at the Shakespeare gravesite. The taste and modesty of the grave marking caused Plant to feel "an uncustomary surge of near-religious respect for such genius . . ." Before he left the nave, Plant examined the choir and noted the gargoyle-like carvings on the arms of the seats there. As he continued his prowling, he bumped into Harvey Schoenberg who, upon leaving the church, found it "weird to be walking on graves."

After looking around the church, which is noted for the beauty of its architecture, return along the tree-lined walk to Old Town Road. Turn left and follow Old Town Road; you will soon cross Southern Lane. Next, you will come to Hall's Croft on your right; this is one of the most interesting of the Shakespeare Trust properties. It was the home of Dr. John Hall, a Puritan physician who married Susanna Shakespeare in 1607 and brought her to live in this triple-gabled house with its walled garden. Among other exhibits displayed here is his *Select Observations on English Bodies,* a collection of cases that he successfully treated. It was published after Hall's death.

Church Street intersects Old Town Street just beyond Hall's Croft. Looking down Church to the right you will see the Shakespeare Institute on the left-hand side of the street. Across the street and down a ways next to the Guildhall are the Almshouses, which have housed the pensioners of Stratford since 1427.

On the corner of Old Town and Church is Mason Croft, now the Brimingham University Shakespeare Institute, but once the home of novelist Marie Corelli. Her books were sensational and slightly naughty and attracted a wide following. She counted Gladstone and Tennyson among her fans, and Queen Victoria is said to have appalled the Empress Frederick by announcing that Marie Corelli would be remembered when novelists like Dickens and George Eliot had been forgotten. Corelli was responsible for the appellation "Mighty Mite," which Frances Chesterton humorously, we assume, applied to her husband—writer, journalist, and creator of Father Brown—the renowned heavyweight, G. K. Chesterton. He, too, was a Corelli fan.

Continue along Old Town, which has become Chestnut Walk, to Rother Street. If you are taking the side trip to Shottery, cross Rother Street and Grove Road, which converges into Rother Street (to the left it is Evesham Road), and follow the footpath marked Anne Hathaway's Cottage. The footpath leads between houses.

Continue the Stratford walk by turning right into Rother Street (a left turn here will take you into Evesham Place and the bus stop for Stratford tours). Walk north past the squat modern buildings that house Mason's Court and the police station and courts on the left. It was here in Detective Sergeant Lasko's cluttered office that Grimes's Superintendent Jury lounged, feet on desk, perusing the Stratford telephone directory in hopes of locating Jenny Kennington.

As you walk along Rother Street you will note that this is

"bed-and-breakfast row." Most of the houses and small hotels offer inexpensive lodging and tasty breakfasts. Some also serve dinner by arrangement. They are not unlike the Diamond Hill Guest House, where the Grimes's ill-fated Gwendolyn Brace-girdle elected to stay.

Follow Rother Street to Greenhill Street. Turn left and take Greenhill to Alcester Road and jog right into Station Road and on to the railway station.

POSSIBLE SIDE TRIPS

The following side trips are suggested not for their mystery associations, but because travel to Stratford-upon-Avon indicates an interest in William Shakespeare and the other historical riches of this Cotswold area.

Shottery

Shottery lies one mile west of Stratford. The walk is a pleasant one along a well-marked footpath. Anne Hathaway's Cottage, your destination, has changed very little since the days when the Bard came courting. The cottage was occupied until 1899 by a member of the Hathaway family.

Begin your walk to Shottery at the west end of Chestnut Street, where it intersects Rother Street and Grove Road. Cross the two streets and follow the posted path to Anne Hathaway's Cottage, which leads between the houses. The walk takes you across a derelict railroad line, through a housing development of fairly new homes, and across three roads. After the third road you will come into a large recreation field called Shottery Fields. After about a hundred yards the path will divide. Follow the right-hand fork to Cottage Lane, which will lead you to the Hathaway cottage. There is a pleasant tearoom across from the cottage where you may refresh yourself before returning the way you came. If you wish to go directly to the railway station, follow the left-hand path through Shottery Fields recreation grounds and alongside the College of Further Education grounds. You will cross a road marked The Willows and the derelict rail line. Continue following the left-hand path to Alcester Road; cross Alcester Road to Station Road, which leads to the station.

Wilmcote

The walk to the home farm of William Shakespeare's mother is about three miles long. You can walk just one way and catch one of the frequent trains back to Stratford, or you can walk both ways.

A good place to start this walk is at the Gower Memorial. Turn left along Bridge Foot, crossing the road at the pedestrian crossing. Walk in front of the bus station and bear to the right to walk along Warwick Road. Follow Warwick Road past Paxton Street to the Stratford Canal. Cross the bridge and go through a gap on the right to the canal towpath. Turn right again and follow the towpath under the road bridge. Follow the towpath for about three miles.

After passing under bridge No. 65, you will see a marina on the left and the old gas works on the right. Continue along the path as it passes through the industrial heart of Stratford.

At the next lock, you will see the Bishopton Spa Lodge just ahead. Spa Lodge was part of the Victoria Spa Baths project, which was opened in 1837 with the intention of rivaling nearby Leamington. The buildings stand today as they did when Victoria was a princess.

After the Bishopton Lane Bridge and the Spa buildings, the towpath becomes a vehicle track when it passes under the Northern bypass. Past Lock No. 40 (the top lock), with its old lock-keepers cottage, cross the bridge and follow the track that winds to the right of farm buildings. Wilmcote Manor Farm is on the left, and the village of Wilmcote is on the right. The path leads to a road at a stile to the right of a gate, and after following a private road for about a hundred yards, you will reach a county road. Turn right and walk past the Victorian school and church, both built of stone from local quarries. Turn right at the Swan Hotel and walk along Station Road. On the left is Mary Arden's Tudor farmhouse. The property is open on weekdays and on Sunday afternoons during the summer months. From November to March it is open weekday mornings and afternoons.

After Mary Arden's house, follow Station Road to the canal bridge, which is just past the last house on the right-hand side. About a hundred yards beyond this point is the railway station where, every day but Sunday, you can catch one of the frequent trains back to Stratford. Of course, should you choose, you may return the way you came—on foot. (Take Birmingham Road to Arden Street, follow Arden Street to Alcester Road, turn right and take Alcester Road to Station Road, turn right once more. Station Road takes you to the railway station and the end of the walk.)

13

THAMES RIVER

BACKGROUND

The Thames River got its name from an ancient Celtic word meaning "dark or mysterious." It crosses the center of England from west to east for 215 miles so that, historically, whoever controlled the river had command of the country. From earliest recorded history, the river was also London's first and most important highway, and twice a day the tides brought her the salty smell of the North Sea. Thanks to the Thames, London also became a great trading center. By the nineteenth century it was the largest port in the world.

The Tower of London was built beside the Thames on the site of a Roman, then Norman, fort commanding the river. London Bridge was the crucial link between north and south England. Originally London Bridge was narrow and hard to go past, making a dam that let the river freeze for the famous Frost Fairs of the seventeenth and eighteenth centuries. The river also provided a livelihood for many people.

Passenger ships used to dock at London from all parts of the world, but by 1975 only one line sailed from Millwall Dock in London to Madeira and Las Palmas. Since the Thames at London was near the North Sea, smuggling was a time-honored Thames River occupation. Smuggling is still alive in mysteries like *Gideon's River* by J. J. Marric (aka John Creasey). There have been many real-life murderers associated with the river communities like the East End's Whitechapel and Limehouse. They included the eighteenth-century murders along the Ratcliffe Highway near Wapping Old Stairs, described by P. D. James and T. A. Critchley in *The Maul and the Pear Tree,* and the gruesome killings of Victorian Jack the Ripper.

By peaceful contrast, the large mute swans on the Thames from Windsor to Greenwich belong either to two ancient City Guilds, the Dyers and the Vintners, or to Her Majesty the Queen. Each season in a traditional ceremony the cygnets are marked by the companies; "unnicked" swans are the property of the Queen.

The Thames was once a major thoroughfare where kings, lords, and commons "took water" to get from Westminster to Richmond or Greenwich. Great palaces once lined the shores, each with its own dock, or "water steps," some with a water gate or private harbor. London's wharves and warehouses and sailors' hostels, described by Charles Dickens, were built as waves of immigrants turned the East End into a slum.

Today, gentrification of the Pool of London docks beyond the Tower has made living by the river fashionable again. The great London papers have moved their new printing plants there, especially media mogul Rupert Murdoch, who publishes not only the high-class *Times* but also the "sexy" *News of the World,* read by John Mortimer's lawyer Rumpole of the Bailey. Two P. D. James detectives live Thameside: the CID's Adam Dalgliesh, who lives at Queenhithe, and Cordelia Gray, who lives in a converted city warehouse nearby. (See also *Mystery Reader's Walking Guide: London.*) Both murderers and detectives, from Sherlock Holmes to Fu Manchu to the Man Who Was Thursday, have hunted their prey on the river, while many a body has been dumped there in hopes of destroying evidence.

The Thames has also been the scene of spectacular waterborne processions. The Lord Mayor of London used to hold his official progress there; today he goes by coach from Mansion House to Temple Bar, as he did in Marion Babson's *The Lord Mayor of Death*. Handel wrote his Water Music for Hanoverian trips by water. The funeral procession of Elizabeth I came by water from Richmond to Westminster, just as earlier she had come to the Tower by way of Traitor's Gate. Great heroes of the empire, Lord Nelson and much later, Sir Winston Churchill, came from their funerals at Saint Paul's Cathedral by water, too.

Across the Thames from the Isle of Dogs lies Greenwich. It is the home of the Royal Naval College, the Maritime Museum, and the place where Greenwich mean time was calculated in the old Greenwich Observatory. (See Greenwich/Blackheath Walk.) Beyond Greenwich is the new Thames Flood Barrier at Woolwich, a reminder that London itself can still flood and is sinking like Venice. Finally you come to Tilbury and the modern container-cargo Port of London.

The "upriver" Thames River begins at Westminster Pier, and "country" London begins at Chelsea. Kings and nobles once had great estates here; then it became the haunt of artists and writers. Now it is fashionable again. Prime Minister Margaret Thatcher's private house is there, and society's Sloane (Square) Rangers, to which Princess Diana and Duchess Sarah both belonged, lived in Chelsea, too. But lurking on the embankments you still may see houseboats, like the one lived in by Donald MacKenzie's former Scotland Yard Inspector Raven, as well as artists and bums like the characters in Pamela Branch's *The Wooden Overcoat* or Lionel Davidson's *The Chelsea Murders*.

Past Hammersmith, where G. K. Chesterton went to St. Paul's School and Peter Lovesey taught, comes the stretch where racing is a popular event. Eights Week is held one Saturday near Easter when crews from Oxford and Cambridge set out from Putney Bridge and row to Mortlake. E. C. Bentley, author of *Trent's Last Case* and schoolboy friend of G. K. Chesterton, won his Oxford blue there.

Farther upstream past Windsor, the Henley Regatta is an event of the social season, while the river teems all summer long with pleasure boats. Some are used for sinister ends, as in Peter Lovesey's *Swing, Swing Together,* or as three men and a dog followed Jerome K. Jerome's trip in *Three Men in a Boat* for murderous purposes. There have also been both murders and mysteries at Kew, at Richmond, and at Chiswick, en route to Henry VIII's Hampton Court.

Length of Trips: About 45 minutes one way by river from Westminster Pier to Greenwich
About an hour and 15 minutes one way by river from Tower Bridge to Thames River Barrier, Woolwich
About 3½ hours one way from Westminster Pier to Hampton Court

See page 281 for map of the Thames River. See list on page 377 for the books and detectives referred to.

How to Get There

(Always check time of last boat back.)
Down River: Tidal Thames River (01-930-4097)
From Westminster Pier:
> To the Tower
>> (all year) every 20 minutes 10:20 to 4–6 P.M.
>> Sailing time 30 minutes
> To Greenwich Pier
>> (all year) every 30 minutes 10:30 to 4–5 P.M.
>> Sailing time 45 minutes
> Circular cruises (01-237-1322)
>> (April–October) every 30 minutes 11:15 A.M.
>> Sailing time 1 hour round trip
> Thames Flood Barrier (01-740-8263)
>> (April–October) 10, 11:15, 12:30, 1:30, 2:45, 4
>> (November–March) 11:15, 1:30, 2:45
>> Sailing time about 1¼ hours one way
> Evening cruises (01-930-4721)
>> (May–September) 7:30, 8:15
>> Sailing time 1¾ hours (no landing)

From Charing Cross Pier:
To Tower and Greenwich Piers
(all year) every 30 minutes 10:30 to 4–4:30
Sailing time to Tower 20 minutes
to Greenwich Pier 45 minutes

Up River Thames (01-930-2063)
From Westminster Pier:
To Kew and Putney
(April–October) every 30 minutes 10:15–12:30, 2–3:30
Sailing time about 1½ hours

To Richmond
(April–October) 10:30, 11:15, 12:00, 12:30
Sailing time about 2½ hours

To Hampton Court
(April–October) 10:30, 11:15, 12:00, 12:30
Sailing time about 3–4 hours

Dogs may travel by boat if kept on leashes.

For longer river trips, contact:

Salter Brothers, Folly Bridge, Oxford (023421)

French Brothers, The Runnymede Boathouse, Windsor, Road, Old Windsor, Berks (0753) 851900

Turk Launches, Thames Side, Kingston-on-Thames, Surrey (01-546-5775)

British Rail: Return trip from Greenwich to Charing Cross Station
Return trip from Hampton Court to Waterloo Station

Nearly all the Thames-side towns mentioned can also be reached by the London Underground or British Railway.
For more information contact the Thames Passenger Services Federation (01-519-4872) or the London Tourist Board (01-730-3488).

Major River Events

March: Oxford v. Cambridge Boat Race from Putney to Mortlake

April: Devizes to Westminster Inter. Canoe Race

May: Thames Barge Sailing Club Open Days. Barges berthed at Greenwich with displays to view

July: Doggetts Coat and Badge Race from London Bridge to Chelsea

September: Thamesday, South Bank. Fireworks, boat races, etc.

November: Fireworks display from barge opposite HMS President by Victoria Embankment. Finale to Lord Mayor's Parade begins at 5 P.M.

PLACES OF INTEREST

Houses of Parliament, Westminster Bridge.

London Bridge.

Tower of London, Tower Bridge.

Pool of London, the East End.

Thames Flood Barrier, Woolwich.

Southwark Cathedral, Bankside.

Lambeth Palace, Lambeth.

South Bank.

Royal Hospital, Chelsea.

Crosby Hall, Chelsea.

Chelsea Old Church (All Saints), Chelsea.

Hampton Court.

PLACES TO STAY/EAT

London is so near that you will naturally want to stay there. For hotel recommendations in Greater London, see the British Tourist Authority at Victoria Station or Lower Regent Street. There are hundreds of famous Thames-side pubs at every town, of which we list a few below.

Prospect of Whitby, 57 Wapping Wall, East End (01-481-1095). Historic pub with courtyard. Associated with Hanging Judge Jeffreys, who put down Monmouth Rebellion. Good pub food, real ale. French restaurant.

Angel, 101 Bermondsley Wall East, Bankside (01-237-3608). Sixteenth-century pub with riverside terrace. Built on old pilings next to site of Shakespeare's Globe Theatre. Bare wood floors and open coal fires. Pub food on ground floor, international restaurant upstairs with view of St. Paul's Cathedral. Hangout of Dr. Samuel Johnson, whom G. K. Chesterton often portrayed in costume.

Anchor, Bankside (01-407-1577). Near Southwark Bridge. Dates from 1750, on site of earlier inn, where Samuel Pepys watched the Great Fire. Five bars and three restaurants. Good pub food.

National Theatre Restaurant, Upper Ground, South Bank (01-928-2033). Good view of the river. English food. Reservations needed.

Kings Head and Eight Bells, 50 Cheyne Walk, Chelsea (01-352-1820). Four-hundred-year-old inn, rebuilt in the 1930s. Pub meals.

—— WESTMINSTER TO WOOLWICH ——

Begin your Thames River Trip by "taking water" at Westminster Pier. It was this ride that Josephine Tey's hospitalized Inspector Alan Grant promised as a treat to his young American researcher in *The Daughter of Time.* Grant told Carradine that they would see some very fine architecture and a fine stretch of muddy river.

Go down the steps at Westminster Pier and choose a seat on the left (port) side of the boat so that you can see the northern shore of the city. Get a single ticket if you mean to land either at the Tower of London or Greenwich and take the train back, or a return (round trip) if you want to come back by river. Although the pilot will tell you some of the major sights, it is a good idea to bring along your own map.

As you leave the pier by the Houses of Parliament and Westminster Bridge, you will go north toward a spectacular view of St. Paul's and London's Wren spires. Next you will pass the Victoria Embankment, where you can see the massive red-and-white Norman Shaw building that was once New Scotland Yard. Shortly afterwards you will pass Cleopatra's Needle, the Egyptian obelisk given to Queen Victoria. In G. K. Chesterton's *The Man Who Was Thursday,* the poet

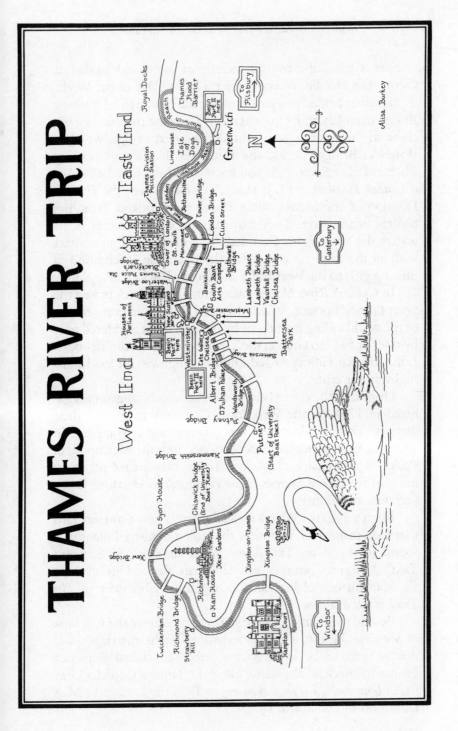

THAMES RIVER TRIP

West End   East End

Alisa Burkey

281

Gabriel Syme came by tug secretly at night and landed at Cleopatra's Needle, where he met a fellow Day of the Week.

The first bridge you pass under is the Hungerford Railway Bridge from Charing Cross Station. Then the river takes a big curve to the right as you go under the next bridge, which is Waterloo Bridge. Beside the bridge is the famous floating Thames Police Station. As you learn from Josephine Bell's *Port of London Murders* and J. J. Marric's *Gideon's River,* the Thames Division of the Metropolitan Police (of Scotland Yard) has control of the river. They maintain a continual patrol of its waters day and night. Commander Gideon came in contact with all the cases up and down the river from Richmond (a missing girl) to the West India and Surrey Docks (smuggling).

In *Gideon's River* Marric (aka John Creasey) celebrated the great Port of London, which then had ships from every corner of the world sailing in and out by day and night, hindered only by tides or fog. To Gideon the Thames River was the lifeline of London from Tilbury to Teddington, a highway for food and a highway for crime.

Originally the river police were a semi-official group organized in 1798 by the West India Company to protect their cargoes. Their headquarters was downstream at Wapping. In 1839 the river police were incorporated into the Metropolitan Police as the Thames Division. Today they patrol fifty-four miles of river from Staines (near Windsor) to Dartford Creek just west of Tilbury.

But it was to the Waterloo headquarters near Scotland Yard that Commander Gideon sent the stolen industrial diamonds found in the river. The River Police also helped Scotland Yard's Assistant Commissioner Sir Denis Nayland Smith chase Fu Manchu out of his Limehouse tunnel laboratory in *The Trail of Fu Manchu.*

Behind the floating police station you can see the vast bulk of Somerset House, where all records of births, marriages, and deaths used to be kept. Many detectives visited Somerset House to check a fishy story, like P. D. James's Cordelia Gray in *An Unsuitable Job for a Woman,* or Dorothy L. Sayers's Miss Climpson in *Unnatural Death.*

Beyond the floating police station as you pass the Temple Gardens, you will see three floating maritime museums—the HQS *Wellington,* HMS *Chrysanthemum,* and HMS *President.* They are moored by the riverbank just before Blackfriars Bridge.

Your view now is of the City itself, with St. Paul's Cathedral still dominating the skyline, in spite of modern skyscrapers built since the wartime bombing. The Fleet River, which rises in Hampstead Heath to the north, flows into the Thames here. It gave its name to Fleet Street, where mystery writers Edgar Wallace, G. K. Chesterton, and E. C. Bentley worked.

It was just past Blackfriars Bridge that playwright-director Peregrine Jay had his warehouse flat that overlooked Bankside and the mythical Dolphin Theatre in Ngaio Marsh's *Killer Dolphin.* Later, in Marsh's *Light Thickens,* the Jays entertained Superintendent Roderick Alleyn on their riverside terrace and watched the tour boats go past.

Another, unnamed, railway bridge crosses the river after Blackfriars Bridge. Then, beyond St. Paul's Cathedral, you come to the original London docks below Upper Thames Street. Many are now being rebuilt as residential flats. Among them is Queenhithe, where P. D. James's Adam Dalgliesh lived.

Next you come to Southwark Bridge, which leads directly across the Thames to Bankside, where Shakespeare's Globe Theatre once stood. Beyond Southwark Bridge is the Cannon Street Railway Bridge with trains coming from Cannon Street Station in the City.

Next you will pass by Old Swan Lane and Old Swan Wharf and come to the imposing bulk of Fishmongers Hall. Fishmongers Hall is the nineteenth-century headquarters of an ancient livery company that was granted its charter in 1272. Their Bargemaster still runs the annual Doggett's Coat and Badge Race on the Thames. At this point Upper Thames Street, which runs parallel to the river, becomes Lower Thames Street.

Now you come to London Bridge, the best-known bridge of all. There has been a bridge here since Roman times, and it was the only one in London until 1749. The stone bridge of the nursery rhyme "London Bridge is falling down" was built in 1176. It had 138 shops, houses, and a church dedicated to St. Thomas à Becket. Later it also had fortified gates with pikes for traitors' heads. That bridge looked much like Florence's Ponte Vecchio, and it was very dangerous to navigate under when the tide was going out. Its damlike qualities caused both floods and frosts. Famous people like Cardinal Wolsey preferred to disembark when they reached the bridge and walk on land to the other side.

London Bridge fell in the late fifteenth century and has been replaced by two others. The second one, built in 1831, stood here until 1973, when it was dismantled and shipped to an American buyer, who rebuilt it in Arizona, USA. The one you see was opened by Elizabeth II in 1973.

Just beyond London Bridge you can see the tall column of the Monument, where the Great Fire began in 1666. It also marks the end of the old London Bridge. Next to it on Lower Thames Street is the white Wren spire of St. Magnus the Martyr Church, which T. S. Eliot described in *The Waste Land*. Part of that poem, which talked about "death having undone so many," was quoted by Nigel Strangeways in Nicholas Blake's *End of Chapter*, in which senior editor Stephen Prothero is a kind of T. S. Eliot look-alike.

Beyond St. Magnus until recently was the Billingsgate Market, a fish market since A.D. 870 and the Customs House, a successor to one that stood there when poet (and mystery writer) Geoffrey Chaucer worked for Edward III. Edward III appeared as a major character in Patrick Doherty's *The Death of a King*. (See Canterbury Walk.)

You know that your boat has passed the official boundary of the City of London when you see the four capped towers of the White Tower of London. Its water gate is called Traitors' Gate, because so many famous people like Elizabeth I entered that way as prisoners. Traitors' Gate was the site of the murder in John Dickson Carr's *The Mad Hatter Mystery*. (See *Mystery Reader's Walking Guide: London*.)

It was to the Tower Stairs, where you can land if you wish to explore on dry land, that the body of Sir Winston Churchill was brought after his state funeral in St. Paul's Cathedral in 1965. His cortege then went by water to Waterloo Bridge and the railway station. Carter Dickson (aka John Dickson Carr) created his "HM," or "the Old Man," Sir Henry Merrivale, as a kind of Churchillian look-alike.

The greatest unsolved mystery in English history, of course, is the question of who murdered the Princes in the Tower (Edward V and Richard, Duke of York). The first account was written by Sir Thomas More, but now there are whole societies devoted to the topic. Elizabeth Peters wrote her entertaining thriller, *The Murders of Richard III,* about such a group. Guy Townsend argued for Richard III as villain in his mystery *To Prove a Villain.* In 1978 Audrey Williamson won a Crime Writer's Gold Dagger for an update on the controversy, called *The Mystery of the Princes,* but most mystery buffs still think the best defense of Richard III against Sir Thomas More and William Shakespeare was Josephine Tey's *The Daughter of Time.*

Once past the Tower you are in the stretch of river called the Pool of London, the oldest port area. On the left bank you are looking at the notorious East End and ahead of you looms the familiar high towers of Tower Bridge. After Tower Bridge you pass the St. Katherine and London Dock area, recently restored after heavy wartime bombing. In Ian Stuart's *Sandscreen,* the Arab terrorist flew her helicopter along the Thames from the East End dockyards to Whitehall to bomb the president of the United States.

In Freeman Wills Crofts's Golden Age classic, *The Cask,* Tom Broughton of the Insular and Continental Steam Navigation Company was sent to St. Katherine's Dock to check on a consignment of wines from the Continent. Young Broughton walked from his Fenchurch Street office in the City east across Tower Hill and down to the river, where the Bullfinch was moored in St. Katherine's Basin. One cask being unloaded hit the deck and spilled out some gold sovereigns. The foreman broke it open and found a dead body inside, but before Scotland Yard could get to the scene, a carter had made off with the cask, contents and all.

North of the dock area, running parallel with the river, is St. Katherine's Way, which shortly becomes Wapping High Street. There are special East End walking tours available that take you to the Whitechapel area north of St. Katherine's Way, and show you the Jack the Ripper murder sites. But after reading Albert Borowitz's *The Jack the Ripper Walking Tour Murder,* you may be safer seeing the area by boat and not on foot.

In Anthony Price's *The Old Vengeful,* the mystery about all the British naval ships that had been called the *"Vengeful,"* retired B. N. Commander Loftus used to make regular trips to Whitechapel tube station from his home in the country. Loftus always carried a heavy briefcase, and was picked up there an hour later by a cabbie. Whitechapel was also the seedy neighborhood where Dorothy L. Sayers's Lord Peter Wimsey took Cattery secretary Joan Murchison to learn to burglarize a safe in *Strong Poison.*

Just east of St. Katherine's Dock on the riverbank is the area called Wapping. Founded by the Saxons, or Waeppa's people, Wapping High Street originally was a road through market gardens until the docks were built at the time of the Napoleonic Wars. At one of the riverside pubs here near Wapping Old Stairs on the riverfront, "Hanging" Judge Jeffreys, the henchman of James II, was captured disguised as a seaman and taken to the Tower. (See Dorchester Walk.)

It was near Wapping Old Stairs at fictional "Fiddlers Steps" in J. J. Marric's *Gideon's River* that the Thames Division patrol rescued a young man and a girl being chased by hoods and found a waterproof container floating in the river that contained stolen industrial diamonds.

The Wapping wharves are being redeveloped for residential use. The northern end of the Thames Tunnel, built in the mid-nineteenth century, is near the Wapping Underground Station, and it is possible to climb down there to smell the river and see the old river floodgates where refuse collected. Somewhere along here is a likely spot for the opening scene in Anne Perry's *Bluegate Fields,* where the body of a young man of good family was found in a Thames storm sewer near a portside slum. (There is another tunnel just east of Wapping at King Edward VII Memorial Park that goes across the Thames to Rotherhithe on the south bank.)

The original (and main) headquarters of the Thames Division Police Station is in Wapping High Street, marked by an old-fashioned blue police light. Its main entrance is by the river. It has a museum with early uniforms and souvenirs, but like Scotland Yard itself, it is difficult to see, since it is only open to visitors by written permission.

Just before you sail by the King Edward VII Memorial Park at the end of Wapping High Street, you will see the old inn, the Prospect of Wapping, at 57 Wapping Wall. Founded in 1520, the inn still has an open coachyard and flagstoned ground floor, and a riverside terrace that has a view of St. Anne's Limehouse to the east. Just beyond the pub was Execution Dock, where condemned pirates were hanged, among them Captain Kidd.

The neighborhood north of the riverbank between the park and Limehouse is Shadwell. The northern boundary of Shadwell is the road called the Highway (or Ratcliffe Highway). It was once a notorious hangout for thieves and cutthroats. In Conan Doyle's story "Black Peter," Sherlock Holmes hunted for clues to the murder of Peter Carey near "the Highway."

More recently, P. D. James and T. A. Critchley, her coauthor from the Home Office, reexamined the evidence about the infamous 1811 Ratcliffe Highway Murders in *The Maul and the Pear Tree.* These were the brutal clubbing murders of two households. The public outcry over them led to the establishment of the London Metropolitan Police Force (Scotland Yard) as a replacement for the ineffective Bow Street Runners, but these murders also led Thomas De Quincey to write his classic essay, "On Murder Considered as One of the Fine Arts." In her epilogue, P. D. James pointed out that most of the sites associated with the Ratcliffe Highway Murders are gone, bombed in World War II or torn down since; the docks are deserted, and the Highway is only a haunt of truck traffic.

Just past Shadwell, the Thames curves sharply to the south in what is known as Limehouse Reach. Along the far shore you will see Limehouse, which was built up in housing for sailors and shipbuilding yards by the sixteenth century. By the late nineteenth century, it had become London's sinister Chinatown. Their gambling and opium dens made Limehouse notorious and mysterious, even after Chinatown moved west to Soho.

Charles Dickens spent a great deal of time near this part of the Thames and wrote his novel *Our Mutual Friend* about Limehouse and the pleasant little pub called the Grapes, located on Narrow Street just east of the Highway and the Limehouse Basin. Dickens called the pub "the Six Jolly Porters."

Limehouse Basin is part of the Grand Union Canal system, which stretches all the way across London to Little Venice west of Paddington Station. The playwriting heroine of Dorothy L. Sayers's comedy, *Love All,* rented a flat on the Grand Union Canal. In *A Taste for Death* P. D. James "murdered" a baronet and a tramp inside her fictitious St. Matthew's Paddington, a Victorian Gothic church by the canal. From the river you can see the steeple of St. Anne's Limehouse, built by Wren's pupil, Hawksmoor. It has the highest church clock in London. Antonia Fraser named her mythical Oxford College Hawksmoor College in *Oxford Blood.* (See Oxford Walk.)

Limehouse was the headquarters of Sax Rohmer's perfidious Oriental, Fu Manchu, whose gang used Sam Pak's Restaurant as a den with a secret entrance to his underground tunnel/laboratory with its eerie blue light visible at night on the Thames. The laboratory was known as The Pit and the Furnace, and in it Chinese coolies plied the roaring furnace like creatures out of Dante's *Inferno.*

In Agatha Christie's *The Big Four,* naive Hastings was easily lured to Limehouse with a telegram saying that his wife had been kidnapped. Led through these "mean streets," Hastings felt himself wrapped all about by the atmosphere of the East—tortuous, cunning, sinister—when suddenly he was in a chamber with silk-covered divans and exquisite Chinese carpets. He was rescued from a watery death in the Thames by Hercule Poirot, who bombed the premises.

Just south of the Limehouse on the Isle of Dogs peninsula, you will pass the West India Docks. In *The Trail of Fu Manchu,* Dr. Petrie, the Egyptologist, was driven to the West India Docks, where he went on board the Jamaican ship, the *Queenstown Bay.* Then Dr. Petrie disembarked in disguise to save the life of Dr. Fu Manchu in a bargain for Petrie's kidnapped daughter, Fleur. Later, after the Limehouse explosion engineered by Scotland Yard, a docker saw a group of Chinese emerge from a manhole near the West India Docks. It was Fu Manchu escaping once again to match wits with Assistant Commissioner Nayland Smith.

Past the West India Docks on the Isle of Dogs your boat passes Millwall and its docks. In *Gideon's River,* more stolen industrial diamonds turn up on a barge opposite the Millwall Docks on a lighter and a Dutch coaster. About the same time in *Gideon's River,* Marric's Commander Gideon was told that the body of a young man, who had been tortured and murdered in the West India Docks area, had floated to Dead Man's Rest, a place bodies come to rest if thrown into the Thames between Wapping and Limehouse.

In Ngaio Marsh's *Scales of Justice,* Chief Inspector Alleyn and his faithful team of Fox, Bailey, and Thompson, left Scotland Yard by night to investigate a murder in the village of Swevenings. As they drove off it was a still, hot night with sheet lightning playing over the East End. Alleyn asked ironically why they didn't join the River Police, whose life was "one long water carnival."

The East India Dock Road runs east of Limehouse at the northern end of the Isle of Dogs, a large peninsula that extends from Limehouse Reach to Greenwich Reach to Blackwall Reach. To the west the East India Dock Road becomes the Commercial Road. Ngaio Marsh first arrived at London by ship from her native New Zealand. Her account in *Black Beech and Honeydew* of that magical ride from the East End harbor along Whitechapel's Commercial Road into the City matches exactly the trip of her young heroine, Roberta Gray, in *A Surfeit of Lampreys*.

The East India Dock Road was the probable route taken by Julian Symons's amateur Sherlock, TV star Sheridan Haynes in *A Three Pipe Problem*. Haynes came by night to sleuth about the East India Docks, tracking clues to the Karate Killings in the West End. Haynes only overheard two "yuppies" in a pub, talking about gentrifying East End real estate. But later, nosing about the dock warehouses, Haynes was jumped and had to be rescued by a night watchman and his dog.

Across the river from the Isle of Dogs is Greenwich, where you can land and explore on foot. (See Greenwich/Blackheath Walk.) If you choose to continue by river east to the Thames Barrier, you end up near Woolwich on the south bank, where you can get a train back to central London.

Beyond the Isle of Dogs on the northern bank of the Thames you will come to the Royal Docks. They cover 230 acres and are among the largest in the world. They include the Royal Victoria, the Royal Albert, and the King George V. These docks used to handle both passengers and cargo from Russia and the Far East.

Ngaio Marsh set the opening of *Singing in the Shrouds* at the Royal Albert Docks when a real pea-souper (fog) made dockside lights swim like moons in their own halos and the cranes above the shipping were lost to sight.

Young Police Constable Moir, on duty at the Royal Albert Docks, was thinking about marriage and promotion, and missed seeing the latest murder by the worst sex killer since Jack the Ripper. This murderer sang as he strangled his victims, all young girls, then showered their bodies with flowers. PC Moir did find the latest body in a dark alley off the passageway between the wharf and the passenger entrance to the docks, but his report to headquarters was too late. The *Cape Farewell* had sailed at midnight for South Africa via Las Palmas with a murderer on board. Much to the captain's dismay, Scotland Yard ordered his ship to wait off Portsmouth in the foggy English Channel until the pilot cutter brought her another passenger, Superintendent Roderick Alleyn.

In *The Sign of Four,* Conan Doyle's Sherlock Holmes pursued the *Aurora,* which was hiding across from the Tower in Jacobson's Yard, downriver. The *Aurora* was caught at Barking Level on your left and ran aground at the Plumstead Marshes on your right. Below on the riverbed lay the Agra treasure, lost forever in the deep mud.

These marshes were near the modern Thames River Flood Barrier in the section of the Thames called Woolwich Reach. The Thames Barrier was put up because, like Venice, London is sinking and the Thames's high tides can cause damaging floods. The Flood Barrier has ten gigantic gates mounted between its shining stainless-steel piers. The gates swing up to block the flow of water, then, to let ships pass, sink to rest on their concrete beds on the river floor.

Much-bombed Woolwich is on the south bank of the Thames near the Flood Barrier. After World War II, Ngaio Marsh grandly "took water" with theatrical producer Tyrone Guthrie and his wife to inspect a war-bombed theater at Woolwich. They had the idea of mounting Shakespeare productions for the Festival of Britain in an old theater there. Marsh thought that it would be grand for theater-goers to take water, too, to get to the productions, as her beloved Elizabethans had done. At Woolwich the Guthries and Marsh got the keys for the theater at a local pub and went to look. But the theater was too badly damaged to repair. Instead, Marsh created the fictitious "Dolphin Theatre" and gave it a rich Greek benefactor to repair it and an eager young playwright-director, Peregrine Jay, to run it. She then wrote two mysteries about the Dolphin, *Killer Dolphin* and *Light Thickens.*

Still farther east on the river at Tilbury is the main Port of London, where ships dock with container loads. Queen Elizabeth I reviewed her troops at Tilbury before the threatened invasion by the Spanish Armada in 1588. In *Black Beech and Honeydew,* Ngaio Marsh wrote that she knew she had arrived in England when her ship had passed Tilbury. In Nicholas

Blake's *End of Chapter*, senior editor Stephen Prothero (a T. S. Eliot look-alike) threw a bag off Hungerford Bridge by Westminster Pier, and the police had to drag the river all the way to Tilbury to find it.

At the Thames Flood Barrier you can get off to return by land to central London, or return by river to Greenwich Pier and then make the return trip by river.

—— GREENWICH TO WESTMINSTER ——

The return trip by boat from Greenwich to Westminster Pier takes you along the south bank of the Thames River. This is an area much like the East End, where you may not want to wander on foot. The trip will take about forty-five minutes, depending on the current. (If you want to explore Greenwich/ Blackheath, use Greenwich/Blackheath Walk.)

Go on board at Greenwich Pier. As the boat heads upstream on the left you will pass the Deptford Power Station on the edge of the village of Deptford. In Martha Grimes's *The Dirty Duck*, American Harvey Schoenberg was a nut on the subject of Shakespeare's contemporary, Christopher Marlowe. He dragged ex-nobleman Melrose Plant to the site of Mistress Bell's Deptford tavern, where Marlowe was killed in a brawl. (See also Cambridge Walk.)

The seventeenth-century diarist John Evelyn lived at Sayes Court in Deptford with a garden that was the envy of his friend and neighboring diarist, Samuel Pepys. Evelyn rented Sayes Court to Admiral Benbow, whose name cropped up in Robert Louis Stevenson's scary *Treasure Island*, then let it to the Russian Czar Peter the Great. Evelyn was the ancestor of Michael Evelyn, who writes legal crime novels under the name of Michael Underwood.

By the time of Henry VIII Deptford had become an important naval center. Beyond it to the west stretched the great Surrey Docks. They were the only docks on the south side of the river and are now closed. In Anthony Price's *The Old Vengeful* Scotland Yard tracked fence Harry Lippman, who had been in Commander Lovat's crew, to a pub called the Jolly Caulkers, opposite the Surrey Docks station.

In *Fear to Tread*, Michael Gilbert, 1987 Grand Master of the Mystery Writers of America, had Wilfred Wetherall, principal of the South Borough High School for Boys, live in Deptford. Gilbert wrote that Wetherall's home was "postally . . . in Blackheath, if spiritually in Deptford." Having missed World War II, the redoubtable Wetherall fought his own war against the gentrification of the postwar black market with the help of his lower-class schoolboys and their families.

In Operation Snakes and Ladders, Michael Gilbert sent agent David Rhys Morgan to track a drug addict in the slums around the abandoned Surrey Docks in *End-Game*. He also located a Doctor Ram Jam who sold drugs from his surgery nearby. When the big blowup came between the gangs and the police, Morgan escaped to his hideout in a tool house in a Rotherhithe park.

Past the Surrey Docks your boat follows the river's bend to the left and comes into the Pool of London again past the southern entrance to Rotherhithe Tunnel. This is a roadway tunnel under the river connecting the south side with Stepney in the East End. Opened in 1908, it, too, might be the tunnel used by the insidious Fu Manchu for his underground laboratory in Sax Rohmer's *The Trail of Fu Manchu*.

This area is called Rotherhithe. In Peter Lovesey's *Abracadaver*, Constable Thackeray was in M Division, stationed at the Paradise Street Police Station, which is on Paradise Street just north of Southwark Park and just south of Jamaica Road in Rotherhithe. When Sergeant Cribb sent for him, Thackeray was trying once again to pass the civil service examination for higher rank. The sergeant and his "Watson" proceeded to investigate a bizarre music-hall murder. They began by attending an evening's entertainment at the Grampian on Southwark Street.

In Lovesey's *A Case of Spirits*, Constable Thackeray was at Paradise Street Police Station, writing a report as his station colleagues held a mock seance, which ended with their "medium" telling Thackeray he had been called to "The Other Side," or Scotland Yard, by Sergeant Cribb. In that mystery the murder victim was a medium who came originally from Blackheath.

Josephine Bell's *The Port of London Murders* also took place in the "slummy area" around Rotherhithe Tunnel, which she called Wood Wharf. A group of poor families lived there under the care of Dr. Ellis, who was involved in illicit drug trade. The heroine, June Harvey, and her little brother lived across the river near Upper Thames Street. Their father was a tugboat captain and during a Guy Fawkes Day fog, Captain Harvey went downriver from Limehouse to Tilbury to collect four lost barges. Both the Thames River Patrol at Wapping and the Friary Road Police Station in Bermondsley became involved in tracking down the murderer and the drugs. Bell's fashionable West End drug dealer died by drowning in the busy Pool of London.

In Peter Dickinson's *Sleep and His Brother* the cast of characters included a Greek tycoon called Mr. Thanatos. Thanatos underwrote the McNair School for cathypnic (sleepy) children in hopes of discovering the secret of eternal life. His efforts were thwarted by ex-Scotland Yard Inspector Jimmy Pibble. Thanatos brought Pibble to his fabulous flat at the top of an old warehouse in South London. There Pibble ate American hamburgers and drank champagne with Thanatos and his secretary, Viscount Catling, an Old Etonian. As a robot vacuumed up their crumbs, they could see the river and the stolid barges and Saint Paul's Cathedral "with an anthology of Wren steeples."

Beyond Rotherhithe your boat passes Cherry Garden Pier, where by prior arrangement, ships sound their signal if they want Tower Bridge to be raised. On your left is Bermondsley with its old Dickensian wharves and piers and occasional pubs. Your boat will pass under Tower Bridge again, coming out into the Pool of London, and head toward Southwark. Moored near the shore between Tower Bridge and London Bridge on the south side of the river at Symons Wharf, Tooley Street, is HMS *Belfast,* a Royal Navy cruiser now a museum with an exhibit about D-day. The murderer Havoc in Margery Allingham's *Tiger in the Smoke* had been to Normandy on a commando raid to prepare for the D-day landings.

Next you come again to London Bridge. From Roman times its southern end at the Borough High Street in Southwark (known familiarly to the police as the Borough) marked the beginning of the great highway to the south and the route to the Continent. It was the way taken by pilgrims to Canterbury and the shrine of St. Thomas à Becket. These pilgrims were made immortal by poet (and mystery writer) Geoffrey Chaucer. Thomas à Becket was reintroduced to the modern world by T. S. Eliot in the play *Murder in the Cathedral,* in which Eliot used a line from Conan Doyle's story "The Musgrave Ritual." (See also Canterbury Walk.)

On the east side of Borough High Street there were several famous medieval inns. One was the White Hart, headquarters of Jack Cade, who invaded London from Blackheath, and the place where Charles Dickens's Mr. Pickwick first met Sam Weller. G. K. Chesterton, a Dickens fan, called his father a "bearded Mr. Pickwick," and it has been suggested that his detective, Father Brown, was derived in part from Mr. Pickwick's round and chubby self. Nearby is the George Inn, the only surviving galleried inn in London. At Talbot Yard once stood the Tabard Inn, where Chaucer's pilgrims began their journey. In Ngaio Marsh's *Light Thickens,* William Smith, who played Macduff's son in the *Macbeth* production, went to the Royal Southwark Drama School. The boy and his mother lived in Tabard Street.

Just west past the bridge and High Street is Southwark Cathedral. It was built by the Augustinian Canons in 1206 as part of their priory, but has been greatly modified. After Westminster Abbey, it is the finest example of Gothic architecture in London. It is also the site of London's celebration each April of Shakespeare's birthday, and Shakespeare's younger brother, Edmund, is buried here.

In *The Dirty Duck,* Martha Grimes's insatiable tourist Harvey Schoenberg dragged Melrose Plant (aka Plantagenet?) down the steps from the Southwark Bridge to look up at the imposing facade of the cathedral. The American then patronizingly told the Englishman that to their south lay the medieval stews and the red-light district. Schoenberg then took Plant to a pub called the Salisbury behind the cathedral.

South of Southwark Cathedral is Guy's Hospital, built on the site of the even earlier St. Thomas Hospital. In Margery Allingham's *Tiger in the Smoke,* Sir Conrad Belfrey, known as the "King Healer," arranged to have killer Havoc taken out of prison and brought here to study his alleged "Number 13" phobia. Havoc killed Sir Conrad and escaped "into the Smoke."

After going under London Bridge your boat will pass St. Saviour's Dock en route to the Cannon Street Railway Bridge. Running parallel to the river on the south bank is Clink Street, the site of the old Clink prison. The term "in the clink," often used in 1920s and 1930s mystery stories, came from this prison. Clink Street runs into Bank End Park Street which marks the beginning of the Bankside area. Between Cannon Street Railway Bridge and Southwark Bridge is the Anchor, a pub that dates from 1750. It is on the site of an earlier inn where Samuel Pepys took refuge from the Great Fire in 1666 and wrote his account of it. It has beamed ceiling, bare floors, and real ale and good bar food. This pub also has Dr. Samuel Johnson associations. Lilian de la Torre has written a series of detective stories about "Dr. Sam."

Bankside, the London area most associated with William Shakespeare, was a favorite site for mystery writer Ngaio Marsh. (Marsh became a Dame of the British Empire, not for writing mysteries like Agatha Christie, but for her New Zealand productions of Shakespeare.)

Just past Southwark Bridge, Shakespeare's Globe Theater is being rebuilt. Beyond it you can see the Bankside Power Station. Bankside was once filled with entertainment, amusement (and bear) gardens, and theaters. Today it is being redeveloped for housing. Marsh set her fictional Dolphin Theatre somewhere near the Globe on fictitious Wharfingers Lane. Young writer-director Peregrine Jay found the bombed theater abandoned. After Jay nearly drowned in a bomb hole onstage, he "resurrected" the Dolphin with the money of Greek millionaire Conducis in *Killer Dolphin*. It was later the scene of the "perfect production" of *Macbeth,* put on by Jay in *Light Thickens.* South of Bankside in Walworth was the South Borough High School run by Michael Gilbert's Wetherall in *Fear to Tread.*

Beyond Bankside your boat will pass again under Blackfriars Bridge, bringing you to a riverside area called Upper Ground. Old warehouses here have been replaced by the South Bank Television Centre, the London Weekend Television building. In Val Gielgud's *Through a Glass Darkly,* the suicide of Simon Hargraves, Managing Director of Gargantua TV, was suspected of being murder. Scotland Yard's offbeat Detective-Inspector Gregory Pellew was brought in to investigate Hargraves's death with the help of his friend, Viscount Hannington, who worked at Gargantua.

Gielgud, brother to actor Sir John, was an old friend of Dorothy L. Sayers and the producer of her BBC plays. Gielgud described the Gargantua TV building as being "the latest and loftiest of those vast and architecturally characterless oblongs which were providing London with a new skyline." It seems likely that Gargantua was a stand-in for the real South Bank Television Centre because from Gargantua's opulent twenty stories of glass, Detective-Inspector Pellew could literally look down upon landmarks such as the Old Vic and Lambeth Palace.

Behind the Centre is Waterloo Station, while on the river ride, the next complex of buildings that stretch on either side of Waterloo Bridge is the South Bank Arts Complex. The complex includes the Festival Hall, the Queen Elizabeth Hall, the National Theatre, the National Film Theatre, and the Hayward Gallery, all emphatically modern in style.

The idea for the complex came from the Festival of Britain, which was held in 1951 just south of Hungerford Footbridge. The festival celebrated the return of peace and prosperity. It used the grounds of what is now called the Silver Jubilee Gardens, laid out in 1977 to celebrate the twenty-five years of Queen Elizabeth II. (You can walk the Jubilee Walk along the south riverbank from Lambeth to Southwark Cathedral.)

In 1986 there was a centennial exhibit of the work of G. K.

Chesterton at the complex. In *Cast for Death* Margaret Yorke's Oxford don Patrick Grant helped to chase some East Germans along the Hungerford Footbridge one evening just before the theaters and concert halls emptied out. Then two shots rang out and a body fell into the Thames. Grant later discovered that the murdered man was his friend, Sam, an actor.

In Nicholas Blake's *End of Chapter* Liz Wenham of the publishing firm of Wenham & Geraldine went to a concert at Royal Festival Hall the night author Millicent Miles was murdered at the firm offices in the Adelphi. (See also *Mystery Reader's Walking Guide: London.*)

Waterloo Station is just behind Jubilee Gardens. It is one of the main stations from which you take a boat train to go abroad. In *Unnatural Death,* Dorothy L. Sayers's Robert Fentiman pretended to sight an elusive suspect named Oliver there, then followed him to France. Musical-comedy actress Ray Markable took the boat train to Southampton from Waterloo Station in Josephine Tey's *The Man in the Queue*.

Just past Waterloo Station is the Old Vic, or Old Victoria Theatre. It became famous for doing the classics, especially Shakespeare, at popular prices. In her autobiography, *Black Beech and Honeydew,* Ngaio Marsh described how before World War II, fresh from New Zealand, she went to every Old Vic production. In the 1950s her secretary-companion attended its famous drama school.

In Marsh's *A Surfeit of Lampreys,* coming out of Scotland Yard one night, Superintendent Alleyn talked with the police constable on duty at Westminster Bridge. The PC told Alleyn he had been to see *Macbeth* done at the Old Vic and gave Alleyn a clue to the murders.

Beyond the Jubilee Gardens on the south bank just before Westminster Bridge, you will pass the modern Shell Centre and the massive London County Hall. Their glittering lights stained the Thames the night that Margery Allingham's couple, David Field and Frances Ivory, walked to Westminster Bridge to replight their troth at the end of *Black Plumes*. Land at Westminster Pier to end this section of the trip.

—WESTMINSTER TO HAMPTON COURT—

To "take water" upstream to Hampton Court, you must get on a boat leaving from Westminster Pier. Along the route you can get off at Kew or Richmond. On this trip we will describe mystery sites *on both sides* of the Thames because we suggest that you plan to take the train from Hampton Court back to London's Waterloo Railway Station.

Just beyond Westminster Bridge on your right are the private terraces of the Houses of Parliament. In Dorothy L. Sayers's *Murder Must Advertise,* a Pym's Publicity artist was sent there to draw MPs wearing a client's shoe.

On your left is St. Thomas's Hospital. St. Thomas's location on the south bank not far from Battersea makes it a likely choice for Dorothy L. Sayers's fictitious St. Luke's Hospital. In *Whose Body?* its staff included the distinguished neurosurgeon, Sir Julian Freke. St. Thomas's Hospital began in 1213 and was moved here from Southwark in the mid-nineteenth century. It is adjacent to Lambeth Palace, the official London residence of the Archbishop of Canterbury.

Lambeth Palace is one of the most important medieval buildings in London. It has been the town house of the Archbishop of Canterbury since the thirteenth century, but its handsome red-brick Tudor gatehouse was built in 1495. Next to it is the Palace Library with a timbered roof and the 1660 Great Hall (now the library) with a hammerbeam roof supported by Gothic angels. The palace picture gallery and chapel are open weekdays. You can see parts of the palace from the river as your boat passes under Lambeth Bridge.

In *An Unsuitable Job for a Woman,* P. D. James's private eye Cordelia Gray rented a bed-sitter from her boss, Bernie Pryde, at No. 15 Cremona Road, Lambeth. She caught the underground at Lambeth North Station but, because of a breakdown on the Bakerloo Line, was slow getting to work the day Pryde committed suicide. Pryde left Cordelia his "private eye" practice and his gun.

Dorothy L. Sayers's Lord Peter Wimsey lived in Lambeth when he went underground to catch a gang in "The Adventurous Exploit of the Cave of Ali Baba." Sayers was also a friend of William Temple, wartime Archbishop of Canterbury, who once offered her an honorary doctor of divinity degree, which she turned down.

In Agatha Christie's short story "The Golden Ball," George Dundas successfully grasped the "golden ball of opportunity" by winning a rich debutante. He then asked his flabbergasted uncle whether he should go to Lambeth Palace or Doctors Commons for a Special License (to be married).

In John Creasey's *Holiday for Inspector West* "handsome" Inspector Roger West of Scotland Yard drove to Lambeth to check out the security ordered for MP George Henby. Henby lived on Lambeth Road in a terrace of houses, most of which had been destroyed by bombs in 1942.

Beyond Lambeth Bridge you are heading toward Vauxhall Bridge. The Albert Embankment is to your left and Millbank to your right. Charles Williams's heroine, Lester Furnival, met her husband on Millbank just after she had been killed in a plane crash in *All Hallows Eve*.

You also pass by the famous Tate Gallery. It was built on the site of the Millbank Penitentiary, where Sherlock Holmes and Dr. Watson landed after crossing the Thames River in Conan Doyle's *The Sign of Four*. The Tate has an outstanding collection of British paintings, including drawings by William Blake, whose biography was written by G. K. Chesterton. In Jessica Mann's *Grave Goods* her sleuth, Tamara Hoyland, was taken to lunch by a German art dealer at the Tate's classy Rex Whistler Restaurant. Hoyland was chasing the lost regalia of Charlemagne, known as the Horn Treasure. Your authors in turn took Jessica Mann to lunch there.

On your left, where the Albert Embankment begins today, were the pleasure gardens of Vauxhall. Popular in the seventeenth and eighteenth centuries, these gardens were famous for fireworks, lantern-lighted groves, music, and Chinese pavilions.

To your right on the north bank, Millbank becomes Grosvenor Road. Then you will pass Pimlico's St. George's Square, where Dorothy L. Sayers's old detective "pussy," Miss Climpson, lived in *Unnatural Death*. There are only industrial buildings on the south bank until you come to Chelsea Bridge.

Historically, Chelsea, located on the north bank beyond Pimlico, was first associated with the Tudors' saintly Sir Thomas More, the chancellor of Henry VIII, who was executed for not agreeing to the King's divorce.

More recently, Chelsea was called London's Latin Quarter, reflecting its reputation as the home of artists, actors, and writers. This is the Chelsea you find in classic mystery stories, but it has been "gentrifying" since the turn of the century. In the 1960s, with designers like Mary Quant, the King's Road became and remains the center of the swingers, as well as one of London's fashionable neighborhoods. John Le Carré's Smiley lived with his unfaithful but aristocratic wife, Lady Ann, on Bywater Street off King's Road.

Chelsea was clearly becoming fashionable in the early 1930s, as noted by Margery Allingham in *Mystery Mile*. Her Oriental villain, Simister, explained to his captive, Albert Campion, that he went where he liked and lived as he chose. He had a villa with a hanging garden on the Bosphorus, and the most delightful Queen Anne house in Chelsea, where he had moved from Mayfair when the fashion changed.

Agatha Christie, who collected houses the way other people collect her mysteries, lived in two places in Chelsea. After her painful divorce, she lived at No. 22 Creswell Place in a small mews flat, which she then loaned to archeologist Sir Leonard Wolley. Sir Leonard in turn introduced her to her second husband, Max Mallowan, in 1929. In 1948 Christie came to live off the King's Road at No. 48 Swan Court, when Mallowan gave his inaugural address as Professor of the Chair of Western Asiatic Archeology at the University of London. While the Mallowans lived there Christie worked on *Witness for the Prosecution, Crooked House,* and *A Murder Is Announced.*

The Pegasus bookshop run by Octavius Browne in Ngaio Marsh's *False Scent* was in Pardoner's Place off the King's Road. It was next door to the elegant home of actress Mary

Bellamy who was murdered. Bram Stoker, author of the horror story *Dracula*, also lived in Chelsea, as did noted Shakespearean actor, Laurence Olivier, now Lord Olivier.

Chelsea's modern popularity really began at the Restoration when the court of Charles II used it as a resort. Society physician Sir Hans Sloane, the head of the Royal Society, not only moved there, but owned most of the real estate. His collections of books, fossils, plants, and rocks were the beginning of the British Museum. In Sloane Square's Royal Court Theatre, Sir Harley Granville-Barker put on the avant-garde plays of G. B. Shaw, debating crony of G. K. Chesterton, at the Royal Court Theatre. On the west side of Sloane Square is Peter Jones Department Store, where in Martha Grimes's *Jerusalem Inn* Superintendent Jury saw an elegant Christmas display of the Three Wise Men.

The Chelsea Builder's Yard, where a small blue van delivered a blue lacquer cabinet from the Westminster flat of Scotland Yard's Sir Denis Nayland Smith, was probably located on the river just east of Chelsea Bridge. In *The Trail of Fu Manchu*, Fu Manchu was hidden inside the cabinet.

On your right after Chelsea Bridge is Ranelagh Gardens, where Agatha Christie's socialite Virginia Revel played tennis in *The Secret of Chimneys*. Mrs. Revel put off her tennis one morning to hear what her pompous cousin, the Honorable George Lomax of the Foreign Office, had to say about affairs in oil-rich Herzoslovakia.

Next to Ranelagh Gardens you see the spacious grounds of the Royal Hospital, the military retirement home established by Charles II. (Greenwich's Royal Naval Hospital was its opposite number.) The Royal Hospital was built by Sir Christopher Wren. In the middle of the square formed by the chapel and Great Hall is Figure Court, with a statue of Charles II in a Roman toga. On Founder's Day in May, 450 retired or invalid soldier pensioners gather there wearing their bright red coats to give three cheers for Charles. They also parade on Sundays at 10:30 in Royal Hospital Road. Visitors may attend the chapel service there at 11 A.M.

Just west of the Royal Hospital grounds, Tite Street runs

to the Chelsea river embankment. The painter James Whistler lived on Tite Street, as did painters John Singer Sargent and Augustus John and writer Oscar Wilde, whose paradoxical style influenced G. K. Chesterton. Tite Street was famous for a number of specially built studio-houses, among them the Tower House, which may have been the model for the Chelsea home of Ngaio Marsh's Troy and Roderick Alleyn.

In *Black as He's Painted* this house was described as being in a cul-de-sac with a garden and a detached studio built for a Victorian Academician (the Royal Academy of Art) of preposterous fame. It had an absurd entrance with a flight of steps with a canopy held by two selfconscious plaster caryatids that Troy thought too funny to remove. The whole setup suited one of her sitters, the Boomer, Alleyn's African-dictator prep-school friend, to perfection.

Just beyond Tite Street on the river you will pass the Chelsea Physic Garden, established by the Apothecaries Society in 1673. Sir Hans Sloane gave them the land, with the understanding that two thousand specimens of plants grown there, well dried and preserved, should be sent yearly to the Royal Society in batches of fifty. The request is still carried out. Until very recently when it was opened to the public on Wednesday and Sunday afternoons, access was limited to specialists only.

The Chelsea Physic Garden was the scene of the crime in Detection Club President Harry Keating's "Mrs. Craggs Gives a Dose of Physic." In that story his Cockney cleaning woman, Mrs. Craggs, saved the life of the poisoned curator by dosing him with lobelia, a common plant from the garden. She had saved the day before the Special Team from Scotland Yard got there. (Nearby is Swan House, built by Norman Shaw, architect of the old New Scotland Yard, now occupied by a private combat unit.)

At the western end of the Chelsea Physic Garden, Flood Street intersects with Royal Hospital Road. Until recently the private house of Prime Minister Margaret Thatcher was in Flood Street. Detective Mason in Davidson's *The Chelsea Murders* saw a copper outside her door.

If you disembarked to walk up Flood Street, you would come to Flood Walk, which was the location of Pamela Branch's hilarious mystery story *The Wooden Overcoat* (slang for *coffin*). In the late 1950s Branch described Flood Walk as a narrow elm-lined street with semidetached cottages, whose streetlights were still lit by a lamplighter on a bike.

On Flood Walk Branch described two grimy, creeper-matted houses separated by walled gardens. One contained the Asterisk Club, run by Clifford Flush for an exclusive group of acquitted murderers; the other was occupied by two sets of young married Bohemians, a charlady, and regular visitor Mr. Beesum, the Rodent Officer.

The Asterisk Club at No. 13 had a blue plaque that said that Tennyson once stayed there. One of the amateurs at No. 15 said the Asterisk Club had probably only READ Tennyson, since their name came from his line, "We against whose familiar names not yet the fatal asterisk of death is set." At No. 15 they put up a phony blue marker saying that Dante Gabriel Rossetti had planted their monkey puzzle tree. These amateurs found themselves coping with corpses dumped on them by their professional neighbors.

Just beyond Flood Street along the river Chelsea's famous riverside Cheyne Walk begins. Sir Thomas More built a celebrated house there which may be the model for his *Utopia*. Later Henry VIII built a palatial manor house here, and his daughter, Elizabeth I, lived there. Like More, his royal master found Chelsea a convenient place from which to row downstream to Westminster.

Cheyne Walk now has lovely eighteenth-century riverside houses that have been occupied by many famous people, from Henry James, author of the spooky *The Turn of the Screw,* to poet Hilaire Belloc, friend of G. K. Chesterton, who used to visit him there to play with the Belloc children, to T. S. Eliot, author of *Murder in the Cathedral.* (See also Canterbury Walk.)

In Davidson's *The Chelsea Murders,* Detective Mason walked there from Flood Street. He went past the huge gated mansions made of marvelous brick, pockmarked with plaques indicating their illustrious residents. Detective Mason rattled them off: George Eliot, Rossetti, Swinburne, Whistler—all the lads. Suddenly he realized that the Chelsea murder victims were ordinary people who shared the initials of these Chelsea greats.

According to Peter Lovesey in *Bertie and the Tinman,* the Prince of Wales (Bertie) and his Watson, Charlie Buckfast, were set upon as they drove to the London house of the Dowager Duchess of Montrose on Cheyne Walk. Both men were thrown in the river. The Prince of Wales managed to swim ashore and appeared soaking wet at the Duchess's home, but Buckfast's body was picked up in Battersea Reach.

In *The Unpleasantness at the Bellona Club* Dorothy L. Sayers placed the studio home of potter Marjorie Phelps on the river in Chelsea. Much later in *Busman's Honeymoon* the Dowager Duchess took Lord Peter and Harriet to dine with her brother, Paul Delagardie, who lived on Cheyne Walk.

Ngaio Marsh's plump little Lord Robert (Bunchy) Gospell lived (and was murdered) at No. 200 Cheyne Walk in *Death in a White Tie.* Glamorous leading lady Destiny Meade, who played Shakespeare's Dark Lady for Peregrine Jay in Marsh's *Killer Dolphin,* also lived on Cheyne Walk in an apartment Superintendent Roderick Alleyn found sumptuous to a degree and in maddeningly good taste.

In Georgette Heyer's *Death in the Stocks* the madcap Vereker twins, Antonia and Kenneth, lived at fictitious No. 3 Grayling Street with their old nurse Murgatroyd when their wealthy step-brother was murdered. They shared a studio flat over a garage, where Antonia kept her prize bull terriers, which she walked by the river. John Creasey's Inspector West lived on Bell Street in Chelsea, and Patricia Moyes's Chief Inspector Henry Tibbett and his wife, Emily, had a flat there in a Victorian house.

To your left on the south side of the Thames just before Chelsea Bridge is the mighty silhouette of the Battersea Power Station. It has become "redundant," but instead of being torn down, it is destined to house a pleasure complex. In Patricia Moyes's *Who Is Simon Warwick?* Inspector Reynolds tracked a murder suspect by seeking signatures on a petition to preserve it.

Past Chelsea Bridge on the left-hand side (south bank of the river) your boat will pass Battersea. In *The Trail of Fu Manchu* Sax Rohmer described Battersea as one of London's oddest suburbs, Communist by vote, but filled with thousands of honest citizens. Dr. Petrie left his cab in Vauxhall Bridge Road to walk to a certain dingy Battersea house filled with Victoriana, where he met Sam Pak and got the elixir of life to administer to Fu Manchu in return for his daughter's life.

Past the Battersea Power Station, you can see the huge 200-acre Battersea Park. It was the site of a duel between the Prime Minister, the Duke of Wellington, and the Marquess of Winchelsea on March 21, 1829. Georgette Heyer described the Duke at Waterloo in her novel *An Infamous Army*.

G. K. Chesterton and his wife, Frances, lived in a Battersea workman's flat in Overstrand Mansions soon after they were married in 1901. In Sayers's *Whose Body?* the Thippses found a dead body in their bath at No. 59 Queen Caroline Mansions, opposite the park. Sayers's Sir Julian Freke lived nearby at No. 50 Overstrand Mansions.

Agatha Christie's Miss Wheeler lived in Battersea in *The Secret Adversary*. In E. X. Ferrar's *Last Will and Testament* a key suspect, Paul Goss, who had a job working for a textbook publisher, had taken a flat in Battersea. One incredibly weird student hostel in Battersea was the Holy Group, to which Josephine Bell's Leslie Rivers was lured when she arrived in London in *A Deadly Place to Stay*. In Lionel Davidson's *The Chelsea Murders,* many of the students (and suspects) at the Chelsea School of Art lived at the Comyns Hall of Residence, which was one of a group of hostels in the Albert Bridge Road. The art school itself was across the Albert Bridge near the King's Road on Manresa Road.

In John Dickson Carr's *Below Suspicion,* Dr. Gideon Fell gave a helping hand to young Irish barrister Patrick Butler when he defended Joyce Ellis for murder. Ellis had been a paid companion for rich old Mrs. Taylor, who lived in a mansion in Balham. Balham lies south of Battersea near Tooting Bec Common. Dr. Fell and Butler found an eighteenth-century chapel there which was being used as headquarters by a witch cult.

On the north side of the river you are still passing Cheyne Walk, which extends from the Albert Bridge past Battersea Bridge to an area called World's End. One of the most famous riverside pubs, the four-hundred-year-old King's Head and Eight Bells, is located at No. 50 Cheyne Walk. It was probably the model for Pamela Branch's pub, the Ten Bells, where her amateurs liked to meet.

Beyond the Albert Bridge, a one-hundred-year-old suspension footbridge, you pass the home of writer Thomas Carlyle on Cheyne Row, where Charles Dickens and Alfred, Lord Tennyson, once visited. Then you come to war-bombed Chelsea Old Church (All Saints), where there is a memorial to Sir Thomas More. His body's whereabouts is uncertain. His head, which was cut off and displayed on London Bridge, was later buried at Canterbury in the family tomb of his son-in-law, William Roper. More's statue now stands outside the church. (See Canterbury Walk.)

More's Chelsea house lay just past the church, close to the mansion of Henry VIII, which was given by his son Edward VI to the Duke of Northumberland. As a result, Queen Lady Jane Grey also lived here as a girl. A little farther west on Danvers Street is Crosby Hall, which is now part of the hostel of the British Federation of University Women. The great medieval hall once stood in Bishopsgate as part of a wool merchant's house, and was rented by the Duke of Gloucester, later Richard III. Much later it was moved here to the land once owned by Sir Thomas More, an ironic coincidence duly noted by Josephine Tey's Inspector Alan Grant in *The Daughter of Time*. Grant's young American researcher, Carradine, took a special bus trip just to see the hall with its medieval painted roof.

At the Battersea Bridge, which is an extension of Beaufort Street in Chelsea, the amateurs in Pamela Branch's *The Wooden Overcoat* tried to dump a corpse they called the Loved One into the Thames. Unfortunately, the tide was out and the Loved One simply landed on the muddy shore.

Your boat now takes a sharp turn to the left into Battersea Reach, which extends to the Wandsworth Bridge. On your left it passes the police helicopter pad from which P. D. James's two detectives, Adam Dalgliesh and his aristocratic assistant, Massingham, flew to East Anglia in *Death of an Expert Witness.* (See Ely Walk.) The Duke and Duchess of York took off from there after their wedding in 1986.

On the right or north side of the river, you will pass Fulham, where Antonia Fraser's Chloe once lived in *A Splash of Red* and where Patricia Wentworth's Henry Eustasius inherited an antique shop from his godfather in *The Case Is Closed.*

The next bridge on the Thames is the Putney Bridge. In Georgette Heyer's Regency mystery *The Quiet Gentleman,* her staid heroine, Drusilla Morland, told the Earl of St. Erth that feminist Mary Wollstonecraft threw herself off Putney Bridge and was picked up by a passing boat. Wollstonecraft later married free-thinker William Godwin. Julian Symons classified Godwin's 1794 novel, *Caleb Williams,* as the first detective story. The Godwins were the parents of Mary Shelley, wife of the poet and author of the classic thriller *Frankenstein.*

(If you want to walk along this part of the Thames River from Putney to Richmond, there is a towpath walk by way of Kew. It goes through an industrial area, into a pathway lined with eighteenth-century residences and modern recreational areas.)

A little past Putney Bridge you will come to the stone marker for the beginning of the famous annual Oxford and Cambridge University Boat Race, which runs upstream to Mortlake's Ship Inn. Across the river on your right you can catch a glimpse of the fifteenth-century Fulham Palace of the Bishops of London. There is a famous St. Mary's Church in Putney, where Charles Dickens placed the wedding of David Copperfield. Cromwell's army camped nearby in 1647 when Charles I was held prisoner upriver at Hampton Court. (Mystery writer Antonia Fraser is also the author of biographies of the Royal Stuarts and the Puritan Protector Oliver Cromwell.)

Along the river from now on, your boat is taking the route followed by Jerome K. Jerome in his *Three Men in a Boat,* but reversing their route. Jerome began his pleasure voyage at Kingston-on-Thames, and the same route was taken by Sergeant Cribb and Constable Thackeray in Peter Lovesey's *Swing, Swing Together*. Constable Hardy and Harriet Shaw of Elfrida College went the same way in pursuit of the three men in a boat who had murdered a tramp. Their chief clue was Jerome K. Jerome's book.

Beyond Putney the Thames bends to the right toward Hammersmith Bridge. Hammersmith was the site of St. Paul's School, a red-brick Victorian pile on Hammersmith Road where mystery writers E. C. Bentley and G. K. Chesterton were schoolmates. Hammersmith was famous for its artists, from William Morris at Kelmscott House to William Hogarth a little farther west at Hogarth's House. There is a famous riverside pub, The Dove, beside Hammersmith Pier.

Beyond Hammersmith on the right, as the Thames goes into another big loop to the left, is Chiswick. Hogarth is buried here in St. Nicholas's Church. It was at Chiswick in *The Man Who Was Thursday* that G. K. Chesterton's poet Gabriel Syme met the Anarchists at a dingy pub with a secret steel-lined basement. Syme was elected to be Thursday, then took a dark, dwarfish steam-launch that looked like a baby dragon with one red eye and sailed downstream to land past Westminster Pier at Cleopatra's Needle.

Past Barnes and the new Public Records Office building on your left, your boat will come to Kew, where there is a royal palace set in the famous Royal Botanic Gardens. They were founded around 1759 by Princess Augusta, the mother of George III, who lived at Kew. Chesterton's journalist hero, William Cobbett, was a garden-boy there. This three-hundred-acre garden is famous for its all-year-round greenhouses.

Peter Lovesey's *Waxwork* is the story of Miriam Jane Cromer, wife of Howard Cromer, a society photographer who lived and had his studio at Park Lodge, Kew Green. Cromer confessed to poisoning her husband's assistant with photographic chemicals because he was blackmailing her, but Sergeant Cribb and his sturdy Constable Thackeray were ordered to reinvestigate the poisoning. They visited the photographer's home at Kew and strolled after clues in the Botanic Gardens.

Across the river from Kew on the northern bank is the estate called Syon House, the stately riverside home of the dukes of Northumberland. Their most famous medieval ancestor, Hotspur, was a main character in *The Bloody Field* by Edith Pargeter (aka Ellis Peters). (See Shrewsbury Walk.) The original Syon House was a monastery, but the present-day mansion was built on the site in the sixteenth century, and redone by Robert Adam in the eighteenth century. Open to the public, Syon House makes a satisfactory substitute for the numerous riverside stately mansions invented by mystery writers. Margery Allingham, for example, put her "Caesar's Court" on the Thames in *The Fashion in Shrouds,* and Dorothy L. Sayers created a mansion owned by Major Milligan that was a secret haunt of society drug dealers in *Murder Must Advertise.* It was also at a Kew theater during World War II that Dorothy L. Sayers's feminist comedy *Love All* had its last production.

Past Kew, around the next bend of the river on the left, you will come to Richmond, one of the prettiest riverside towns in all England. It is built uphill and its lovely Georgian green surrounded by a group of early Georgian houses is visible from the river. The site of the royal palace of Richmond was on the north side of the green. The Tudor gatehouse is all that is left standing. Richmond Palace was once called Sheen Palace, where Edward III, the real villain of Patrick Doherty's *The Death of a King,* died of old age. After defeating Richard III and seizing his throne, the Tudor Henry VII rebuilt the palace and renamed it for his family estate in Yorkshire.

Elizabeth I died here in 1603 and her body was taken by water to Westminster for burial. Sir Robert Carey rode north that night to tell Mary Stuart's son James that he was now king of Great Britain. James I (about whom both Antonia Fraser and Charles Williams wrote biographies) was fascinated by magic. Ngaio Marsh's favorite Shakespeare play, *Macbeth,* was written for him. Richmond Park's 2400 acres were enclosed by Charles I and stocked with deer, making it the largest royal park now open to the public in the entire London area.

The recently renovated St. John's Church had T. S. Eliot,

author of *Murder in the Cathedral* and "Macavity: The Mystery Cat" as a parishioner in World War II. Eliot's friends Leonard and Virginia Woolf lived at Hogarth House in Paradise Street, Richmond, where they founded their Hogarth Press and published Eliot's poem *The Waste Land*. Leonard Woolf went to St. Paul's School, where he was a friend of G. K. Chesterton's brother Cecil and a member of their famous literary club, the J.D.C.

In J. J. Marric's *Gideon's River,* a thirteen-year-old girl disappeared at Richmond. While Scotland Yard searched for her, even dragging the river, she was being kept captive in an old unused riverside quarry.

In Peter Lovesey's *A Case of Spirits* a medium from Blackheath named Brand held fashionable seances at a respectable house on Richmond Hill. Lovesey opened each chapter with a verse from Robert Browning's poem "Mr. Sludge, the Medium."

In Lovesey's mystery, Scotland Yard's Sergeant Cribb and the faithful Thackeray visit the elegant home of Dr. Probert on Richmond Hill, where a painting of nude ladies had disappeared. Probert's house was tall, detached, and Georgian, and stood almost at the top of the hill opposite the terrace, so that Sergeant Cribb could see above the river mist as he pulled the doorknob.

In Josephine Bell's *The Port of London Murders,* society drug dealer Gordon Longford drove shopgirl June Harvey to Richmond Park to seduce her. June insisted that Longford buy her an expensive tea on the hill, then when he drove to the river to "see the sun set," the fog came in. His plans thwarted, Longford was taking her home, when she "ditched" him at a tobacco shop and got home on her own.

Beyond Richmond Bridge on the north side of the river your boat will go around Eel Pier Island and pass Twickenham. You are now past the tidal Thames and in the part of the river where the boats enter and leave each stretch through a series of locks.

Just beyond Twickenham you can see the ornate, "Gothick" Strawberry Hill, built by Horace Walpole. He was the son of Sir Robert Walpole, who first organized the Metropolitan Police Force, who were affectionately known in his honor as "bobbies." Horace Walpole, with help from Sir Walter Scott, started the eighteenth-century craze for Gothick horror and mystery by writing *The Castle of Otranto*. Mystery writer Jane Austen parodied the craze in *Northanger Abbey,* as did Georgette Heyer in *Sylvester or the Wicked Uncle* and *The Quiet Gentleman*. Horace Walpole himself was a minor character in Heyer's *The Convenient Marriage*.

In Josephine Bell's *Treachery in Type,* the body of young Chris Trotter, who had stolen the novel written by Mrs. Grosshouse (aka Anita Armstrong) turned up in the Thames. His nude body was caught at low tide between Richmond and Teddington Lock, but since the body could not have gone through the lock by itself, Scotland Yard theorized that it had been dumped in the river elsewhere. They finally discovered a riverside mansion called Meadowside, where Sir Edgar Seven had wild parties.

Past Teddington Lock on the south (left) side of the river your boat will come to Kingston-on-Thames. Kingston is a Royal Borough where seven Saxon kings were crowned. Their coronation stone is displayed outside the Guildhall.

Then, around the next bend of the river, on your right you come to princely Hampton Court. When you see its charming red-brick Tudor beauty, it will be no mystery why Henry VIII hankered for this palace built by Cardinal Wolsey and took it from him.

Hampton Court was and is the grandest private house in England. Parts of it, like Windsor and Kensington Palaces, today are lived in by Royal Pensioners, in what are known as Grace and Favor quarters. Sadly, one of them burned herself up and nearly burned the palace down when we were in London researching this book in 1986. She had been using a candle for light at night.

With its many other treasures, Hampton Court also has a famous garden maze here, which was planted in William III's time. Characters in Georgette Heyer's Regency novels often got lost there and so did one of Jerome K. Jerome's *Three Men in a Boat*.

Beyond Hampton Court on the Thames you would come to Staines, then go past Runnymede, where the barons made King John guarantee their rights by signing Magna Carta. In John Creasey's *Theft of Magna Carta* Inspector West saved the Sarum copy of the Great Charter. There is a part of Runnymede that is forever American, given by Elizabeth II in memory of President John F. Kennedy. Then you would come to Windsor. (See Windsor/Eton Walk.)

Between Windsor and Oxford on the left bank of the river you would pass Maidenhead and then Cookham. Mr. John Turk, the hereditary Swan Keeper to Her Majesty the Queen, has his boathouse here. In P. D. James's *A Taste for Death,* there was a fashionable inn called the Black Swan at Cookham. All the principal characters, including murder-victim baronet Sir Paul Berowne, liked to drive out there for a late London supper, and several of them fell into the river.

Across the Thames from Cookham is Clivedon, a mansion with spectacular gardens, which now is run by the National Trust. Once famous foreign policy weekends were held here, very like the ones at Chimneys in Agatha Christie's *The Secret of Chimneys*. Beyond Cookham you would come to Henley-on-Thames, the site of the fashionable London season rowing regatta, which occurs yearly about Ascot Week. Peter Lovesey's river mystery, *Swing, Swing Together* (its title taken from the Eton Boating Song) began on the Thames River near Henley, where Harriet Shaw's Elfrida College for the Training of Female Elementary Teachers was located. Harriet went skinny-dipping on a dare and became involved in murder.

In Dick Francis's *Blood Sport* Gene Hawkins was taken by his boss for a day on the river in his motor cruiser. He went on board at Henley and met Dave Teller, an American, who wanted Hawkins to help solve the disappearance of some famous race horses. Near Henley on the return trip, Teller was hit with a punt pole, knocked into the weir, and rescued by Hawkins.

Past Henley and the other riverside towns you will finally come to Oxford.

The river boats from London end their trip at Hampton Court. You can disembark, explore Hampton Court, then take the train at the station across the Thames back to Waterloo Station in London to end your Thames River Trip.

14

WINDSOR/ETON/ ASCOT

BACKGROUND

Windsor has been the chief residence of the British monarchy for 850 years, and it is the only royal residence in Europe still in continual use. It is also one of the largest castles ever built. It is a day's march from London, making it suitably far from the bustle of city life. Windsor's royal history began when the Norman William the Conqueror built the first castle on a chalk cliff above the Thames River. His son Henry I was the first of many of the Royal Family to be married there in 1124. It was Henry's daughter, the Empress Matilda, who fought with her cousin, King Stephen, for the crown. Their struggle is the background for Ellis Peters's medieval mysteries about Brother Cadfael. Matilda's son, Henry II, added to the Norman keep, which was extended to its present size by Henry III and Edward III.

Both Edward III, victor of Crécy, a battle described in P. C. Doherty's *The Death of a King,* and Henry VI, described disparagingly in Josephine Tey's *The Daughter of Time,* were born at Windsor. Many English kings are also buried here. Some are entombed in state in the Chapel of St. George, but Queen Victoria and her consort, Prince Albert, are buried in the

Frogmore Mausoleum in Windsor Great Park. In *Bertie and the Tinman* Peter Lovesey described a filial visit made there by the Prince of Wales and his mama. Other members of the Royal Family are buried in the Royal Cemetery nearby.

The present castle still shows its original "motte and bailey" design. It has two large courtyards and a motte, or hill, where the Norman Keep towers above the river and the town. Windsor Castle was extensively restored by Wyatville under the great royal rebuilder, the portly Prince Regent, later George IV. (See also Brighton Walk.)

The castle also has important connections with English literature. Medieval storyteller Geoffrey Chaucer was Master of the Works at Windsor. Chaucer supervised repairs on an early chapel on the site of the present Albert Memorial Chapel. G. K. Chesterton wrote a biography of Chaucer, and mystery writer Catherine Aird insists Chaucer is a mystery writer, too.

England's most famous writer, William Shakespeare, revived Prince Hal's boon companion, Sir John Falstaff, here to amuse Queen Elizabeth I. Falstaff reappeared in the farce *The Merry Wives of Windsor*. The play's first performance was associated with Garter Day or the Feast of St. George in 1597. In the play the "fairy queen," played by Mistress Quickly, told her fairies to scour the several chairs of order, a clear reference to the Stalls of the Knights of the Garter. (See also Shrewsbury and Stratford Walks.)

Queen Victoria, crushed by the untimely death of Prince Albert, lived here so much she became known as the Widow of Windsor. Later the castle gave its name to her descendants, the House of Windsor. Queen Elizabeth II and her sister, Princess Margaret, lived here as girls during World War II. In 1986, American Wallis Simpson, Duchess of Windsor and widow of the star-crossed Edward VIII was buried near Frogmore beside her husband, finally achieving the royal status that eluded her in life. If the Royal Standard is flying from the Keep the Royal Family is in residence.

Windsor itself looks just the way an English town should look. Its winding, cobbled streets are lined with Regency and Victorian houses, as well as fascinating stores, pubs, and tea shops. The Home Park, partly open to the public, stretches to the south and east of the castle. Beyond the Home Park lies Windsor Great Park, through which you may take a ten-mile walk that includes Runnymede.

Virginia Water, a lake in Windsor Great Park, was the creation of the notorious Duke of Cumberland, son of George II, and butcher of Bonnie Prince Charlie's royal hopes at Culloden Field. In Robert Player's *Oh, Where Are Bloody Mary's Earrings?* the peculiar and unpleasant personality of Victoria's grandson, the Duke of Clarence (Prince Eddie), was attributed by the queen to his resemblance to the Duke of Cumberland. Some authorities have also identified Prince Eddie with London's infamous Jack the Ripper.

Across the Thames north of Windsor is the small village of Eton, which is the home of the most famous public school in England. Eton College was founded in 1440 by Henry VI. Public school (boys' boarding school) life is familiar to all Americans who watch BBC shows on public television, especially James Hilton's *Goodbye, Mr. Chips.* But instead of typical caps and blazers, Etonians wear broad (Eton) collars and tailcoats; once graduated, they are known as Old Etonians and wear the Old School Tie.

Eton has legendary status in English life. The Duke of Wellington, whom mystery writer Georgette Heyer portrayed in *An Infamous Army,* went there and is said to have declared that "the battle of Waterloo was won on the playing fields of Eton." Eton's guidebook itself states that Wellington said that he owed "his spirit of enterprise to the tricks he had played in the (Eton) garden."

The true essence of Eton's claim to fame was summed up by Agatha Christie in *The Secret of Chimneys.* Her adventurer hero Anthony Cade appeared at the front door of socialite Virginia Revel, pretending to be an unemployed veteran like Tommy Beresford. Virginia just happened to have a body to dispose of, so she said she might have a job for Cade. When she asked, "Are you—I mean—" Cade reassured her by replying, "Eton and Oxford . . . That's what you wanted to ask me, vasn't it?"

Among the many famous graduates of Eton, those interesting to mystery readers are writers Eric Blair (aka George Orwell), whose *Nineteen Eighty-Four* was set in the same year as G. K. Chesterton's *The Napoleon of Notting Hill,* and Percy "Mad" Shelley, the poet, whose wife, Mary, wrote *Frankenstein.*

Mystery writers find English boarding schools represent as nicely "closed" a community as an English village for crime. Some mystery writers like Edmund Crispin and Nicholas Blake not only went to boarding schools, but were also schoolmasters there.

Some school mysteries take place in preparatory schools, where small boys are sent at age seven or eight to prepare them for schools like Eton, whose students are about the same age as those in an American high school. These lower schools share most of the characteristics of the upper, or public, schools for older boys. Both lower and upper schools have the familiar Headmaster and schoolmasters (married or single), Matron, and Houses (or dormitories) where the boys live under the thumb of older students known as prefects. One upper-form boy is Head Boy, and, the epitome of the true blue Englishman, he almost never commits murder. These schools share a basic ambiance: they are single-sex schools, where Latin and Greek are studied and the emphasis is on team sports like cricket and rowing. In keeping with the Old Boy/Old School Tie motif of boys together, mystery writers often make mere women either victims or murderers.

A murder typically occurs on a day when parents are expected to make an appearance and when games and/or plays are performed for their amusement. The school plays tend to be Shakespeare. In Josephine Bell's *Curtain Call for a Corpse,* her detective, Dr. David Wintringham, and his wife, Jill, had come to Denbury School to visit Jill's sister, the Headmaster's wife, when a member of a professional players group was killed during a performance of *Twelfth Night.*

In Edmund Crispin's *Love Lies Bleeding,* Castrevenford School was putting on a production of *Henry V* for Speech Day. In this case the victims were schoolmasters. Fortunately,

Dr. Gervase Fen of Oxford University was on hand to give out the prizes and solve the murder. In Leo Bruce's mystery, *Death at St. Asprey's School,* Carolus Deene began his investigation into odd happenings just before school sports day to prevent the parents' removing their sons.

In Michael Innes's *Hare Sitting Up* one of the two Juniper brothers, who were identical twins, had disappeared. The missing brother was either a famous scientist or a Headmaster of Splaine School. Sir John Appleby had to discover if the disappearance meant the scientist had defected to Russia, so he arrived at the school disguised as a parent. Later his wife, Judith, searched the school by organizing a bizarre "game" of hide-and-seek with the boys left there over summer vacation.

Michael Gilbert wrote about a boys' school in *The Night of the Twelfth*. Trenchard House School turned out to be the center of an area where an appalling number of small boys were being tortured and killed. Since the son of a very high-ranking Israeli diplomat was one of the school's three head boys, Scotland Yard Detective Manifold was sent to take the place of one of the masters.

Robert Barnard even dealt with the sticky social issue of the private school that was not classy enough to be called a "public school" in his witty *School for Murder*. Burleigh School, owned by Headmaster Crumwallis and his appalling wife, Enid, was a monument to snobbery, a school where parents can brag their sons were privately educated, without even having necessary textbooks.

Far fewer mystery stories take place in girls' schools, but Josephine Tey's *Miss Pym Disposes* was set in a girls' training college, while Antonia Fraser set the first Jemima Shore mystery, *Quiet as a Nun,* in Blessed Eleanor's Convent, an imaginary Roman Catholic girls' school very similar to her own alma mater in South Ascot.

North of Eton, the High Street becomes the road to Slough (A355), which is only about two miles away at the crossroads with the M4 from London. In his *Autobiography,* G. K. Chesterton and his wife, Frances, meant to spend a day in Slough (where you change for Windsor) but, in typically

absentminded Chestertonian fashion, they arrived at nearby
Beaconsfield. They liked Beaconsfield so much they later returned there to live.

South of Windsor and its 48,000 acres of parkland is the
town of Ascot with the Royal Heath and its internationally
famous racecourse, where so many of Dick Francis's sleuthing
jockeys rode. During Ascot Week in the June Season the
Queen rides from Windsor to Ascot in an open carriage attended by the master and huntsmen of the Royal Buckhounds
to attend the races. The chief event of Ascot Week is Gold Cup
Day on Thursday.

Both Ascot and Beaconsfield are included in this walk as
places where a mystery reader may want to go after seeing the
major sights of Windsor and Eton.

How to Get There

British Rail: Trains to Windsor's Central Station from London's
  Paddington (change at Slough) every half hour. Trains to
  Windsor's Riverside Station, Datchet Road, from London's
  Waterloo Station.
  Trains from London's Waterloo Station to Ascot via Staines
  (no direct link with Windsor).
  Trains to Beaconsfield from London's Marylebone Station.

Bus to Ascot: from Windsor take the White Bus at Tourist Office
  behind Central Railway Station. No service Sunday or Public
  Holidays. Marvelous ride through Windsor Great Park takes
  about three quarters of an hour.

For more information contact: White Bus Services, C. E. Jeatt
& Sons, Ltd., North Street Garage, Winkfield, Windsor, Berk.
SL4 4TF. Call Winkfield Row (0344) 882612. (Our thanks to
Mr. D. E. R. Jeatt for this information.)

See also Alder Valley buses between Brachnell and Maidenhead, which go to Eton, Windsor, and Ascot. Get bus at the
Windsor Parish Church on Windsor High Street. For more
information contact: Alder Valley, Halimote Road, Aldershot,
Hants GU11 3EG (0800) 2200.

Automobile: Windsor/Eton: Take the M4 Motorway where it divides from the old Great West Road (A4) at Chiswick. Bypass Slough on Slough West exit and take A308. 21 miles from London.

Ascot: Take A4 Great West Road from London, then A329; 25 miles from London.

Beaconsfield: M40 from London (25 miles); A355 from Windsor (10 miles).

River: Windsor/Eton: May through September, take steamer from Kingston-upon-Thames.

For more information, contact: Turk Launches, Thames Side, Kingston-upon-Thames (01-546-5775); French Brothers, the Runnymede Boathouse, Windsor Road, Old Windsor, Berks (0753) 851900; Salter Brothers, Folly Bridge, Oxford (0865) 43421.

Length of walk: About 2 miles from Windsor to Eton and back. (This does not count touring inside Windsor Castle, touring Eton College, walking in the Home Park, or visiting Ascot or Beaconsfield. Additional walk around Windsor Great Park is 10 miles long.)

See map on page 325 for the boundaries of this walk, and page 386 for a list of detectives and stories referred to.

PLACES OF INTEREST

Windsor

Windsor Castle, Castle Hill. Royal Castle; State Apartments; Round Tower; Queen Mary's Doll House; St. George's Chapel. (Open weekdays 11–3, 4, 5 P.M. Sunday in summer, unless the Court is in residence, when the Royal Standard is flown from the Keep.) Admission charge. Lower Ward, North Terrace, and part of East Terrace open daily. Free.
St. George's Chapel open February through December, Monday–Saturday 10:45–3:45; Sunday 2–3:45. Closed January, Garter Days. Admission charge, but free for services.

Nell Gwynne's House, Church Street. C. 1670. Mistress of Charles II.

Theatre Royal, Thames Street. Built 1793. May be theater at
Windsor where young actress-wife of Professor Bonner-Hill in
Lovesey's *Swing, Swing Together* played the lead in a Pinero
play.

The Guildhall, High Street. Classical building with covered
portico completed by Christopher Wren. Collection of royal
portraits and local history museum.

Windsor Parish Church, High Street. Rebuilt in the nineteenth
century. Carvings by Grinling Gibbons, painting of the Last
Supper given by George III, eighteenth-century monuments.

Windsor Great Park

Eton

Eton College, High Street, Famous public school founded in 1440
by Henry IV, which has produced twenty Prime Ministers. See
School Yard with statute of Henry VI, Lypton's Tower
(1517), the Cloisters, College Hall (1450), Upper School
(1694), Lower School (1443), Eton College Chapel, College
Dining Hall (1450), College Library (1729), and the Museum
of Eton. Admission charge.

The Cock Pit, High Street. Half-timbered building c. 1420.
Knucklebone cockpit floor, spurs and hoods used for this
sport. Now a restaurant. Outside see stocks, whipping post,
and 100-year-old pillar (mail) box.

Ascot

Ascot Racecourse, High Street (0990) 22211. See the Royal
Enclosure where men wear top hats and morning coats and
women smart hats and dresses. Ascot Week: four days in the
third week in June, Gold Cup Race on Thursdays.

Beaconsfield

Top Meadow, Grove Road and Station Road. Home of G. K.
Chesterton. (Open by appointment only.)

Overroads, Grove Road (across from Top Meadow). First home of
GKC.

Public Cemetery, Shepherd's Lane, G. K. Chesterton's grave with
Eric Gill monument.

The Royal White Hart, London End. GKC's pet pub.

Catholic Church of St. Theresa, Warwick Road. Statue of Virgin Mary donated by Chestertons, who supported building of the church itself. Memorial plaque.

Bekonscot, famous miniature village. Admission charge.

For more information: Tourist Information Centre, Windsor Central Railroad Station, Thames Street (95) 52010.

PLACES TO STAY/EAT

There are so many places to eat that we have included only a few of those we liked. As for hotels, most visitors to Windsor/ Eton come for the day from London.

Windsor

Wren Old House, Thames Street (07539) 613540. Hotel located by the river in a historic house built by Sir Christopher Wren. Restaurant, bar, and terrace by the river. Inexpensive.

Castle Hotel, High Street (07535) 51011. First-class eighteenth-century hotel run by Trusthouse Forte. Two restaurants; Castle Coffee Shop faces High Street. Licensed. Inexpensive.

The Courtyard, 8 George V Place, Thames Avenue (07535) 58338. In a narrow alley off Thames Avenue. Tiny tea shop serving coffee, lunch, or tea. Homemade pies and cakes. Inexpensive.

Eton

Christopher Hotel, 110 High Street (07535) 52359. Old coaching inn with modernized, elegant rooms. Victorian public bar and contemporary saloon bar. Real ale. Expensive.

Ascot

The Horse and Groom, High Street. Pub with good cold lunch table, pleasant open barroom. Inexpensive.

The White Stag, 63 High Street. Pub with daily hot lunch specials. Saloon and public bars still separated. Mahogany trim, thick carpets, marble fireplace with a ten-point stag's head above it, and a wall full of Royal Family photographs.

Beaconsfield

The White Hart, Aylesbury End, Old Town (Cress Hotel chain).
G. K. Chesterton's favorite pub. White stag over door, low
beamed ceilings, G. K. Chesterton Museum. Good hot pub
lunches, roast beef and Yorkshire pudding.

Saracen's Head, Windsor End (across the center). Another white
half-timbered pub patronized by GKC.

─────── WINDSOR/ETON WALK ───────

Begin your walk at the Windsor-Eton Central Railway Station
on High Street. To the rear of the station is the Tourist Information Centre, as well as the place to get the White Bus Lines
to Ascot. If you arrive in Windsor at the Riverside Railway
Station on Datchet Road, take Datchet Road to the right.
Datchet Road will become Thames Avenue, leading to Thames
Street. Turn left and follow Thames Street to Windsor Castle.

As you come out of the Central Station, straight ahead of
you up the hill is Windsor Castle. In Robert Player's *Oh,
Where Are Bloody Mary's Earrings?* Sir Henry Ponsonby, personal secretary to Queen Victoria, arrived at Windsor Station,
bringing with him from the Tower of London the Tudor
Tiara. It had been designed by Prince Albert for the Crystal
Palace Exhibition of 1853.

Royal family opinion varied as to whether Prince Albert
had created a masterpiece or a monstrosity, but everyone from
Queen Victoria to the Prince of Wales to his unspeakable son
and heir, Prince Eddie, wondered who owned the tiara and
how much money it would bring. The gems of greatest value
were the earrings Philip II of Spain brought to (Bloody) Mary
Tudor as his wedding present.

Sir Henry's rail coach, complete with a tea basket in his
private compartment, had been routed straight to Windsor
without changing at Slough the way the rest of us have to do.
The Windsor station master, used to receiving royalty, did not
spend much time on Sir Henry, but quickly let his coachman
drive Sir Henry to the castle.

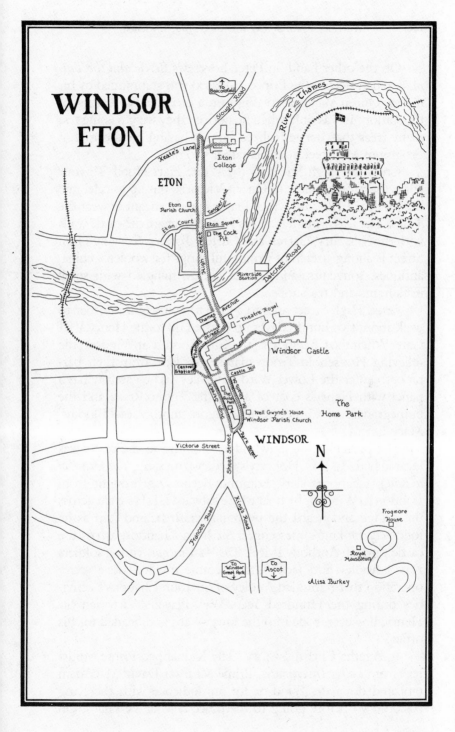

WINDSOR
ETON

To Beaconsfield

Slough Road

River Thames

Keate's Lane

Eton College

ETON

Eton Parish Church

Tangier Lane

Eton Court

Eton Square

The Cock Pit

High Street

Riverside Station

Datchet Road

Thames Avenue

Theatre Royal

Thames Street

Central Station

Windsor Castle

Castle Hill

To Supply Co.

The Guild Hall

High Street

Nell Gwyne's House

Windsor Parish Church

The Home Park

Victoria Street

River Street

Park Street

WINDSOR

N

Frances Road

Kings Road

Frogmore House

Royal Mausoleum

To Windsor Great Park

To Ascot

Alisa Burkey

On the other hand, in Peter Lovesey's *Bertie and the Tin-man,* when Bertie (the Prince of Wales) was summoned by his mama, Queen Victoria, to Windsor, a carriage was waiting at the station. It was only when he noticed they were passing too many trees that Bertie realized he was having his meeting at Frogmore Mausoleum at his father's tomb.

Cross the High Street by the White Hart Hotel. To your left is the bronze statue of Queen Victoria, put up to celebrate the Jubilee of 1887 for which Player said she meant to wear the Tudor Tiara. To your left across High Street are the castle walls with the Salisbury, Garter, and Curfew Towers. Curving High Street is a long stretch of wonderful shops for woolens, china, antiques, souvenirs, and leather goods, mingled with small restaurants and tea shops.

Cross High Street and go a little to your right in order to walk about two hundred feet up Castle Hill to the Henry VIII Gate. When the Changing of the Guard occurs at Windsor, the relieving Household Troop marches by here from their bar-racks to enter the Lower Ward (or bailey). The gateway has a panel with Henry's coat of arms, the Tudor Rose, and the pomegranate of Catherine of Aragon, mother of "Bloody" Mary I.

The portcullis, or drawbridge, entrance to the castle was located here. In P. C. Doherty's medieval mystery, *The Death of a King,* Chancery clerk Edmund Beche was brought from London to Windsor by boat to see Edward III. He went across the bridge and heard the portcullis crash behind him as he followed the king's messenger, Sir John Chandos, across the castle yard. In Anthony Price's *The '44 Vintage,* young soldiers David Audley and Jack Butler became involved in a secret operation that reminded Audley of Sir John Chandos's activi-ties during the Hundred Years War. Player's Victorian Sir Henry, however, rode into the lower ward and headed for his office.

In Agatha Christie's story "The Kidnapped Prime Minis-ter" from *Poirot Investigates,* Prime Minister David MacAdam motored down to Windsor for an audience with the King (George V) before going to the peace talks at Versailles. On the way back to London, the Prime Minister was shot and wounded, but went on to France, where he then was kidnapped. The Leader of the House of Commons and a member of the War Cabinet then appeared at Poirot's London flat to ask his aid.

In the lower ward to your left are the quarters of the Poor Knights, pensioners of the crown. Beyond them is the Horseshoe Cloister, built by Edward IV. To your right you can look up the long green to the Norman Keep on its motte. Beyond the keep lies the still higher Upper Bailey and the State Apartments. Directly across from Henry VIII's gate is the gorgeous Perpendicular Gothic St. George's Chapel.

Cross the courtyard to enter the chapel. It is one of the great showpieces of English architecture, ranked with King's College Chapel at Cambridge and Henry VII Chapel at Westminster. St. George's Chapel was begun by Edward IV and completed under the Tudors. It was built in the light and airy Perpendicular style, with great soaring arches holding up huge stained-glass windows. The chapel is dedicated to England's patron saint, St. George, the Knight of the Red Cross, and is the official Chapel of the Order of the Garter.

Edward III, who ordered the clerk Edmund Beche to search for the facts about the murky death of his father, Edward II, in Doherty's *The Death of a King,* began the Order of the Garter in 1348. In Doherty's mystery, Beche met Edward III in a chamber off an earlier chapel on the site of the Albert Memorial Chapel just beyond St. George's Chapel. Doherty mentioned that this original chapel had recently been rebuilt, but he did not add that the rebuilding was overseen by poet (and mystery writer) Geoffrey Chaucer, who probably lived in the Winchester Tower on the north wall.

A number of English kings are buried in St. George's Chapel, among them archenemies "White Rose" Edward IV and "Red Rose" Henry VI, Henry VIII and his third wife, Jane Seymour, the beheaded Charles I, mad "Farmer" George III, America's last king, his son the Prince Regent, and most recently, George V. The chapel choir has the Stalls of the Knights of the Garter, which are hung with their banners.

According to Wilfred Scott-Giles, who wrote *The Wimsey Family* using his correspondence with Dorothy L. Sayers, the Garter stall-plate of Gerald de Wimsey, fifth Earl of Denver, c. 1450, is unaccountably missing. As an official herald called the Fitzalan Pursuivant of Arms, who took part in the installation of the present Prince of Wales, Scott-Giles drew the Garter stall-plate from a drawing at the Wimsey seat at Bredon Hall. It is the frontispiece of *The Wimsey Family*. A later Paul Wimsey, Duke of Denver, was made a Knight of the Garter for his services to Charles II as well as Hereditary Keeper of the Privy Stair. His family gracefully gave up this position when Queen Victoria insisted it be held by a female.

When you come out of St. George's Chapel, turn to your left and walk uphill to the Round Tower (the Norman Keep). The top ramparts were added by George IV but the oldest parts of the tower date back to 1170. The Royal Archives are housed in the lower part above the dungeons, where there is an ancient well to be used in case of siege. In Player's *Oh, Where Are Bloody Mary's Earrings?* Sir Henry Ponsonby wanted to lock up the Tudor Tiara in the dungeons.

If it is open, climb the tower for a spectacular view northward over the Thames, Eton School, and the little church of Stokes Poges, immortalized by Eton poet Thomas Gray in his "Elegy Written in a Country Churchyard." To the south you can see the Long Walk and the statue of George III on Snow Hill. Sir Henry Ponsonby and his wife lived in the Norman Tower in Player's mystery.

Go past the Round Tower, bearing left toward the gateway that lets you into the North Terrace. To your right is the Norman Gateway, built in 1359. It once housed captive French and Scottish kings; today the Governor of Windsor Castle lives there. Enter the North Terrace, which has another panoramic view over Eton and its playing fields.

The North Terrace is a courtyard where you gain admission to the various parts of the castle open to the public like the Round Tower, the State Apartments, and Queen Mary's Doll House. In Player's *Oh, Where are Bloody Mary's Earrings?* the office of Sir Henry Ponsonby was here and could be reached from the private royal apartments along the East and South Terraces. During the mystery, the Prince of Wales, Queen Victoria, Princess Beatrice of Battenberg (grandmother of the Lord Mountbatten who was the victim of an IRA bomb), and loathsome Prince Eddie all came secretly to the North Terrace to see Sir Henry.

The route you take in the State Apartments may change from year to year, depending upon renovations. Whatever order you enter them, the major sights are the Grand Staircase, with a suit of armor made for Henry VIII and a statue of George IV (the Prince Regent), who redid Windsor the way he redid Buckingham Palace and Brighton's Royal Pavilion. (See Brighton Walk.)

The big state rooms are the Throne Room (or Garter Room), where the annual Garter investitures are held, the Grand Reception Room for banquets with Gobelin tapestries, and the 185-foot-long St. George's Hall, once the banqueting hall of the Knights of the Garter, whose shields decorate the ceiling and window recesses. The Private Chapel is here at one end. The Waterloo Chamber was created from a twelfth-century courtyard in 1830. It was the place in Player's mystery where Queen Victoria in 1887 had been almost festive, seeing performances by Jenny Lind, Ellen Terry, and Henry Irving, much to the annoyance of Sir Henry, who liked peace and quiet.

Among the apartments dating from the seventeenth century are the Queen's Guard Chamber, where the Yeomen of the Guard were stationed, the Queen's Presence Chamber, a Baroque anteroom for official visitors, and the Queen's Ballroom, where major receptions are held. More private quarters are the Queen's Drawing (or withdrawing) Room, the King's Dressing Room and the King's Closet, where he had private meetings with his (privy) council, the King's Drawing Room, and the Dining Room, which is the official dining room of the Royal Family.

In Player's mystery you can follow Sir Henry, his wife, Mary, and various members of Queen Victoria's family and guests about the private apartments in a way you cannot do unless you are a friend of the Royal Family. In the story, everyone went back and forth along the Great Corridor, which runs along the east side of the castle and looks out on the Upper Ward. The Corridor linked the various private chambers and apartments. With a Regency ceiling and white marble busts, it was described as majestic, if middle-class. It was there that the Royal Family all took a good look at the Tudor Tiara displayed on its black velvet cushion.

According to Player, on the afternoon of June 19, 1887, the day before her Jubilee, Queen Victoria took the air on the South Terrace, then received the Prince of Wales in her Gold Room, which Player described as a typically bourgeois parlor stuffed with photographs and mementos of her enormous royal brood. That night the royal party ate in the Green Drawing Room, with the smaller Winterhalters. The lower staff and guests ate next door in the Green Dining Room with the smaller Landseers. The second, more lowly group had to finish eating the moment the Queen did to join her for coffee and a "treat" in the Corridor.

The "treat" was Sir Henry telling the story of Prince Albert's creation of the Tudor Tiara. Unfortunately her guest, the Maharajah of Kashgar, who wanted to be made a Knight of the Garter, told the Queen that "Bloody" Mary's earrings were fakes. This discovery meant that the tiara might not provide adequate collateral for a loan by the Rothschilds to the Prince of Wales. It also meant that "Bloody" Mary's earrings were missing and raised the interesting question of who had taken them and when.

All during Queen Victoria's long widowhood, everything in the Blue Room, which had been Prince Albert's bedroom, was kept exactly as it had been when he died. Every night his clothes were laid out by his valet as if he would come and change into them, and every night Queen Victoria came there to say her prayers. In the mystery it turned out that she had also squirreled away the genuine Tudor Tiara there.

Later, when the chase was up for the earrings, the Prince of Wales convened a business meeting in the Windsor State Dining Room to sort out the facts about the earrings' disappearance. This strange gathering included the future Kaiser, Prince William of Prussia, Sir Frederick Rogers, Commissioner of Police from Scotland Yard, Field Marshal Lord Wilson, Constable of the Tower of London, the Prime Minister, and assorted others, including Baron Ferdinand Rothschild and Mr. Friedman of Garrards of Regent Street, jewelers to the Queen. The Prince of Wales ended the meeting by exclaiming, "Oh, where the hell are Bloody Mary's earrings?"

In addition to the State Apartments, Windsor Castle has two other attractions. One is Queen Mary's Doll House, given to the Queen in 1923 by the nation. It is perfectly scaled to fit persons six inches high. G. K. Chesterton was one of the authors who contributed a tiny piece of writing. (It was also for Queen Mary's birthday that Agatha Christie wrote the BBC radio play *The Mousetrap,* which is still playing in London's West End.)

The other attraction, which you can also enter from the North Terrace, is the Exhibition of Old Masters' Drawings from the Royal Collection. It has wonderful works by Da Vinci, Holbein, Raphael, Michelangelo, Hogarth, and many others. To leave the Upper Ward of the castle, go through St. George's Gateway into the Middle Ward by the Round Tower, and continue downhill back to the Henry VIII gate.

Once outside the castle gate, cross Castle Hill to St. Albans Street on the opposite side. As you walk along St. Albans Street, the Royal Stables are to your left and you will pass one of the numerous houses occupied by Nell Gwynne, the actress-mistress of Charles II. In Anthony Price's *Soldier No More,* the large and luscious Lady Alexandria Perowne (Lexy) was a descendant of an actress-mistress of that monarch who might well have been Nell Gwynne. (See Newmarket Walk.) Follow St. Albans Street as it curves to the right back to High Street. You will cross Church Street and Market Street. Both of these old lanes are cobblestoned and have interesting old houses.

At the corner of St. Albans Street and Park Street, turn right on High Street to walk back toward the Castle Hotel and Central Station. You pass the Windsor Parish Church, which was rebuilt in the nineteenth century. It has some Grinling

Gibbons carvings and a painting of the Last Supper given by George III, who ended his days talking to the trees in Windsor Great Park. This is the place to get the Alder Valley buses from Slough and Eton to Ascot.

Just beyond the church along High Street is a cobblestoned open-air market next to the classical Guildhall with its covered portico. The Guildhall was designed by Sir Thomas Fitz and completed by Sir Christopher Wren in 1707. It has statues of Queen Anne and her consort, Prince George of Denmark, a collection of Royal portraits, and a museum of local historical and archeological objects.

Walk down High Street past the castle walls until High Street turns sharply right to become Thames Street. Follow Thames Street past River Street on your left to the Theatre Royal. This theater dates from the late eighteenth century. It may have been "the Playhouse Theatre" at Windsor where the young wife of Merton College don Bonner-Hill acted in a Pinero play in Lovesey's *Swing, Swing Together*. Later in the mystery, when Mrs. Bonner-Hill arrived from Windsor at the Oxford mortuary to identify her murdered husband, she was swathed in deep mourning as if she were Queen Victoria. She was accompanied by Jacob Goldstein, manager of the Playhouse, who was young and dark-complected and wearing an expensive overcoat, rather like the young Benjamin Disraeli, who became Queen Victoria's favorite Prime Minister. (See Oxford Walk.)

Past the theater, follow Thames Street, which turns left, and walk toward the Thames River. Off to your right below the castle is St. George's School, which is attended by the Chapel's choirboys. On the left off Thames Street you come to a courtyard called George V Place. At the back is a tiny tea shop called the Courtyard, which serves coffee, tea, and lunch, with superb homemade scones, cakes, and pies. Cream teas are their specialty.

Cross Thames Avenue. On the right is Dachet Road, where the London trains from Waterloo Station come in at the Riverside Railway Station. (If you come into Riverside Station from London you don't have to change trains.) On Thames

Avenue on your left as you walk toward the river is the Old Wren House. The small Hotel is a late seventeenth-century red-brick house, built and lived in by Sir Christopher Wren. It has a dining room and an outdoor terrace overlooking the Thames.

Next you will come to the banks of the Thames River, where the old cast-iron footbridge takes you across to Eton. You can see gulls and royal swans on the river. Boat clubs and terraces to sit on in summertime line the riverbanks.

The Eton College Boat Club is on the Eton side of the river. It is the largest club of its kind in the world. Dorothy L. Sayers's Lord Peter Wimsey probably learned to scull at Eton, although he did not show off his prowess until he was at Oxford in *Gaudy Night*.

The Eton College Boating Song (played on the hour by the chimes of Fortnum & Mason's on Piccadilly, London) was written in 1863 for the College's annual celebration of the Glorious Fourth of June, which is the birthday of its patron, George III. According to Wilfred Scott-Giles in *The Wimsey Family*, the nursery song about "Three Blind Mice" came from a lampoon about "Farmer" George III and a Duke of Denver. The Duke had unsuccessfully tried to win a place for a kinswoman in the Royal Household. The mice, of course, were the mice on the Wimsey coat of arms.

Once you cross the Thames you are on Eton High Street. Eton is even more delightfully English than Windsor. Walk along the right-hand side of the High Street toward Eton College. You will pass hotels, pubs, tea shops, school-clothing shops, china and gift shops, and bookstores.

Keep on walking until you come to the Cock Pit, a fifteenth-century black-and-white half-timbered building now used as a restaurant. Outside there are an old pair of wooden stocks and a whipping post, as well as one of the three oldest pillar-boxes (for mail) in England. In Georgette Heyer's mystery *Death in the Stocks* the first murder victim, Arnold Vereker, was lured into sitting in some stocks, then stabbed to death.

From the window you can see the knucklebone cockpit floor and the spurs and hoods worn by the fighting gamecocks. Cockfighting was a rough sport much enjoyed by "low types" like Charles II. In Georgette Heyer's Regency mystery *The Quiet Gentleman,* Martin Frant, the surly younger brother of the new Earl of St. Erth, was caught sneaking out to go cocking in the village.

First cross Eton Square, then Tangier Lane. (If you took Tangier Lane it would take you back to the Thames, Eton's playing fields, Romney Lock, and part of the [Windsor] Home Park.) On High Street you come next to another crossroads, called Baldwin's Shore, which goes around the south side of Eton College. At this point High Street becomes the Long Walk and you are passing by the high walls of the College itself. In a niche on the wall is a statue of Bishop Waynflete, who was an Eton Provost (or Headmaster).

The College was founded in 1440 by Lancastrian Henry VI to provide scholars for King's College, Cambridge. He made it lavish grants of land, which were taken away from the College in 1461 when his rival, the Yorkist Edward IV, became king. According to Eton tradition Edward IV's most famous mistress, Jane Shore, persuaded Edward to restore some of Eton's lands, then Bishop Waynflete saved the chapel by having it roofed and finished in the Perpendicular style of the Chapel of St. George at Windsor. In Tey's *The Daughter of Time,* Inspector Alan Grant commented ironically on the kindness of Richard III in letting Jane Shore marry a London goldsmith. Lady Antonia Fraser named her TV investigator Jemima Shore after Jane Shore, whom she admires.

Eton College began as a religious foundation where seventy scholars received a free education. Today, there are still seventy Collegers or Scholars, who win their places by open examination. In addition there are over a thousand Oppidians (or townies) who originally lived in private houses, but now live in twenty-five Houses on the Eton campus. The students range in age from thirteen to eighteen. There are 125 full-time masters, a Provost (or Headmaster) and a Vice-Provost, as well as ten nonresident Fellows who are the successors to the ten priests of Henry VI's original Foundation. Like all English public schools, Eton College is really a private school, open to anyone who can pass the entrance examination and pay the fees.

Walk until you reach the archway of the Upper School, built in 1694 and badly damaged in World War II. Enter the gateway, where you will find the School Office. You can join a guided tour or simply pay to go inside on your own, purchasing a guidebook. Eton College is open only on weekday afternoons, so plan accordingly.

As you walk into the cobblestoned quadrangle called School Yard, to your left is Eton's oldest building, Lower School. Lower School's ground floor has a long hall with facing benches and tables, which is the oldest classroom still in use in the world. Above it was the Long Chamber, the original dormitory where the seventy King's Scholars slept and worked.

On your right in School Yard is the Eton College Chapel. It has many mementos of the Etonians who have died defending England. War has touched the College itself, for the bomb that hit Upper School blew out most of the chapel's stained-glass windows, which have been replaced with modern ones. The old wooden roof was replaced by a handsome fan-vaulted steel and concrete ceiling, a replica of the original roof planned for this shrine to St. Mary. Behind the carved pews are some fifteenth-century wall paintings of the life of the Virgin as well as classical heroes. These paintings were whitewashed by the Puritans, then later rediscovered and restored.

When you have seen Lower School and the Chapel, come out into School Yard again. Straight ahead of you is a statue of the School's founder, Henry VI. The King is in his Garter robes, wearing a crown. Beyond Henry VI is Lupton's Tower, a handsome Tudor Gatehouse built in 1520 that leads to the second quadrangle called the Cloisters.

In the Cloisters you can see College Hall, a tall raftered hall built in 1450 for the Masters' and Scholars' use, and the 1729 College Library with treasures like a Gutenberg Bible. Beyond the second quad you may wish to make your way to the left to the playing fields, or to your right, where you will find the old kitchen and the College Museum.

The young James Hilton wrote an early mystery called *Was It Murder?* that took place at an English public school called Oakington. In it, university graduate Colin Revell (who had just published the obligatory novel defaming Oxford) was asked by the Headmaster to investigate a series of surprising deaths in one family of boys at the school. As an Old Boy, Revell was able to linger about and wound up playing Dr. Watson to Scotland Yard's Detective Guthrie. Although Oakington was clearly not as ancient and venerable as Eton, Hilton's descriptions of student life, from compulsory chapel to the private lives of the masters, gave his reader as good a sense of public school life as his later classic *Goodbye, Mr. Chips.*

There have been several real-life Old Etonians who wrote mysteries, like Detection Club member Monsignor Ronald Knox, who preached the eulogy for his close friend and fellow Club member, G. K. Chesterton. In *Oh, Where Are Bloody Mary's Earrings?* Robert Player's Maharajah vividly remembered being bullied when sent to Eton. The boys at the terrible private school in Robert Barnard's *School for Murder* complained to their master about their miserable lot, only to be told that the eighteenth-century Eton of poet Thomas Gray had probably been much much worse.

In *Bonecrack*, Dick Francis's Neil Griffon was sent to Eton. Griffon ran away at sixteen to sweep floors at Sotheby's (the auction house) in London until he knew enough to set himself up in the antique business. In Georgette Heyer's Regency mystery *The Quiet Gentleman*, the Earl of St. Erth had sent his two sons to Eton, following the family tradition, but sent his orphaned nephew Theo to Winchester, making him feel second-rate.

In Peter Dickinson's *Sleep and His Brother*, a mystery about a special school run for cathypnic children, the Greek millionaire who supported the school's research has a private secretary, Viscount Catling, whose tie makes it clear to detective Jimmy Pibble that the viscount is an Old Etonian. The same was true of P. D. James's Chief Inspector John Massingham, who worked for Commander Adam Dalgliesh. In Michael Innes's *Candleshoe*, Lord Scattergood had gone to "the large school near Windsor." Later in the same mystery, the rich American, Mrs. Feather, who wanted to purchase the manor of Candleshoe, also wanted to send the housekeeper's boy, Jay, to Eton because it was the best place "to teach one to play a prominent position on life's stage."

Dorothy L. Sayers's Wimsey family traditionally sent its sons to Eton, so that both Lord Peter's nephew, Lord St. George, and Lord Peter's brother, Gerald, Duke of Denver, went there. Presumably, Lord Peter and Harriet's three sons, Bredon, Roger, and Paul, all of whom appeared in "Talboys" went there, too.

The epitome of the proper Etonian was Lord Peter. The account of his school days was written by his maternal uncle, Paul Delagardie. According to Delagardie, Lord Peter was a shrimp of a boy with the devil's own pluck, but more skill than brawn. He grew up liking books and music, with the result that life at home and at school was hell, and his classmates called him "Flimsy." Then an Eton games master discovered that Lord Peter was a natural cricketer. All his mannerisms were forgiven him and he became instead The Great Flim. Years later his very walk when he had played in the all important Eton-Harrow Match at Lords was remembered by a doddery old client of Pym's Publicity in *Murder Must Advertise*.

By the time Wimsey was in Eton's Sixth Form, he had become the fashion—athlete, scholar, arbiter elegantiarum—a role he played later at Balliol, judging from his contemporary's remarks when they met sculling on the Isis in *Gaudy Night*. His Uncle Paul also introduced him to Edwardian sex by setting him up with a charming Parisian mistress. The details about this affair remain unpublished in the sequel to *Busman's Honeymoon* called *Thrones, Dominations*.

Once you have explored Wimsey's Eton College, go out Upper School gate again to the High Street. To your right the High Street soon will become Slough Road, passing more modern Eton buildings like Savile House. Across the street are the New Schools, built in 1861, and, beyond Common Lane, the Boer War Memorial Buildings built in 1908.

G. K. Chesterton, who went to St. Paul's School but never

subscribed to the Old Boys' network, won his spurs writing articles against the Boer War. (His St. Paul's schoolmate and fellow mystery writer, E. C. Bentley, never forgot the sight of his nervous friend when he had to read his prize-winning poem at Speech Day at St. Paul's.)

If you do not plan to drive directly north to Slough and Beaconsfield, cross Eton High Street and turn left to go back toward Windsor. Cross Keate's Lane (named for a seventeenth-century Eton Provost, not the poet), and continue past the post office (useful for stamps for postcards) until you come to the Church of St. John the Evangelist, the Eton Parish Church. It was built in the mid-nineteenth century, but its parish records date to the sixteenth century.

Next cross Eton Court, where you will come to the Christopher, a small hotel-cum-pub that began life as a coaching inn. It has two bars—a Victorian public bar, and a contemporary one that matches its updated rooms. If you do not wish to stop off at the Christopher, keep on walking to the Thames and cross the bridge back to Windsor. Follow Thames Street to High Street and the Central Railway Station, where you can end your walk or catch a bus to Ascot or Beaconsfield. You have walked about two miles in Windsor/Eton, not counting the time spent inside the castle itself.

──────── ASCOT WALK ────────

Get a bus for Ascot either behind Central Station, Windsor, or on Windsor High Street by the Windsor Parish Church. The trip will take about three quarters of an hour and goes through parts of Windsor Great Park. Local people are the main customers, hopping on and off at little clumps of houses or tiny villages along the route. The White Bus takes King's Road, which will give you a glimpse of the Royal Mausoleum in the Home Park, where Queen Victoria is buried.

To the south lies Windsor Great Park. It began as a deer enclosure made by William the Conqueror in 1086, but the castle and the park were kept separate until the time of Charles II. George III supervised the laying-out of roads and appointed himself Ranger. Queen Victoria was very partial to the park and Prince Albert made many improvements. A model village for royal staff was built there in 1948 by George VI, but the deer were removed during World War II and returned only as recently as 1979.

It is possible to walk through Windsor Great Park from Windsor Castle to the Obelisk and back, roughly ten miles. You leave the castle and walk away from Windsor toward Datchet Road on the Thames, then go left to follow a footpath south for about four miles, crossing Albert Bridge, then passing Old Windsor Church. Old Windsor was the original Saxon town before the Conqueror built the castle.

Beyond Old Windsor you come to Runnymede, where the barons made King John sign Magna Carta in 1215. G. K. Chesterton's friend, Hilaire Belloc, always argued that John was one of England's better kings. This unconventional approach was echoed by Chesterton in *A Short History of England,* where he stated that Richard Coeur-de-Lion may have gained glory for England by fighting in the Crusades, but King John devoted himself conscientiously to domestic politics. In John Creasey's *Theft of Magna Carta,* Inspector West became involved in a plot to steal the Sarum copy of the famous charter. (See Salisbury Walk.) Three acres at Runnymede are now American soil, given by Elizabeth II for a memorial to American President John F. Kennedy when he was assassinated.

The path then goes south and somewhat to your right past the Savill Garden toward the Obelisk. The Obelisk was erected by George II to celebrate the 1747 victory of his son, the Duke of Cumberland, over Bonnie Prince Charlie at Culloden. Both the Obelisk and the ornamental lake called Virginia Water were created to give the duke's veterans work.

The Duke of Cumberland had depraved habits, which reminded everyone in Robert Player's *Oh, Where Are Bloody Mary's Earrings?* of the unspeakable Prince Eddie, suspected of being Jack the Ripper. Marie Belloc-Lowndes, sister of G. K. Chesterton's friend, Hilaire Belloc, wrote the first fictional account of that East End murderer in *The Lodger.*

Reunited at last in *The Skeleton in the Clock,* John Dickson Carr's lovers, Martin Drake and Lady Jenny, drove to see the sun rise over Virginia Water. In *Forfeit* Dick Francis's sportswriter James Tyrone visited a man who owned a racehorse somewhere near Virginia Water. Tyrone, whose wife was afflicted with polio (like Dick Francis's own wife), also met the owner's half-black niece and became her lover.

The crooked financial wizard, Randall Blackett, in Michael Gilbert's *End-Game* also lived at Virginia Water. In that mystery, at the end of "Operation Snakes and Ladders," agents Susan Perronet-Conde and David Rhys Morgan met again at Blackett's lovely, lavish, and impersonal mansion.

Turn right at the Obelisk to start back through the Park toward the castle. You will pass Cumberland Lodge, built by Charles II and once the home of the first Duke of Marlborough, Sir Winston Churchill's illustrious ancestor, and then the Royal Lodge, the weekend home of Queen Elizabeth, the present Queen Mother, whose most famous jockey was Dick Francis. It was here that Elizabeth and her husband, the Duke of York, waited out the abdication crisis of Edward VIII, which brought the Duke to the throne as George VI.

Beyond the Royal Lodge you can see the Copper Horse (George III in a Roman toga) on Snow Hill. It stands at the top of the famous Long Walk created for Charles II. As you walk down the Long Walk toward Windsor Castle, to your right you will see the Royal Mausoleum, built in 1862 to hold the body of the Prince Consort. Queen Victoria was later buried there. When they die, the royal family are now buried in the Royal Cemetery in the garden.

If you take the bus to Ascot, Windsor High Street soon becomes Sheet Street, then King's Road as you sail along, passing Adelaide Square with its terrace of attractive Regency houses. At the junction of Osborne and Albert Roads on the right is the Brigidine Convent School, a reminder that Antonia Fraser attended another girls' school called St. Mary's in South

Ascot. She wrote us that she based the fictional convent school called Blessed Eleanor's Convent on St. Mary's. In the first Jemima Shore mystery, *Quiet as a Nun,* it was Jemima's classmate, Sister Miriam, the wealthy daughter of a Lord Mayor of London, who was found murdered there.

As you ride through the lovely wooded countryside, remember that in Agatha Christie's *Partners in Crime,* Alfred, Tommy and Tuppence Beresford's office boy, caught a crook on the Ascot Road.

Christie was partial to the Ascot Road as a site for mayhem. In the Poirot adventure called "The Kidnapped Prime Minister," the Prime Minister had been shot as he left Windsor after his audience with King George (V), en route back to London and the Versailles Peace Conference after World War I. The Prime Minister's secretary, Captain Daniels, had a maiden aunt who lived at Ascot, so later Poirot and the faithful Hastings followed the cold trail from Windsor to Ascot to visit the maiden aunt. They then drove back to London, stopping at every cottage hospital on the way.

At the sign "Ascot, 1 mile," the road curves suddenly, and on your left you can see Ascot racecourse. The Queen drives there in a carriage from Windsor every day during June's Ascot Week. Just past the racecourse the bus comes into Ascot High Street, where you should get off.

The racecourse itself is on your left. You will see signs for the entrances to the Royal Enclosure, the press box, and the stands. Across the High Street to your left are the white rail fences of the racing world, with signs indicating the parking lots, stables, and other buildings.

Ascot is a very social place to see and be seen. In Dorothy L. Sayers's *Gaudy Night* Harriet Vane went to Ascot with a witty young woman writer and her barrister husband, partly for fun and partly to get color for a short story where a victim fell dead in the Royal Enclosure while all eyes were glued on the finish. Scanning those sacred (and expensive) precincts from without the pale, Harriet saw Lord Peter in a gray top hat, being amused by a bevy of social butterflies. She told herself she was pleased that he was so well occupied, but she was also happy when he rang her up the next day to invite her out.

In Nicholas Blake's *The Smiler with the Knife* Georgia Strangeways was recruited by Nigel's uncle at Scotland Yard to uncover the identity of the Fascist leader of a plot to subvert England. She went to a houseparty in Berkshire where her hosts were trainers. They took her to Ascot, where she met the epitome of the true British nobility, Lord Chilton Canteloe.

According to Saul Panzer, the beautiful and titled exwife of sleazy newspaper mogul Ian MacLaren had met him at "that fancy racetrack—Ascot," in Robert Goldsborough's latest Nero Wolfe called *Death on Deadline*.

The Ascot associations for Dick Francis fans are legion. Francis himself, while the Queen Mother's jockey, wrote in his autobiography, *The Sport of Queens,* that the new course at Ascot, officially flat, had an upward pull. He also mentioned being advised by the Queen Mother's friend, Lord Abergavenny, who was later the Queen's representative at Ascot, to "retire at the top." Francis did so, to write best-seller mysteries.

In *Nerve,* Francis's jockey Rob Finn, whose parents were both world-class musicians, was supposed to race a horse called Template at the Midwinter Cup Day at Ascot. Finn was beaten up and had freezing water poured on him, but he was rescued by his cousin and a London cabbie who revived him, so that he won the race on "Ascot's blasted heath." At Ascot Finn went a lot of places the public cannot go: the jockey changing room and weighing room, the stalls, the trophy table. The racecourse itself can be seen in the racing season.

In Francis's *Enquiry,* "warned off" (disqualified) jockey Kelly Hughes met his owner's daughter, Roberta Cranfield, at the Ascot Jockeys' Fund Dance. The dance was held in the Royal County Hotel along the road from Ascot racecourse. All the Stewards and racing VIPs were there. Both Hughes and Roberta were ignored or stared at. But Hughes learned some useful facts for his investigation because, while driving home, something went wrong with his car, and he was nearly killed at a railway crossing.

In Francis's *Blood Sport* a private detective trying to solve the disappearance of some valuable racehorses went to Ascot on Gold Cup Day to recruit a stable lad to help the search. Ascot was also the racecourse where Neil Griffon finally went to make peace with his domineering father in *Bonecrack,* but the reunion was something less than warm. In *Reflex* photographer-jockey Philip Nore rode at Ascot and came in third. He was trying to solve the murder of another photographer who he thought had been a blackmailer.

In Francis's more recent mysteries, *Break In* and *Bolt,* champion jockey Kit (for Christmas) Fielding rode for the Princess Casilia, Mme. de Brescou. She had her own box at most of the better-known racecourses like Ascot, which a designer decorated in her favorite pale peach and coffee. When Fielding raced at Ascot in blinding sleet (rather like the storm we met in April) he won on the Princess's horse, Icefall. He also found out that the son of newspaper magnate Lord Vaughnley had sold his family stock to pay racing debts. Fielding drove the Princess's niece, Danielle (with her highness's gracious approval), to Henley-on-Thames en route back to Eaton Square in London.

Neither the Princess nor her niece Danielle seemed to be very class-conscious, and they proved to be useful co-conspirators. By *Bolt,* in spite of the snobbish opposition of Princess Casilia's sister-in-law, Beatrice de Brescou, Kit Fielding had become engaged to Danielle and was very much a part of the family. At Ascot with the Princess, Danielle, and the annoying sister-in-law all in attendance, Fielding found that his archenemy, Maynard Allardeck, was still trying to get him in official racing trouble. (See also Newmarket Walk.)

In Jeffrey Archer's revenge story, *Not a Penny More, Not a Penny Less,* the conspirators learned that their prey, American millionaire Harvey Metcalfe, had arrived in England and had gone to Ascot to see his filly, Rosalie, run in the King George VI and Queen Elizabeth Stakes. Metcalfe also had a private box at Ascot for Ascot Week, so one of the conspirators, Stephen Bradley, a visiting lecturer at Oxford, chose Ascot Week as his chance to approach Metcalfe to issue a phony Oxford invitation.

Bradley scraped an acquaintance with Metcalfe by pretending to be a Professor Porter. He then watched the Royal Entrance, the National Anthem, and the special parade for the King George VI Stakes from the Metcalfe box in the Royal Enclosure. Metcalfe's horse won the race, making its owner so euphoric that he would do anything, including accept a phony invitation to the University Garden Party. (See Oxford Walk.)

Ascot High Street has many shops, including a bookstore selling Dick Francis mysteries, and several handsome pubs with a nice horsey flavor reminiscent of Newmarket. The one nearest the bus stop is the Horse and Groom. It has a bountiful cold luncheon table. A little farther along High Street is a corner pub called the White Stag. This is the perfect racing pub, with furnishings out of the Edwardian era of that great sportsman, Edward VII. It still has separate public and private bars, a wall covered with photographs of the Royal Family, lots of Toby jugs and horse prints on deep mauve wallpaper, a marble fireplace with a ten-point stag head over it, and dark oak tables and benches. The pub has good hot and cold food and very friendly bar help, who made your sleet-frozen authors some hot coffee "after hours."

After you have gone to the races, or seen enough local color, catch the bus back to Windsor or go to your left across the High Street to follow the sign to the Ascot train station. You can get a train from Ascot back to Windsor, via Staines, where you will have to change lines, or you can go directly from Ascot back to Waterloo Station, London.

The return bus trip to Windsor follows a different route than the one coming. It takes you deeper into Windsor Great Park through South Ascot, where Lady Antonia Fraser went to St. Mary's. You pass the little towns of Sunnyhill and Sunningdale, then suddenly get a glorious view of the Copper Horse (statue of George III in Roman toga) on top of Snow Hill. Beyond it you can see Charles II's Long Walk, which leads to the South Terrace of Windsor Castle.

Back in Windsor, take High Street from the bus stop back to the Central Railway Station to end your walk.

Beaconsfield

Arrive at Beaconsfield by car from Windsor/Eton by way of the Slough Road (A355), or take the train from London's Marylebone Station. Beaconsfield, a charming old town of 12,000, is where G. K. Chesterton went to live in 1909 to find some peace and quiet to write, while his wife, Frances, gardened. Authorities differ as to whether GKC missed the hurly-burly of his beloved London's Fleet Street, but one thing is certain— he loved Beaconsfield and often wrote about it.

If you arrive by car, you will come into Beaconsfield at the southern end. Follow the A355 to the M40, then take the clover leaf exit north (straight ahead) to the A40 (London-Oxford Road). Go left to follow the A40 as it becomes London End. At the crossroads in the center of the Old Town (see GKC on the two towns of Beaconsfield in his *Autobiography*) you will see the White Hart and the Saracen's Head pubs and can get out and walk, reversing the route of the people who come by train. There are parking places near the town square and by the pubs.

Arriving by train, leave the railroad station, which is down in a hollow, and climb the stairs to Station Road. (You are in New Town here with several modern shopping centers and shops.)

Turn left and follow Station Road across Maxwell Road to the point where it splits into Grove Road and Station Road. Take Grove Road to your right and follow it around a curve that eventually leads you back to Station Road at the point where there is a film studio. Dorothy Collins, GKC's last and best secretary, once went to this studio and told them that they were making so much noise that "Mr. Chesterton can't write." According to Aidan Mackey, Chairman of the Chesterton Society, GKC insisted that the reply was "We are well aware of that!"

Grove Road has pleasant suburban villas and open spaces, mostly red-brick or timbered, like the older buildings in Old Town. Toward the end of Grove Road on your left, as it approaches Station Road again, is a sign saying "Overroads," indicating the house the Chestertons first rented in Beacons-field. Across Grove Road there once was a meadow with a big tree, around which Chesterton built a studio. Now you see the red-brick wall and roofs of his home, Top Meadow, created by enlarging the studio.

Top Meadow, which was left to the Roman Catholic Church by Frances Chesterton, is the property of the Con-verts' Aid Society and not open to the public except by special request. It is a large, rambling house with a tiny closet where Chesterton worked until he was nagged into building a real study overlooking Frances's garden. The dining area is still elevated above the living room, a remainder of the days when it was the stage for Chestertonian theatricals. Dorothy Collins, his secretary and literary executor, lives at Top Meadow Cot-tage at the end of the garden on Station Road.

Turn right on Station Road, which soon becomes Ayles-bury End, and walk to the crossroads of the Old Town, where four main highways meet: London End, Aylesbury End, Windsor End, and Wycombe End. Along the way you will pass some medieval and Georgian houses, as well as narrow alleyways, one known as Burke's Corner.

This part of Beaconsfield from Top Meadow to the Old Town was once a part of the estate of the famous orator and statesman Edmund Burke. Another, later politician, Benjamin Disraeli, who was Queen Victoria's favorite Prime Minister, had connections with the town, from which he took the title of Lord Beaconsfield.

At the place where the Ends meet, the White Hart is on your left between Aylesbury End and Shepherd's Lane. Across London End is the white-timbered Saracen's Head, another pet GKC pub. Straight ahead across Windsor End is the green with the War Memorial. There is no proof that Father Brown ever came to Beaconsfield, but the Chestertons' great friend, Father John O'Connor, certainly did and saw Chesterton slashing flowers with his sword in the garden at Top Meadow.

The gleaming Royal White Hart, with a great deer above the entrance, has a special GKC museum room and a drink called the Dorothy Collins. An old coaching inn, it has excellent English food and hotel accommodations.

Outside the Royal Hart turn to your left on narrow Shepherd's Lane and walk about three blocks past a new housing development. You will come to the public cemetery where the Chestertons are buried beneath a monument designed by his artist friend, Eric Gill.

Back at the White Hart, cross the intersection to look at the Saracen's Head on the corner of the London End. Go left along London End to the barber shop, where GKC had his hair cut and see the chair, which is still there.

Return to your left and cross Windsor End to look at the War Memorial on the village green. Chesterton described how it came to be put up in his *Autobiography*. Turn right to cross Wycombe End, then right again to take Aylesbury End, which becomes Station Road, back to the railroad station.

Go past the station on Penn Road to Warwick Road. Turn right to walk to St. Theresa's Church. This is the Roman Catholic Church that the Chestertons helped to build and to which GKC donated a statue of the Virgin Mary. There is a plaque to Chesterton beside the door.

Across Warwick Road is Bekonscot, a famous toy village to which Queen Mary brought Queen Elizabeth and her sister, Princess Margaret, when they were little girls. Then turn right on Warwick to Penn Road. Go left on Penn Road back to the railway station. This walk is about two miles long.

SPECIAL
HELPS

AUTHORS, BOOKS, AND SLEUTHS BY WALK

BATH WALK: AUTHORS

Austen, Jane	Northanger Abbey
Austen, Jane	Persuasion
Carr, John Dickson	Problem of the Green Capsule, The
Chaucer, Geoffrey	Canterbury Tales, The
Creasey, John	Theft of Magna Carta
Defoe, Daniel	—
Dickens, Charles	Pickwick Papers
Fielding, Henry	Tom Jones
Francis, Dick	Rat Race
Girvan, Ian, and Margaret Royal	Local Ghosts
Gosling, Paula	"Mr. Felix"
Heyer, Georgette	Bath Tangle
Heyer, Georgette	Lady of Quality
Heyer, Georgette	Sylvester or the Wicked Uncle
Livingston, Nancy	Fatality at Bath & Wells
Lovesey, Peter	Rough Cider

Parish, Frank — **Fire in the Barley**
Pepys, Samuel — **—**
Peters, Elizabeth — **Camelot Caper, The**
Price, Anthony — **Our Man in Camelot**
Royal, Margaret, and Ian Girvan — **Local Ghosts**
Shelley, Mary — **Frankenstein**
Sheridan, Richard Brinsley — **Rivals, The**

BATH WALK: BOOKS

Bath Tangle — Heyer, Georgette
Camelot Caper, The — Peters, Elizabeth
Canterbury Tales, The — Chaucer, Geoffrey
Fatality at Bath & Wells — Livingston, Nancy
Fire in the Barley — Parish, Frank
Frankenstein — Shelley, Mary
Lady of Quality — Heyer, Georgette
Local Ghosts — Royal, Margaret, and Ian Girvan
"Mr. Felix" — Gosling, Paula
Northanger Abbey — Austen, Jane
Our Man in Camelot — Price, Anthony
Persuasion — Austen, Jane
Pickwick Papers — Dickens, Charles
Problem of the Green Capsule, The — Carr, John Dickson
Rat Race — Francis, Dick
Rivals, The — Sheridan, Richard Brinsley
Rough Cider — Lovesey, Peter
Sylvester or the Wicked Uncle — Heyer, Georgette
Theft of Magna Carta — Creasey, John
Tom Jones — Fielding, Henry

BATH WALK: SLEUTHS

DR. GIDEON FELL — Carr
JACK KEMP — Livingston
DAN MALLETT — Parish

MR. PRINGLE	Livingston
DAVID RANDALL	Peters
THEO SINCLAIR	Lovesey
JESSICA TREGARTH	Peters
SUPERINTENDENT ROGER WEST	Creasey

BRIGHTON WALK: AUTHORS

Ainsworth, Harrison	—
Allingham, Margery	"Evidence in Camera"
Blake, Nicholas	Thou Shell of Death
Byrne, Muriel St. Claire, and Dorothy L. Sayers	Busman's Honeymoon
Carr, John Dickson	Bride of Newgate, The
Carr, John Dickson	Problem of the Green Capsule, The
Carr, John Dickson	To Wake the Dead
Chesterton, G. K.	Orthodoxy
Christie, Agatha	Pocketful of Rye, A
Christie, Agatha	Poirot Investigates
Christie, Agatha	"Rajah's Emerald, The"
Collins, Wilkie	Moonstone, The
Creasey, John	Holiday for Inspector West
Dickens, Charles	Bleak House
Dickens, Charles	Dombey and Son
Dickens, Charles	Oliver Twist
Doyle, Sir Arthur Conan	—
Francis, Dick	Break In
Francis, Dick	Danger, The
Francis, Dick	Dead Cert
Francis, Dick	Rat Race
Fraser, Antonia	Splash of Red, A
Frome, David	Black Envelope, The
Greene, Graham	Brighton Rock
Grimes, Martha	I Am the Only Running Footman
Hardwick, Mollie	Malice Domestic
Heyer, Georgette	Conqueror, The
Heyer, Georgette	Corinthian, The

Heyer, Georgette	Infamous Army, An
Heyer, Georgette	No Wind of Blame
Heyer, Georgette	Penhallow
Heyer, Georgette	Regency Buck
Heyer, Georgette	Royal Escape
Heyer, Georgette	Spanish Bride, The
Heyer, Georgette	Talisman Ring, The
Heyer, Georgette	Unknown Ajax, The
Hodge, Jane Aiken	Watch the Wall, My Darling
James, P. D.	Death of an Expert Witness
Johnson, Dr. Samuel	—
Kipling, Rudyard	—
Lovesey, Peter	Mad Hatter's Holiday
Moody, Susan	Penny Dreadful
Peters, Ellis	Knocker on the Door, The
Sayers, Dorothy L., and Muriel St. Claire Byrne	Busman's Honeymoon
Sayers, Dorothy L.	Love All
Smith, Shelley	Grave Affair, A

BRIGHTON WALK: BOOKS

Black Envelope, The	Frome, David
Bleak House	Dickens, Charles
Break In	Francis, Dick
Bride of Newgate, The	Carr, John Dickson
Brighton Rock	Greene, Graham
Busman's Honeymoon	Sayers, Dorothy L., and Muriel St. Claire Byrne
Conqueror, The	Heyer, Georgette
Corinthian, The	Heyer, Georgette
Danger, The	Francis, Dick
Dead Cert	Francis, Dick
Death of an Expert Witness	James, P. D.
Dombey and Son	Dickens, Charles
"Evidence in Camera"	Allingham, Margery
Grave Affair, A	Smith, Shelley
Holiday for Inspector West	Creasey, John
I Am the Only Running Footman	Grimes, Martha

Infamous Army, An	Heyer, Georgette
Knocker on the Door, The	Peters, Ellis
Love All	Sayers, Dorothy L.
Mad Hatter's Holiday	Lovesey, Peter
Malice Domestic	Hardwick, Mollie
Moonstone, The	Collins, Wilkie
No Wind of Blame	Heyer, Georgette
Oliver Twist	Dickens, Charles
Orthodoxy	Chesterton, G. K.
Penhallow	Heyer, Georgette
Penny Dreadful	Moody, Susan
Pocketful of Rye, A	Christie, Agatha
Poirot Investigates	Christie, Agatha
Problem of the Green Capsule, The	Carr, John Dickson
"Rajah's Emerald, The"	Christie, Agatha
Rat Race	Francis, Dick
Regency Buck	Heyer, Georgette
Royal Escape	Heyer, Georgette
Spanish Bride, The	Heyer, Georgette
Splash of Red, A	Fraser, Antonia
Talisman Ring, The	Heyer, Georgette
Thou Shell of Death	Blake, Nicholas
To Wake the Dead	Carr, John Dickson
Unknown Ajax, The	Heyer, Georgette
Watch the Wall, My Darling	Hodge, Jane Aiken

BRIGHTON WALK: SLEUTHS

SERGEANT CRIBB	Lovesey
ANDREW DOUGLAS	Francis
HOWELL EVANS	Hardwick
DR. GIDEON FELL	Carr
SUPERINTENDENT RICHARD JURY	Grimes
MISS JANE MARPLE	Christie

George Felse	Peters
Mr. Pinkerton	Frome
Hercule Poirot	Christie
Matt Short	Francis
Penny Wanawake	Moody
Inspector Roger West	Creasey
Lord Peter Wimsey	Sayers
Alan York	Francis

Cambridge Walk: Authors

Allingham, Margery	Mystery Mile
Allingham, Margery	No Police at the Funeral
Anderson, J. R. L	Death in a High Latitude
Bell, Josephine	—
Bentley, E. C.	—
Blake, Nicholas	—
Brand, Christianna	Tour de Force
Bunyan, John	Pilgrim's Progress
Butterworth, Michael	Man in the Sopwith Camel, The
Chesterton, G. K.	Ballad of the White Horse, The
Childers, Erskine	Riddle of the Sands, The
Christie, Agatha	—
Clinton-Baddeley, V. C.	Death's Bright Dart
Daniel, Glyn	Cambridge Murders, The
Francis, Dick	Rat Race
Francis, Dick	Whiphand
Fraser, Antonia	Oxford Blood
Gloag, Julian	Sleeping Dogs Lie
Grimes, Martha	Dirty Duck, The
Heyer, Georgette	Detection Unlimited
Heyer, Georgette	Lord John
James, P. D.	Death of an Expert Witness

James, P. D.	Unsuitable Job for a Woman, An
Kelly, Nora	In the Shadow of Kings
Kenney, Susan	Garden of Malice
Mann, Jessica	Funeral Sites
Marlowe, Christopher	Tamburlaine
Milne, A. A.	Red House Mystery, The
Moyes, Patricia	Johnny Underground
Pepys, Samuel	—
Postgate, Raymond	Verdict of Twelve
Price, Anthony	Soldier No More
Priestley, J. B.	Salt Is Leaving
Sayers, Dorothy L.	Clouds of Witness
Sayers, Dorothy L.	Documents in the Case, The
Sayers, Dorothy L.	Five Red Herrings, The
Sayers, Dorothy L.	Gaudy Night
Sayers, Dorothy L.	Have His Carcase
Sayers, Dorothy L.	Murder Must Advertise
Sayers, Dorothy L.	Nine Tailors, The
Sayers, Dorothy L.	Whose Body?
Sayers, Dorothy L., and Wilfrid Scott Giles	Wimsey Family, The
Snow, C. P.	Death Under Sail
Snow, C. P.	Search, The
Stuart, Ian	Garb of Truth, The
Taylor, Andrew	Caroline Minuscule
Tey, Josephine	Daughter of Time, The
Woolf, Virginia	Room of One's Own, A
Yorke, Margaret	—

CAMBRIDGE WALK: BOOKS

Ballad of the White Horse, The	Chesterton, G. K.
Cambridge Murders, The	Daniel, Glyn
Caroline Minuscule	Taylor, Andrew
Clouds of Witness	Sayers, Dorothy L.
Daughter of Time, The	Tey, Josephine
Death in a High Latitude	Anderson, J. R. L.

Death of an Expert Witness	James, P. D.
Death's Bright Dart	Clinton-Baddeley, V. C.
Death Under Sail	Snow, C. P.
Detection Unlimited	Heyer, Georgette
Dirty Duck, The	Grimes, Martha
Documents in the Case, The	Sayers, Dorothy L.
Five Red Herrings, The	Sayers, Dorothy L.
Funeral Sites	Mann, Jessica
Garb of Truth, The	Stuart, Ian
Garden of Malice	Kenney, Susan
Gaudy Night	Sayers, Dorothy L.
Have His Carcase	Sayers, Dorothy L.
In the Shadow of Kings	Kelly, Nora
Johnny Underground	Moyes, Patricia
Lord John	Heyer, Georgette
Man in the Sopwith Camel, The	Butterworth, Michael
Murder Must Advertise	Sayers, Dorothy L.
Mystery Mile	Allingham, Margery
Nine Tailors, The	Sayers, Dorothy L.
No Police at the Funeral	Allingham, Margery
Oxford Blood	Fraser, Antonia
Pilgrim's Progress	Bunyan, John
Rat Race	Francis, Dick
Red House Mystery, The	Milne, A. A.
Riddle of the Sands, The	Childers, Erskine
Room of One's Own, A	Woolf, Virginia
Salt Is Leaving	Priestley, J. B.
Search, The	Snow, C. P.
Sleeping Dogs Lie	Gloag, Julian
Soldier No More	Price, Anthony
Tamburlaine	Marlowe, Christopher
Tour de Force	Brand, Christianna
Unsuitable Job for a Woman, An	James, P. D.
Verdict of Twelve	Postgate, Raymond
Whiphand	Francis, Dick
Whose Body?	Sayers, Dorothy L.
Wimsey Family, The	Sayers, Dorothy L., and Wilfrid Scott-Giles

CAMBRIDGE WALK: SLEUTHS

ALBERT CAMPION	Allingham
DR. DAVIE	Clinton-Baddeley
WILLIAM DOUGAL	Taylor
DETECTIVE EDWARD GISBORNE	Kelly
CORDELIA GRAY	James
DAVID GRIERSON	Stuart
SID HALLEY	Francis
TAMARA HOYLAND	Mann
ERNEST KITTERIDGE	Butterworth
SUPERINTENDENT ROBERTSON-MACDONALD	Daniel
ROSAMUND SHOLTO	Mann
JEMIMA SHORE	Fraser
CHIEF INSPECTOR HENRY TIBBETT	Moyes
HARRIET VANE	Sayers
LORD PETER WIMSEY	Sayers

CANTERBURY WALK: AUTHORS

Aird, Catherine	Dead Liberty, A
Aird, Catherine	Henrietta Who?
Aird, Catherine	Late Phoenix, A
Aird, Catherine	Parting Breath
Aird, Catherine	Religious Body, The
Austen, Jane	Northanger Abbey
Barham, Canon Richard Harris	Ingoldsby Legends, The
Belloc, Hilaire	Road to Rome, The
Buchan, John	Thirty-Nine Steps, The
Cadell, Elizabeth	Remains to Be Seen
Chaucer, Geoffrey	Canterbury Tales, The
Collins, Wilkie	Woman in White, The
Conrad, Joseph	Secret Agent, The
Creasey, John	Theft of Magna Carta

Defoe, Daniel	**Robinson Crusoe**
Dickens, Charles	**David Copperfield**
Doherty, Patrick C.	**Death of a King, The**
Eliot, T. S.	**Murder in the Cathedral**
Gilbert, Michael	**Smallbone Deceased**
Grimes, Martha	**Dirty Duck, The**
Heyer, Georgette	**Lord John**
Heyer, Georgette	**Sylvester or the Wicked Uncle**
Marlowe, Christopher	—
Marsh, Ngaio	**Death in a White Tie**
Marsh, Ngaio	**Surfeit of Lampreys, A**
Maugham, Somerset	**Ashenden or the British Agent**
Maugham, Somerset	**Of Human Bondage**
Moody, Susan	**Penny Dreadful**
Sayers, Dorothy L.	**Zeal of Thy House, The**
Tey, Josephine	**Daughter of Time, The**
Underwood, Michael	**Uninvited Corpse, The**
Walpole, Horace	**Castle of Otranto, The**
Williams, Charles	**Thomas Cranmer of Canterbury**
Williamson, Audrey	**Mystery of the Princes, The**

Canterbury Walk: Books

Ashenden or the British Agent	Maugham, Somerset
Canterbury Tales, The	Chaucer, Geoffrey
Castle of Otranto, The	Walpole, Horace
Daughter of Time, The	Tey, Josephine
David Copperfield	Dickens, Charles
Dead Liberty, A	Aird, Catherine
Death in a White Tie	Marsh, Ngaio
Death of a King, The	Doherty, Patrick C.
Dirty Duck, The	Grimes, Martha
Henrietta Who?	Aird, Catherine
Ingoldsby Legends, The	Barham, Canon Richard Harris

Late Phoenix, A	Aird, Catherine
Lord John	Heyer, Georgette
Murder in the Cathedral	Eliot, T. S.
Mystery of the Princes, The	Williamson, Audrey
Northanger Abbey	Austen, Jane
Of Human Bondage	Maugham, Somerset
Parting Breath	Aird, Catherine
Penny Dreadful	Moody, Susan
Religious Body, The	Aird, Catherine
Remains to Be Seen	Cadell, Elizabeth
Road to Rome, The	Belloc, Hilaire
Robinson Crusoe	Defoe, Daniel
Secret Agent, The	Conrad, Joseph
Smallbone Deceased	Gilbert, Michael
Surfeit of Lampreys, A	Marsh, Ngaio
Sylvester or the Wicked Uncle	Heyer, Georgette
Theft of Magna Carta	Creasey, John
Thirty-Nine Steps, The	Buchan, John
Thomas Cranmer of Canterbury	Williams, Charles
Uninvited Corpse, The	Underwood, Michael
Wimsey Family, The	Sayers, Dorothy L., and Wilfrid Scott-Giles
Woman in White, The	Collins, Wilkie
Zeal of Thy House, The	Sayers, Dorothy L.

CANTERBURY WALK: SLEUTHS

CHIEF DETECTIVE INSPECTOR RODERICK ALLEYN	Marsh
INSPECTOR ALAN GRANT	Tey
RICHARD JURY	Grimes
C. D. SLOAN	Aird
PENNY WANAWAKE	Moody
SUPERINTENDENT ROGER WEST	Creasey
LORD PETER WIMSEY	Sayers

Dorchester/Charmouth Walk: Authors

Austen, Jane	Persuasion
Branston, Frank	Sergeant Ritchie's Conscience
Elkins, Aaron	Murder in the Queen's Armes
Fowles, John	French Lieutenant's Woman, The
Hardy, Thomas	Far from the Madding Crowd
Hardy, Thomas	Mayor of Casterbridge, The
Hardy, Thomas	Return of the Native, The
Hardy, Thomas	Three Strangers, The
Hardy, Thomas	Under the Greenwood Tree
Hardy, Thomas	"Withered Arm, The"
Household, Geoffrey	Rough Shoot, A
Iles, Francis	Before the Fact
James, P. D.	Black Tower, The
James, P. D.	Skull Beneath the Skin, The
Marsh, Ngaio	Death and the Dancing Footman
Marsh, Ngaio	Hand in Glove
Marsh, Ngaio	Overture to Death
Maybury, Anne	Pavilion at Monkshood, The
Price, Anthony	Gunner Kelly

Dorchester/Charmouth Walk: Books

Before the Fact	Iles, Francis
Black Tower, The	James, P. D.
Death and the Dancing Footman	Marsh, Ngaio
Far from the Madding Crowd	Hardy, Thomas
French Lieutenant's Woman, The	Fowles, John
Gunner Kelly	Price, Anthony
Hand in Glove	Marsh, Ngaio
Mayor of Casterbridge, The	Hardy, Thomas

Murder in the Queen's Armes	Elkins, Aaron
Overture to Death	Marsh, Ngaio
Pavilion at Monkshood, The	Maybury, Anne
Persuasion	Austen, Jane
Return of the Native, The	Hardy, Thomas
Rough Shoot, A	Household, Geoffrey
Sergeant Ritchie's Conscience	Branston, Frank
Skull Beneath the Skin, The	James, P. D.
Three Strangers, The	Hardy, Thomas
Under the Greenwood Tree	Hardy, Thomas
"Withered Arm, The"	Hardy, Thomas

Dorchester/Charmouth Walk: Sleuths

Dr. Gideon Oliver	Elkins
Roderick Alleyn	Marsh
Roger Taine	Household

Ely Walk: Authors

Allingham, Margery	No Police at the Funeral
Bell, Josephine	Fall over Cliff
Brontë, Emily	Wuthering Heights
Cannel, Dorothy	Thin Woman, The
Chesterton, G. K.	"Blue Cross, The"
Chesterton, G. K.	Flying Inn, The
Chesterton, G. K.	"Sins of Prince Sarradine, The"
Childers, Erskine	Riddle of the Sands, The
Christie, Agatha	Pocketful of Rye, A
Daniel, Glyn	Cambridge Murders, The
Gash, Jonathan	Tartan Sell, The
Giroux, E. X.	Death for a Darling
Greene, Graham	—
Haymon, S. T.	Stately Homicide
Heyer, Georgette	Quiet Gentleman, The
Hunter, Alan	Gently Between the Tides

James, P. D.	**Death of an Expert Witness**
Kenney, Susan	**Garden of Malice**
Marsh, Ngaio	**Clutch of Constables, A**
Peters, Ellis	**St. Peter's Fair**
Player, Robert	**Oh, Where Are Bloody Mary's Earrings?**
Sayers, Dorothy L.	**Nine Tailors, The**
Sayers, Dorothy L.	**"Teaching of Latin, The"**
Sayers, Dorothy L.	**Thrones, Dominations**
Sayers, Dorothy L., and Wilfrid Scott-Giles	**Wimsey Family, The**
Snow, C. P.	**Death Under Sail**

ELY WALK: BOOKS

"Blue Cross, The"	Chesterton, G. K.
Cambridge Murders, The	Daniel, Glyn
Clutch of Constables, A	Marsh, Ngaio
Death for a Darling	Giroux, E. X.
Death of an Expert Witness	James, P. D.
Death Under Sail	Snow, C. P.
Fall over Cliff	Bell, Josephine
Flying Inn, The	Chesterton, G. K.
Garden of Malice	Kenney, Susan
Gently Between the Tides	Hunter, Alan
Nine Tailors, The	Sayers, Dorothy L.
No Police at the Funeral	Allingham, Margery
Oh, Where Are Bloody Mary's Earrings?	Player, Robert
Pocketful of Rye, A	Christie, Agatha
Quiet Gentleman, The	Heyer, Georgette
Riddle of the Sands, The	Childers, Erskine
St. Peter's Fair	Peters, Ellis
"Sins of Prince Sarradine, The"	Chesterton, G. K.
Stately Homicide	Haymon, S. T.
Tartan Sell, The	Gash, Jonathan
"Teaching of Latin, The"	Sayers, Dorothy L.
Thin Woman, The	Cannel, Dorothy

Thrones, Dominations	Sayers, Dorothy L.
Wimsey Family, The	Sayers, Dorothy L., and Wilfrid Scott-Giles
Wuthering Heights	Brontë, Emily

ELY WALK: SLEUTHS

SUPERINTENDENT RODERICK ALLEYN	Marsh
FATHER BROWN	Chesterton
ALBERT CAMPION	Allingham
INSPECTOR ADAM DALGLIESH	James
ROBERT FORSYTHE	Giroux
ROZ HOWARD	Kenney
LOVEJOY	Gash
MISS JANE MARPLE	Christie
SUPERINTENDENT ROBERTSON-MACDONALD	Daniel
LORD PETER WIMSEY	Sayers
DR. DAVID WINTRINGHAM	Bell

GREENWICH/BLACKHEATH WALK: AUTHORS

Bell, Josephine	**Death on the Borough Council**
Bell, Josephine	**Port of London Murders, The**
Bell, Josephine	**Trouble in Hunter Ward, The**
Blake, Nicholas	**Worm of Death, The**
Buchan, John	**Thirty-Nine Steps, The**
Christie, Agatha	**Murder of Roger Ackroyd, The**
Creasey, John	**Gideon's River**
Dickens, Charles	**Our Mutual Friend**
Granger, Bill	**November Man, The**
Heyer, Georgette	**Lord John**
Perry, Anne	**Paragon Walk**
Peters, Ellis	**House of Green Turf, The**

Sayers, Dorothy L.	**Five Red Herrings, The**
Sayers, Dorothy L.	**Gaudy Night**
Symons, Julian	**Blackheath Poisonings, The**
Symons, Julian	**Bland Beginning**
Symons, Julian	**Three Pipe Problem, A**

Greenwich/Blackheath Walk: Books

Blackheath Poisonings, The	Symons, Julian
Bland Beginning	Symons, Julian
Death on the Borough Council	Bell, Josephine
Five Red Herrings, The	Sayers, Dorothy L.
Gaudy Night	Sayers, Dorothy L.
Gideon's River	Creasey, John
House of Green Turf, The	Peters, Ellis
Lord John	Heyer, Georgette
Murder of Roger Ackroyd, The	Christie, Agatha
November Man, The	Granger, Bill
Our Mutual Friend	Dickens, Charles
Paragon Walk	Perry, Anne
Port of London Murders, The	Bell, Josephine
Thirty-Nine Steps, The	Buchan, John
Three Pipe Problem, A	Symons, Julian
Trouble in Hunter Ward, The	Bell, Josephine
Worm of Death, The	Blake, Nicholas

Greenwich/Blackheath Walk: Sleuths

Commander Gideon	Creasey
Sheridan Haynes	Symons
Charlotte Pitt	Perry
Nigel Strangeways	Blake
Dr. David Wintringham	Bell

NEWMARKET WALK: AUTHORS

Aird, Catherine	—
Allingham, Margery	Mystery Mile
Allingham, Margery	No Police at the Funeral
Allingham, Margery	Sweet Danger
Bradley, Sheila	Chief Inspector's Daughter, The
Butterworth, Michael	Man in the Sopwith Camel, The
Christie, Agatha	Secret Adversary, The
Clinton-Baddeley, V. C.	Only a Matter of Time
Creasey, John	Theft of Magna Carta
Daniel, Glyn	Cambridge Murders, The
Dickens, Charles	Pickwick Papers
Francis, Dick	Bolt
Francis, Dick	Bonecrack
Francis, Dick	Break In
Francis, Dick	Enquiry
Francis, Dick	Rat Race
Francis, Dick	Whiphand
Fraser, Antonia	—
Heyer, Georgette	Behold, Here's Poison
Heyer, Georgette	Lord John
Heyer, Georgette	Regency Buck
Hunter, Alan	Gently Between the Tides
James, P. D.	Unnatural Causes
James, P. D.	Unsuitable Job for a Woman, An
Kenney, Susan	Garden of Malice
Lovesey, Peter	Bertie and the Tinman
Moyes, Patricia	Down Among the Dead Men
Oliver, Anthony	Elberg Collection, The
Perry, Anne	—
Rendell, Ruth	Dark-Adapted Eye, A
Sayers, Dorothy L.	Have His Carcase
Sayers, Dorothy L., and Wilfrid Scott-Giles	Wimsey Family, The

Taylor, Andrew	**Caroline Minuscule**
Tey, Josephine	**Brat Farrar**
Tey, Josephine	**Daughter of Time, The**

Newmarket Walk: Books

Behold, Here's Poison	Heyer, Georgette
Bertie and the Tinman	Lovesey, Peter
Bolt	Francis, Dick
Bonecrack	Francis, Dick
Brat Farrar	Tey, Josephine
Break In	Francis, Dick
Cambridge Murders, The	Daniel, Glyn
Caroline Minuscule	Taylor, Andrew
Chief Inspector's Daughter, The	Bradley, Sheila
Dark-Adapted Eye, A	Rendell, Ruth
Daughter of Time, The	Tey, Josephine
Down Among the Dead Men	Moyes, Patricia
Elberg Collection, The	Oliver, Anthony
Enquiry	Francis, Dick
Garden of Malice	Kenney, Susan
Gently Between the Tides	Hunter, Alan
Have His Carcase	Sayers, Dorothy L.
Lord John	Heyer, Georgette
Man in the Sopwith Camel, The	Butterworth, Michael
Mystery Mile	Allingham, Margery
No Police at the Funeral	Allingham, Margery
Only a Matter of Time	Clinton-Baddeley, V. C.
Pickwick Papers	Dickens, Charles
Rat Race	Francis, Dick
Regency Buck	Heyer, Georgette
Secret Adversary, The	Christie, Agatha
Sweet Danger	Allingham, Margery
Theft of Magna Carta	Creasey, John

Unnatural Causes	James, P. D.
Unsuitable Job for a Woman, An	James, P. D.
Whiphand	Francis, Dick
Wimsey Family, The	Sayers, Dorothy L., and Wilfrid Scott-Giles

NEWMARKET WALK: SLEUTHS

TOMMY & TUPPENCE BERESFORD	Christie
BERTIE	Lovesey
ALBERT CAMPION	Allingham
INSPECTOR ADAM DALGLIESH	James
DR. DAVIE	Clinton-Baddeley
WILLIAM DOUGAL	Taylor
INSPECTOR GENTLY	Hunter
CORDELIA GRAY	James
NEIL GRIFFON	Francis
SID HALLEY	Francis
ROZ HOWARD	Kenney
CHARLOTTE PITT	Perry
MATT SHORT	Francis
CHIEF INSPECTOR HENRY TIBBETT	Moyes
JOHN WEBBER	Oliver
SUPERINTENDENT ROGER WEST	Creasey
LORD PETER WIMSEY	Sayers

OXFORD WALK: AUTHORS

Addison, Joseph	—
Archer, Jeffrey	**Not a Penny More, Not a Penny Less**
Austen, Jane	—
Bentley, E. C.	—

Blake, Nicholas	—
Buchan, John	**Thirty-Nine Steps, The**
Byrne, Muriel St. Claire, and Dorothy L. Sayers	**Busman's Honeymoon**
Carroll, Lewis	**Alice's Adventures Underground**
Chaucer, Geoffrey	**Canterbury Tales, The**
Chesterton, G. K.	**Ballad of the White Horse, The**
Crispin, Edmund	**Moving Toyshop, The**
Crispin, Edmund	**Swan Song**
Cross, Amanda	**No Word from Winifred**
Cross, Amanda	**Question of Max, The**
De Quincy, Thomas	**"On Murder Considered as One of the Fine Arts"**
Dexter, Colin	**Dead of Jericho, The**
Dexter, Colin	**Last Bus to Woodstock**
Dexter, Colin	**Service of All the Dead**
Fraser, Antonia	**Oxford Blood**
Grahame, Kenneth	—
Hardy, Thomas	**Jude the Obscure**
Innes, Michael	**Hare Standing Up**
Innes, Michael	**Seven Suspects**
James, Henry	**Portraits of Places**
James, Henry	**Turn of the Screw, The**
James, P. D., and T. A. Critchley	**Maul and the Pear Tree, The**
Johnson, Dr. Samuel	—
Knox, Ronald	—
Lewis, C. S.	—
Lovelace, Richard	—
Lovesey, Peter	**Swing, Swing Together**
Masefield, John	—
McClue, James	—
Morice, Anne	**Murder Post-dated**
Penn, John	**Deadly Sickness, A**
Penn, John	**Mortal Term**
Peters, Ellis	**Mourning Raga**
Pope, Alexander	—

Price, Anthony   **Alamut Ambush, The**
Pym, Barbara   **Crampton Hodnet**
Robinson, Robert   **Landscape with Dead Dons**
Sayers, Dorothy L.   **Gaudy Night**
Sayers, Dorothy L., and   **Busman's Honeymoon**
  Muriel St. Claire Byrne
Shelley, Percy Bysshe   —
Waugh, Evelyn   **Brideshead Revisited**
Wilde, Oscar   —
Williams, Charles   **Place of the Lion, The**
Yeats, William Butler   —
Yorke, Margaret   **Cast for Death**

OXFORD WALK: BOOKS

Alamut Ambush, The   Price, Anthony
Alice's Adventures   Carroll, Lewis
  Underground
Ballad of the White Horse,   Chesterton, G. K.
  The
Brideshead Revisited   Waugh, Evelyn
Busman's Honeymoon   Byrne, Muriel St. Claire, and
                                    Dorothy L. Sayers
Busman's Honeymoon   Sayers, Dorothy L., and
                                    Muriel St. Claire Byrne
Canterbury Tales, The   Chaucer, Geoffrey
Cast for Death   Yorke, Margaret
Crampton Hodnet   Pym, Barbara
Dead of Jericho, The   Dexter, Colin
Deadly Sickness, A   Penn, John
Gaudy Night   Sayers, Dorothy L.
Hare Standing Up   Innes, Michael
Jude the Obscure   Hardy, Thomas
Landscape with Dead Dons   Robinson, Robert
Last Bus to Woodstock   Dexter, Colin
Maul and the Pear Tree, The   James, P. D., and T. A.
                                    Critchley

Mortal Term	Penn, John
Mourning Raga	Peters, Ellis
Moving Toyshop, The	Crispin, Edmund
Murder Post-dated	Morice, Anne
No Word from Winifred	Cross, Amanda
Not a Penny More, Not a Penny Less	Archer, Jeffrey
"On Murder Considered as One of the Fine Arts"	De Quincy, Thomas
Oxford Blood	Fraser, Antonia
Place of the Lion, The	Williams, Charles
Portraits of Places	James, Henry
Question of Max, The	Cross, Amanda
Service of All the Dead	Dexter, Colin
Seven Suspects	Innes, Michael
Swan Song	Crispin, Edmund
Swing, Swing Together	Lovesey, Peter
Thirty-Nine Steps, The	Buchan, John
Turn of the Screw, The	James, Henry

Oxford Walk: Sleuths

Dominic Felse	Peters
Stephen Bradley	Archer
James Brigsley	Archer
Inspector Cribb	Lovesey
Tony Dinsley	Penn
Kate Fanzler	Cross
Dr. Gervase Fen	Crispin
Nicholas Flower	Robinson
Dr. Patrick Grant	Yorke
David Kessler	Archer
Chief Inspector Morse	Dexter
Inspector Robin Price	Morice
Harriet Vane	Sayers
Lord Peter Wimsey	Sayers

SALISBURY WALK: AUTHORS

Austen, Jane	Northanger Abbey
Bell, Josephine	—
Branston, Frank	Sergeant Ritchie's Conscience
Creasey, John	Theft of Magna Carta
Cutter, Leela	Who Stole Stonehenge?
Dickens, Charles	Martin Chuzzlewit
Elkins, Aaron	Murder in the Queen's Armes
Fielding, Henry	—
Foxe, John	Book of Martyrs
Gilbert, Michael	Close Quarters
Goldsmith, Oliver	Vicar of Wakefield, The
Green, William M.	Salisbury Manuscript, The
Hardy, Thomas	Jude the Obscure
Hardy, Thomas	Tess of the D'Urbervilles
Household, Geoffrey	"Abner of the Porch"
Pepys, Samuel	—
Peters, Elizabeth	Camelot Caper, The
Price, Anthony	Gunner Kelly
Price, Anthony	Our Man in Camelot
Rutherford, Edward	Sarum
Sayers, Dorothy L.	—
Stewart, Mary	Crystal Cave, The
Tey, Josephine	Daughter of Time, The
Trollope, Anthony	—
Walton, Izaak	—
Wordsworth, William	—

SALISBURY WALK: BOOKS

"Abner of the Porch"	Household, Geoffrey
Book of Martyrs	Foxe, John
Camelot Caper, The	Peters, Elizabeth
Close Quarters	Gilbert, Michael
Crystal Cave, The	Stewart, Mary
Daughter of Time, The	Tey, Josephine

Gunner Kelly	Price, Anthony
Jude the Obscure	Hardy, Thomas
Martin Chuzzlewit	Dickens, Charles
Murder in the Queen's Armes	Elkins, Aaron
Northanger Abbey	Austen, Jane
Our Man in Camelot	Price, Anthony
Salisbury Manuscript, The	Green, William M.
Sarum	Rutherford, Edward
Sergeant Ritchie's Conscience	Branston, Frank
Tess of the D'Urbervilles	Hardy, Thomas
Theft of Magna Carta	Creasey, John
Vicar of Wakefield, The	Goldsmith, Oliver
Who Stole Stonehenge?	Cutter, Leela

SALISBURY WALK: SLEUTHS

J. D. HILESBECK	Cutter
DR. GIDEON OLIVER	Elkins
DAVID RANDALL	Peters
SERGEANT RITCHIE	Branston
JESSICA TREGARTH	Peters
SUPERINTENDENT ROGER WEST	Creasey
LETTIE WINTERBOTTOM	Cutter

SHREWSBURY WALK: AUTHORS

Bell, Josephine	Murder on the Medical Board
Bell, Josephine	Trouble at Wrexin Farm
Bentley, E. C.	Complete Clerihews, The
Blake, Nicholas	Smiler with the Knife, The
Brett, Simon	Murder in the Title
Butler, Samuel	Erewhon

Byrne, Muriel St. Claire, and Dorothy L. Sayers — Busman's Honeymoon

Byrne, Muriel St. Claire (ed.) — Lisle Letters, The

Chesterton, G. K. — "Lord Clive"

Chesterton, G. K. — Ballad of the White Horse, The

Chesterton, G. K. — Innocence of Father Brown, The

Chesterton, G. K. — Return of Don Quixote, The

Critchley, T. A., and P. D. James — Maul and the Pear Tree, The

De Quincy, Thomas — "On Murder Considered as One of the Fine Arts"

Dickens, Charles — "Christmas Carol, A"

Dickens, Charles — Pickwick Papers

Francis, Dick — Enquiry

Greville, Fulke — —

Heyer, Georgette — Beauvalet

Heyer, Georgette — Infamous Army, An

Heyer, Georgette — Lord John

Heyer, Georgette — Royal Escape

Higgins, Jack — Dark Side of the Street

Houseman, A. E. — —

James, P. D., and T. A. Critchley — Maul and the Pear Tree, The

Johnson, Dr. Samuel — —

Mann, Jessica — Deadlier Than the Male

Milton, John — Comus

Peters, Elizabeth — Murders of Richard III, The

Peters, Ellis — Black Is the Colour of My True-Love's Heart

Peters, Ellis (Edith Pargeter) — Bloody Field, The

Peters, Ellis — City of Gold and Shadows

Peters, Ellis — Dead Man's Ransom

Peters, Ellis — Death and the Joyful Woman

Peters, Ellis — Devil's Novice, The

Peters, Ellis — Excellent Mystery, An

Peters, Ellis — Flight of a Witch

Peters, Ellis	House of Green Turf, The
Peters, Ellis	Knocker on the Door, The
Peters, Ellis	Leper of St. Giles, The
Peters, Ellis	Monk's Hood
Peters, Ellis	Morbid Taste for Bones, A
Peters, Ellis	One Corpse Too Many
Peters, Ellis	Pilgrim of Hate, The
Peters, Ellis	Raven in the Foregate, The
Peters, Ellis	Rose Is Rent, The
Peters, Ellis	Sanctuary Sparrow, The
Peters, Ellis	St. Peter's Fair
Peters, Ellis	Virgin in the Ice, The
Poe, Edgar Allan	Purloined Letter, The
Sayers, Dorothy L.	Gaudy Night
Sayers, Dorothy L., and Muriel St. Claire Byrne	Busman's Honeymoon
Sayers, Dorothy L., and Wilfred Scott-Giles	Wimsey Family, The
Scott, Sir Walter	Kenilworth
Shakespeare, William	Henry IV, Part One
Sidney, Sir Philip	—
Stevenson, Robert Louis	Black Arrow, The
Stevenson, Robert Louis	Treasure Island
Tey, Josephine	Daughter of Time, The
Tey, Josephine	Franchise Affair, The
Tey, Josephine	Miss Pym Disposes
Townsend, Guy M.	To Prove a Villain
Webb, Mary	—
Weyman, Stanley	Shrewsbury

SHREWSBURY WALK: BOOKS

Ballad of the White Horse, The	Chesterton, G. K.
Beauvalet	Heyer, Georgette
Black Arrow, The	Stevenson, Robert Louis
Black Is the Colour of My True-Love's Heart	Peters, Ellis

Bloody Field, The	Peters, Ellis (Edith Pargeter)
Busman's Honeymoon	Sayers, Dorothy L., and Muriel St. Claire Byrne
"Christmas Carol, A"	Dickens, Charles
City of Gold and Shadows	Peters, Ellis
Complete Clerihews, The	Bentley, E. C.
Comus	Milton, John
Dark Side of the Street	Higgins, Jack
Daughter of Time, The	Tey, Josephine
Dead Man's Ransom	Peters, Ellis
Deadlier Than the Male	Mann, Jessica
Death and the Joyful Woman	Peters, Ellis
Devil's Novice, The	Peters, Ellis
Enquiry	Francis, Dick
Erewhon	Butler, Samuel
Excellent Mystery, An	Peters, Ellis
Flight of a Witch	Peters, Ellis
Franchise Affair, The	Tey, Josephine
Gaudy Night	Sayers, Dorothy L.
Henry IV, Part One	Shakespeare, William
House of Green Turf, The	Peters, Ellis
Infamous Army, An	Heyer, Georgette
Innocence of Father Brown, The	Chesterton, G. K.
Kenilworth	Scott, Sir Walter
Knocker on the Door, The	Peters, Ellis
Leper of St. Giles, The	Peters, Ellis
Lisle Letters, The	Byrne, Muriel St. Claire (ed.)
"Lord Clive"	Chesterton, G. K.
Lord John	Heyer, Georgette
Maul and the Pear Tree, The	James, P. D., and T. A. Critchley
Miss Pym Disposes	Tey, Josephine
Monk's Hood	Peters, Ellis
Morbid Taste for Bones, A	Peters, Ellis
Murder in the Title	Brett, Simon

Murder on the Medical Board	Bell, Josephine
Murders of Richard III, The	Peters, Elizabeth
One Corpse Too Many	Peters, Ellis
"On Murder Considered as One of the Fine Arts"	De Quincy, Thomas
Pickwick Papers	Dickens, Charles
Pilgrim of Hate, The	Peters, Ellis
Purloined Letter, The	Poe, Edgar Allan
Raven in the Foregate, The	Peters, Ellis
Return of Don Quixote, The	Chesterton, G. K.
Rose Is Rent, The	Peters, Ellis
Royal Escape	Heyer, Georgette
Sanctuary Sparrow, The	Peters, Ellis
Shrewsbury	Weyman, Stanley
Smiler with the Knife, The	Blake, Nicholas
St. Peter's Fair	Peters, Ellis
To Prove a Villain	Townsend, Guy M.
Treasure Island	Stevenson, Robert Louis
Trouble at Wrexin Farm	Bell, Josephine
Virgin in the Ice, The	Peters, Ellis
Wimsey Family, The	Sayers, Dorothy L., and Wilfrid Scott-Giles

Shrewsbury Walk: Sleuths

Father Brown	Chesterton
Brother Cadfael	Peters
Chavasse	Higgins
Chief Inspector George Felse	Peters
Inspector Alan Grant	Tey
Kelly Hughes	Francis
Jacqueline Kirby	Peters
Charles Paris	Brett
Nigel Strangeways	Blake
Lord Peter Wimsey	Sayers

STRATFORD-UPON-AVON WALK: AUTHORS

Archer, Jeffrey	Not a Penny More, Not a Penny Less
Christie, Agatha	"Philomel Cottage"
Corelli, Marie	—
Crispin, Edmund	Love Lies Bleeding
Dickens, Charles	Bleak House
Dickens, Charles	Mystery of Edwin Drood, The
Dickens, Charles	Pickwick Papers
Francis, Dick	Trial Run
Grimes, Martha	Dirty Duck, The
Hall, Dr. John	Select Observations on English Bodies
Peters, Elizabeth	Murders of Richard III, The
Potter, Jeremy	Trail of Blood, A
Sayers, Dorothy L., and Wilfrid Scott-Giles	Wimsey Family, The
Shakespeare, William	—
Tey, Josephine	Daughter of Time, The
Townsend, Guy M.	To Prove a Villain
Williamson, Audrey	Mystery of the Princes, The
Wright, Eric	Death in the Old Country
Yorke, Margaret	Cast for Death

STRATFORD-UPON-AVON WALK: BOOKS

Bleak House	Dickens, Charles
Cast for Death	Yorke, Margaret
Daughter of Time, The	Tey, Josephine
Death in the Old Country	Wright, Eric
Dirty Duck, The	Grimes, Martha
Love Lies Bleeding	Crispin, Edmund
Murders of Richard III, The	Peters, Elizabeth
Mystery of Edwin Drood, The	Dickens, Charles
Mystery of the Princes, The	Williamson, Audrey
Not a Penny More, Not a Penny Less	Archer, Jeffrey

"Philomel Cottage"	Christie, Agatha
Pickwick Papers	Dickens, Charles
Select Observations on English Bodies	Hall, Dr. John
To Prove a Villain	Townsend, Guy M.
Trail of Blood, A	Potter, Jeremy
Trial Run	Francis, Dick
Wimsey Family, The	Sayers, Dorothy L., and Wilfrid Scott-Giles

STRATFORD-UPON-AVON WALK: SLEUTHS

JAMES BRIGSLEY	Archer
RANDALL DREW	Francis
DR. PATRICK GRANT	Yorke
DETECTIVE SUPERINTENDENT RICHARD JURY	Grimes
DR. GERVASE FEN	Crispin
CHARLIE & MAUD SALTER	Wright
LORD PETER WIMSEY	Sayers

THAMES RIVER TRIP: AUTHORS

Allingham, Margery	Black Plumes
Allingham, Margery	Fashion in Shrouds, The
Allingham, Margery	Mystery Mile
Allingham, Margery	Tiger in the Smoke
Austen, Jane	Northanger Abbey
Babson, Marian	Lord Mayor of Death, The
Bell, Josephine	Deadly Place to Stay, A
Bell, Josephine	Port of London Murders, The
Bell, Josephine	Treachery in Type
Bell, Josephine	Trouble in Hunter Ward, The
Belloc, Hilaire	—
Belloc-Lowndes, Marie	Lodger, The

Bentley, E. C.   **Trent's Last Case**

Blake, Nicholas   **End of Chapter**

Borowitz, Albert   **Jack the Ripper Walking Tour Murder, The**

Branch, Pamela   **Wooden Overcoat, The**

Brett, Simon   **Amateur Corpse, An**

Byrne, Muriel St. Claire, and Dorothy L. Sayers   **Busman's Honeymoon**

Byrne, Muriel St. Claire (ed.)   **Lisle Letters, The**

Carlyle, Thomas   —

Carr, John Dickson   **Below Suspicion**

Carr, John Dickson   **Mad Hatter Mystery, The**

Carr, John Dickson   **Skeleton in the Clock, The**

Chaucer, Geoffrey   —

Chesterton, G. K.   **Man Who Was Thursday, The**

Christie, Agatha   **"Golden Ball, The"**

Christie, Agatha   **Big Four, The**

Christie, Agatha   **Crooked House, The**

Christie, Agatha   **Murder Is Announced, A**

Christie, Agatha   **Secret Adversary, The**

Christie, Agatha   **Secret of Chimneys, The**

Christie, Agatha   **Witness for the Prosecution**

Critchley, T. A., and P. D. James   **Maul and the Pear Tree, The**

Creasey, John   **Gideon's River**

Creasey, John   **Holiday for Inspector West**

Creasey, John   **Theft of Magna Carta**

Creasey, John   **Toff and the Deadly Parson, The**

Crofts, Freeman Wills   **Cask, The**

Davidson, Lionel   **Chelsea Murders, The**

De Quincy, Thomas   **"On Murder Considered as One of the Fine Arts"**

Dickens, Charles   **David Copperfield**

Dickens, Charles   **Our Mutual Friend**

Dickens, Charles   **Pickwick Papers**

Dickinson, Peter   **Sleep and His Brother**

Doherty, Patrick C.   **Death of a King, The**

Doyle, Sir Arthur Conan	"Black Peter"
Doyle, Sir Arthur Conan	"Musgrave Ritual, The"
Doyle, Sir Arthur Conan	Sign of Four, The
Eliot, T. S.	"Macavity: The Mystery Cat"
Eliot, T. S.	Murder in the Cathedral
Eliot, T. S.	Waste Land, The
Evelyn, John	—
Ferrar, E. X.	Last Will and Testament
Francis, Dick	Blood Sport
Fraser, Antonia	Splash of Red, A
Gielgud, Val	Through a Glass Darkly
Gilbert, Michael	End-Game
Gilbert, Michael	Fear to Tread
Godwin, William	Caleb Williams
Grimes, Martha	Anodyne Necklace, The
Grimes, Martha	Dirty Duck, The
Grimes, Martha	Jerusalem Inn
Heyer, Georgette	Convenient Marriage, The
Heyer, Georgette	Death in the Stocks
Heyer, Georgette	Infamous Army, An
Heyer, Georgette	Quiet Gentleman, The
Heyer, Georgette	Sylvester or the Wicked Uncle
James, Henry	Turn of the Screw, The
James, P. D.	Death of an Expert Witness
James, P. D.	Taste for Death, A
James, P. D.	Unsuitable Job for a Woman, An
James, P. D., and T. A. Critchley	Maul and the Pear Tree, The
Jerome, Jerome K.	Three Men in a Boat
Johnson, Dr. Samuel	—
Keating, H. R. F.	"Mrs. Craggs Gives a Dose of Physic"
Keating, H. R. F.	Mrs. Craggs Crimes Cleaned Up
Le Carré, John	—
Lovesey, Peter	Abracadaver

Lovesey, Peter	Bertie and the Tinman
Lovesey, Peter	Case of Spirits, A
Lovesey, Peter	Swing, Swing Together
Lovesey, Peter	Waxwork
MacKenzie, Donald	—
Mann, Jessica	Grave Goods
Marsh, Ngaio	Black as He's Painted
Marsh, Ngaio	Black Beech and Honeydew
Marsh, Ngaio	Death in a White Tie
Marsh, Ngaio	False Scent
Marsh, Ngaio	Killer Dolphin
Marsh, Ngaio	Light Thickens
Marsh, Ngaio	Man Lay Dead, A
Marsh, Ngaio	Scales of Justice
Marsh, Ngaio	Singing in the Shrouds
Marsh, Ngaio	Surfeit of Lampreys, A
More, Sir Thomas	Utopia
Mortimer, John	—
Moyes, Patricia	—
Moyes, Patricia	Who Is Simon Warwick?
Pepys, Samuel	—
Perry, Anne	Bluegate Fields
Peters, Elizabeth	Murders of Richard III, The
Peters, Ellis (Edith Pargeter)	Bloody Field, The
Player, Robert	Oh, Where Are Bloody Mary's Earrings?
Price, Anthony	Old Vengeful, The
Rohmer, Sax	Trail of Fu Manchu, The
Sayers, Dorothy L.	"Adventurous Exploit of the Cave of Ali Baba, The"
Sayers, Dorothy L.	Love All
Sayers, Dorothy L.	Murder Must Advertise
Sayers, Dorothy L.	Strong Poison
Sayers, Dorothy L.	Unnatural Death
Sayers, Dorothy L.	Unpleasantness at the Bellona Club, The
Sayers, Dorothy L.	Whose Body?
Sayers, Dorothy L., and Muriel St. Claire Byrne	Busman's Honeymoon

Shakespeare, William	—
Shaw, George Bernard	—
Shelley, Mary	**Frankenstein**
Stevenson, Robert Louis	**Treasure Island**
Stoker, Bram	**Dracula**
Stuart, Ian	**Sandscreen**
Symons, Julian	**Blackheath Poisonings, The**
Symons, Julian	**Three Pipe Problem, A**
Tennyson, Alfred Lord	—
Tey, Josephine	**Daughter of Time, The**
Tey, Josephine	**Man in the Queue, The**
Townsend, Guy M.	**To Prove a Villain**
Underwood, Michael	—
Wallace, Edgar	—
Walpole, Horace	**Castle of Otranto, The**
Wentworth, Patricia	**Case Is Closed, The**
Wilde, Oscar	—
Williams, Charles	**All Hallows Eve**
Williamson, Audrey	**Mystery of the Princes, The**
Woolf, Virginia	—
Yorke, Margaret	**Cast for Death**

Thames River Trip: Books

Abracadaver	Lovesey, Peter
"Adventurous Exploit of the Cave of Ali Baba, The"	Sayers, Dorothy L.
All Hallows Eve	Williams, Charles
Amateur Corpse, An	Brett, Simon
Anodyne Necklace, The	Grimes, Martha
Below Suspicion	Carr, John Dickson
Bertie and the Tinman	Lovesey, Peter
Big Four, The	Christie, Agatha
Black as He's Painted	Marsh, Ngaio
Black Beech and Honeydew	Marsh, Ngaio
"Black Peter"	Doyle, Sir Arthur Conan
Black Plumes	Allingham, Margery
Blackheath Poisonings, The	Symons, Julian
Blood Sport	Francis, Dick

Bloody Field, The	Peters, Ellis (Edith Pargeter)
Bluegate Fields	Perry, Anne
Busman's Honeymoon	Sayers, Dorothy L., and Muriel St. Claire Byrne
Caleb Williams	Godwin, William
Case Is Closed, The	Wentworth, Patricia
Case of Spirits, A	Lovesey, Peter
Cask, The	Crofts, Freeman Wills
Cast for Death	Yorke, Margaret
Castle of Otranto, The	Walpole, Horace
Chelsea Murders, The	Davidson, Lionel
Convenient Marriage, The	Heyer, Georgette
Crooked House, The	Christie, Agatha
Daughter of Time, The	Tey, Josephine
David Copperfield	Dickens, Charles
Deadly Place to Stay, A	Bell, Josephine
Death in a White Tie	Marsh, Ngaio
Death in the Stocks	Heyer, Georgette
Death of a King, The	Doherty, Patrick C.
Death of an Expert Witness	James, P. D.
Dirty Duck, The	Grimes, Martha
Dracula	Stoker, Bram
End-Game	Gilbert, Michael
End of Chapter	Blake, Nicholas
False Scent	Marsh, Ngaio
Fashion in Shrouds, The	Allingham, Margery
Fear to Tread	Gilbert, Michael
Frankenstein	Shelley, Mary
Gideon's River	Creasey, John
"Golden Ball, The"	Christie, Agatha
Grave Goods	Mann, Jessica
Holiday for Inspector West	Creasey, John
Infamous Army, An	Heyer, Georgette
Jack the Ripper Walking Tour Murder, The	Borowitz, Albert
Jerusalem Inn	Grimes, Martha
Killer Dolphin	Marsh, Ngaio
Last Will and Testament	Ferrar, E. X.

Secret of Chimneys, The	Christie, Agatha
Sign of Four, The	Doyle, Sir Arthur Conan
Singing in the Shrouds	Marsh, Ngaio
Skeleton in the Clock, The	Carr, John Dickson
Sleep and His Brother	Dickinson, Peter
Splash of Red, A	Fraser, Antonia
Strong Poison	Sayers, Dorothy L.
Surfeit of Lampreys, A	Marsh, Ngaio
Swing, Swing Together	Lovesey, Peter
Sylvester or the Wicked Uncle	Heyer, Georgette
Taste for Death, A	James, P. D.
Theft of Magna Carta	Creasey, John
Three Men in a Boat	Jerome, Jerome K.
Three Pipe Problem, A	Symons, Julian
Through a Glass Darkly	Gielgud, Val
Tiger in the Smoke	Allingham, Margery
Toff and the Deadly Parson, The	Creasey, John
To Prove a Villain	Townsend, Guy M.
Trail of Fu Manchu, The	Rohmer, Sax
Treachery in Type	Bell, Josephine
Treasure Island	Stevenson, Robert Louis
Trent's Last Case	Bentley, E. C.
Trouble in Hunter Ward, The	Bell, Josephine
Turn of the Screw, The	James, Henry
Unnatural Death	Sayers, Dorothy L.
Unpleasantness at the Bellona Club, The	Sayers, Dorothy L.
Unsuitable Job for a Woman, An	James, P. D.
Utopia	More, Sir Thomas
Waste Land, The	Eliot, T. S.
Waxwork	Lovesey, Peter
Who Is Simon Warwick?	Moyes, Patricia
Whose Body?	Sayers, Dorothy L.
Witness for the Prosecution	Christie, Agatha
Wooden Overcoat, The	Branch, Pamela

Thames River Trip: Sleuths

Superintendent Roderick Alleyn	Marsh
Father Brown	Chesterton
Albert Campion	Allingham
Miss Climpson	Sayers
Mrs. Craggs	Keating
Sergeant Cribb	Lovesey
Inspector Adam Dalgliesh	James
Dr. Gideon Fell	Carr
Drs. Fisher and Thompson	Bell
Detective-Inspector Frost	Bell
Commander Gideon	Creasey
Inspector Alan Grant	Tey
Dr. Patrick Grant	Yorke
Cordelia Gray	James
Gene Hawkins	Francis
Sheridan Haynes	Symons
Sherlock Holmes	Doyle
Tamara Hoyland	Mann
Detective Superintendent Richard Jury	Grimes
Detective Mason	Davidson
Sir Henry Merrivale	Carr
David Rhys Morgan	Gilbert
Drusilla Morland	Heyer
Charles Paris	Brett
Inspector Gregory Pellew	Gielgud
Inspector Jimmy Pibble	Dickinson
Hercule Poirot	Christie
Raven	MacKenzie
Inspector Reynolds	Moyes
Horace Rumpole	Mortimer
George Smiley	Le Carré
Sir Denis Nayland Smith	Rohmer
Nigel Strangeways	Blake
Sergeant Cribb	Lovesey

CHIEF INSPECTOR HENRY TIBBETT	Moyes
THE TOFF	Creasey
SUPERINTENDENT ROGER WEST	Creasey
MISS WHEELER	Christie
DETECTIVE-INSPECTOR WHIMPLE	Bell
LORD PETER WIMSEY	Sayers
DR. DAVID WINTRINGHAM	Bell

WINDSOR/ETON/ASCOT WALK: AUTHORS

Aird, Catherine	—
Archer, Jeffrey	Not a Penny More, Not a Penny Less
Barnard, Robert	School for Murder
Bell, Josephine	Curtain Call for a Corpse
Belloc, Hilaire	—
Belloc-Lowndes, Marie	Lodger, The
Blake, Nicholas	Smiler with the Knife, The
Bruce, Leo	Death at St. Asprey's School
Byrne, Muriel St. Claire, and Dorothy L. Sayers	Busman's Honeymoon
Carr, John Dickson	Skeleton in the Clock, The
Chaucer, Geoffrey	—
Chesterton, G. K.	Autobiography (Chesterton)
Chesterton, G. K.	Napoleon of Notting Hill, The
Chesterton, G. K.	Short History of England, A
Christie, Agatha	"Kidnapped Prime Minister, The"
Christie, Agatha	"Mousetrap, The"
Christie, Agatha	Partners in Crime
Christie, Agatha	Poirot Investigates
Christie, Agatha	Secret of Chimneys, The
Creasey, John	Theft of Magna Carta

Crispin, Edmund	Love Lies Bleeding
Dickens, Charles	Child's History of England, A
Dickinson, Peter	Sleep and His Brother
Doherty, Patrick C.	Death of a King, The
Francis, Dick	Blood Sport
Francis, Dick	Bolt
Francis, Dick	Bonecrack
Francis, Dick	Break In
Francis, Dick	Enquiry
Francis, Dick	Forfeit
Francis, Dick	Nerve
Francis, Dick	Reflex
Francis, Dick	Sport of Queens, The
Fraser, Antonia	Quiet as a Nun
Gilbert, Michael	End-Game
Gilbert, Michael	Night of the Twelfth, The
Goldsborough, Robert	Death on Deadline
Gray, Thomas	"Elegy Written in a Country Churchyard"
Heyer, Georgette	Death in the Stocks
Heyer, Georgette	Infamous Army, An
Heyer, Georgette	Quiet Gentleman, The
Hilton, James	Goodbye, Mr. Chips
Hilton, James	Was It Murder?
Innes, Michael	Candleshoe
Innes, Michael	Hare Sitting Up
James, P. D.	—
Lovesey, Peter	Bertie and the Tinman
Lovesey, Peter	Swing, Swing Together
Orwell, George	Nineteen Eighty-Four
Peters, Ellis	—
Player, Robert	Oh, Where Are Bloody Mary's Earrings?
Price, Anthony	'44 Vintage, The
Price, Anthony	Soldier No More
Sayers, Dorothy L.	Gaudy Night
Sayers, Dorothy L.	Murder Must Advertise
Sayers, Dorothy L.	Thrones, Dominations

Sayers, Dorothy L., and Muriel St. Claire Byrne	**Busman's Honeymoon**
Sayers, Dorothy L., and Wilfrid Scott-Giles	**Wimsey Family, The**
Shakespeare, William	—
Shelley, Mary	**Frankenstein**
Shelley, Percy Bysshe	—
Tey, Josephine	**Daughter of Time, The**
Tey, Josephine	**Miss Pym Disposes**

WINDSOR/ETON/ASCOT WALK: BOOKS

Autobiography (Chesterton)	Chesterton, G. K.
Bertie and the Tinman	Lovesey, Peter
Blood Sport	Francis, Dick
Bolt	Francis, Dick
Bonecrack	Francis, Dick
Break In	Francis, Dick
Busman's Honeymoon	Sayers, Dorothy L., and Muriel St. Claire Byrne
Candleshoe	Innes, Michael
Child's History of England, A	Dickens, Charles
Curtain Call for a Corpse	Bell, Josephine
Daughter of Time, The	Tey, Josephine
Death at St. Asprey's School	Bruce, Leo
Death in the Stocks	Heyer, Georgette
Death of a King, The	Doherty, Patrick C.
Death on Deadline	Goldsborough, Robert
"Elegy Written in a Country Churchyard"	Gray, Thomas
End-Game	Gilbert, Michael
Enquiry	Francis, Dick
Forfeit	Francis, Dick
'44 Vintage, The	Price, Anthony
Frankenstein	Shelley, Mary

Gaudy Night	Sayers, Dorothy L.
Goodbye, Mr. Chips	Hilton, James
Hare Sitting Up	Innes, Michael
Infamous Army, An	Heyer, Georgette
"Kidnapped Prime Minister, The"	Christie, Agatha
Lodger, The	Belloc-Lowndes, Marie
Love Lies Bleeding	Crispin, Edmund
Miss Pym Disposes	Tey, Josephine
Mousetrap, The	Christie, Agatha
Murder Must Advertise	Sayers, Dorothy L.
Napoleon of Notting Hill, The	Chesterton, G. K.
Nerve	Francis, Dick
Night of the Twelfth, The	Gilbert, Michael
Nineteen Eighty-Four	Orwell, George
Not a Penny More, Not a Penny Less	Archer, Jeffrey
Oh, Where Are Bloody Mary's Earrings?	Player, Robert
Partners in Crime	Christie, Agatha
Poirot Investigates	Christie, Agatha
Quiet as a Nun	Fraser, Antonia
Quiet Gentleman, The	Heyer, Georgette
Reflex	Francis, Dick
School for Murder	Barnard, Robert
Secret of Chimneys, The	Christie, Agatha
Short History of England, A	Chesterton, G. K.
Skeleton in the Clock, The	Carr, John Dickson
Sleep and His Brother	Dickinson, Peter
Smiler with the Knife, The	Blake, Nicholas
Soldier No More	Price, Anthony
Sport of Queens, The	Francis, Dick
Swing, Swing Together	Lovesey, Peter
Theft of Magna Carta	Creasey, John
Thrones, Dominations	Sayers, Dorothy L.
Was It Murder?	Hilton, James
Wimsey Family, The	Sayers, Dorothy L., and Wilfrid Scott-Giles

WINDSOR/ETON/ASCOT WALK: SLEUTHS

SIR JOHN APPLEBY	Innes
EDMUND BACHE	Doherty
TOMMY & TUPPENCE BERESFORD	Christie
FATHER BROWN	Chesterton
ANTHONY CADE	Christie
BROTHER CADFAEL	Peters
SERGEANT CRIBB	Lovesey
CAROLUS DEENE	Bruce
DR. GERVASE FEN	Crispin
KIT FIELDING	Francis
ROB FINN	Francis
INSPECTOR ALAN GRANT	Tey
NEIL GRIFFON	Francis
DETECTIVE GUTHRIE	Hilton
KELLY HUGHES	Francis
DAVID KESSLER	Archer
DETECTIVE MANIFOLD	Gilbert
SIR HENRY MERRIVALE	Carr
PHILIP NORE	Francis
INSPECTOR JIMMY PIBBLE	Dickinson
HERCULE POIROT	Christie
COLIN REVELL	Hilton
JEMIMA SHORE	Fraser
NIGEL STRANGEWAYS	Blake
HARRIET VANE	Sayers
SUPERINTENDENT ROGER WEST	Creasey
LORD PETER WIMSEY	Sayers
DR. DAVID WINTRINGHAM	Bell
NERO WOLFE	Goldsborough

BIBLIOGRAPHY

Ashley, Harry. *Dorset*. Newbury, Berkshire, England: Local Heritage Books, 1985.

Birnbaum, Stephen. *Great Britain and Ireland 1986*. Boston: Houghton Mifflin Co., 1985.

Crowl, Philip A. *The Intelligent Traveller's Guide to Historic Britain*. New York: Congdon & Weed, 1983.

Cunliffe, Barry. *The City of Bath*. New Haven and London: Yale University Press, 1986.

Dale, Alzina Stone. *Maker and Craftsman, The Story of Dorothy L. Sayers*. Grand Rapids, MI.: Wm. Eerdmans, 1978.

Dale, Alzina Stone. *The Outline of Sanity*. Grand Rapids, MI.: Wm. Eerdmans, 1982.

Dale, Alzina Stone, and Barbara Sloan Hendershott. *Mystery Readers' Walking Guide: London*. Lincolnwood, IL.: Passport Books, 1986.

Draper, Jo. *Thomas Hardy's England*. Edited and introduced by John Fowles. London, England: Jonathan Cape, 1984.

Fletcher, Geoffrey. *London at My Feet*. London: The Daily Telegraph, 1980.

Hall, Michael. *Oxford*. Cambridge, England: The Pevensey Press, 1985.

Hanson, Neil, ed. *The Best Pubs of Great Britain*. 14th ed. Charlotte, NC: The East Woods Press, 1986.

Hatts, Leigh. *Country Walks Around London*. London: David & Charles, 1983.

Hodge, Jane Aiken. *The Private World of Georgette Heyer*. London: The Bodley Head, 1984.

Jenkins, Simon. *The Companion Guide to Outer London*. London: William Collins & Sons, 1981.

Kane, Robert. *Britain at Its Best*. Lincolnwood, IL.: Passport Books, 1986.

Lucas, Katie. *London Walkabout with Kate Lucas*. London: Settle & Benball, 1983.

Mann, Jessica. *Deadlier Than the Male*. New York: Macmillan Company, 1981.

Morgan, Janet. *Agatha Christie, A Biography*. New York: Alfred A. Knopf, 1985.

Nagel's Encyclopedia Guide: Great Britain. Geneva, Switzerland: Nagel Publishers, 1985.

Ousby, Ian. *Blue Guide: Literary Britain and Ireland*. New York: W. W. Norton, 1985.

Perrott, David, ed. *Nicholson the Ordinance Survey Guide to the River Thames and the River Wey*. London: Robert Nicholson Publications, 1984.

Reveley, Betty, and Allan Wendt. *Historic Walks in London, Bath, Oxford and Edinburgh*. London: W. H. Allen, 1985.

Seymour, John. *The Companion Guide to East Anglia*. London: William Collins & Sons, 1971.

Sitwell, Edith. *Bath*. London: Century, in association with the National Trust, 1952.

Steinbicker, Earl. *Daytrips from London by Rail, Bus or Car*. New York: Hastings House, 1983.

Summerville, Christopher. *Twelve Literary Walks*. London: W. H. Allen, 1985.

Town Walks. Farum House. Basingstroke, Hampshire, England: The Automobile Association, 1984.

Turner, Christopher. *Outer London Step by Step*. London: Faber & Faber, 1986.

White, John Talbot. *Country London*. London: Routledge & Kegan Paul, 1984.

INDEX